Shakespeare's First Folio

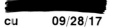
ᴐ'S

First Folio

Four Centuries of an Iconic Book

EMMA SMITH

OXFORD
UNIVERSITY PRESS

OXFORD
UNIVERSITY PRESS

Great Clarendon Street, Oxford, ox2 6dp,
United Kingdom

Oxford University Press is a department of the University of Oxford.
It furthers the University's objective of excellence in research, scholarship,
and education by publishing worldwide. Oxford is a registered trade mark of
Oxford University Press in the UK and in certain other countries

Published in the United States of America by Oxford University Press
198 Madison Avenue, New York, NY 10016, United States of America

British Library Cataloguing in Publication Data
Data available

Library of Congress Control Number: 2015945824

ISBN 978-0-19-875436-7

Printed in Great Britain by
Clays Ltd, St Ives plc

Contents

Acknowledgements

I have been working on this book for a long time and gathered many debts. The Sprint for Shakespeare campaign at the Bodleian Libraries in 2012 was a real boost to my thinking about one particular First Folio's past and present. It was a project involving fundraising, conservation, imaging, and digital services, and thanks are due to Nicole Gilroy, Christine Madsen, Margaret Czepiel, Sarah Thomas, and especially to Pip Willcox, as well as all the other people, including the many donors, who made it possible to put the book online. Colleagues in the Bodleian, particularly Sarah Wheale and the staff of the reserve in the Upper Reading Room, have been unfailingly helpful during a time of enormous and stressful change at the library. Other library colleagues elsewhere who particularly have helped me with access to this awkwardly valuable book and to related material in different contexts include Jocelyn English, Alice Ford-Smith, Susan Killoran, Tim Kirtley, Calista Lucy, Janet McMullan, Bryan Maggs, Martin Maw, Jun Ota, John Pollack, Georgia Prince, Alice Roques, Amanda Saville, Niall Sheekey, Sue Usher, Betsy Walsh, Martin Wills, and Georgianna Ziegler. Clare Asquith, Helen Barr, Judy Beckett, Giles Bergel, Claire L. Bourn, Karen Collis, Derek Dunne, Sascha Förster, Arthur Green, Tracey Hill, Kevin Hilliard, Peter Holland, Andrew Honey, Adam Hooks, Ian Jackson, Andy Kesson, Zachary Lesser, Sjoerd Levelt, Robert Lloyd George, Samuel Horsley, Katherine Lunn-Rockliffe, Elizabeth Macfarlane, Laurie Maguire, Peter Marx, Jean-Christophe Mayer, Barry Murnane, Catherine Richardson, Shef

Rogers, Viv Smith, Lyn Tribble, Kate and Rupert Wallace, Sarah Werner, Anthony James West, Abigail Williams, Henry Woudhuysen, and Akihiro Yamada have all asked, or answered, questions, helped me find materials, and read parts of the book. Without Noriko Sumimoto's patience, kindness, and expertise I could not have made a trip to Meisei; without Tom Bishop, the generosity of the Alice Griffin trustees, and colleagues at Auckland, I would not have got to New Zealand; without Missing Bean I would not have got to work at all. I am grateful to university and general audiences at Sussex, Birkbeck, Cambridge, Auckland, the Wells Literary Festival, London's Guildhall, the West Sussex Oxford Society, and the Friends of the Bodleian Library for the chance to try out parts of this material. I have disagreed on many points of detail and occasionally of substance with Eric Rasmussen and Anthony James West's *The Shakespeare Folios: A Descriptive Catalogue* (2012), but I could not have developed this project without their invaluable work.

I have consulted a large number of Folio copies and have tried particularly to shift the Folger-centrism of previous studies of this fascinating book. I am grateful to the staff and trustees of the Shakespeare Birthplace Trust, the New York Public Library, the Morgan Library New York, the Furness Library at the University of Pennsylvania, Senate House Library University of London, the British Library, the Victoria and Albert Museum, Trinity College Cambridge, the University Library Cambridge, King's College Cambridge, Queen's College Oxford, Wadham College Oxford, Birmingham City Library, Auckland City Libraries, Meisei University Tokyo, Eton College, Winchester College, Glasgow University Library, National Library of Scotland, Dulwich College, Sir John Soane Museum, Folger Shakespeare Library, Universität zu Köln, University of New South Wales, London Guildhall Library, The Craven Museum Skipton, Universität Stuttgart, John Rylands Library Manchester, Brotherton Library Leeds, The Getty Library at Wormsley, the Quaritch archive,

Oxford University Press archives, and La Bibliothéque de l'Aglommeration at St-Omer.

The Principal and Fellows of Hertford College, Oxford, our English students over many years, and my closest colleagues Charlotte Brewer and David Dwan, have all made my work more collegial and enjoyable: I am lucky to be there.

This book is for Elizabeth Macfarlane, with thanks for the Norton, and for everything else too.

Note on the Texts

In quoting from the First Folio I have used the copy I discuss at length in Chapter 1 from the Bodleian Library, available online at www.http://firstfolio.bodleian.ox.ac.uk. When citing Shakespeare lines or scenes, I have provided the act, scene, and where appropriate, line reference from the *Oxford Shakespeare*, ed. Stanley Wells and Gary Taylor (1986). For ease of reference I have used Anthony James West's numbering system for individual Folio copies—West 1, West 2 etc—as developed in his *The Shakespeare First Folio: The History of the Book: Volume 2. A New Worldwide Census of Folios* (2001) and expanded in Eric Rasmussen and Anthony James West, *The Shakespeare First Folios: A Descriptive Catalogue* (2012). Unless otherwise stated my account of these copies is based on my own work with them.

List of Illustrations

✦

(information about copyright ownership is in brackets)

Sir Edward Dering goes Shopping

Jorge Luis Borges once observed that 'when writers die, they become books', adding 'which is, after all, not too bad an incarnation'.[1] Shakespeare's bibliographic embodiment appeared on the London bookstalls some seven years after his death in 1616. His fellow playwright Ben Jonson wrote in a dedicatory poem: 'Thou art a Moniment, without a tombe, | And art alive still, while thy Booke doth live'. This posthumous collection of his plays—known now as the First Folio—printed in 1623, had had a long gestation. Some of its contents had had their first theatrical presentation some thirty years previously; others must have had their genesis in Shakespeare's experiences or reading decades before that. Its nine hundred printed pages had been in preparation at the print shop of William Jaggard for almost two years. *Mr. William Shakespeares Comedies, Histories, & Tragedies* was a volume, therefore, that looked backwards. Many accounts of the First Folio confirm this retrospection by suggesting that everything that is most interesting about the book precedes its appearance in print. My emphasis here turns in the other direction: it is resolutely

---

[1] Quoted on the occasion of Borges' death in 'The Talk of the Town', *The New Yorker*, 7 July 1986, pp. 19–20.

focused on what happened next. Who bought it, both immediately and over the following centuries, and why? What did it mean to them and what did they do with it? Because this study is concerned with almost four centuries of buyers, readers, actors, and other users of the first collected edition of Shakespeare's plays, it finds its beginning with the first attested purchase of the First Folio on 5 December, 1623. Here the book begins its four-century history of reception.

On that day, Sir Edward Dering's outgoings were, in almost all respects, typical of his shopping habits that autumn. Like most fashionable young gentlemen and would-be courtiers, he had left his country seat of Surrenden Dering in Kent to spend the legal season of Michaelmas term in London. In town, the twenty-five-year-old Dering dedicated himself to the related interests of conspicuous consumption and active networking in the circle round the royal favourite, George Villiers, the Duke of Buckingham. For 5 December, he records various miscellaneous expenses: a pair of boot hose for ten shillings, a shilling box of marmalade, ten shillings on his own meals, plus a further shilling and four-pence for victualling his servant.[2] He gave sixpence to a beggar, paid the same amount for 'travel by water', perhaps to cross the river to see a play (one shilling and sixpence paid) on the south bank of the Thames at the Globe theatre, or perhaps simply to make his way across the city more swiftly than the muddied streets of a miserably wet autumn would allow.[3] He visited one of his habitual London haunts, the churchyard of St Paul's. Paul's Churchyard was the information hub of early modern London

[2] All references to Edward Dering's accounts cite Laetitia Yeandle, *Sir Edward Dering, 1st bart., of Surrenden Dering and his 'Booke of Expences' 1617–1628*, published online by Kent Archaelogical Society at http://www.kentarchaeology. ac/authors/020.pdf (accessed April 2015).

[3] On the weather during the last months of 1623, see *The Letters of John Chamberlain* ed. N. E. McClure (Philadelphia: The American Philosophical Society, 1939), vol. II, pp. 518, 520.

where print, ideas, gossip, and news were all exchanged. In this centre of the book trade, Dering bought two playbooks for one shilling and fourpence. These were individual plays published in the small quarto format, but their titles, like those of almost all the hundred and forty or more playbooks he bought during this particular London trip, are not known. He bought a book in Latin by the Jesuit preacher and rhetorician Drexelius, and a book of 'Jhonson's playes' for nine shillings (probably the 1616 folio edition of Ben Jonson's *Workes* that included plays for the public theatre alongside poems and court masques). In addition to these older titles, he also bought a new book, which had only just reached the booksellers of London: *Mr. William Shakespeares Comedies, Histories, & Tragedies*.

Dering's is the first recorded purchase of the iconic book we now know as the First Folio, to distinguish it from later editions of Shakespeare's collected plays, which were published in 1632 (the Second Folio), 1663/4 (Third), and 1685 (Fourth). It marks, therefore, its birthday: the beginning of the book's life and the launch of an extensive history of interactions with different owners, readers, and contexts over almost four centuries. Dering's particular configuration of political, literary, and familial relationships allow us to contextualize his First Folio laterally and to suggest what the book might have meant to him. Dering's example serves to set out some of the possibilities for the generations of owners who follow him in the Folio's long life ever since.

Firstly, just what did Dering buy? His new Shakespeare book was a large, double-columned work in the folio format that measured about thirty-three by twenty-one centimetres. Most books in this period were sold unbound so that their owners could specify the livery in which they should be presented. Dering's accounts record payments for binding his individual play quartos into volumes for durability and convenient library storage (a later record of the Surrenden library suggests there were twenty-six such volumes), but he does not seem to have been bothered to specify a bespoke binding for his new Folio purchases.[4] Evidence in another extant copy of the First Folio suggests that its original, unbound, price was probably fifteen shillings.[5] Dering's accounts suggest that this enthusiastic shopper bought two copies of Shakespeare's collected plays, at a total cost of £2: perhaps one, like some of the other books he buys, was to be a gift (earlier in the autumn he acquires 'Camdens remains for my aunt Skeffington' and 'Spanish mandevill for my cousin Biddulph'). The price makes it likely that Dering bought these copies already bound in plain brown calf, most probably at the shop of one of its publishers, Edward Blount, whose retail premises at the sign of the Black Bear in Paul's Churchyard seem to have offered on-site binding facilities.[6] Although most of the copies of the First Folio still in existence have been rebound at some later point in their history, examples of this original binding do still survive, notably in one of the many copies in the Folger Shakespeare Library in Washington DC, and the copy held by the Getty family in their collection at Wormsley, Buckinghamshire.[7]

Dering's new book contained thirty-six plays—probably. It may be that early copies consisted of the thirty-five plays named on its

---

[4] See Nati H. Krivatsy and Laetitia Yeandle, 'Sir Edward Dering', in R. J. Fehrenbach and E. S. Leedham-Green (eds.), *Private Libraries in Renaissance England: A Collection and Catalogue of Tudor and Early Stuart Book-Lists* (Binghamton, New York; Marlborough: Medieval & Renaissance Texts & Studies; Adam Matthew Publications: 1992), pp. 137–269.

[5] Peter W. M. Blayney, *The First Folio of Shakespeare* (Folger Library Publications: Washington DC: 1991), p. 28.

[6] Blount's preface to a 1620 publication encourages the reader that 'if the Booke please you, come home to my Shop, you shall have it bound ready to your hand'. 'To the Reader' in [Grey Brydges], *Horae Subsecivae. Observations and Discourses.* (London: 1623), sig. A3–v.

[7] All references to individual copies of the First Folio draw on my own research but use the cataloguing system outlined in Eric Rasmussen and Anthony James West (eds), *The Shakespeare First Folios: A Descriptive Catalogue* (Basingstoke: Palgrave Macmillan, 2012). The Folger volume in early binding is West 68; the Getty copy is West 33.

catalogue page. After extended negotiations with stationers holding the rights to publish certain Shakespeare titles, there had been
an apparently intractable problem in acquiring the rights for one
final play, *Troilus and Cressida*, which had previously been published by the stationer Henry Walley in 1609. Either because
Troilus was a commercially successful title and so he did not
want to sell the rights, or more likely because it had been a flop
and he was still trying to recover his initial outlay by selling the
copies, Walley seems to have made difficulties over the permis-
sions negotiations. The catalogue page listing the book's contents
had already been printed, without mention of *Troilus*, before the
dispute was settled, and so perhaps the earliest copies to be sold,
including Dering's, did not in fact have this late addition, squeezed
in the unbound sheets making up individual copies of the book
between the last history, *Henry VIII*, and the first tragedy,
Coriolanus.

The significance of the folio format for publishing these plays
was twofold. Firstly, it conferred some economic advantages in
that it enabled large amounts of text to be printed while making
efficient use of the expensive imported commodity of paper (in this
way a modern telephone directory is a useful comparison, making
use of a larger format to present a lot of information in the most
efficient possible way).[8] But more significantly, it also had status
implications. The folio format represented a different kind of
publication, one associated with more high-status religious, topographical or historical contents than with the down-market products of the London theatre (here we might think of an exhibition
catalogue or photographic 'coffee table' book as the modern folio
equivalent). This was not the standard format for play publication,
as the lawyer and anti-theatrical controversialist, William Prynne,

---

[8] See Steven K. Galbraith, 'English literary folios 1593–1623: studying shifts in
format', in John N. King (ed.), *Tudor Books and Readers: Materiality and the
Construction of Meaning* (Cambridge: Cambridge University Press, 2010),
pp. 46–67.

noted in horror in 1632. For Prynne, that 'some play books are grown from Quarto into Folio' had turned his enemies from 'pygmies' to 'giants', and he notes the specific referent for that 'some' in the margin: 'Shakespeare's plays are printed in the best crown paper, far better than most bibles'.[9]

The Folio also had some notable exclusions. It is a collaboration between the stationers, Isaac Jaggard and Edward Blount, and the veteran King's Men actors, John Heminge and Henry Condell, and, as such, the volume omits all of Shakespeare's poetry, even the popular *Venus and Adonis*, which had already been through a dozen editions. Also missing are other plays generally considered to be at least partly Shakespeare's: *Pericles*, and *The Two Noble Kinsmen*, not to mention the large corpus of possible, or apocryphal plays since attributed to him.[10] Half of the plays included in the volume had not been previously published. The volume has prefatory verses by Ben Jonson and other writers, the now-familiar engraved portrait by Martin Droeshout of a balding Shakespeare wearing a square ruff, and a dedication to the Earls of Pembroke and Montgomery, William Herbert and his brother Philip.

The plays published in the Folio are constructed of nuanced, detailed interpersonal relationships: that is the stuff of Shakespearean drama. But what may be more surprising is to think of the book itself in similar terms. That the First Folio even appeared on London bookstalls testifies to a series of cultural, economic, and ultimately personal interactions between men of the theatre and men of the book trade, between noble patrons, stationers, and poets, and between the author, his proxies in the theatre, and the printing shop. Readers extend this sociable network of interpersonal relations centred on the book. For Edward Dering,

[9] William Prynne, *Histriomastix, The players scourge or actors tragedy... Wherein it is largely evidenced... that popular stage plays... are sinful, heathenish, lewd, ungodly spectacles and most pernicious corruptions* (London: 1632), sig * * 6v.

[10] See Jonathan Bate et al. (eds), *William Shakespeare and Others: Collaborative Plays* (Basingstoke: Palgrave Macmillan, 2014).

recording the purchase of the First Folio was part of a sustained programme of personal self-fashioning and social self-advancement, captured in his account books. Like all his other purchases, the Shakespeare book makes a statement about his intellectual, cultural, and political priorities, the networks he aspired to join, the person he wanted to become. Dering's Shakespeare exists alongside works of political philosophy and lavishly fashionable suits; in the mundane world of tooth powder and candles and the social whirl of courtly London; in the aftermath of the return of his patron Buckingham from the foreign policy debacle that was the so-called Spanish Match; and the ongoing concerns of running his Kent estates and laying out a new garden at Surrenden. Thus, a work that has often been understood as a monument to the individual genius of Shakespeare immediately emerges, in the hands of its first recorded purchaser, as a text in animated conversation with a range of adjacent ideological concerns.

The overlap between play audiences and playbook buyers in this period has not been definitively analysed, but in Dering's case the activities are absolutely aligned. His account books covering the period 1619 to 1626 record almost thirty visits to plays. Often he also indicates that he was accompanied by people he wanted to impress, or by members of his extended family as he used his London stays to affirm and consolidate his wider network. In December 1623, he also records payments to boy actors: the 'little Thomson there' to whom he gave two shillings and sixpence was probably John Thompson, a young boy attached to the King's Men who played women's roles, including that of the Cardinal's mistress Julia in Webster's *The Duchess of Malfi*, according to a cast-list published with that play in 1623; and 'little Borne ye boy there' two days later may have been the young Theophilus Bird, associated with Queen Henrietta's Men at the Cockpit theatre.[11] Dering also bought playbooks in large quantities, often on the

---

[11] T. N. S. Lennam, 'Sir Edward Dering's Collection of Playbooks, 1619–1624', *Shakespeare Quarterly* 16 (1965), pp. 145–53; p. 147.

same day as a theatre visit, apparently constructing a complete collection from the back catalogue of the Paul's Churchyard booksellers. Some 272 individual dramatic titles were published between 1580 and 1623.[12] Dering's expenses book counts purchases of at least 220 playbooks during the early 1620s, often buying ten or more at a time: he bought thirty playbooks, for instance, on 28 November 1623 at a total cost of £1. He seems, that's to say, to have set about acquiring a copy of just about all drama in print. Only two plays are ever mentioned by title: the anonymous Cambridge comedy *Band, Ruff and Cuff* that Dering may have seen as a young man at Magdalene College, and Beaumont and Fletcher's *The Woman Hater*—both of which he bought in multiple copies, perhaps as gifts.[13]

In part, then, we can see the purchase of the Shakespeare Folio in this context of a sustained collection of printed plays. Since eighteen of the plays included in the collected edition of 1623 had not been previously available, it must have been an attractive bulk purchase to the young enthusiast. In addition to buying plays and visiting the theatre, we know that Dering was also interested in amateur theatricals. Earlier in 1623, his accounts record a payment to a local clergyman for secretarial work, 'writing out the play of King Henry IV', a script that survives in the Folger Shakespeare Library in Washington DC. The manuscript presents Dering's own adaptation of Shakespeare's two plays on the reign of Henry IV, which had been first published in 1598 and 1600. Dering, like many later adapting directors, combined a majority of material from the first part with key scenes and the ending of the second part in which the scapegrace Prince Hal finally succeeds to the

---

[12] Figures from Alan B. Farmer and Zachary Lesser, *Database of Early English Playbooks (DEEP)*: http://deep.sas.upenn.edu (accessed April 2015).

[13] It is possible that the Beaumont and Fletcher play was, like *The Spanish Curate* (discussed below), bought in multiple copies for amateur performance, but that hypothesis is less convincing in explaining the six copies of *Band, Ruff and Cuff*, a play which has only three eponymous speakers.

throne and regally banishes from his presence his former companion Falstaff. This produced a new single play more seriously and
closely focused on the play's royal material.[14] It was apparently
intended for performance by friends and family at Surrenden.
We know that Dering also put on an amateur performance of
Fletcher's play, *The Spanish Curate*. Further, the mysterious
payments for 'heads of hair and beardes' and 'a false beard'
(10 December 1623, costing one shilling) is reminiscent of the
eager amateur actor, Bottom, in *A Midsummer Night's Dream*
whose first question on being allocated the role of Pyramus is to
wonder 'what beard were I best to play it in?' [1.2.83–4]. Dering
clearly considered a collection of fake facial hair to be the secret of
successful performance.

   This Shakespeare Folio purchase, then, has affiliations with its
owner's attested interests in drama as performance and as print—
and this is the context in which Dering's account book has received
most attention from literary historians. A few of Dering's other
books acquired at this time would also now be judged literary—he
buys Sir Philip Sidney's prose romance *Arcadia*, and Arthur Gold-
ing's influential translation of Ovid's *Metamorphoses*, for
example—but plays are clearly his favourite. More obvious from
the accounts is an active policy of buying books of statecraft and
policy. Dering buys John Hayward's *Lives of the Three Norman
Kings of England* (1613) and Francis Bacon's *History of Henry VII*
(1622, both dedicated to Prince Charles), Machiavelli's *The Prince*,
and Hubert Languet's tract on resistance to tyrannical government
published in a number of editions across Europe as *Vindiciae contra
Tyrannos*. Like the terrestrial globe he purchased, along with
atlases by John Speed and others, these titles attest to his political
interests in the lessons of history and the nature of government.
He also buys how-to books to learn new skills: works on

---

[14] Peter Holland, 'Shakespeare Abbreviated', in Robert Shaughnessy (ed.), *The
Cambridge Companion to Shakespeare and Popular Culture* (Cambridge: Cambridge
University Press, 2007), pp. 26–45.

gardening, for example, and a title on childbirth just before his
son was born—probably a translation of the French obstetrician,
Jacques Guillemeau, since he immediately also buys the oil of lilies
the book recommends as a general panacea for infant ailments.[15]

The prominence of works of political philosophy and history
shines a bibliographic light on Dering's personal ambitions. His
second marriage in 1625 to Anne Ashburnham sealed his links
with her kinsman Buckingham, and that year he became MP for
Hythe in Kent, again under Buckingham's patronage. In 1627,
Charles I created him a baronet, and he became a gentleman-
extraordinary of the King's privy chamber. These posts required
assiduous cultivation of himself and of others. Part of this attention to status was expressed and honed through the purchase of
up-to-date books on heraldry and genealogy, including Augustine
Vincent's *Discovery of Errors* (1622)—from Jaggard's, the same
printing house as the Shakespeare Folio, and printed concurrently
with it. Dering bought book-plates with his coat of arms, stamping
the covers of works in his library with the saltire, his personal seal,
and commissioned painted escutcheons for his property and his
coach, and the engraving of arms on silver plate including platters
and cutlery (Figure I.1).[16]

The Shakespeare Folio, marked with the familial insignia of
Dering's armorial bookplate or his stamp, thus became an emblem
of Dering's preoccupation with pedigree, just as his antiquarian
researches were concerned to establish and, where necessary, rose-
tint the history of his own family, and just as his purchases register
his care for his son and heir, Anthony. Dering buys the boy toys,
books including Aesop's *Fables*, and elaborate 'mini-me' clothing.

---

[15] Jacques Guillimeau, *Child-Birth, or the Happy Deliverie of women* (London:
1612), pp. 51, 58.

[16] Examples of Dering's book-stamps can be seen in the *British Armorial
Bindings Database*: http://armorial.library.utoronto.ca and at St John's College,
Cambridge: http://www.joh.cam.ac.uk/library/special_collections/early_books/
pix/provenance/dering/dering.htm (accessed April 2015).

The book of expenses is itself a careful index of social aspiration, prompted by, and attempting to live up to, its inaugurating entry. Dering's account book traces the arc of a new chapter in the young man's life by beginning, in January 1618, with his payment of the substantial sum of £160 plus £43 expenses for the 'price of knighthood'. Maintaining his contacts and position required constant attention. Later, he paid £1 2s at the 'Mermaid in the Old Bailey' to Sir Thomas Wotton, before witnesses, 'upon this condition that when he is Warden of the Cinque Ports I may be his lieutenant'. In a phrase highly influential for our ideas of social and cultural formation in the early modern period, Edmund Spenser suggested that his national poetic epic *The Faerie Queene* would 'fashion a gentleman or noble person':[17] for Dering, Shakespeare's works, alongside his other extensive library accessions, may have been part of a similarly aspirational development, albeit one achieved as much through well-targeted expenditure as the study of an allegory of moral virtue.

FIG. 1.1.   Edward Dering binding
The bookplate of Edward Dering
before he became a baronet in 1627,
and therefore likely to have adorned
his First Folio copy.

Shakespeare's name distinguishes these plays in the accounts from all the other anonymous play titles except Jonson's. It thus serves as a proper noun among many others in Dering's expense records that document familial and other alliances. The name of little Anthony, but also of Nurse Simonson and her maid, Thomas Hart and Goodwife Codwell, Dering's cousins Richard, Lettice, and Cicely Skeffington, who are the recipients of stockings, gloves,

[17] Edmund Spenser, 'Letter to Ralegh', in *The Faerie Queene*, ed. A. C. Hamilton (New York and London: Longman, 1977), p. 737. On the significance of this for the period's literary production more generally, see Stephen Greenblatt, *Renaissance Self-Fashioning: From More to Shakespeare* (Chicago and London: University of Chicago Press, 1980), pp. 157–92.

and other small presents, his brothers Robert and Charles, and
servants Nicholas, Stephen, and Elizabeth Banks, transform economic transactions into intimate interactions. Little details in the
accounts bring this extended community to life. It cost Dering
seven shillings and six pence 'for a porter to carry a letter from
London to Surrenden in haste when my cousin Skeffington was
sick' in July 1622; he paid one of his regular estate workers,
Theophilus Tilghman, nine shillings 'for work which he did for
John Barton when his eye was sore, which John Barton was to pay
but that I forgave it him'. The man who bought gardening books,
seed, and specialist cherry trees gives a shilling to 'John ye gardener
when he first shewed me how to graft'. At the beginning of 1621,
he records £1 3s 'given my wife this quarter besides her allowance,
which she lost at cards'. The details here are narrative rather than
documentary, in excess of their purpose in the account book.[18]
Shakespeare's name, then, is interpolated in these human stories,
interleaved with the names of relatives, servants, associates, and
neighbours. The First Folio bears a prominent picture of the
author and its dedications suggest that he lives on within its
pages ('This Booke,' wrote Leonard Digges in his prefatory
poem, 'When Brasse and Marble fade, shall make thee looke |
Fresh to all Ages'). It is further humanized by the company it
keeps in Dering's account books. We might adapt here Don
McKenzie's resonant concept of the 'sociology of texts'—the
'human motives and interactions which texts involve at every
stage of their production, transmission, and consumption'—to
focus attention as well on their 'sociability'—their participation,
even (to risk anthropomorphism), their enjoyment of these interpersonal interactions.[19]

[18] Adam Smyth, *Autobiography in Early Modern England* (Cambridge: Cambridge University Press, 2010), p. 97.
[19] D. F. McKenzie, *Bibliography and the Sociology of Texts* (Cambridge: Cambridge University Press, 1999), p. 15. On books and their friends, see Helen Smith,
'"Rare poemes ask rare friends": Popularity and Collection in Elizabethan England',

The First Folio is also redrawn as a desirable, fashionable possession by the company it keeps in Dering's account book. Later that same December, for example, Dering paid out £8 and £6 for two suits, with the exquisite particulars of silk, buckram, taffeta, stiffenings, and buttons all enumerated. Perhaps the detail suggests sensual pleasure in the perfect components, or self-justification at the expense. He buys fashionable accessories, including 'an earring with rubies' and 'a clock with an alarum' (at four times the cost of the Shakespeare Folio). He had a 'new crystal' set into his watch, the luxury item Shakespeare's steward Malvolio had fantasized about owning as the husband of a rich wife in *Twelfth Night* [2.5.58]. Some of the prestige and luxury of these non-necessities may attach itself to the purchase of a book of Shakespeare's plays: like them, it is a fashionable refinement, indicating—even as it helps to construct—the evident wealth and taste of its owner. A later theorist of economic behaviour, writing at the end of the nineteenth century, would influentially name this phenomenon: 'conspicuous consumption'.[20] Dering's copy of Shakespeare takes its place among his other purchases as an item of cultural value—in more sociological terms, as an objectified form of cultural capital, those social assets that promote and demonstrate the ambition and aspiration of their owners.[21]

Time has spared almost none of these items. Just as Dering's own reputation and his carefully achieved social position were irreparably damaged by his controversial defection to the parliamentarians during the civil war, so too the possessions that had built that status, particularly his library, were dispersed. The extensive collection at Surrenden was one of the county's glories

in Andy Kesson and Emma Smith (eds), *The Elizabethan Top Ten: Defining Print Popularity in Early Modern England* (Farnham: Ashgate, 2013), pp. 79–100.

[20] Thorstein Veblen, *The Theory of the Leisure Class*, ed. Martha Banta (Oxford: Oxford University Press, 2007), pp. 86ff.
[21] On 'cultural capital' see Pierre Bourdieu, *Distinction: A Social Critique of the Judgement of Taste* (Routledge: London, 2010), pp. 48ff.

for more than a century. Writing his *History of Kent* in 1719, John Harris noted that the first baronet had 'built the finely situated and elegant Seat at Surenden; where is a very good good [*sic*] Library, the Use of which I do hereby, with all Respect and Gratitude, acknowledge was kindly afforded me, and from whence I had some good Helps towards the Compiling of this History'.[22] But this 'good good' collection was ultimately broken up, slowly at first, and then more decisively at an auction in 1811 and a series of subsequent sales in the 1850s. A handful of Dering's copies can be traced in scattered libraries in the UK and the US: an edition of Milton in the Beinecke Library at Yale, religious works in York Minster, St John's College, Cambridge, and in the General Theological Seminary in New York, and volumes stamped with Dering's seal in the British Library and in the collection built up in Washington DC in the early twentieth century by Henry Clay Folger. The bookseller Joseph Lilly included a copy of the First Folio in a sale advertised as including (unspecified) works from Dering's library, but as this copy had been recently rebound and missing leaves replaced in facsimile any evidence that it might once have belonged to Dering has been erased.[23] The Elizabethan manor house of Surrenden Dering burned down in 1952. It is thus impossible to trace what happened to Sir Edward Dering's copies of the First Folio.

One attractive possibility is that one of these copies is now in the University Library in Padua. This book is in its original binding, and includes annotations to three plays—*Macbeth*, *Measure for Measure* and *The Winter's Tale*—that seem to prepare them for performance.[24] There is some tantalizing overlap with the names in Dering's performance copy of the Fletcher play, *The*

---

[22] John Harris, *The History of Kent* (London: 1719), p. 240.
[23] Joseph Lilly, *A Catalogue of a most interesting and valuable assemblage of rare, curious, and useful old books* (London: 1862).
[24] West 198.

Spanish Curate, and perhaps Padua's Mr Carlile, TS and Mr K are the same performers as 'John Carlile', 'Tho: Slender' and 'Mr Kemp' in SC. But perhaps—and more likely—not.[25] The wish to connect this theatrical copy with the attested amateur dramatics interests of Sir Edward Dering attests to the strong appeal of Shakespearean provenance narratives; the disappointment that the Padua copy cannot be confidently identified as Dering's registers the real difficulties of tracing any of the extant Folios from the seventeenth century to the present day. While the First Folio registers across the centuries as a constant material presence, reconstructions of the itineraries of individual copies are contingent and often complicit, serving to legitimize ownership, corroborate pre-existing interpretations, or increase financial value.

With Sir Edward Dering, the first collected edition of Shakespeare's plays finds its first attested owner. Dering's network of interests, contacts, and purchases situates this book in an immediate context of aspirational self-presentation, interpersonal bonds, and luxury shopping. The Folio is here closely collocated with estate management, with courtly networking, fashionable clothing, and the acquisition of a serious library of printed books and manuscripts. A picture now in the Frick collection in New York may capture something of Dering's aspirations (Figure I.2).

It is a painting not of Dering himself, but of his more glamorous near-contemporary, Sir John Suckling, cavalier poet and prodigal (1609–41). Suckling is painted by Anthony van Dyke, sporting an elaborate, rather theatrical costume and 'all at length, leaning

---

[25] On the argument that these annotations could plausibly be connected to Surrenden Dering, see G. Blakemore Evans (ed.), *Shakespearean Prompt-books of the Seventeenth Century* (Charlottesville, Virginia: 1960), vol. 1.i., p. 8; on the discovery of another theatrically-marked printed play that is clearly later in the period and therefore suggests that the Dering attribution is unlikely, see the same author's 'New Evidence on the Provenance of the Padua Prompt-Books of Shakespeare's *Macbeth*, *Measure for Measure* and *Winter's Tale*', *Studies in Bibliography* 20 (1967), pp. 239–42.

FIG. I.2. Anthony van Dyck, *Sir John Suckling*
It's not clear whether Suckling poses here with a First or Second Folio, but the large Shakespeare volume, open at *Hamlet*, is key to his self-presentation.

against a rock, with a play-booke, contemplating', as John Aubrey put it when he saw the portrait in the 1660s.[26] The pictured playbook is in fact an open folio marked with the word 'Shakespere', its pages double-columned and with the running title 'Hamlet' across the top of the text. The painting has been dated to 1638, the highpoint of Suckling's own literary success in the London theatre, and thus it is not possible to be sure that the book is a First Folio rather than the Second (printed in 1632). But nevertheless it is, as Malcolm Rogers points out, the earliest painted example of an identifiable, secular vernacular text in English portraiture, and one with a significant implication.[27]

Suckling's public construction of selfhood in his portrait pose deploys Shakespeare in two historically distinct ways. The specific and legible choice of *Hamlet* points to an influential modern model of subjectivity that prioritizes the Prince's traits of alienation, introspection and individuality. On the other hand, the specific connotations of the book itself identify a distinctly early modern selfhood secured through carefully chosen and curated objects and possessions. This is

[26] John Aubrey, *Aubrey's Brief Lives*, ed. Andrew Clark (Oxford: Clarendon Press, 1898), vol. II, p. 244.

[27] Malcolm Rogers, 'The Meaning of Van Dyck's Portrait of Sir John Suckling', *The Burlington Magazine* 120 (1978), pp. 739–45.

a model of the self that registers the conceptual and etymological connections between property, prop, and the sense of 'proper' via the French '*propre*' ('own') that the *Oxford English Dictionary* glosses as, 'Belonging or relating to a specified person or thing distinctively or exclusively; characteristic; particular'.[28] Thus the crucial material prop for the construction of the sitter as poet, lover, royalist, and aesthete is Shakespeare's Folio. Dering's persona as well-connected antiquarian and courtier may be less flamboyant—and he had his own portrait taken by the Dutch-trained Cornelius Johnson or Jansen rather than the court celebrity, van Dyke—but it is no less dependent on a range of props, including the one he bought in December 1623.

This book develops the implications of Dering's initial purchase to construct a biography of Shakespeare's First Folio across almost four centuries. It explores the ways people have interacted with it, what they got from that encounter, and how individual copies document stages in its life. It identifies different and overlapping contexts for the First Folio—sometimes understood alongside other earlier and later editions of Shakespeare's works, sometimes amid fine bindings or other bibliographic treasures, sometimes as a token of cultural or social ambition, sometimes as a financial investment or conspicuous display of wealth, sometimes as patriotic or imperial totem. Mine is a work of reception, in part because so much existing research, building on heroic detective work by Charlton Hinman after the Second World War discussed in Chapter 3, has already brilliantly detailed the making of the First Folio.[29] There is a methodological point too, however. Literary

---

[28] 'proper, adj., n., and adv.'. OED Online. September 2014. Oxford University Press. http://www.oed.com/view/Entry/152660?rskey=HNPxTA&result=1&is Advanced=false (accessed April 2015).

[29] Charlton Hinman, *The Printing and Proof-Reading of the First Folio of Shakespeare* (Oxford: Clarendon Press, 1963). See also Peter Blayney's updating of Hinman's introduction in the second edition of *The First Folio of Shakespeare* (London and New York: W.W. Norton, 1996).

criticism in the later twentieth century has turned away from a focus on authorial literary production and instead to an interest in readerly literary reception. The posthumous character of the Shakespeare book, published seven years after its author's death, makes it a suggestive case study for Roland Barthes' provocative concatenation of the death of the author with the birth of the reader.[30] Or, as Michel de Certeau put it, 'whether it is a newspaper or Proust'—or, he might have added, Shakespeare—'a text has a meaning only through its readers; it changes along with them; it is ordered in accordance with codes of perception that it does not control. It becomes a text only in its relation to the exteriority of the reader.'[31] But as this book makes clear, many—perhaps a majority—of encounters with the First Folio would not be classified as 'reading': exterior agents including booksellers, librarians, collectors, curators, bookbinders, legatees, and other owners and users of the First Folio make and change it in diverse and discontinuous ways, and this book explores a variety of these transformative encounters.

In stressing users of the First Folio, then, this book is not concerned with the discussions of how the Folio came to be published, the provenance of its texts, or the technicalities of its production. Rather, we begin where traditional bibliography ends—in the retail bookshop, probably belonging to the cosmopolitan publisher Edward Blount, to which Dering went in Paul's Churchyard in 1623—but where traditional biography starts—with the emergence of its subject into the world. This is thus a 'biblio-biography'—not, as that portmanteau term can sometimes signify, a (self-)portrait of an individual person in which personal experience and classic reading are brought into conversation, but rather an attempt to reconstruct the history of one particular book

---

[30] Roland Barthes, 'The Death of the Author', in *Image-Music-Text*, trans. Stephen Heath (London: Fontana, 1977).

[31] Michel de Certeau, *The Practice of Everyday Life*, trans. Steven Rendell (Berkeley CA and London: University of California Press, 1988), p. 170.

as a specimen of life-writing. Owen Gringerich's account of the first edition of Copernicus' astronomical treatise *De revolutionibus*, 'the story of how an intensely technical sixteenth-century treatise launched a revolution...and how the copies have evolved into million-dollar cultural icons' is one model, although the current book, readers may be relieved to discover, eschews Gringerich's engaging accompanying genre of 'personal memoir'.[32] Other recent models for this kind of work have tended to focus on the characters, plot, or language of the originating text rather than, as here, on its material form. Kevin Birmingham's account of Joyce's *Ulysses* 'is the biography of a book', but is—properly—more interested in the genesis, development, and dissemination of that book's contents than in the movement of specific copies.[33] It is likewise intrinsic to the argument of Edith Hall's cultural history of Euripedes' *Iphigenia at Tauris* and to Beverly Lyon Clark's 'afterlife' of Louisa May Alcott's *Little Women* that their texts exist in highly 'mutable' forms which variously express their translation into new historical contexts and different media.[34] Works abound on the extraordinary spread of Shakespeare across the globe, and across media, and on his reception in different times and places, and some parts of this current book intersect with that rich critical seam.

But my focus is absolutely not on how Shakespeare transcended the first publication of his collected plays of 1623, but on a more insistently material question of transmission: how that very book has moved through time, space, and context. Here, I draw on the work on cultural biography by art historians, archaeologists,

---

[32] Owen Gringerich, *The Book Nobody Read: Chasing the Revolutions of Nicolaus Copernicus* (London: William Heinemann, 2004), p. x.

[33] Kevin Birmingham, *The Most Dangerous Book: The Battle for James Joyce's 'Ulysses'* (London: Head of Zeus, 2014), p. 2.

[34] Edith Hall, *Adventures with Iphigenia in Tauris: A Cultural History of Euripides' Black Sea Tragedy* (New York: Oxford University Press, 2012); Beverly Lyon Clark, *The Afterlife of 'Little Women'* (Baltimore: Johns Hopkins University Press, 2014), p. 2.

economists and phenomenologists. Chris Gosden and Yvonne Marshall helpfully outline the ways that the cultural biography of objects 'seeks to understand the way objects become invested with meaning through the social interactions they are caught up in. These meanings change and are renegotiated through the life of an object.'[35] The cultural geographer, Tim Cresswell, adds to this: 'value is produced by the passage of things in and out of different *regimes of value* ... objects have biographies that are formed as they pass through these regimes of value'.[36] The First Folio accrues and bestows such meanings through its multiple historical lives through multiple regimes of value. I hope this current book can contribute to ongoing conversations about the convergence of two fields that still often proceed separately: the interest in the material lives of books as objects; and more interpretative histories of literary reception. I am keen to see how scholars can further develop current interesting and sophisticated ideas about the early modern reading and publishing context for playbook production into a more extended reception narrative about how those books continue to move through time, space, and ownership.

We are used to the humanistic idea that an encounter with Shakespeare changes individuals; the contention of this book is that the effect works the other way. Marks in copies of the First Folio—be they pen, pencil or crayon, grubby fingers, food and drink stains, library stamps, booksellers' notes, tipped-in cuttings, bibliographical comparisons, price labels, muddy pet paws, candle wax or tobacco burns—are only visible signs of the ways the book itself, and therefore its contents, have been invisibly modified by its various historical itineraries and relationships. In his influential study, Marcel Mauss identified inalienability as a defining characteristic of gift relations, where the gift is inalienably linked to the

---

[35] Chris Gosden and Yvonne Marshall, 'The Cultural Biography of Objects', *World Archaeology* 31 (1999), pp. 169–78; p. 170.

[36] Tim Cresswell, 'Value, Gleaning, and the Archive at Maxwell Street, Chicago', *Transactions of the British Geographical Society* 37 (2012), pp. 164–76; p. 169.

giver and a means of cementing the relationship between donor and receiver.[37] By contrast, the property that can be transferred without ties from one owner to another is the pure commodity: 'In a commodity transaction the object is alienated from the person who gave it.'[38] Although the rising price and increasing commercial sales of Shakespeare First Folios from the mid-eighteenth century onwards make clear that these objects did indeed become saleable commodities, the marks they bear of their human history also mean that they continue to retain something of Mauss's inalienability. The genealogies of provenance that can be attempted for each copy and are often partially inscribed within them, are a modern equivalent of the exemplary Maori gift in Mauss's study which, 'even when it has been abandoned by the giver, it still possesses something of him'.[39]

This, then, is a history of the book that reified Shakespeare's posthumous reputation: a reception history and a study of interactions between owners, readers, forgers, collectors, actors, scholars, and the book through which we understand and recognize Shakespeare. Its wider theme is the kinds of value attributed to this book at different times by different people, and thus it proceeds through a range of associated examples and case studies rather than a strict chronology. Throughout, it draws on close work with individual copies of the First Folio now located around the world to discuss five major themes: owning, reading, decoding, performing, and perfecting.

In the first chapter, I discuss how and why people have wanted to own this book across four centuries, and some specific instances of its global reach as copies reached Europe, America, Australasia, Africa and Asia. Three particular copies have their longitudinal

---

[37] Marcel Mauss, *The Gift: The Form and Reason for Exchange in Archaic Societies*, trans. W. D. Halls (London: Routledge, 2002).

[38] James G. Carrier, *Gifts and Commodities: Exchange and Western Capitalism since 1700* (London: Routledge, 1995), p. 27.

[39] Mauss, p. 15.

history traced, to introduce some major themes and individuals, and to explore some of the theories and practical difficulties of tracing provenance narratives. Shakespeare's Folio has played some particular, sometimes troubling roles in cultural debates, colonial policies, and global commerce, where owning this book has signalled wealth, cultural capital, and national or regional pride. The implications of a general move from private to institutional ownership during the twentieth century, the rising prices, and the motivation of collectors are analysed. The second chapter examines habits of reading, focusing on how we can interpret the marks made by readers in copies of the First Folio during the first century of its life. It surveys a wide range of examples and provides case studies of early female engagement with the book, as well as identifying a range of marks that reveal readerly preoccupations and predispositions in this period. The third chapter takes up the specific forms of intense scholarly engagement with Shakespeare's book I categorize as 'decoding'. A copy of Shakespeare's Folio was an indispensable weapon in the editorial arms race that gripped eighteenth-century publishing: collating these editors' practice in their editions with their treatment of their own Folios shines new light on the kinds of authenticity these intellectual reiterations conferred on the book. I continue the story to consider the role of the Folio text for later editorial practice, as well as the curious structural similarities between the detailed attention paid by scholars to its nuances, and by early cryptographers convinced that its irregularities contained secret codes. In Chapter 4, I turn to the uses of the Folio in the theatre from the 1620s onwards, its role in re-establishing Shakespeare at the Restoration, and the evidence from copies owned by actors and theatre managers. More recently, the Folio has played a part in the rise of 'original practices' theatre, and I discuss the investment many theatre practitioners have made in the specifically theatrical implications of its orthography and punctuation. The final chapter deals with the phenomenon of 'perfecting' the Folio: from early pen facsimiles to nineteenth-century forgeries, and from early experiments with technologies from photolithography to digital surrogate, to the kitsch ubiquity of the Droeshout engraving of Shakespeare reproduced from its title page.

Throughout, I am concerned to understand how and where this book has fitted into the individual and ideological circumstances of its time, and how those who have owned, read, decoded, performed, and reproduced it have endowed it with different types of value. And while I am conscious that this focus on the First Folio enacts the same fetishization that it is so concerned to anatomize, my aim in this book is always to contextualize the material Shakespeare. I try to understand and interrogate, rather than reproduce as natural or inevitable, the cultural work the Folio has undertaken at different ideological moments, and the ways this work is registered in the materiality of particular copies. I have wanted to connect the wider history of Shakespeare's critical transmission with the more specifically material history of a book. This biography is about the many ways in which an object that is not particularly rare came to be so uniquely important to individuals, institutions, and nations.

CHAPTER I

Owning

Unpacking his books in Berlin in 1931, the critic and book collector, Walter Benjamin (1892–1940), declared that 'the period, the region, the craftsmanship, the former ownership—for a true collector the whole background of an item adds up to a magic encyclopedia whose quintessence is the fate of his object'.[1] Assembling such a magic encyclopedia for First Folio objects requires the reconstruction of copies' divergent fates. All these journeys share a common embarkation point: the printshop of William Jaggard and his son Isaac in the Barbican, where the sheets of the book were printed across many months in 1622 and 1623, and where they were finally gathered together for sale in the autumn of 1623. Many of them have ultimately found their way back together to the same destination: a third of extant First Folios are now housed in a single institution, the Folger Shakespeare Library in Washington DC, thanks to the particular centripetal collecting energy of Henry Clay Folger at the turn of the twentieth century. But the provenance of First Folios takes in diverse geographical, social, institutional, and domestic locations. The Folio, once a book for reading and recreation, is now a museum object, even a secular relic. Researchers in the collection of the Kodama Memorial Library in Meisei near Tokyo wear facemasks to consult

---

[1] Walter Benjamin, 'Unpacking my Library', in *Illuminations* (London: Fontana Press, 1992), p. 62.

books that are marked with food and drink stains from previous owners, who read them over supper. Professional security, plus temperature, light, and humidity controlled conditions are required from American libraries hoping to host one of Folger's copies on loan during the four hundredth anniversary of Shakespeare's death in 2016; the label on the box of the Huntington Library copy reads 'Shakespeare, | First Folio, 1623 | Bridgewater Copy, | RB 56421 | Not to be Touched'.[2] These are used books that have survived for centuries through a variety of strategies from benign neglect to active reconstruction. The reverence with which Folio copies are now treated often belies those earlier existences, when readers annotated or corrected their copies, actors and theatre managers marked them up for performance, editors and scholars explored their hidden meanings, owners boasted about their dimensions and qualities, and booksellers and publishers worked to construct perfect versions. All of these forms of interaction are discussed in more detail in the chapters which follow.

In economic terms, it is clear that the First Folio had lost its immediate use-value by the later seventeenth century. Within sixty-five years, three further editions of the plays were published, including, in 1663/4, the Third Folio, which added in previously unpublished plays in an attempt to supersede its predecessors. Engaged readers were more likely to want a new edition than to understand a first edition as intrinsically valuable. At sales in the seventeenth century, the First Folio was a second-hand rather than an antiquarian book, which sold for less than its original price.[3] For early eighteenth-century consumers, smart, contentious Shakespeare editions were being published every decade or so: again, readers had a choice of modern edition, and the First Folio was an

---

[2] West 56.

[3] Anthony James West, *The Shakespeare First Folio: The History of the Book. Volume 1. An Account of the First Folio Based on its Sales and Prices, 1623–2000* (Oxford: Oxford University Press, 2001), p. 18.

apparent irrelevance. Thousands of versions of Shakespeare have
since entirely usurped the original use-value of this volume of
collected plays. What has happened instead is that the First
Folio has become pure exchange value, the definition of a commodity: a thing, rather than an object.

But something else has also happened. In anthropological,
rather than economic, terms the First Folio has acquired the
particular symbolic weight that actually restricts effective circulation in the marketplace. Recent sales of First Folios by institutions,
including Oriel College, Oxford, Dr Williams's Library, and the
unsuccessful attempt by Senate House Library in London in 2013,
have met with considerable public resistance. This has often taken
the form of a strongly articulated sense that these books are not
items that can or should be monetized. Contributors to an online
petition against the sale of the Folio that was given by Sir Louis
Sterling to Senate House Library in 1956 decried 'a short-sighted
market-oriented act of cultural vandalism', and argued that
'Shakespeare's folios need to be protected—they belong to all of
us and should not be for sale' and 'these folios are quite simply
priceless'.[4] Many of the signatories noted that in selling off a gift,
the Library broke faith with the donor. Here, it seems that books
with long and specific histories are popularly understood as inalienable possessions, as in the concept of the gift in the classic
structural anthropology of Marcel Mauss. 'What makes a possession inalienable', writes Annette Weiner in her study of the 'paradox of keeping-while-giving' in Oceanic cultures, 'is its exclusive
and cumulative identity with a particular series of owners through
time. Its history is authenticated by fictive or true genealogies,
origin myths, sacred ancestors, and gods. In this way, inalienable
possessions are transcendent treasures to be guarded against all the

[4] https://www.change.org/p/senate-house-library-university-of-london-reconsider-
the-proposed-sale-of-its-first-four-shakespeare-folios Petition | Senate House Library,
University of London: Reconsider the proposed sale of its first four Shakespeare Folios
(accessed September 2013).

exigencies that might force their loss.'[5] Even those First Folios that are not literally gifts, as the Sterling one is, or those that have been uprooted from these interpretative contexts and circulated in the marketplace, continue to bear the inalienable marks of these prior histories with and in them.

If Folio copies amass these histories, they also take on different characteristics in different contexts. Owning a First Folio has made different sense for different collectors at different times, and part of the meaning the book carries is, in context, its constellation in relation to other objects. In the introduction, we saw Edward Dering's First Folio purchases in the context of estate expenses in Kent and fashionable and luxurious shopping and entertainment in London. At around the same time, the Norfolk gentleman John Buxton (1608–1660) was spending about three pounds annually on books, mostly vernacular poetry, plays, and theology. He spent far more, however, on domestic paraphernalia bought at Stourbridge fair, and on clothes and personal accessories bought in London: his First Folio exists alongside skillets, chafing dishes, beaver hats, and other necessities, including several gallons of sack and claret to wet the head of his baby daughter, Isabel, in 1628.[6] One private owner, who was generous enough to allow me to view his copy in a modern Regency-style library, also walked me round his arboretum planted up in the design of a Union Flag to mark the Queen's Diamond Jubilee in 2012.[7] These two copies of the same book have quite different cultural meanings from these contexts, and it is the aim of this study to trace these changes.

Charles Jennens, the eighteenth-century librettist and non-juror, kept a First Folio alongside a range of Shakespearean,

---

[5] Annette Weiner, *Inalienable Possessions: The Paradox of Keeping-While-Giving* (Berkeley; Los Angeles; Oxford: University of California Press, 1992), p. 33.

[6] David McKitterick, '"Ovid with a Littleton": The Cost of English Books in the Early Seventeenth Century', *Transactions of the Cambridge Bibliographical Society* 11 (1997), pp. 184–234.

[7] West 229.

juridical, and religious material in his library at Gopsall in
Leicestershire, and used this as a working collection with which
he attempted to break into the unforgiving world of Shakespearean
editing and scholarship (see Chapter 3). The African-American
song-writer, Paul Francis Webster, bought the same copy at
Sotheby's in the summer of 1965, the year of his Oscar-winning
song 'The Shadow of your Smile', and resituated it in his
California collection. His set of the four seventeenth century folios
'like giant redwoods of the surrounding forest' stood 'unsophisti-
cated and prime' among a collection particularly rich in the
American musical tradition. Webster had collected, for instance,
a holograph draft of 'The Battle Hymn of the Republic' by Julia
Ward Howe, and signed copy of Samuel Francis Smith's patriotic
'My country, 'tis of thee'.[8] In 1985 his Folio was sold at Sotheby's
for $638,000, reported by the *New York Times* to be 'the second
highest price for a printed book sold in America, and the second
highest for a work by Shakespeare'.[9] The bidder was the Japanese
university of Meisei, where Jennens' and Webster's book now joins
eleven other copies of the First Folio in a strong-room panelled to
resemble an Edwardian English library. The point here is that
even the same Shakespeare Folio is a different object in each of
those contexts: working document, mark of individual success,
cultural trophy. And it is important not to overstate this teleology,
nor to sentimentalize these differences. I do not suggest that earlier
readers engaged with the contents of the book in an unmediated
way, unburdened by later appreciations: rather, I acknowledge that
each of the book's historic identities has its own specific authenticity, anchored in its continued materiality. These stories of
ownership are not narratives of decline from a moment of privil-
eged and personal communion with Shakespeare to a dusty or
dead collection. Instead, they trace the ways these volumes have

---

[8] [Paul Francis Webster], *'Multum in Parvo': The Small Select Library of Paul
Francis Webster* (privately printed, Beverly Hills, California: 1972), n.p.

[9] *New York Times*, 25 April 1985.

gathered a kind of cultural mass, and how that snow-balling process has shaped and been shaped by our understandings of what Shakespeare should be.

Annette Weiner notes of ritual objects in aboriginal cultures that their 'density accrues through an object's association with its owner's fame, ancestral histories, secrecy, sacredness, and aesthetic and economic values'.[10] Copies of the First Folio have both experienced and recorded a similar thickening: they are themselves the dominant witnesses to their changing cultural identity. A book that is part of a library of other playbooks and vernacular literature is different from one that is part of an art gallery of classical sculpture, just as a book kept chained in a library is different from one kept in a domestic chest: and these differences still—or especially—pertain when the book is the same title in each case. Tracing the history of twentieth-century First Folio prices compared with those of luxury cars, caviar, and high-end shotguns, constructs the book as a distinct kind of artefact—one that is different in kind from a First Folio housed along with a summer opera season and a perfect cricket pavilion (Getty's 'quintessentially English' estate of Wormsley in Buckinghamshire) or in a suburban house with David Bowie's 'Heroes' playing on the radio (my experience of a private collection).[11] 'We have to follow the things themselves, for their meanings are inscribed in their forms, their uses, their trajectories', writes Arjun Appadurai in the important collection, *The Social Life of Things*.[12] Following the things themselves reveals the different ways in which Folio copies have absorbed their environments. The historian of the book,

[10] Annette Weiner, quoted in Fred R. Myers, 'Introduction: The Empire of Things', in *The Empire of Things: Regimes of Value and Imperial Culture*, ed. Myers (Santa Fe: School of American Research Press, 2001), pp. 3–64; p.9.

[11] West (2001), p. 33; http://www.wormsleycricket.co.uk (accessed April 2015); West 225.

[12] Arjan Appadurai, 'Introduction: Commodities and the Politics of Value', in Arjun Appardurai (ed.), *The Social Life of Things: Commodities in Cultural Perspective* (Cambridge: Cambridge University Press, 1986), pp. 3–63; p. 5.

Roger Chartier, in conversation with the French sociologist of value, Pierre Bourdieu, states that 'a book changes by the fact that it remains changeless while the world changes'.[13] But here the book is always changing, marked by its encounter with a changing world. What did it mean to the person who wrote 'August 4th 1914 war declared on Germany' and then in pencil below 'Nov 11th 1918 armistice signed at 5am' to record this in the binder's leaf of a Shakespeare First Folio, and how is this different from or similar to the motives, occasion, and sense of the book that produced the child's inscription 'Elizabeth Okell her Book 1729' in the same copy?[14] Sometimes, as in this copy, the mark of the encounters with the world are visible, in annotations, in greasy or inky stains, or small burns from tobacco, in armorial bindings, in library stamps, even in the rusted imprint left by a pair of reading glasses left inside the pages of *The Winter's Tale*.[15] Often they are less visible, or less easily interpretable, but still evident. As this book shows, First Folio copies are objects that can be coaxed and interpreted to reveal their itineraries and the personal, institutional, and social histories that have added to their symbolic weight.

The value of individual First Folio copies, and of the edition itself, derives from this complex historical process of accrual. Its economic and cultural value is not really related to its rarity. It is important to be clear at the outset that, notwithstanding perennial newspaper and auction catalogue reports, the First Folio is not a very rare book. Describing the 'amiable mania' of the nineteenth century for collecting First Folios, the self-identified 'Literary Man', Percy Fitzgerald, expressed some puzzlement:

It is difficult to account for this craze, or indeed to define the element that is priced so highly. It is not the text, for that is accessible in facsimile

---

[13] Quoted in Roger Chartier, 'Laborers and Voyagers: From the Text to the Reader', trans. J. A. Gonzalez, *Diacritics* 22 (1992), pp. 49–61; p. 56.

[14] West 136.

[15] West 104.

reprints; nor is it the scarcity, for there are other works far more rare, yet not so costly. It seems really a compliment to the surpassing merit of the bard himself combined with the other elements. Fine choice copies are also extraordinarily few and bring increasing prices.[16]

As early as 1793, George Steevens had described the First Folio as 'the most expensive single book in our language'.[17] Writing to the Provost of the University of Pennsylvania, William Pepper, about the cost of a working campus library, Horace Howard Furness added: 'I do not here include any fictitiously valuable books, such as ... the First Folio of Shakespeare'.[18] A few years later, Sidney Lee presented his census of over one hundred and fifty extant copies with a flourish, predicting that 'the general numerical result will create widespread surprise' given 'the width of the interval that separates the popular estimate of the volume's rarity from the precise testimony to its existing plenitude'.[19] But Lee's demonstration, reiterated and much amplified by later and fuller surveys, that the First Folio is not, by early modern standards, a particularly rare book, did not undermine its hyperinflation. Rather, it hothoused the desire, already overheated by the wealth of Golden Age America, to possess a copy: for at least one collector, Lee's *Census* was effectively a mail-order catalogue for First Folios.[20] The

---

[16] Percy Fitzgerald, *The Book Fancier or the Romance of Book Collecting* (London: Sampson Lowe, Marston, Searle and Rivington, 1886), p. 256. Fitzgerald owned a First Folio himself, now in the Folger (West 90).

[17] George Steevens (ed.), *The Plays of William Shakspeare in Fifteen Volumes* (London: 1793), vol. 1, p. 447.

[18] Horace Howard Furness to William Pepper, 13 Nov 1890. *The Letters of Horace Howard Furness* (Boston: Houghton Mifflin, 1922), vol. 1, p. 264.

[19] Sidney Lee, *Shakespeare's Comedies, Histories, & Tragedies: A Supplement to the Reproduction in Facsimile of the First Folio Edition (1623) from the Chatsworth copy in the Possession of the Duke of Devonshire, KG. Containing a Census of Extant Copies with some Account of their History and Condition* (Oxford: Clarendon Press, 1902), p. 7.

[20] Folger, see Stephen H. Grant, *Collecting Shakespeare: The Story of Henry and Emily Folger* (Baltimore: Johns Hopkins University Press, 2014), p. 99.

paradox of the valuable but relatively common book continues. Newspaper accounts of a newly discovered copy in the Jesuit library of St-Omer in 2014 struggled to reconcile the required excitement at the discovery with the known fact that there were already over two hundred copies elsewhere, and a number on public display. *The Guardian* wrote dutifully that it was 'one of the rarest books in the world' and then confessed that '233 copies of the book are believed to survive in the world':[21] implicit in the contradictory statements is the assumption that the Folio must be interesting because it is rare.

The opposite is more true. Take any ten-year period since the beginning of the nineteenth century, and it is clear that at least one copy of the First Folio has been sold at public auction, and, while the price has been extremely high and rising, any collector of sufficient means has had the opportunity to add the book to their collection for two centuries. The book-dealer, Hans P. Kraus, reflecting in 1978 on a career spent buying and selling rare print and manuscript items, particularly to post-war American institutions, noted that the Shakespeare Folios, 'though desirable, are of only moderate rarity. They can be obtained whenever one is able to pay the price.'[22] To compare this with, say, the first edition of *Venus and Adonis*, which exists in a single copy (now in the Bodleian library), or of *Titus Andronicus* (the single edition was bought by Henry Folger in 1905), or with the 1640 Bay Psalm book, the first book to be printed in America and which did not appear at any auction for over a century, is to compare an expensive but available book with one that cannot be bought for any money. Nor is the First Folio a record-breakingly expensive book. Anthony West points out that the price of

---

[21] 'Shakespearean meet Shakespeare: Mark Rylance views first folio': http://www.theguardian.com/books/2015/feb/24/shakespeare-rare-first-folio-french-library-mark-rylance-globe-theatre

[22] H. P. Kraus, *A Rare Book Saga: The Autobiography of H. P. Kraus* (London: Deutsch, 1979), p. 286.

Gutenberg bibles has consistently out-stripped that of First Folios; in recent years the elephant folio text of Audubon's *Birds of America* has taken the prize for the most expensive book.[23] Around one third of the estimated original print run of 750 copies are extant. As Fitzgerald acknowledges, therefore, the book's value is not in its rarity. Nor is it in its contents, which are widely and cheaply available in facsimiles which reproduce, with varying degrees of accuracy depending upon their technology, the text and layout of the book. It is not a technically complicated book, nor is it unique—although, as Chapter five discusses, one way in which its value has been corroborated has been by high-lighting the individual aspects of each copy. The value placed on copies of the First Folio—culturally as well as economically—does not quite compute.

In part, of course, the value that has accrued to the book is a reflection of the value of Shakespeare himself. Writing of the expansive tastes of the American collector, J. P. Morgan, one biographer observed that 'provenance was important and he acquired Leonardo da Vinci's notebooks, Catherine the Great's snuff box, Shakespeare first folios, a letter from George Washing-ton, and Napoleon's watch' (spot the odd one out in this list of possessives).[24] Similarly, a First Folio was a key prop when, in November 1994, the BBC broadcast the first ever British National Lottery draw live on television. The programme involved a studio audience in a range of games, which worked effortfully to recast the major attraction of the lottery as patriotic philanthropy, rather than individual greed or need. One game, related to the charitable purposes of the lottery proceeds, focused on the preservation of the national heritage. Contestants had to identify which of a group of items was the most valuable. The iconic items included one of

---

[23] West (2001), vol. 1, p. 65.
[24] Ron Chernow, *The House of Morgan* (London: Simon & Schuster, 1990), p. 117.

Churchill's cigars, the Duke of Wellington's boots, a drum from the Battle of Trafalgar, a celebrated signed cricket bat, and Charlie Chaplin's cane, alongside, 'From the Shakespeare birthplace trust, one of the original copies of the First Folio of Shakespeare's collected plays published in 1623'.[25] The lucky winner of the competition is pictured hugging the host of the programme, Noel Edmonds, behind the open book as the audience erupts into applause: the Folio's financial value, stated at a million pounds, is cleverly instrumentalized as the material and decorous embodiment of the lottery jackpot, and the potential for venality is deflected into culturally-sanctioned value. Offstage, the Shakespeare Birthplace Trust librarians were wincing at the liberties taken with their book, having agreed with the producers that it should not be touched.[26] In both the description of Morgan's interests, and the game devised for the lottery show, the 'Shakespeare' in 'Shakespeare's First Folio' comes to denote provenance and personal association. The Folio's value here is clearly that it can be connected with Shakespeare. A regular cigar, cricket bat, or snuff box has negligible value without its celebrity association; the paradox of including the Shakespeare in these two discursive sets is that the author can neither be directly associated with the book—it was published seven years after his death—nor ever dissociated from it.

But Shakespeare's own reputation can be mapped, economically and geographically, against the distribution of this book. The promotion of Shakespeare to become 'both symbol and exemplar of British national identity' in Garrick's 1769 Jubilee took a while to map onto interest in the Folio itself—not surprisingly, since Garrick's veneration of Shakespeare as a cultural icon was curiously

[25] *The National Lottery Live: The First Draw*, broadcast 19 November 1994. British Film Institute ref. 433428.

[26] Recollection by Richard Morris at http://theshakespeareblog.com/2011/11/still-harping-on-first-folios-with-eric-rasmussen/ (accessed April 2015).

independent of his actual plays.[27] But by the time George Bernard Shaw was cheerfully exclaiming, in his *Three Plays for Puritans* of 1901, 'so much for Bardolotry', the value of First Folio copies and the imperial spread of Shakespeare were in expensive step.[28]

In tracing some individual biographies of specific copies, this chapter explores the ways by which an ordinary print commodity sold in the busy commercial market of St Paul's churchyard accumulated its particular and exceptional cultural density. This chapter will first develop case studies, three entries in Benjamin's magic encyclopedia, three itinerant Folio copies. The first, bought by the Sheldon family at some point within thirty years of its publication, passed through various hands, including the Victorian philanthropist and collector, Angela Burdett Coutts, to the Folger library in Washington DC. The second was part of a library kept by the uxorious Thomas Hervey, who wrote his and his wife's name, Isabella, in an extensive book collection kept at Ickworth in Suffolk. It passed to the fashionable literary Lyttelton family at Hagley Hall, and then ultimately to Meisei University in Japan. The third went from the stationers in London to Oxford's Bodleian Library early in the new year of 1624, and thence was sold eventually to a playbook enthusiast, tangled with an insatiable Folio collector, and was returned back to the Bodleian by public subscription, where it has since been digitized and put onto the library's website. These are exemplar narratives of the accumulation of value, as each copy gathers owners and their histories to itself, but they are also stories inscribed on the copy of the First

---

[27] Michael Dobson, *The Making of the National Poet: Shakespeare, Adaptation and Authorship 1660–1769* (Oxford: Clarendon Press, 1992), p. 185.
[28] George Bernard Shaw, *Plays for Puritans*, in *The Works of Bernard Shaw* (London: Constable, 1930–2), vol. 9, p. xxxiv. Among the many books on the rise of Shakespeare's reputation, see Gary Taylor, *Reinventing Shakespeare: A Cultural History from the Restoration to the Present* (London: Hogarth, 1990), Louis Marder, *His Exits and His Entrances: The Story of Shakespeare's Reputation* (London: John Murray, 1963), and Michael Dobson, *The Making of the National Poet: Shakespeare, Adaptation and Authorship 1660–1769* (Oxford: Clarendon Press, 1992).

Folio itself as testimony to changing patterns of use, location, and estimation.

The first case study concerns the copy of the First Folio associated with the Sheldon family of Long Compton in Warwickshire. It was probably acquired by 1650, either by William Sheldon (1589–1659) or his eldest son, Ralph Sheldon (1623–84), the Catholic antiquary who was born in the year of its publication. There are a few clues in the volume to its seventeenth-century ownership, either Sheldon's or unknown prior owners. Its only marks are an inconclusive note beginning 'Pretium' (price) and ending in the paper's torn top corner and a curtailed signature 'Ja. Ha', a memorandum of a sale of 'three score pounde off sugre' [sugar] dated 28 November 1628, and a series of commonplacing marks suggesting lines of particular note. Whichever Sheldon first acquired the book, he marked his own possession of the volume by stamping the family coat of arms, featuring three sheldrakes, in gilt on the front and back covers of its dark calf binding. Ralph was known to write his name in other of his books, but he does not appear to have done so in the First Folio, although it does bear his motto 'In Posterum'.[29] Someone has added the missing play title 'Troilus & Cressida' in ink to the Catalogue page.

Sheldon gathered a large library at Beoley in Worcestershire, catalogued by his friend and fellow antiquary, Anthony Wood, who reported that he 'did put [Ralph Sheldon's] library in that order, and made two such exact catalogues of his books that nothing could be purloyn'd thence or taken away, but it could be with little ease straight discovered'. One of these catalogues, now extant, is a list of plays in the Sheldon collection. It does not make any reference to the Shakespeare volume.[30] Wood continued: 'This

---

[29] David Pearson, 'English Book Owners in the Seventeenth Century: A Work in Progress Listing', http://www.bibsoc.org.uk/content/english-book-owners-seventeenth-century (accessed April 2015).

[30] Albert Baugh, 'A Seventeenth-Century Play List', *Modern Language Review* 13 (1918), pp. 401–11.

library he setled in a larg square waincot roome over the entrie into the hall; which continuing there until 1682, and then Mr Sheldon causing the room at the north end of the gallery to be new waincoted, translated them thence'.[31] In this new physical arrangement, Sheldon was following a Restoration fashion for housing books in a separate dedicated library room. Samuel Pepys is associated with an innovative design for tall glazed bookshelves in the 1660s: before this, books were usually kept in a closet or chest with their fore-edge rather than the spine outermost. One writer suggested in 1680 that these developments were an affectation: 'But among those few persons (especially those of quality) that pretend to look after books, how many are there that affect rather to look upon them then in them? Some covet to have libraries in their houses as Ladies desire to have Cupboards of plate in their chambers, only for shew; as if they were only to furnish their roomes and not their mindes.'[32] Sheldon's serious collection—of books, manuscripts belonging to the herald John Vincent, and of other curiosities—probably exempts him from Waller's charge of creating a library for decoration only.

For Sidney Lee, writing in 1923, the value of Sheldon's copy was that it was the only one for which he felt he could tell a continuous, and aristocratic narrative.[33] Lee's was an attractive story but not strictly true: there are questions about the ownership of the book before it came into the Sheldon family, for instance, and Lee's own version of its subsequent history also had some unevidenced or incorrect assumptions. But we do know that Sheldon's library was dispersed at a sale at Weston House in 1781. Copies of books with Sheldon's coat of arms, sold in 1781,

[31] Andrew Clark (ed.), *The Life and Times of Anthony Wood* (Oxford: Oxford Historical Society at the Clarendon Press, 1894), vol. 3, pp. 103–5.
[32] William Waller, quoted in J. T. Cliffe, *The World of the Country House in Seventeenth-Century England* (New Haven; London: Yale University Press, 1999), p. 168.
[33] Lee (1924), p. 86.

are now spread widely in libraries from Windsor Castle to Illinois University. The copy of the auction catalogue marked up with prices and buyers in the Christie's archive marks the First Folio 'imperfect', although the volume now appears to be complete.[34] Significantly, the book was not apparently yet a singular commodity: it was bundled with a copy of *Paradise Lost* and one further unnamed volume in a lot selling to the London bookseller, Vandenberg, who bought a number of other lots that day, for £2. 4s. The First Folio thence made its way into the collection of the controversial radical politician, John Horne Tooke (1736–1812). Tooke's contentious public life, and his involvement in radical causes, including constitutional reform and American independence, was summarized approvingly by William Cobbett: 'His is a history of the damned hypocritical tyrannies of this jubilee reign.'[35] An account of his book-collecting was less flattering, dubbing him 'a turbulent antagonist of all constituted authority' and noting that there was no bible in his library.[36] One of James Gillray's satirical etchings pictured Tooke wearing the *tricolore* sash of the revolutionaries across the channel, standing speechifying in front of a list of the rights of man ('Droit de l'homme').[37]

Tooke's influence on the status of the First Folio was also significant. His uncompromising view that 'the first Folio, in my opinion, is the only edition worth regarding' was expressed in his

[34] *Catalogue of the Sale of the Contents of Weston House* (1781). Xerox of Christie's copy marked up with ms. prices and other notes in the Bodleian Library at Bod. Facs. c.22.

[35] William Cobbett to John Wright, 8 January 1810. Lewis Melville (ed.), *The Life and Letters of William Cobbett in England and America* (London: John Lane, the Bodley Head, 1913), vol. 2, p. 38.

[36] *Contributions towards a Dictionary of English Book-Collectors* 3 (London: Bernard Quaritch, 1892), n.p.

[37] National Portrait Gallery NPG D12640: http://www.npg.org.uk/collections/ search/portrait/mw62233/John-Horne-Tooke-Prsident-dAdministration-Municipale? LinkID=mp04517&search=sas&sText=tooke&role=sit&rNo=17 (accessed April 2015).

book *Epea pteroenta. Or, the Diversions of Purley.* It was much quoted in sales catalogues and newspaper reports throughout the nineteenth century and even written into some Folio flyleaves, including that belonging to John Forster, Charles Dickens' literary adviser.[38] Tooke continued:

And it is much to be wished, that an edition of Shakspeare were given literatim according to the first Folio: which is now become so scarce and dear, that few persons can obtain it. For, by the presumptuous licence of the dwarfish commentators, who are for ever cutting him down to their own size, we risque the loss of Shakspeare's genuine text; which that Folio assuredly contains; notwithstanding some few slight errors of the press, which might be noted, without altering.[39]

Despite his scorn for the 'dwarfish commentators', Tooke certainly retrofitted his Folio with manuscript annotations recording later editorial emendations. At the moment when the champion wrestler, Orlando, falls in love with Rosalind at court, early in *As You Like It*, for instance, Tooke notes in the margin of his Folio a gloss for the unfamiliar word 'quintine' [1.2.240]: 'See an excellent note of Malone quoting Stowe's Survey of London'. Tooke here clearly recognized the seriousness with which Malone took this interpretation in his 1790 edition of the plays. Malone's lengthy challenge to the standard definition of this word as 'lifeless block' spread across the foot of three consecutive pages and extrapolated the larger editorial moral: 'it is a common but a very dangerous mistake, to suppose, that the Interpretation which gives most spirit to a passage is the true one'.[40] (Malone cited authorities including Stowe to demonstrate that 'quintine' referred to a 'mere rustick sport'.) Tooke also noted his own editorial interventions into the

---

[38] West 26.

[39] John Horne Tooke, *Epea pteroenta. Or, the Diversions of Purley*, vol.2 (printed for the author, 1798–1805), p. 52.

[40] Edmond Malone (ed.), *The Plays and Poems of William Shakspeare in Ten Volumes* (London: 1790), vol. 4, p. 134.

text of the plays. For instance, at the beginning of Act 5 of *Much Ado About Nothing*, Tooke tussles with a line in Leonato's speech of grief over the assumed death of his daughter Hero. The Folio reads 'If such a one will smile and stroke his beard, | And sorrow, wagge, crie hem, when he should grone' [5.1.16]. In a handwritten marginal note on the page, Tooke cites Book 11 of *Paradise Lost* as a syntactic parallel: 'Milton. Send them forth, though sorrowing, yet in peace', and offers his own emendation of the Folio line to 'sorrowing, crie hem, when he should grone. J. Horne Tooke.' In *The Merchant of Venice* he emends the Folio's gnomically abbreviated line, which reads 'The Ewe bleate for the Lambe' [4.1.73], with his own metrical filler: 'And bid him, as the Ewe, bleate for the Lambe. J.H.T'.[41]

Tooke's great political disciple was the radical reformist MP, Sir Francis Burdett (1770–1844), dubbed 'an implicit follower of Robespierre' by the family chaplain.[42] When Tooke, whose politics had all been conducted outside parliament, was finally and discreditably returned as MP for the rotten borough of Old Sarum in 1801, it was Burdett who took the aged man to his seat on the benches. Tooke's own light was fading, whereas for the next two decades Burdett was the most recognizable of the radical politicians, much caricatured by James Gillray and other satirists. And if Tooke transmitted his political radicalism to Burdett, he also gave him something more concrete—and perhaps not ideologically unconnected: his Shakespeare First Folio. Edmond Malone's 1790 edition (discussed in Chapter 3) was actively constructing a reassuringly middle class Shakespeare 'just when, as Burke recognized, the middle classes needed reassurance in view of

[41] West 68.

[42] Quoted by Marc Baer, 'Burdett, Sir Francis, fifth baronet (1770–1844)', *Oxford Dictionary of National Biography*, Oxford University Press, 2004; online edn, May 2009 [http://www.oxforddnb.com/view/article/3962, accessed April 2015].

events in France'.[43] (Malone sent Edmund Burke a copy of his 1790 edition and received in return a copy of *Reflections on the Revolution in France*.[44]) Coleridge's contemporaneous Lectures argued for a politically disinterested Shakespeare, or even a reactionary one—'a philosophical aristocrat, delighting in those hereditary institutions which have a tendency to bind one age to another'.[45] Tooke's championing of the First Folio can be read as an implicit attempt to strip Shakespeare of this politically conservative commentary and return to a more radical text.

The book passed through the family to the daughter of Francis Burdett and Sophia Coutts, heiress of the banking family. Angela Burdett Coutts (1814–1906) was a society philanthropist to whom Dickens dedicated *Martin Chuzzlewit* 'with the True and Earnest regard of the author'. She was later ennobled for her philanthropy as Baroness Burdett Coutts (the first woman to be recognized as a Baroness in her own right). She became one of the most famous First Folio owners of the nineteenth century, but not, however, because of the Sheldon copy inherited from her father. She also acquired, at a record price and with much publicity, another copy at the sale of George Daniel of Islington amid the cultural fever of the tercentenary year of Shakespeare's birth. The price was a record sum, £714. Daniel had bought the copy only five years previously for £100, and carried it home to Islington wrapped, at his insistence, in one of the seller's 'best silk handkerchiefs'.[46] The *Gentleman's Magazine* praised it as 'a matchless volume of unrivalled beauty'. The auction room in July 1864, according to the bookseller Frederick Ellis, had 'the atmosphere of the black hole of

---

[43] Jonathan Bate (ed.), *The Romantics on Shakespeare* (London: Penguin, 1992), p. 19.

[44] Peter Martin, *Edmond Malone: Shakespearean Scholar: A Literary Biography* (Cambridge: Cambridge University Press, 1995), p. 137.

[45] Bate, p. 20.

[46] *Contributions towards a Dictionary of English Book-Collectors* 10 (London: Bernard Quaritch, 1897), p. 2.

Calcutta', 'crowded to suffocation, crammed to a degree that the writer has never witnessed anywhere before or since (except at a boxing match in New York)'.[47] It was, wrote Percy Fitzgerald with more enthusiasm than accuracy, 'the really great day for the folio—the greatest since Mr Herringman issued his volume in 1623' (Herringman was in fact the publisher of the Fourth Folio in 1685).[48]

The sale, and the sum involved, continued to be cited in newspaper articles and book catalogues as the high-water mark of Folio prices. Bernard Quaritch's catalogue of 1888 advertised a copy as 'equal in size and in every other respect to the famous Daniel copy... the only first-rate first folio which has been seen since the Daniel sale'.[49] Joseph Lilly wrote across the hemispheres to George Grey, the bibliophile governor of New Zealand: 'I suppose you heard of the most enormously high prices which rare & curious books obtained last year at the sale of the library of Mr G. Daniel'.[50] Cuttings about the sale were often tipped into Folio copies, including in West 155, now at the University of Nebraska, West 141, at Georgetown University, and West 93, at the Folger. Halliwell-Phillips wrote a survey of prices on the binder's leaf of his copy in 1870, noting that 'the highest price yet reached was Daniel's which sold for six hundred and eighty-two guineas, purchased by Miss Burdett-Coutts', and he repeated this observation in his introduction to the facsimile edition of 1876.[51] Surveying book prices across the century in 1898, Henry Wheatley noted that 'the amount was paid on account of the height of the book and of its great beauty' and added 'but this

[47] *Contributions* 10 (1897), p. 3.   [48] Fitzgerald, p. 270.

[49] Bernard Quaritch, *Catalogue* 93 (London: 1888), p. 177.

[50] Joseph Lilly to George Grey, Grey Archives, Auckland Public Libraries GL: L26.

[51] West 225; *The First Edition of Shakespeare. The Works of William Shakespeare in reduced facsimile from the Famous First Folio edition of 1623 with an introduction by J.O. Halliwell-Phillips* (London: Chatto & Windus, 1876), p. xi.

sale had the effect of raising the price of all copies permanently'.[52] While the price was indeed in itself noteworthy, there was a particular frisson in the knowledge that this sum had been paid by a woman.

Chapter 2 discusses a significant number of female signatures in copies of the First Folio in the first century or so after it was published, including those readers who have transcribed on a flyleaf the lines, 'To the Ladies' by Mary Chudleigh with their uncompromising instruction, 'Value your selves and men despise' (the copy has thus been dubbed, somewhat gauchely, the Feminist Folio).[53] But almost no woman appears to have been publicly involved in book-collecting during the nineteenth and early twentieth centuries. The memberships of bibliophile clubs, such as the British Roxburghe and its American equivalent, the Grolier, were entirely male. When Charlotte Porter and Helen Clarke published in Boston an edition of Shakespeare based on the First Folio at the beginning of the twentieth century, the work of 'these two advanced ladies' was greeted with some concern across the Atlantic at the Oxford University Press.[54] An editorial old guard tried to recruit the Folio's great textual advocate, Alice Walker, to the team to kickstart their own misadventured edition.[55] These were, however, rare exceptions to the presiding masculinism of First Folio scholarship and connoisseurship. Even Emily Folger, wife of the pre-eminent collector, with her MA thesis directed by Horace

---

[52] Henry B. Wheatley, *Prices of Books: An Inquiry into the Changes in the Price of Books which have Occurred in England at Different Periods* (Detroit: Gale Research Co: 1970), p. 223.

[53] *The Poems and Prose of Mary, Lady Chudleigh*, ed. Margaret J. Ezell (New York: Oxford University Press, 1993), pp. 83–4; Rasmussen and West, p. 345.

[54] Sir Walter Raleigh, 24 January 1905, Oxford University Press Archives, 019/00045.

[55] See Laurie E. Maguire, 'How Many Children Had Alice Walker?' in Douglas A. Brooks (ed.), *Printing and Parenting in Early Modern England* (Aldershot: Ashgate, 2005), pp. 327–50.

Howard Furness on 'The True Text of Shakespeare' and her evidently hands-on approach to collecting and then to library matters after her husband's death, is usually relegated to the role of helpmeet.

While women have not, then, been very visible in the history of the Folio in more modern times, some bibliophiles were obviously also hostile. William Blades' much reprinted *Enemies of Books* (1880) had listed the dangerous depredations of fire, water, dust, ignorance, vermin, book-binders and collectors, but Andrew Lang added, caustically, women:

Almost all women are the inveterate foes, not of novels, of course, nor peerages and popular volumes of history, but of books worthy the name ... broadly speaking, women detest the books which the collector desires and admires. First, they don't understand them; second, they are jealous of their mysterious charms; third, books cost money; and it really is a hard thing for a lady to see money expended on what seems a dingy old binding, or yellow paper scored with crabbed characters.[56]

Women in twentieth-century collecting and bibliophile circles seem to have been rare and exotic creatures, such as Belle de Costa Greene (1883–1950), J. P. Morgan's powerful librarian, an intelligent, stylish, and commercially astute woman of African-American heritage, who became the first director of the Morgan museum. 'The cleverest girl I know', as the *Chicago Tribune* reported: 'She wears her hair long, does not use glasses, runs to Europe on secret missions, and is the terror of continental collectors' agents'.[57] Or as *The World Magazine* put it in May 1911, '"Fifty thousand dollars for that book!" quietly said Miss Belle de Costa Green, the Bachelor Girl, still in her twenties, who as J. Pierpont Morgan's librarian has charge of one of the finest

---

[56] Andrew Lang, *The Library* (London: Macmillan, 1881), p. 61.

[57] Article transcribed from a newspaper article reproduced in Heidi Ardizzoni, *An Illuminated Life: Belle de Costa Greene's Journey from Prejudice to Privilege* (New York and London: W.W. Norton, 2007), n.p.

private collections of costly volumes in the world—how she engages with bibliophiles and museum curators in battles of thousands.'[58] These descriptions reveal how very unusual it seems to have a woman in this role, and the fascination of calibrating her long-haired femininity with her intellectual and financial acumen. These attitudes persist. Even at the end of the twentieth century, an admiring account of the collector, Mrs Abbie Pope of Brooklyn, who as a young unmarried woman in the 1880s, according to an anonymous note in a sales catalogue now in the Morgan Library, 'bought a first folio Shakspere of Ellis @ £750', could not resist the italic strangeness of the modifier '*femme bibliophile*'.[59] (Pope's First Folio was later bought up by those *hommes bibliophiles*: first Robert Hoe and then Henry Folger.)[60]

Perhaps one of the reasons women seem so unusual in this context is the popular gendered image of the collector. Russell Belk, reviewing the psychological literature on collecting, notes that the 'competitive and aggressive characteristics of collecting ... accord well with masculine gendering': one much retold anecdote about the Duke of Roxburghe acquiring a First Folio at auction in 1790 may serve:

A friend was bidding for him in the sale-room: his Grace had retired to a distance, to via the issue of the contest. Twenty guineas and more were offered, from various quarters, for the book: a slip of paper was handed to the Duke, in which he was requested to inform his friend whether he was 'to go on bidding'—His Grace took his pencil, and wrote underneath, by way of reply—

———————— lay on Macduff!
And d———d be he who first cries 'Hold, enough!'

[58] *The World Magazine* (New York), May 21, 1911.
[59] Charles Ryskamp, 'Abbie Pope: Portrait of a Bibliophile XXIV', *The Book Collector* 33 (1984), pp. 39–52; p. 39.
[60] West 72.

Such a spirit was irresistible, and bore down all opposition. His Grace retired triumphant, with the book under his arm.[61]

These lines are quoted from the climax of *Macbeth*, the Shakespeare play most concerned with ideas of masculinity. This sense of the auction as a contest, serious sport or hunt constructs bookcollecting within a masculine world of money, rivalry, and strong language.

Belk summarizes the conventionally masculine aspects of fictional treatments of the collector, which generally portray him as 'strange, obsessive-compulsive, antisocial, or someone who prefers things to people' or suggesting that 'collecting arises from sublimated sexual desire'.[62] Somehow these gendered prejudices and expectations combined in the excitement about the Daniel sale and the Folio's dashing female purchaser, Burdett Coutts, an unmarried woman who, since her glamorous appearance at Victoria's coronation, had long been a figure of erotic speculation. Of her fictional alter ego 'the greatest heiress in England' Adriana, in Benjamin Disraeli's satirical novel *Endymion* (1880), it is observed: 'her books interested her, and a beautiful nature, but she liked to be alone ... She was impressed with the horrible and humiliating conviction, that she was courted and admired only for her wealth.'[63] Burdett Coutts did not, however, remain alone. Only months after Disraeli's *roman à clef*, she married, to considerable adverse comment, her American assistant William Bartlett. Bartlett was aged twenty-nine to her sixty-six. Just as Burdett Coutts' pursuit of a First Folio inverted established gendered norms, so too did this apparently contented marriage of a young

---

[61] Russell Belk, 'Collectors and Collecting' in *Collecting, Luxury and the Production of Consumer Desire*, ed. Soren Askegaard (Los Angeles: SAGE, 2014), p. 97; T.F. Dibdin, *Bibliomania; or Book-Madness; A Bibliographical Romance* (London: Chatto & Windus, 1876), p. 53.

[62] Russell Belk, *Collecting in a Consumer Society* (London: Routledge, 1995), p. 19.

[63] Benjamin Disraeli, *Endymion* (London: Longmans, Green, 1881), p. 135.

American to a wealthy English baroness and art collector reverse an emerging cultural trope of the new 'transatlantic traffic in wealth and culture', which tended to see American heiresses married into the impoverished English nobility.[64]

Burdett Coutts' estate passed at her death to her widower, but William's own interests seemed less in bibliography than in horse-breeding, and he did not add to the collection. Both Folio copies, along with a range of other art objects, books and literary manuscripts, were sold at auction on William Burdett Coutts' death in 1922. The Daniel copy, bought for such a thrilling price in 1864, was sold for £8,600. The Sheldon copy that had come from Tooke, made £5,400. These were both record sums for the book at auction. In each case, the buyer was the same: the Philadelphian bookseller and collector, A. S. W. Rosenbach, who outbid the London bookseller Maggs. Rosenbach worked for all the big American collectors across a range of old books, but one of his particular specialisms is indicated by the names he gave his boats, *First Folio I* and *First Folio II*.

Rosenbach's client for both the Folio copies acquired at the Burdett Coutts sale was Henry Clay Folger (1857–1930), the man who has become synonymous with this particular book, and whose collection is housed in the Folger Shakespeare Library in Washington DC. Folger, chairman of Standard Oil, began his lifelong association with Shakespeare at a lecture by Ralph Waldo Emerson while he was an undergraduate at Amherst College. He bought a facsimile of the book early in his marriage to Emily Jordan (1858–1936), a Vassar literature graduate, but began his collecting career in earnest in 1889, when he bought a copy of the fourth folio of 1685 (he would acquire thirty-five more copies of this book over the course of his life, along with fifty-eight examples of the second folio and twenty-four of the third). He bought his first copy of the First Folio in 1893.

---

[64] Jean Strouse, *Morgan: American Financier* (London: Harvill, 1999), p. 385.

Folger was by no means the first serious American Shakespearean book collector. From at least 1836 onwards, newly wealthy American collectors had been buying English books, particularly Shakespeare Folios.[65] James Lenox (1800–1880) acquired thirteen copies, including two First Folios, for his library on Fifth Avenue, beginning with the copy bought from the sale of James Baker's library in 1855. Lenox Library became a semi-public library for scholars in 1870 and, in 1895, it was consolidated with other trusts to form the New York Public Library.[66] Quaritch lamented that this 'destroy[ed] the individual character of the collection'.[67] (The NYPL now holds six copies.) But, by the turn of the twentieth century, this westward transfer had become a cause of concern. Sidney Lee's census in 1902 described a First Folio topography still centred on private owners in the UK, with about a third of extant copies in the US. But he saw that the balance was shifting and predicted that the transatlantic ratio would be reversed within a quarter century.[68] Writing an update in a 1923 volume to celebrate the Folio's tercentenary, Lee's tone was more urgent, calling on 'English millionaires' to imitate Henry Huntington's plan to make his collection available to the public: 'Otherwise there is a likelihood that all the forty privately owned copies of the volume still in this country will make tracks across the Atlantic.' Lee noted:

Unlike our rich men the American millionaire is usually fired, when his bank balance grows substantial, with a holy zeal to acquire a copy of the First Folio. I honour this aspiration on the part of America's plutocrats, although it is having the effect of draining this country of original copies of

---

[65] On American sales, see West, vol. 1, pp. 32–4.

[66] Carl L. Cannon, *American Book Collectors and Collecting From Colonial Times to the Present* (New York: H. W. Wilson Company, 1941), pp. 74–5.

[67] *Contributions towards a Dictionary of English Book-Collectors* 8 (London: Bernard Quaritch, 1896), n.p.

[68] Sidney Lee, *Notes & Additions to the Census of Copies of the First Folio* (London: Oxford University Press, 1906), p. 30.

the volume. English owners are exposed in these days of heavy taxation and of death duties to real temptation from America, and I am in doubt whether any copy of the First Folio now in private hands has a solid chance of escaping an early voyage across the Atlantic.[69]

Folger's enormous collection grew by stealth. He was not so wealthy that it was without effort, however. Whereas other super-rich American collectors such as J. P. Morgan could pay out vast sums seemingly without a second thought, Folger's Shakespeare purchases were always acquired through a more complicated and careful process of haggling, borrowing, repayment, and instalments. His cash income and expenditure were always strained. He frequently took out loans to acquire new books, and owed half a million dollars on these at the time of his death. The Folgers did not live a lavish personal lifestyle, and frequently excused themselves from other charitable contributions because of the extent of their financial commitments to Shakespeare. The collection grew, but remained secret. Folger was worried that a publicized interest in First Folios would inflate their price, and also concerned that his senior colleagues at Standard Oil, especially John D. Rockefeller, found the extent of his purchases a worrying sign of misdirected profligacy. Stephen H. Grant tells the story of Rockefeller's question to Folger about whether he had really paid $100,000 for a book (the Pavier quartos of 1619, with which Folger is pictured in his portrait by Frank Salisbury). Folger replied, evasively, that newspapers exaggerate. Rockefeller was relieved: 'we wouldn't want to think that the president of one of our major companies would be the kind of man foolish enough to pay $100,000 for a book'.[70] This reticence meant that the extent of his growing collection went largely unnoticed. Folger was hardly

---

[69] Sidney Lee, 'A Survey of First Folios', in *1623–1923: Studies in the First Folio Written for the Shakespeare Association* (London: Oxford University Press, 1924), pp. 78–105; p. 105; p. 99.
[70] Grant, p. xii.

on Sidney Lee's radar at the time of the census of Folio copies in
1902, although by 1906 Lee issued an update: 'Mr Folger is to be
congratulated on having acquired in the last few years as many as
eight copies of the First Folio in all—a record number for any
private collector.'[71] The extent of his purchases over the next few
years is extraordinary. In 1914, Folger wrote in a private letter, 'My
collection is, perhaps, unnecessarily strong in First Folios—yet
every one of the 47 copies seems to have an excuse for its
presence.'[72]

How might the aggregate of those individual excuses stack up?
Belk defines collecting as 'the process of actively, selectively, and
passionately acquiring and possessing things removed from ordinary use and perceived as part of a set of non-identical objects
or experiences'.[73] Actual collectors tended to prefer to mythologize
their activities, and to understand themselves as informed or
judicious cultural curators and the items in their collection as
revered treasures. Folger wrote in 1915 that 'I hope to use my
collection in the line of literary work and have not made it for the
purposes of exhibition, or to satisfy the ambitions of the mere
collector.'[74] The last phrase acknowledges the possible negative
associations of 'mere' collecting. Victorian observers of the age of
collecting had identified book collecting as a particular pathology.
The bibliographer, Thomas Dibdin, diagnosed a 'bibliomania'
traceable from the mid-eighteenth century and suggested its
vivid scenes might furnish a modern Holbein with a new panel
in a 'Dance of Death'. He prescribed a dose of public libraries as
'intellectual hospitals' for sufferers.[75] More recent fictional treatments of collectors —epitomized in the troubling title character of
John Fowles' 1963 debut novel *The Collector*—were creepier and
less amusing, and 'tend', wrote one analyst, 'to identify a repressed

[71] Lee (1906), pp. 29–30.   [72] Grant, 97.   [73] Belk (1995), p. 67.
[74] Quoted in Grant, p. 116.   [75] Dibdin, pp. 30–1, 551.

figure compensating for emotional lack'.[76] The wish/lack vocabulary of the key given to Emily Folger's 1896 numerical ranking of
the 1,200 Shakespeare books the couple most wanted to acquire
for their collection seems to partake of something similar, if less
pathological:

1. I wish under any circumstances,
2. I lack but think I can get,
3. I have, but think there may be better than mine,
4. I do not wish.[77]

Whatever emotional work Shakespeare First Folios did for the
couple is not retrievable. Folger's collection did, however, curiously
recapitulate one of the major themes of his business life. The
Standard Oil Company of New Jersey was indicted in 1911 for
monopolistic practices: the company 'with its vast accumulation of
property, because of its potency for harm and the dangerous
example which its continued existence affords, is an open and
enduring menace to all freedom of trade and a byword and
reproach to all modern economic methods'.[78] The Supreme
Court judgment found that the company had broken anti-trust
laws and ordered its immediate dissolution. Henry C. Folger was
one of the executives named in the indictment, and, as secretary,
signed the company order to break up Standard Oil into thirty-
four separate companies. As Folger acquired First Folios, so
Standard Oil acquired smaller companies: both instincts were
monopolistic, designed to drive out competitors from the market.
In retaining the integrity and secrecy of his growing collection of
First Folios, Folger compensated in bibliographic terms for the
failure to preserve the mega oil corporation from journalistic and
legal scrutiny, and dissolution. Writing in 1894, William Roberts
described the rare book market as 'a stock exchange in miniature',

---

[76] Belk (2014), p. 19.   [77] Grant, p. 82.
[78] Supreme Court judgment quoted in *New York Daily Tribune*, 16 May 1911.

but Folger was only buying.[79] The Folger Folios were not simply the cultural dividend from the system of plutocratic aggregation and monopolistic trading that was so characteristic of early twentieth-century American corporate business: they were its bibliographic synecdoche.

One self-justification for collectors is the reconceptualization of their objects. Withdrawn from the market, the objects in the collection are decontextualized within 'an economy of romance rather than an economy of commodities'. Within this mythology, the collector sometimes sees himself 'as a savior, risking much in order to rescue treasures that others fail to appreciate'.[80] Rescue narratives in which the romantic collector discovered an unloved First Folio, often being cheerfully neglected by provincial English peasants or mishandled by careless librarians, abounded. These stories served to establish the American buyer as the energetic champion of English cultural heritage, rather than its monied despoiler.

Introducing the catalogue of the collection of bibliophile and printing-press magnate, Robert Hoe, who had died in 1909, for example, Beverly Chew recalled a justificatory anecdote:

Mr Hoe once told me, on his return from Europe, of a visit he had made to one of the great Libraries, and of his feelings of surprise and disgust at the utter lack of reverence and appreciation he found as shown in the want of care given to the great monuments of printing. The catalogue of this library was rich in the masterpieces of the early printers, and when he asked for them, volume after volume was brought to him covered with dust, with leaves stained and bindings broken, and in every way proclaiming the effects of indifference and neglect.

---

[79] Quoted in Joseph F. Loewenstein, 'Authentic Reproductions: The Material Origins of the New Bibliography', in Laurie E. Maguire and Thomas L. Berger (eds), *Textual Formations and Reformations* (Newark: University of Delaware Press, 1998), pp. 23–44; p. 28.

[80] Belk (2014), p.20.

Hoe's will arranged for the break up of his collection at auction because he 'loved his books and wished them to pass after his death to those who would continue to cherish and care for them, and that they in their turn should transmit them to the booklovers of the future'.[81] (The most prominent of these booklovers at the New York sale of Hoe's books in 1911 was another substantial collector, Henry E. Huntington.) Here the collector appears to recognize the collection as corporally contiguous with himself: on his death it is deconstituted, returning to a series of individual items or auction lots like those from which it was originally compiled. Other American collectors faced down similarly unworthy British owners from whom valuable objects needed to be liberated. A. S. W. Rosenbach recalled tea with the Countess of Caledon whose unbookish husband had bought Bishop Percy's scholarly collection wholesale to furnish his beautiful new Nash library. She confided in him that she 'had known of [their] First Folio of Shakespeare but had always been doubtful whether the scribbled notes in the margins were written by Shakespeare or not'.[82] In fact they were almost certainly by Joseph Batailhey writing at the turn of seventeenth century, who has written his name at several points in the volume.[83] The encounter is a scene from Henry James—an etiolated and intellectually torpid Old World burdened with cultural lumber meets a vigorously inquiring and monied New World. It is not surprising that James wrote a play, later a novella, *The Outcry* (1911), on the encounter between an American art collector (a portrait of J. P. Morgan) and a washed-up English nobility living impecuniously at the morbidly named 'Dedborough Hall'.

[81] Beverly Chew, 'Foreword', *Catalogue of the Library of Robert Hoe of New York Auction beginning 24 April 1911* (New York: Anderson Auction Company, 1911), n.p.

[82] Leslie A. Morris, *Rosenbach Redux: Further Book Adventures in England and Ireland* (Philadelphia: Rosenbach Museum and Library, 1989), p. 32.

[83] West 134.

Such stories of ignorant and unappreciative owners who did not deserve the privilege of cultural stewardship were common currency. One indicative anecdote of finding a First Folio in the library of a country house, serves, as often, to confirm the teller's own connoisseurship and suavity:

I took down at random a tall old book, bare-backed, but with faded green sides, opened it, then looked quickly for the title-page and portrait. All were there. When my hostess returned I threw my bomb. 'If I may suggest it,' I said, 'I should have this repaired and find a place for it on the shelves. It would easily make the reputation of a library by itself.' She looked politely interested. 'Really? What have you found?' 'A book which I believe to be worth some three thousand pounds.' Then her interest ceased to be merely polite. 'Good heavens!' she said, 'what can that be?' I replied, 'A first-folio Shakespeare'. That bomb was not a 'dud'.[84]

Referring to the prevalence of such biblio-romance, Sidney Lee assured readers that his *Census* dealt in 'hard unromantic fact' and cited 'an American biographer of Shakespeare' who had told him he 'was better fitted for statistics than aesthetics'. Nevertheless, along with his attempt to establish a quasi-scientific bibliographic hierarchy of copies, he still described his search for books as 'a quest' that was 'exhilarating and not without adventure' amid aristocratic and eccentric owners.[85] More recently, one of the jacket quotations for Eric Rasmussen's pacy account of how 'a team of First Folio hunters' 'uncovered a fascinating world between the covers of one of the world's most expensive books, one populated with thieves, masterminds, fools, and eccentrics, all of whom have risked fortunes and reputations to possess a coveted First Folio' identified its popular generic appeal: 'Indiana Jones... pursues the Bard'.[86] Some of this residual romance narrative

[84] Maurice Hewlett, *Extemporary Essays* (London and New York: Humphrey Milford, Oxford University Press, 1922), pp. 121–2.

[85] Lee (1924), pp. 78, 80.

[86] Eric Rasmussen, *The Shakespeare Thefts: In Search of the First Folios* (Basingstoke: Palgrave Macmillan, 2011), pp. xi, xv.

resurfaced in the coverage of the discovery of a First Folio in the library at the Jesuit College in St-Omer in France in 2014: 'An extremely rare First Folio of the plays of William Shakespeare has been uncovered in France, having sat undisturbed for more than 400 years in the library of St-Omer near Calais', wrote the *Huffington Post*. Bringing the book back to London on tour, the French chevalier-librarian, Remy Cordonnier, poetically called this 'forgotten' copy 'Sleeping Beauty', with the faint associations of unspoilt, even virginal perfection.[87] In fact, the main claim to scholarly interest of this copy was less its undefiled condition, but, more, its extensive range of manuscript annotations in different hands, some of them apparently directed towards performance, and largely dating from the eighteenth and nineteenth centuries (see Chapter 4). But the romance of discovery—even when that discovery was in a library, hardly the last place anyone might look for a rare book—continued to drive the news story.

In one of his very few forays into print on the subject of his collection, 'A Unique First Folio', Henry Folger described a heroic quest at Canwick Hall in Lincolnshire, seat of the Sibthorp family. Folger cited his agent's account:

having finished work in the library, I was taken to the coach-house, in which was a large case of books. On the top of the case, outside, were stacked a great number of folios covered with dust. These were passed to me by an assistant who lived on the estate. On throwing down a volume which was tightly tied around with cord, he remarked, 'That is no good sir, it is only old poetry.' I unloosed the string, opened the books and, at a glance, saw what a treasure was found.[88]

---

[87] http://www.huffingtonpost.co.uk/2014/11/25/shakespeare-first-folio-discovered-in-french-library-having-been-overlooked-for-400-years_n_6221838.html (accessed April 2015).

[88] Henry Folger, in *Outlook*, 23 November 1907, quoted by Rosenbach in *Henry Clay Folger*, p. 91.

In fact the rescue narrative here elides a more extended and hard-nosed commercial interaction in which the price and terms of acquisition were negotiated by trans-Atlantic cable. The Sibthorp folio had an early and immediate provenance that made it extremely desirable for Folger. While he was printing the First Folio in 1622, William was also involved in the latest stage in a publishing skirmish on the contentious subject of heraldry. His friend Augustine Vincent was a herald and antiquary who had published, with Jaggard, *A Discovery of Errors*, a book criticizing a previous work on genealogy by Ralph Brooke. This book was also acquired by the aspiring Edward Dering in the early 1620s. In *A Discovery of Errors*, Jaggard defended himself against Brooke's claim that the mistakes in his book were due to printer error. In return it appears that the Jaggards made Vincent a gift of a copy of the Shakespeare First Folio: the Sibthorp copy carries the inscription 'Ex Dono Willi. Jaggard Typographi. ao 1623'.[89] This is in Vincent's writing, not William Jaggard's, who had died only weeks before the First Folio finally reached the London bookstalls. This early provenance blinded Folger to other, less desirable aspects of the book, which had been restored and perfected by the bookseller A. B. Railton, including supplying missing leaves from other copies, and of the flyleaf and final leaf in facsimile. Folger bargained hard with Sibthorp over a period of years to get hold of this prize, finally agreeing with his British agent to 'buy without fail even at ten thousand cash but arrange time payments if you can' and thus setting a new high for Folio prices.[90] It was categorized in his library as Folio 1 in recognition of its perceived importance in the collection.

Folger's own self-construction as the unassuming but loyal champion of unappreciated bibliographic riches continues to resonate in the biography of his influential library. Michael D. Bristol, discussing Folger in volume nine of the *Great*

---

[89] West 59.   [90] Blayney (1991), pp. 44–5.

Shakespeareans series (2011) observes defensively, that, before Folger, 'many copies of the early editions were held in private collections, mostly on the estates of wealthy British families. The books were not always appreciated or properly cared for, and it was often difficult for scholars to find a convenient way to study them.' This is a partial and romantic history of the collection, based on hindsight. Bristol half-acknowledges that all modern Shakespeareans, including himself, are potentially compromised by the powerful and generous academic patronage exerted on scholarship by the Folger library: 'to portray its creator as a conniving, cigar-smoking, capitalist scoundrel would be more than a bit churlish, to say the least, especially for the present writer, who has certainly benefited greatly from having access to Folger's rare book collection'.[91]

Such access was not open to scholars of Folger's own time, however. These books were kept in storage. If Folger had always planned a research library he did not publicize this ambition before an announcement in 1928, so, as far as scholars and booksellers were concerned, his purchases were entirely inaccessible, withdrawn from circulation, and marked out as distinctly, even selfishly, private property. In her book on the desires and motives of collecting, *On Longing*, Susan Stewart observes that 'the boundary between collection and fetishism is mediated by classification and display in tension with accumulation and secrecy'.[92] During his own lifetime, Folger's Folio acquisitions seemed to be decisively on the wrong side of this demarcation: accumulated rather than classified, secret rather than on display, and thus less a collection than a fetish. Even the ghost of Shakespeare, in a cartoon by Bernard Partridge, seemed disturbed (Figure. 1.1). At a time of enormous bibliographic energy and the renewed attention to

---

[91] Michael Bristol, in Cary DiPietro (ed.), *Bradley, Greg, Folger* (London: Continuum, 2011), pp. 115, 164.

[92] Susan Stewart, *On Longing: Narratives of the Miniature, the Gigantic, the Souvenir, the Collection* (Baltimore: Johns Hopkins University Press, 1984), p. 163.

FIG. 1.1.　Henry Folger as Autolycus, by Bernard Partridge

material texts characteristic of the New Bibliographers such as A. W. Pollard and W. W. Greg, the sequestration of large amounts of important primary material away from the prevailing gentlemanly conventions of scholarship in which book owners, experts, scholars and librarians were in regular communication, was distinctly unpopular. In 1920, Pollard's measured article for *The Library* on the distribution of rare books between Britain and the US noted that the large 'number of copies in Mr Folger's ownership (I wish I could say 'In his library') offers a promise of future possibilities of a really exhaustive collation which is all to the good'.[93] In the circumstances, it was a generous assessment. Pollard had attempted, unsuccessfully, to consult, for his important *A Census of Shakespeare's Plays in Quarto 1594–1709* (co-authored by Henrietta C. Bartlett and printed in 1916), the earliest extant play quarto, the 1594 *Titus Andronicus* which Folger had bought in Sweden in 1905 and 'is now apparently reposing in one of Mr Folger's inaccessible boxes'. Pollard compared Folger's disregard for the academic availability of his purchases to the 'sportsmanlike promptitude' of W. A. White of New York, in allowing a new 1598 edition of *Richard II* to be reproduced in facsimile.[94] The *Titus* quarto was not available for scholarly collation until the eventual opening of the Library in 1932.

The Sheldon copy, then still in the binding stamped with the family arms, made its way from the London auction room of the Burdett Coutts sale in 1922, via Rosenbach as agent, into Folger's 'inaccessible boxes'. But there was a plan to make the material available to scholars. From 1919 onwards, Folger had begun, in his characteristically unshowy way, to acquire land and property on East Capitol Street. His plan, announced in 1929, was for a library

---

[93] A. W. Pollard, 'The Division of Rare English Books between England and the United States', *The Library* 20 (1920), pp. 111–19; p. 113.

[94] H. C. Bartlett and A. W. Pollard, *A Census of Shakespeare's Plays in Quarto 1594–1709* (New Haven: Yale University Press; London: Oxford University Press, 1916), pp. xxiv–xxv.

as a private research institution for professional scholarship rather than a public or educational facility. Folger was not Carnegie; and nor were First Folios directed towards Carnegie's 'gospel of wealth': 'to place within [the community's] reach the ladders upon which the aspiring can rise'.[95]

The new library was opened in 1932, after Henry Folger's death. At his funeral the eulogy anticipated:

His dust will repose in the marble temple that will rise at Washington. His spiritual presence will overshadow it as the years come and go. The golden gates of another Renaissance will open. A new America will come, just as providential in the order of succession as that of Washington or Lincoln; an America which shall do on a wholesale scale what he did individually, which shall take the gifts of the market place and lay them without regard to cost or labor upon the altar of a more spiritualized existence for men and for nations.[96]

The library was designed by the French-Philadelphian architect, Paul Philippe Cret, with a Tudor-style interior including a large panelled reading room with scholars' desks amid a minstrels' gallery, baronial fireplace, and armchairs (Figure 1.2). There are portraits of the Folgers and, now, of Queen Elizabeth II. Speaking to the Meridian Club in 1933, Emily Folger described the relationship between the collection and the building: 'the Library was to be the First Folio, illustrated'.[97] Its marble neo-classical facade was decorated with quotations in First Folio orthography, taken from the book's prefatory material and preserving its particular spelling. These included Jonson's economium 'thou art a moniment without a tombe | And art alive still while thy booke doth live | And we have wits to read, and praise to give', and Heminge

---

[95] Andrew Carnegie, 'Wealth', *North American Review* 148 (June 1889), pp. 653–64; pp. 663–4.
[96] S. Parkes Cadman, *Henry C Folger 18 June 1857–11 June 1930* (New Haven, privately printed 1931), pp. 18–19.
[97] Grant, p. 81.

FIG. 1.2.   Folger Shakespeare Library
The Elizabethan-style interior of the Folger Shakespeare Library, Washington DC.

and Condell in 'To the Great Variety of Readers': 'his wit can no more lie hid | then it could be lost. | Read him therefore and againe and againe'. The building's bas-reliefs of plays, by John Gregory, were also titled in First Folio orthography: 'The Tragedie of King Lear' and 'A Midsommer Nights Dream'. As the Folio memorialized Shakespeare, so the library memorialized Folger.

The library, however rich its collections and aspirational its design, immediately became cash poor. In his *Recollections of the Folger Shakespeare Library* of 1950, Stanley King, the former president of Amhurst College, which had been bequeathed the library in Folger's will, set out its gloomy financial position even before its official opening on April 23 1932: 'this made total charges of two-hundred and sixty-one thousand dollars a year against an income of sixty-five thousand dollars'.[98] However, the library established its scholarly and financial position. A new director, Louis B. Wright, disarmed the guards, developed the continental holdings of the collection, and instituted grants to allow scholars to visit the Folger.[99] During the Second World War, all the Folger's valuable books, including the Sheldon First Folio, were removed from Washington to a vault in Amherst for safety, and Hinman wrote in 1953 that his work collating Folios had been interrupted since 'as a precaution against possible disaster only about half of the irreplaceable Folger copies are being kept in the Library in Washington'.[100] As the Folio evacuation during the confusion in Washington DC on 11 September 2001 further demonstrated, that high prestige location of the library on Capitol Hill was also risky. Whereas the Folger's original mission was consciously elitist in 1960, Wright reasserted that its 'main responsibility is to the few, to the leaders in the humanities, to the scholars who can use most effectively its source materials'—it has since developed an active, public-facing role.[101] One copy of the First Folio is on permanent public display at the Folger, and it has digitized three of its copies for online display. In 2014 it announced a plan for a touring exhibition in 2016 which would send one of its First Folios, open at Hamlet's 'to be or not to be' soliloquy [3.1.58], to every state in the US.

The Sheldon copy may not encapsulate the entirely continuous provenance narrative that Sidney Lee desired, but, in its transfers

[98] Stanley King, *Recollections of the Folger Shakespeare Library* (Ithaca: Cornell University Press for the Trustees of Amherst College, 1950), p. 11.

[99] Frederick Hard (ed.), *Louis B. Wright: A Bibliography and Appreciation* (Charlottesville: University of Virginia Press for the Folger Shakespeare Library, 1968), p. 41. On the early development of the Library collection and organization, see *The Folger Library: A Decade of Growth, 1950–1960* (Washington: The Folger Shakespeare Library, 1960).

[100] Charlton Hinman, 'The Proof-Reading of the First Folio Text of *Romeo and Juliet*', *Studies in Bibliography* 6 (1954), pp. 61–70; p. 61.

[101] Hard (ed.), p. 45.

of ownership, it is implicated in a range of Folio narratives touching on collecting, on gender, on nationality and, above all, on the vital figure of Henry Clay Folger in the biography of this book.

The second biggest collection of First Folios outside the Folger Shakespeare Library is held at Meisei University in Tokyo. One of its dozen First Folios bears, in a clear, almost childlike, script, the ownership mark of 'Tho: and Isabella' (Figure 1.3). This inscription is recognizable from scores of other extant books, many of them still in the library at Ickworth Manor in Suffolk. Thomas Hervey (1625–94), member of parliament for Bury St Edmunds, was a one-time navy commissioner with Samuel Pepys, who described him as 'a very drolle' after an evening's drinking at the Dolphin Tavern in June 1665, but later fell out with him over Hervey's alleged laziness. He married Isabella, daughter of Sir Humphrey May, in 1658. Their memorial in Ickworth described them as exemplars of 'conjugal affection', and their son John described how his widowed father wrote a verse to Isabella's memory every year on the anniversary of her death.[102] This particularly strong bond expresses itself directly in their joint ownership inscription—apparently written by Thomas—which reconfigures their books as a testament to their household intimacy. These are not formal signatures for external readers or marks of possession as the book moves through the world: they rarely include the couple's surname, for instance. Rather, they are witness to the private and shared enjoyment of particular texts.

Even a preliminary assessment of this now scattered library—no early or more recent catalogue exists—makes clear the wide range of their reading interests. The Herveys built a large collection of vernacular, classical, and European works. Their copies of a 1561 edition of Langland's *Piers Plowman*, George Herbert's poetry collection *The Temple* (1633), and John Donne's *Devotions*, like

[102] Hervey, Sir Thomas (1625–94) in *The History of Parliament Online*: http://www.historyofparliamentonline.org/volume/1660-1690/member/hervey-sir-thomas-1625-94 (accessed April 2015).

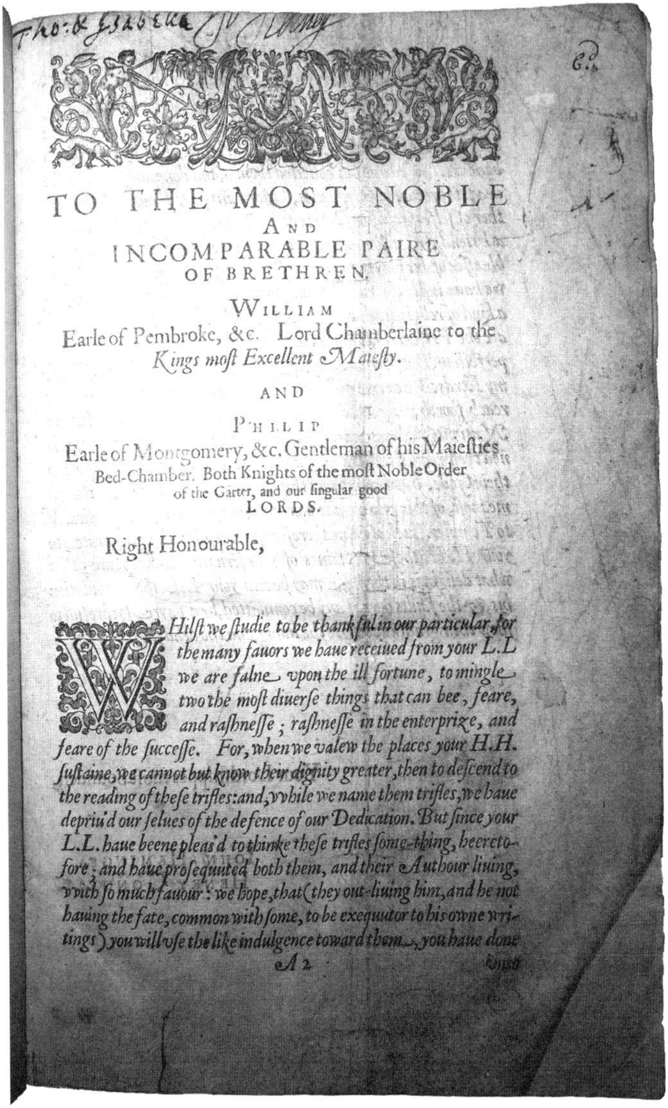

TO THE MOST NOBLE
AND
INCOMPARABLE PAIRE
OF BRETHREN.

WILLIAM
Earle of Pembroke, &c. Lord Chamberlaine to the
Kings most Excellent Maiesty.

AND

PHILIP
Earle of Montgomery, &c. Gentleman of his Maiesties
Bed-Chamber. Both Knights of the most Noble Order
of the Garter, and our singular good
LORDS.

Right Honourable,

Hilst we studie to be thankfull in our particular, for
the many fauors we haue receiued from your L.L
we are falne vpon the ill fortune, to mingle
two the most diuerse things that can bee, feare,
and rashnesse; rashnesse in the enterprize, and
feare of the successe. For, when we valew the places your H.H.
sustaine, we cannot but know their dignity greater, then to descend to
the reading of these trifles: and, vvhile we name them trifles, we haue
depriu'd our selues of the defence of our Dedication. But since your
L.L. haue beene pleas'd to thinke these trifles some-thing, heereto-
fore; and haue prosequuted both them, and their Author liuing,
vvith so much fauour: we hope, that (they out-liuing him, and he not
hauing the fate, common with some, to be exequutor to his owne writings) you will vse the like indulgence toward them, you haue done

A2

FIG. 1.3.   Meisei Thomas and Isabella Hervey
The ownership mark of Thomas and Isabella Hervey of Ickworth in Suffolk, in a
copy now in Meisei, Japan.

copies of the Jacobean city comedy *Northward Ho* (1607), an Italian edition of Machiavelli from 1550, collections of speeches both by Oliver Cromwell and Charles I, a Latin edition of Erasmus' colloquies, scientific works by William Harvey and Robert Hooke, and works by the antiquarians, Richard Verstegan and William Camden, are all co-inscribed. Isabella is therefore not just included in the light, recreational, or English-language material that might be judged more appropriate female reading matter. Rather, she is a full co-creator of, and partner in, the extensive intellectual range represented in the library. Some books that seem to have been owned by Thomas before his marriage have been reinscribed to include her. Thus the Ickworth copy of the writings of the sixteenth-century Protestant writer, Jean Bodin, has been reinscribed: it has the ownership marks 'Tho: Hervey' and then 'Tho: & Isabella' underneath.

The Hervey copy of the First Folio is scattered with common-placing marks, underlinings, manuscript corrections, and other symbols that indicate attention to most of the plays in the book. Perhaps the Herveys together, or individually, planned to work through the whole book systematically: the openings of the first play, *The Tempest*, seem to employ a complicated differentiated system of symbols marking out different aspects of the text. This hieroglyphic perhaps becomes burdensome, and is dropped by the time the drunken Trinculo and Stephano have suborned Caliban, and Ferdinand has been set to work to affirm his love for Miranda, half way through the play [3.1]. Passages of apparent note to the Herveys later in the volume include the taut encounter between Isabella and the corrupt deputy Angelo in *Measure for Measure*, in which many lines including her fervent declaration that she would 'strip my selfe to death, as to a bed' [2.4.102], are underlined. They also noted Ulysses' long speech on degree in *Troilus and Cressida* [1.3.85–123] (marked with a wavy marginal line), many of the lines in Mark Antony's speech over Caesar's body in *Julius Caesar* [3.2.74–106], and the malapropistic comedy of Dogberry and the watch in *Much Ado About Nothing* [2.5]. This sense of reading for comic and poetic pleasure as well as for political or moral philosophy confirms the place of the Herveys' First Folio in an actively used library of literary, historical, political, religious, and scientific works, many of which, like the Shakespeare, are annotated.

These traces of their reading corroborate other evidence of the warmth and affection of their marriage, so as to situate their books, including the First Folio, as affective symbols. A majority of titles remain at Ickworth, rebuilt as a striking and eccentric Italianate folly at the beginning of the nineteenth century, and transferred to the National Trust in lieu of death duties in 1956.[103] The books that have left the collection—the Shakespeare, early modern play quartos, the Donne, the Langland—are an index to the differential value of the books collected in an early modern library in subsequent markets.[104]

It is not entirely clear when the First Folio, or indeed these other volumes, left Ickworth. Thomas and Isabella's son, John Hervey, first Earl of Bristol (1665–1751), developed their collection and added his name to their books, including above the title of *The Tempest* in their First Folio. Perhaps he was also responsible for the swirls and doodles of ink that may represent juvenile pen practice in the volume. John's son, the second Baron Hervey (1696–1743), was a courtier and memoirist cruelly satirized as the sexually ambivalent cherub Sporus by Pope in the memorable phrase in the 'Epistle to Dr Arbuthnot': 'Satire or sense, alas! Can Sporus feel? | Who breaks a butterfly upon a wheel?' The Hervey Folio's next attested owner, Lord Lyttelton (1709–93) was also a prominent figure in the literary drama and quarrels of the first half of the eighteenth century, who wrote a verse epistle to Hervey in 1730 urging him to 'be a country gentleman at heart'.

[103] For the current holdings of the library at Ickworth, see http://www.nationaltrustcollections.org.uk.

[104] The Donne and the Langland are included in Nicholas Barker and Simon Jervis, *Treasures from the Libraries of National Trust Country Houses* (New York: Royal Oak Foundation & The Grolier Club, 1999).

The Whig politician and partisan literary patron was the dedicatee of his schoolmate Henry Fielding's, *The History of Tom Jones, a Foundling* ((1749–50); he may have been the model for Squire Allworthy). He was satirized as the scrawny Sir Gosling Scrag in Smollett's *Peregrine Pickle*, and was the addressee of James Thomson's *The Seasons*, a poem the author revised while at Lyttelton's home, Hagley Hall, in Worcestershire. Lyttelton was in correspondence with Voltaire and, unlike Baron Hervey, was a friend and supporter of Pope. In *An Epistle to Mr Pope*, he used the mouthpiece of Virgil's ghost to urge the poet away from 'meaner satire' and instead to 'join the patriot to the poet's praise'.[105] In return he received from Pope a series of literary busts, including one of Shakespeare, by Peter Sheemakers, whose most famous commission had been the statue of Shakespeare in Poet's Corner in 1740. These joined a commanding painting of Pope and his dog by Jonathan Richardson decorating the library in his fine Palladian house.

Hagley was set in a park fashionably laid out, with advice from Pope, in picturesque style with grottoes and other follies. It was much admired by Horace Walpole and by John Adams travelling in England with Thomas Jefferson. Adams was keen to visit Lyttelton, whom he knew from Pope's works, and found his Worcestershire excursion 'poetical' while seeming to disapprove of the munificence of the nobility in England whose 'residences of greatness and luxury' depended on 'a national debt of two hundred and seventy four millions sterling'.[106] Adams and Jefferson also visited Stratford-upon-Avon, so they may well have been interested to view the Hagley Shakespeare. In later years, Lyttelton collaborated with his friend, the bluestocking Elizabeth Montagu: perhaps she too had cause to consult his First Folio at Hagley

---

[105] George Lyttelton, *The Poetical Works of George Lyttelton* (Edinburgh: 1781), p. 86; pp. 82–3.
[106] John Adams and Charles Francis Adams, *The Works of John Adams, Second President of the United States*, 10 vols (Boston: Little, Brown, 1850–6), vol. 3, p. 395.

during the writing of her defence of Shakespeare's 'dramatic
genius' against some of the editorial commentary of Pope and
Johnson, which was published in 1769 as *An essay on the writings
and genius of Shakespear, compared with the Greek and French
dramatic Poets*.

The Hagley Hall bookplate of the Lyttelton family thus joins
the signatures of Thomas, Isabella and John Hervey in the copy of
the First Folio that passed between them across the centuries. The
book remained in the Lyttelton family at Hagley, surviving the fire
in 1925 that destroyed the library, much of the house, and many of
the fine paintings, of which a catalogue had been published in
1900. It survived also the Folio feeding-frenzy of the early twentieth century, presumably ignoring or rejecting the overture of
Folger, who got his agent to write to all the owners identified in
Lee's 1902 Census asking if they would consider selling. It was
finally put up for sale in 1990, when the ready money was to the
east, not the west, of the UK, and when a minor Tokyo university
was coming to the end of a remarkable bibliophile spending spree.

Meisei University was founded in April 1964, initially as a
merger of smaller engineering and physical sciences institutions
to form a new technical and business higher education institute to
contribute to Japan's astonishing post-war economic boom. The
university expanded to include the humanities—although it has
never had a Department of Literature. Four years after its founding, it bought a copy of Charlton Hinman's newly published
Norton facsimile of the First Folio, sparking an active—and
expensive—round of antiquarian acquisitions under the leadership
of its enthusiastic President Mitsuo Kodama. It gradually acquired
the later folios and boosted its library with a large collection of
5,000 duplicate books from the Folger Shakespeare Library in June
1973. Later purchases from the libraries of scholars Allardyce
Nichol and Alice Walker added to the collection. In 1975, it
bought its first First Folio, a copy that had belonged to the
nineteenth, century collector Thomas Phillips. The Houghton
copy, complete with extensive seventeenth-century annotations

by William Johnstoone (see Chapter 2), was acquired at auction in 1980, by which time this otherwise unremarkable university owned four copies of the First Folio along with numerous copies of the later folios. Five years later, it could list a further five copies of the First Folio in the second volume of its catalogue, *Shakespeare and Shakespeariana*. The third, and final, volume, published in 1993 as the Japanese economy began to stagnate, marked the end of the bibliographic boom which had enabled the library to acquire twelve copies of the First Folio, the largest collection after that of Folger in Washington DC. Meisei's Shakespeare purchases, like the collection of French impressionist paintings it acquired over the same period, were enabled by, and were a triumphant symbol of, Japanese national pride at its economic dominance over the west, and a particular kind of trophy for Kodama, whose own major academic work had produced a study of the post-war Allied occupation of Japan.

The iconography of the world's second largest collection is rather different from that adopted by the Folger: Meisei frequently reproduces photographs of all of its Folios, standing upright, spines outward, their differing sizes drawing attention to their number. By contrast, the Folger has tended to display one exemplary or metonymic copy in its Great Hall, an emphasis on singularity which is, as its then Director admitted, 'a bit misleading, and for us, perhaps even a bit self-serving'.[107] One of these Meisei trophies was the copy that had moved from Thomas and Isabella Hervey's marital library at Ickworth via the Lyttelton family at Hagley Hall. Sold in 1990 along with copies of the other three seventeenth-century Folios for almost a million US dollars, it now acquired the shelf mark MR3570 in the panelled, air-conditioned and temperature controlled strong-room that is the Kodama Memorial library at the university's Hino campus.

---

[107] Blayney (1991), 'Foreword' by Werner Gundersheimer, n.p.

A different magic encyclopaedia can be compiled for the third example: the copy of the First Folio that left Edward Blount's shop in Paul's Churchyard for the Bodleian Library in Oxford at the end of 1623. On the founding of his library at the beginning of the century, the scholar and diplomat, Thomas Bodley, had entered into an agreement with the Stationers' Company that a copy of any book published in London would be provided on request, but, famously, at the same time he instructed his librarian:

I can see no reason to alter my opinion for excluding such books as almanacs, plays, and an infinite number that are daily printed of very unworthy matters and handling ... haply some plays may be worthy the keeping, but hardly one in forty ... [W]ere it so that some little profit might be reaped (which God knows is very little) out of some of our playbooks, the benefit thereof will nothing near countervail the harm that the scandal will bring unto the library, when it shall be given out that we stuff it full of baggage books.[108]

None of the more than sixty individual editions of Shakespeare plays and poems printed before 1623 had found their way into the library in the early seventeenth century.

'Baggage' books were, literally, portable ones, in small formats, and it may have been observing this size distinction that permitted the library to request the 1623 Folio—if, indeed, the book came via this route. Thus the size of the book was more important than its Shakespearean contents. It was received unbound: most copies of the Folio, in common with other books of the period, were sold as a sheaf of gathered pages for binding at separate premises according to the specifications of their owner. The Bodleian sent their book for binding at William Wildgoose's workshop in Oxford, in February 1624. The First Folio was part of a small consignment of ten books sent to Wildgoose, of which all but one were recent, and six were in Latin. Wildgoose's handiwork was

[108] G. A. Wheeler (ed.), *Letters of Sir Thomas Bodley to Thomas James* (Oxford: Clarendon Press, 1926), pp. 221–2.

a plain reversed-calf binding with oblique hatching on the spine, according to Library specifications.[109] On its return, the First Folio was given the shelfmark S.2.17 Art, and was chained, with its fore-edge out from the shelf, in the Arts End of the library, for consultation by readers.

The First Folio seems to have remained in the Bodleian for the next four decades. The library does not appear to have received a copy of the Second Folio when it was printed in 1632, although it did acquire a couple of early Shakespeare quartos in bequests by the author of *The Anatomy of Melancholy*, Robert Burton, and by John Seldon (copies of *Venus and Adonis* and of *Hamlet* respectively). The First Folio is first formally listed in an Appendix Catalogue of 1635. Later accounts suggested it was heavily consulted during that period, although, as will become clear, this aspect of the volume's history may be tendentious, adduced for a particular purpose. But at some point, the book left the library. A catalogue of 1674 lists the 1664 Third Folio but not that of 1623. It is probable that when the Restoration edition, with its promise of additional plays, was acquired, the First Folio was de-accessioned as an obsolete edition. There was then no particular value attached to an earlier over a later edition: indeed, the historian of book-collecting, John Carter, identified as late as 1948 that chronological priority as the overriding interest of bibliphiles was a 'quite modern development'.[110] It was not a priority for diarist Samuel Pepys, for example, who did something similar to the Bodleian later in the century, replacing his Third Folio with a Fourth when

---

[109] Andrew Honey and Arthur Green, 'Met by Chance—A Group of Ten Books Bound for the Bodleian Library in February 1624 by William Wildgoose of Oxford', conference paper given at the *Men and Books: From Microorganisms to Megaorganisms* (Horn II Conference), St. Pölten, Austria, 28 April–1 May 2014, forthcoming in the conference proceedings.

[110] John Carter, *Taste and Technique in Book-Collecting: A Study of Recent Developments in Great Britain and the United States* (Cambridge: Cambridge University Press, 1948), p. 20.

it was published in 1685.[111] When Nicholas Rowe came to present the first edited collection of Shakespeare's plays (discussed in Chapter 3), he based his text not on the earliest but on the Fourth, the most recent Folio. Most likely, the Bodleian's First Folio was included in a job lot of so-called 'superfluous Library books sold by order of the Curators' to the Oxford bookseller Richard Davis in the year 1664.[112] Like many of the institutions associated with the university, the Bodleian was still reeling from the effects of the civil war and the crippling expense of Charles's tenure in Oxford. In addition, the library had taken delivery in 1659 of the last of the polymath John Selden's vast bequest of 8,000 volumes—about half as much again as its current holdings, leading to a crisis of both money and shelving space. The Library's—rational—policy was to purge unwanted volumes and sell off duplicates.[113]

So far as the Bodleian was concerned, the book was lost, until, in January 1905, it was brought, unannounced, to the office of its sub-librarian, Falconer Madan, by an undergraduate, Gladwyn Turbutt, who had brought an old volume of Shakespeare from his family home at Ogston Hall in Derbyshire, to get advice on its restoration. Madan immediately recognized Wildgoose's handi-work, and the rip in the board that indicated the forceful removal of the clip that would have secured the chain to the shelf in the seventeenth-century reading room, confirmed the identification (Figure 1.4). This copy of the First Folio had been lost from the library for two hundred and fifty years. The story of how the Library got it back was connected to a range of larger issues, from the internal politics of the library and the university during a time of institutional change to the fiscal policies of Lloyd

[111] Lee (1924), p. 85.

[112] Falconer Madan and Gladwyn Turbutt, *The Original Bodleian Copy of the First Folio of Shakespeare (The Turbutt Shakespeare)* (Oxford: Clarendon Press, 1905), p. 5.

[113] Ian Philip, *The Bodleian Library in the Seventeenth and Eighteenth Centuries* (Oxford: Clarendon Press, 1983), p. 59.

FIG. 1.4.   Bodleian binding
This binding from 1624 shows the mark where the clip held the book by a chain to
the reading room shelf.

George's government in the early years of the twentieth century, and widespread anxieties about the transfer of culturally valuable objects from England to the USA. Appealing for donations to buy back the Folio marked the university's first real development effort, setting out some of the ongoing issues about institutional priorities, the role of philanthropy in the modern university, and the value of this specific edition and this particular copy.

On an interpersonal level, the discovery of the Bodleian First Folio was bound to increase tensions between Bodley's librarian and his deputy, because it opened up the faultlines in their differing attitudes to their role in the Edwardian university. Falconer Madan (1851–1935), the sub-librarian, was a scholar-librarian in his fifties who had been working at the Bodleian for twenty years, much of it while in post as university lecturer in paleography. His academic credentials were impeccable: having worked on the revision of Liddell and Scott's Greek–English lexicon, he was also the major figure in the Bodleian's great feat of bibliographic consolidation, its Summary Catalogue. He was a founder member of the Bibliographical Society and an acknowledged expert on manuscript cataloguing and on the early book trade in Oxford: a scholar-librarian. Edward Nicholson (1847–1912) had a different background and outlook: as an undergraduate at Trinity College, he was more interested in being librarian of the Oxford Union debating society than in his studies. He pursued a professional career in librarianship as librarian of the London Institute, where he comprehensively overhauled the library and the educational programme, influenced by new developments in American libraries. Nicholson's appointment as Bodley's Librarian in 1881 was thus a real break with academic tradition, championed by the arch-modernizing Vice-Chancellor, Benjamin Jowett. In fact, Nicholson became an active and progressive controversialist in many aspects of the Oxford politics of the *fin-de-siècle*, including women's education (he was pro) and scientific experimentation on animals (he was against). His tenure was not an entire success. The *Times* obituary at his death noted delicately that 'it was a difficult post to fill at a difficult time', and observed 'Oxford, while impatient for reform, is always impatient of reformers'.[114] The reforming Nicholson came to a library which was starved of space and money, and he worked tirelessly to expand its physical footprint and to anticipate its ever-increasing storage needs by developing a modern underground bookstore with rolling bookcases.

Madan and Nicholson thus embodied the contrasting figures of the librarian as scholar and as administrator, or, to adapt the more loaded terms identified by Marjorie Garber in *Academic Instincts*, the librarian as gentlemanly amateur or as career professional.[115] And if Madan was at odds with Nicholson, he was also on a collision course with the Folio's owners. On the proof copy of his pamphlet on the rediscovered Shakespeare First Folio, he made

---

[114] *The Times*, 18 March 1912.
[115] See the discussion of 'gentleman' and 'amateur' in Marjorie B. Garber, *Academic Instincts* (Princeton, NJ: Princeton University Press, 2001), pp. 1–52.

a decisive change: the title had originally been 'The Turbutt First Folio Shakespeare', but Madan changed it to 'The Original Bodleian Copy of the First Folio of Shakespeare' with, in rather smaller letters below, '(The Turbutt Shakespeare)'. The proprietorial claim was unmistakeable. Part of the pamphlet's intent was to maximize the Bodleian provenance of the volume and to minimize the Turbutts' own claims to ownership. Madan's bibliographic enquiries, therefore, were deeply partial, designed to furnish evidence of the care and attention bestowed on the book during its first forty or so years, and to suggest that the clock had stopped at the time it had left the Bodleian and 'lain for a century and a half in the library of Ogston Hall, Derbyshire'.[116]

The volume was almost complete save for a missing verse leaf and some bumped and torn corners, and it had virtually no annotations. The Latin oath for readers to be admitted to the Bodleian in the seventeenth century swore them to treat books carefully and not 'openly or underhand, by way of embezeling, changing, razing, defacing, tearing, cutting, noting, interlining, or by voluntarie corrupting, blotting, slurring or any other manner of mangling or misusing, any one of more of the said books, either wholly or in part'. Thomas Bodley's own English translation here serves, in the act of interdiction, incidentally to record the range of practices that might be unleashed on the early modern book.[117] Madan undertook a detailed description of the wear and tear to each leaf of the book, in order to demonstrate which plays were most popular with early seventeenth-century library readers (the Bodleian's policy was not to allow undergraduates, but only those who had been awarded the Bachelors of Arts degree to use the library). Madan found, based on discolouration, tears, and thinning of the paper, that the most popular play was *Romeo and Juliet*, followed by *Julius Caesar* which 'must have thrilled the

---

[116] Madan and Turbutt, p. 6.
[117] William Clennell, 'The Bodleian Declaration: A History', *The Bodleian Library Record* 20 (2007), pp. 47–60, p. 50.

generation which saw the Civil War'. Overall Madan's assessment was that the tragedies were the most read by Oxford men in the seventeenth century, with the histories, especially the pristine *King John*, the least.

The basis for this assessment was Madan's assumption that the volume had '*not* been subjected to private usage' since it left the library, although the fact that it was apparently purchased in the early eighteenth century by Richard Turbutt to add to a library dominated by theatrical books might suggest otherwise.[118] Richard Turbutt was a regular theatregoer and supporter of the drama: his name appears in a list of subscribers to Henry Brooke's tragedy *Gustavus Vasa* (1739) intended for the Theatre Royal Drury Lane but instead gaining the honour of being the first play banned under the Licensing Act of 1737 (its use of Scandi-navian history seemed dangerously topical and Whiggish, and it was seen as a criticism of Sir Robert Walpole). A member of another branch of the family, Robert Turbutt, was an actor at Drury Lane, alongside David Garrick, in Fielding's *The Wedding Day* (1734), and his name appears in the cast list of numerous plays of the 1730s and 1740s, including some by Shakespeare.[119] Copies of these other dramas were also in Richard Turbutt's library, and it seems therefore reasonable to assume both that he acquired the Shakespeare volume out of a specific interest in its contents and that therefore he might have spent time reading it.[120] There is evidence in the First Folio itself to support this view of a more active post-Bodleian life for the book—evidence strategic-ally suppressed by Madan in a bibliographic description

[118] Madan and Turbutt, pp. 6–7.

[119] Philip H. Highfill, Jr, Kalman A Burnim, and Edward A. Langhans, *A Biographical Dictionary of Actors, Actresses, Musicians, Dancers, Managers & Other Stage Personnel in London, 1660–1800. Vol. 15: Tibbett to M.West* (Carbondale and Edwardsville: Southern Illinois University Press, 1993), pp. 53–5.

[120] Gladwyn Turbutt, *A History of Ogston* (Higham: The Ogston Estates, 1975), pp. 80–1.

concerned only with its early years. At some point in its early history, for example, the book had lost the page facing the portrait with Ben Jonson's verse 'To the reader'. These lines had since been added in flourishing manuscript, quite possibly dating from the period of Turbutt's ownership. On the same leaf an additional unidentified, somewhat unaccomplished pastoral poem takes up a prominent theme of eighteenth-century Shakespearean criticism: 'So Nature once in her Essays of Wit, | In Shakespeare took the Shepherd's lucky leap | But over-straining in the great Effort | In Dryden and the rest, has since fell Short' (Figure 1.5). At the end of *Macbeth* a neat hand has added the historical note: 'Macbeth usurp'd the Crown of Scotland about the Reign of Edward ye Confessor—1042'. There are scattered stains, smears, and pencil crosses to mark particular lines. In addition, a number of eighteenth-century paper repairs, carefully but probably not professionally executed, suggest that the volume was not merely parked in Turbutt's library to await its eventual delivery back to the Bodleian, but was part of an actively used recreational private library.

This extensive collection was left at Richard Turbutt's death in 1758 to future Turbutt generations and numbered over 1,500 volumes in a catalogue of 1768. The first explicit mention of the family 1623 Folio comes from the young Gladwin Turbutt—grandfather to the student who delivered the book to Madan's office seventy years later—who visited the hall at Ogston into which his family was about to move in 1838: 'I rumaged [*sic*] among the old books in the Library, many of which I found to be 3 hundred years old, particularly one which was very valuable, it being the first edition of Shakespeare dated 1623, & I believe a large sum of money has been offered for one of the same sort.'[121]

---

[121] Turbutt, p. 108.

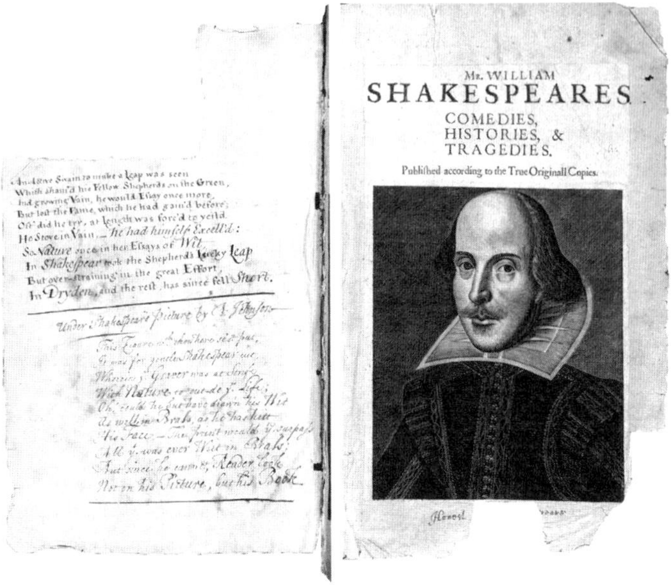

FIG. 1.5. Bodleian title page and added verses
The title page of the Bodleian First Folio with the verse by Ben Jonson and an additional unattributed poem in manuscript.

Madan and Turbutt prepared two publications on the redis-covery: an article on the book for the *Athanaeum* journal, and a pamphlet privately published by subscription, which offered a full bibliographical description of the volume as well as the narrative of its return to the library. Madan commissioned Horace Hart, the printer at Oxford University Press, to produce the letterpress printing pamphlet, in folio size and in an equivalent Folio fount. The pamphlet made one ominous sale. In March 1905, the booksellers Henry Sotheran and Co. wrote to Madan: 'An important foreign customer of ours is anxious to obtain, for purely bibliographical reasons, further particulars respecting the

Shakespeare.'[122] Six months later, acting on behalf of this anonymous but 'important foreign customer', Sotheran wrote to Turbutt Sr. at Ogston Hall to offer to buy the book.

The price he offered—£3,000—was incredible. In the 1890s, the average price of a top condition First Folio at auction was £835. In May 1905, a first Folio was offered by a London bookseller for the exceptional price of £1,350, but the average price of the dozen copies sold at public auction during the period 1903–5 was around £1,000.[123] The offer was, as his son wrote to Madan, too much to pass up. For the Turbutt family at Ogston, as for many contemporary landowners, the agricultural depression of the late nineteenth century meant that capital was short and estate expenses burdensome. Plummeting land values were coupled with increased taxation, especially death duties, under Lloyd George's Liberal administration. 'Damn Lloyd George', J. P. Morgan had murmured comfortingly to Lady Victoria Sackville-West in 1913 as she tried to sell him some seventeenth-century tapestries on the theme of the Seven Deadly Sins to offset family legal bills (he acceded 'to help you, as I have always had the greatest admiration and esteem for you all at Knole').[124] Writing to Sidney Lee in response to his questionnaire to Folio owners in 1902, the 4th Earl of Gosford fumed:

Sir, I beg to state that owing to the outrageous and absolutely illegal working of the Irish Land Commission—by order of this Supreme Court under which we sit and suffer—my income has so reduced that I sold my library including the First Folio Shakespeare—which was purchased, I believe, by Toovey of Piccadilly.[125]

Turbutt senior wrote apologetically to Madan that 'the amount of the offer somewhat alters the opinion which I had previously

---

[122] Bodleian Library Records, b862/57.
[123] West, vol. 1, 36.   [124] Strouse, p. 639.
[125] Papers relating to Sidney Lee's Census, Shakespeare Birthplace Trust, ER85/6/1.

formed of making it a family heirloom because, as you are aware, death duties will continuously make very heavy charges upon the resources of each generation'.[126] Oscar Wilde's Lady Bracknell, reassured that Jack's income is in investments rather than land, voices this contemporary patrician anxiety rather more elegantly: 'What between the duties expected of one during one's lifetime, and the duties exacted from one after one's death, land has ceased to be either a profit or a pleasure. It gives one a position, and prevents one from keeping it up. That's all that can be said about land.'[127] The two decades before the outbreak of the First World War saw estates broken up, land sold off, and a major transfer of art objects and other cultural artefacts to America. As Jean Strouse notes of J. P. Morgan, 'having spent his professional career importing financial capital for the emerging American economy, Morgan turned in the last 20 years of his life to importing cultural capital as well'.[128]

£3,000 for the First Folio was small beer in this wider context: in the same year, 1905, Lord Tweedmouth sold Old Masters worth almost £50,000; the Philadelphia meat magnate P. A. B. Widener took Rembrandt's 'The Mill' off Lord Lansdowne's hands for $500,000; and the Duke of Leeds sold off most of the contents of Hornby Castle, including its Canalettos, but not the library, for £85,000.[129] As Hugh Crimble, 'one of the quite new connoisseurs' in Henry James' *The Outcry* (1911) notes: 'Precious things are going out of our distracted country at a quicker rate than the very quickest—a century and more ago—of their ever coming in'.[130] Many of these aesthetic items—Italian Renaissance

[126] Bodleian Library Records, b.862/10.

[127] Oscar Wilde, *The Importance of Being Earnest* in Robert Ross (ed.), *The Collected Works of Oscar Wilde* (London: Routledge/Thoemmes Press, 1993), vol. 6, p. 42.

[128] Jean Strouse, 'The Collector J. Pierpont Morgan', in Anthony Grafton, Deanna Marcum, and Jean Strouse, *Collectors, Collections and Scholarly Culture* (America Council of Learned Societies Occasional Paper 48, n.d.), p. 29.

[129] David Cannadine, *The Decline and Fall of the British Aristocracy* (New Haven; London: Yale University Press, 1990), p. 115.

[130] Henry James, *The Outcry* p. 49; p. 44.

or Dutch seventeenth-century paintings, for example—had obviously been originally imported to England from impoverished continental aristocrats and so were uneasy nationalistic tokens. Disquiet at the transfer of cultural artefacts across the Atlantic took up instead the exemplary case of the native Shakespeare First Folios as emblems of national and patrician malaise. Some owners were adamant that they would not sell abroad. In 1927, the will of Miss Elizabeth Ann Williams of Clifton, Bristol, was published. Williams had left a First Folio to one of her nieces, 'but if neither wishes to keep it, it shall not be sold to go out of England, but shall be offered to the British Museum or the Shakespeare Museum at Stratford-on-Avon, and sold to whichever of the two shall give the highest price'.[131] The Bodleian/Turbutt copy of the First Folio was thus caught between the declining English squirearchy and the unstoppable American squillionaires, as Bernard Behrenson would dub the new super-rich of the Golden Age.[132]

Young Gladwyn Turbutt wrote ingenuously to Madan: 'Of course I should be overjoyed to see the work once more brought to the Bodleian, but I do not suppose the library will care to give that sum: however we felt we would like to give it first chance as, in its way, the book is one of its greatest possible treasures.'[133] The library did not at all care to give that sum. University finances were parlous: a *Statement of the Needs of the University* in 1899 had estimated some half a million pounds of new expenditure required to maintain academic posts, while current budgets ran in deficit.[134] Further, as Nicholson admitted, the

---

[131] *The Publishers' Circular and Booksellers' Record*, 3 September 1927, p. 290.

[132] Ernest Samuels, *Bernard Berenson: The Making of a Connoisseur* (Cambridge, Mass. London: Belknap Press of Harvard University Press, 1979), p. 428.

[133] Bodleian Library Records, b862.85.

[134] Janet Howarth, 'The Edwardian Reform Movement', in M. G. Brock and M. C. Curthoys, *The History of the University of Oxford*, vol. VII: *Nineteenth Century Oxford*, Part 2 (Oxford: Clarendon Press, 2000), pp. 822–54; p. 822.

library had never paid more than two hundred pounds for a book at this point, and was itself facing a large deficit. The curators of the library were consulted about a fundraising appeal in November 1905 and were not convinced. It was agreed that no public subscription should be undertaken but that library staff could make private communications with potential donors. The Turbutts had given the library a period of a month to trump their buyer, later extended to 31 March 1906, but there was no apparatus for contacting potential donors, no institutional experience of fund-raising, and the wheels of the university ground very slowly. Colleges professed themselves unwilling or unable to give lists of their 'rich men'; many appeared to have felt that the appeal was vulgar.[135]

Money did, however, begin to arrive. The vast majority of the donations were small sums of a guinea or less. Nicholson, described later as 'a man largely incapable of delegation', appears to have written to thank each individual, and, further, was involved in Pooterish exchanges with people who did, or did not, want to be named in a printed list of subscribers.[136] One man wrote in some embarrassment to ask for his guinea back, since he had fallen on hard times. Reverend H. B. Barry of Bath wrote to say that he did not see his name on the list of subscribers, and on consulting the clerical directory, Crockfords, suggested that perhaps the listed clergyman, H. B. Baring, was a misprint he wished to see corrected. A canon of Norwich Cathedral promised half a guinea and suggested Nicholson throw himself on the mercy of 'Mr Carnegie'; a thought which had also occurred to the Dean of Durham and others, recalling the American philanthropist's generosity to libraries and his professed love of Shakespeare. Not everyone

[135] Bodleian Library Records c. 1259.
[136] Giles Barber, 'Libraries', in Brian Harrison (ed.), *The History of the University of Oxford*, Vol. VIII, *The Twentieth Century* (Oxford: Clarendon Press, 1994), pp. 471–84; p. 471.

agreed that the objects were laudable. Warden Spooner of New College wrote to donate a guinea but considered the purchase 'an extravagance'; the King sent an expression of regret that he was unable to respond positively to the appeal; the headmaster of Radley School likewise, feeling the price was too high. One correspondent spoke for many in wondering at the wisdom of undertaking an appeal on such a scale since 'the occurrence of [a First Folio] in a sale is not now very uncommon'. E. W. Bowell wrote from St John's School, Leatherhead, a long letter about why he could not contribute, suggesting 'the present possessor ought to present it to the library' and that 'it is quite absurd that any copy of any book should command such a price. Only the man-eating money-maniacs of America could have started such an inept fashion.' W. A. Hoffman, a Cambridge graduate, sent a covering note with his contribution 'to help this treasure going the way of all our English treasures—to America'. Other contributors suggested that Turbutt should reduce the price on patriotic grounds.[137] Nicholson defended him against the slurs in his fundraising brochure: 'this price was not proposed by him but offered to him... whether we like it or not the price has been offered and the only question is whether it shall be paid to transfer this copy to an American millionaire or to preserve it in England and restore it to the Bodleian'.[138]

The deadline for the raising of the funds was 31 March 1906. By 11 March, only £1,300 of the required £3,000 had been raised. In desperation, Nicholson wrote to *The Times* newspaper to alert 'Oxford Men' to the situation. He warned that 'it is practically certain that the offer comes from the United States' and that the danger was that 'this will be lost for ever not only to us but to Shakespeare's fatherland'. 'That after two and a half centuries we

[137] Bodleian Library Records, c.1261.
[138] Bodleian Library Records, b.862.89.

should have the extraordinary chance of recovering this volume and should lose it because a single American can spare more money than all Oxford's sons or friends who have been helping us, is a bitter prospect.'[139] The *Times* leader encouraged its readers to donate, noting that 'in another country, the Government would help in such a case, but Oxford and the Bodleian live in proud isolation, asking for nothing from the state' (12 March 1906). Edmund Gosse wrote in exasperation to *The Times* asking the identity of the nameless millionaire and suspecting some emotional manipulation in the fundraising for the volume: Nicholson replied that he had no idea who the potential buyer was—and certainly no name appears in any of the archival correspondence. A cartoon in the *Morning Post* showed a faceless tycoon with the Folio under one arm and the Rokeby Venus, also threatened with transportation to America, under the other.

In the end, the money was raised, but at the eleventh hour, helped by a last-minute donation from Turbutt himself which reduced the sum needed by £200. The day before the deadline, Madan wrote to Turbutt to ask him for instructions about where to send the volume—it was still sitting in his office—and seems genuinely to have felt that the target was not going to be reached. But it was, and Nicholson announced in *The Times* that 'the Shakespeare is saved'.[140] Turbutt telegraphed to Madan telling him to deliver the Bodleian First Folio down the corridor to its new owner, Bodley's Librarian. In the event some money was returned to subscribers as being in excess of the sum required, and the list of subscribers includes promises not called in from, among others, the bishop of Oxford and the dean of Christ Church. Some fifty subscribers had their money returned.

[139] *The Times*, 12 March 1906.   [140] *The Times*, 30 March 1906.

The printed list of subscribers to the fund runs to over 800 subscribers, making the average donation just over three pounds. The Bodleian's archive includes Madan's manuscript addition to his copy of the list: a cramped but extensive and heartfelt list of 'Persons who did not subscribe', the neatness of his writing an index of his venom. In fact, the list of shame includes fifty notables of the university, including the Chancellor, Vice Chancellor, and Proctors, the keeper of the archive, the keeper of the Ashmolean Museum, three Regius professors, and thirteen Heads of Colleges. He has underlined for particular opprobrium the name of the professor of English Literature, Walter Raleigh—who was at the time negotiating with Oxford University Press about an edition of Shakespeare to be based on the First Folio text.[141] The Bodleian got its First Folio back not through the efforts of the University's great and the good, then, but through the small-scale donations of former students and members of the public who felt that the book should stay in Britain.

Comparing the fates of the Bodleian copy with the Sheldon one, bought by Folger at the Burdett Coutts sale, Sidney Lee professed it a 'rather more satisfactory outcome'.[142] It is easy to see why, given the anxieties about American ownership, and the uncertainty over Folger's intentions for his collection. But remaining in a general, cash-strapped library like the Bodleian rather than being transferred to the specialist Folger also had its disadvantages for the Turbutt copy. By the end of the twentieth century, it was judged too delicate for scholars to handle and was therefore effectively lost anew to the library's collections. Stimulated by the history of the initial campaign, a new fund-raising effort to digitize the book and create an online surrogate for scholarly use, and widen public access in new ways, was launched in 2012. A campaign for £20 donations with the Olympic-themed title 'Sprint for Shakespeare' was immediately championed by the

---

[141] Bodleian Library Records, b.862.   [142] Lee (1924), p. 89.

press and on social media, and quickly met its fundraising target of
£20,000. The Folio was subjected to new conservation protocols
which, across antique objects from chairs to buildings to books,
have moved away from 'restoration' to 'stabilization'. Thus no
interventions were made except those necessary to keep the book
in its current state of repair and enable it to be digitally scanned
without damage. 'We are finding it an interesting discipline to "sit
on our hands" where, in most of our usual work, we would judge it
was appropriate to do more in-depth treatment', wrote Nicole
Gilroy in a blog on the conservation work.[143] The digital facsimile
was launched on 23 April 2013. An online dedications list gives
some idea why people had contributed: 'In memory of Winifred
Young who taught me to love Shakespeare'; 'I would like to
dedicate my gift to my parents for taking me to see Shakespeare
productions when I was a child'; 'Lizzie . . . other women cloy the
appetites they feed, but she makes hungry where most she satis-
fies'; 'Shakespeare should be available to everyone in the closest
possible form to his original text'.[144] Readers of the Bodleian First
Folio online can turn the pages of the digital copy, read or search a
transcribed text, and download page sets for reuse under a Creative
Commons licence in the latest virtual incarnation of a book that
took on such local and national importance in the early years of the
twentieth century.[145]

The Sprint for Shakespeare campaign also shared another feature with its predecessor. Both fund-raising projects emphasized
the unique qualities of the copy, and suppressed the fact that the
Bodleian already owned another First Folio (received as part of the
estate of Edmond Malone in 1821). The digitization campaign

---

[143] Sprint for Shakespeare Conservation Diary: http://shakespeare.bodleian.ox.
ac.uk/2012/08/06/conservation-diary-day-2/ (accessed April 2015).

[144] Sprint for Shakespeare Supporters: http://shakespeare.bodleian.ox.ac.uk/the-
project/supporters/ (accessed April 2015).

[145] Digital facsimile of the Bodleian First Folio of Shakespeare's plays, Arch.
G c.7: http://firstfolio.bodleian.ox.ac.uk/ (accessed April 2015).

also omitted to mention that there were already a dozen online First Folios, thus perpetuating the disconnect between the fetishization of individual copies and the census information that reveals how common the book actually is. The cultural work of singularizing Folio copies over a longer period is discussed in more detail in Chapter 5.

These three case studies outline some of the ways that Folios follow money, and give some sense of their different interpretative contexts and the different ways these books have been valued during their lifetimes. They show how Folio copies have been transferred between private and institutional ownership, and from England across the world. These proprietorial and geographical shifts stand in for, and punctuate, a larger narrative of transformation, from early modern print commodity to late modern secular relic.

Just as the transfer of First Folios to Folger and the other wealthy collectors of Golden Age America symbolized a shift in the global economic balance, so too First Folios were an index to changing patterns of wealth in the UK. The decline of the country house library during the nineteenth century, since books were seen as easily fungible assets for impoverished noble families, fed new money both in the American book market and at home. In 1848, for example, the sale of assets by the bankrupted Chandos dynasty of the Duke of Buckingham at Stowe in Buckinghamshire, was a *cause célèbre*: 'All the world is talking Stowe', wrote Benjamin Disraeli, and *The Times* drew out the moral.[146] In the year of European revolutions, 'King Mob' had pawed over the ducal treasures and the break up of the collections was seen as 'a painful presage of a wider ruin' that 'we can only compare to the overthrow of a nation or a throne'. The Duke of Buckingham's ruinous extravagance had 'struck a heavy blow

---

[146] Benjamin Disraeli to Lady Londonderry, 5 August 1848, in J. A. W. Gunn (ed.), *Benjamin Disraeli Letters*, vol. 5: *1848–51* (Toronto, Ont.; London: University of Toronto Press,), p. 52.

at the whole order to which he, unfortunately, belongs'.[147] All four seventeenth-century Folios were among more than six thousand books put up for sale.[148] Annette Weiner's anthropological insight on inalienable possessions in aboriginal societies is relevant here:

> possessions that are imbued with the intrinsic and ineffable identities of their owners [...] are not easy to give away. Ideally, these inalienable possessions are kept by their owners from one generation to the next within the closed context of family, descent group, or dynasty. The loss of such an inalienable possession diminishes the self and by extension, the group to which the person belongs.[149]

The transfer of First Folios was a major symbolic element in this process of aristocratic diminishment. The men who had made good amid the wreckage of this dissolute aristocratic class symbolized their new claim to economic and ethical superiority in the ownership of high cultural artefacts, chief among them First Folios.

One of the newly-monied, newly-serious class buying up this ultimate high culture artefact was Thomas Watson (1851–1921), a self-made colliery- and ship-owner in South Wales. Watson listed his recreations in the 1920 edition of *Who's Who in Newport* as 'Collection of early printed books and MSS., being the proud possessor of a Shakespeare first folio; hunting, breeding pedigree shorthorns'.[150] Watson's copy of the First Folio had been owned by James Halliwell and has remained in his family's private ownership: he replied, curtly, to Folger's overture about selling in 1915: 'Sir, In reply to yours of 10th I am not disposed to sell my First

---

[147] *The Times*, 14 August 1848.

[148] *Catalogue of the Library removed from Stowe House, Buckinghamshire* (S. Leigh Sotheby & Co, 1849).

[149] Annette Weiner, *Inalienable Possessions: The Paradox of Keeping-while-Giving* (Berkeley; Los Angeles; Oxford: University of California Press, 1992), p. 6.

[150] Samuel D. Williams (ed.), *Who's Who in Newport* (Newport: Williams Press Ltd, 1920), p. 65.

Folio Shakespeare. Yours Truly T. E. Watson'.[151] Another industrialist First Folio owner was William Gott (1797–1863) of Armley in industrial Leeds. Gott's father, Benjamin (1762–1840), had made his fortune as an entrepreneurial cloth merchant and manufacturer. His Palladian house, Wyther Grange, is now the run-down clubhouse for a municipal golf-course that ranges across the parkland Gott laid out with views to his mills, including Armley Mills on the River Aire, now a museum of Leeds' industrial heritage.

The Gott papers for the early-nineteenth century reveal a cultured household with an extensive library. A son, Benjamin Jr, died in Greece while on the Grand Tour, having sent back a distinctive collection of 'ancient marbles' forming a significant classical sculpture collection now in Leeds museum. A near neighbour asks permission to keep a Hebrew book of psalms a bit longer, and thanks Gott for the loan of a book in Greek. There is extensive correspondence with the society portraitist, Thomas Lawrence, about sittings, frames, and advances of money (Lawrence painted Benjamin and his wife in 1828). A list of the paintings at Wyther Grange in 1823 includes works by Veronese, Caravaggio and Canaletto.[152] Gott's instincts for how to spend his first-generation industrialist riches were ones validated by the aesthetic judgement of history. So too, his son William's taste in books.

William Gott acquired a First Folio by the middle of the nineteenth century: it is not clear where from, but it was certain to be from one of the noble families selling up around the time of the collapse of Stowe. He marked his ownership of the First Folio with his gold roundel bookplate and the family motto 'nec temere ne timide' on its marble endpapers. Gott also marked up the catalogue page of the book with a record of the quarto editions

---

[151] West 225; Rasmussen and West, p. 184.
[152] Gott Papers, Brotherton Library, University of Leeds, MS194.

he owned. There are only the faintest traces of prior owners, including some pen practice copying of words on the first page of *Macbeth*. Displayed amid the classical statuary in Armley, the Gott First Folio is as much a monument to manufacturing success and prosperity in Leeds as Cuthbert Brodrick's grandiose Town Hall, built in the 1850s, or Gott's own steam-powered mills.

William's own son, John Gott (1830–1906), became Bishop of Truro. His book collection was well known and he was generous in allowing access to scholars, sending Pollard rare quartos in the post for his research and loaning his Caxtons to the exhibition at South Kensington Museum in 1877. Folger learned of his collection of play quartos and began a determined strategy to acquire them: although the bishop repeatedly declined these overtures, negotiations with his son-in-law were more productive. As Rosenbach, his agent in this matter, reported: 'The Doctor was in poor health, with a very limited income, leaving nothing for repairing a considerable estate rapidly falling into decay. The son-in-law actually found himself sympathetic with the notion of disposing of the books to a keen American.'[153] The economic wheel of fortune had turned again: the Gotts, on their way up, had caught a Folio dropped from an aristocratic family on their way down; in decline in turn, they themselves handed the book on to a newly rich man, Henry Folger. Folger acquired the quartos privately on the eve of Gott's death, and then the Folio in the sale of 1907. It is now one of the digitized copies on the Folger website.

Focus on the American market for First Folios should also not obscure what a Folger exhibition curated by Anthony West has dubbed the 'diaspora', its wider international travels, long before the nineteenth century.[154] Folger's purchases were only the most sustained and purposive of the Folio's many international transfers

[153] A. S. W. Rosenbach, 'Henry C. Folger as a collector', in *Henry C. Folger 18 June 1857–11 June 1930* (New Haven: privately printed, 1931), pp. 82–3.

[154] See the map at http://titania.folger.edu/exhibitions/diaspora/ (accessed April 2015).

from the seventeenth century onwards. Edward Blount, the Folio publisher, had a related business importing luxury items for preferred customers. Imported books were an important part of the English market: books printed in Barcelona, Burgos, Paris and Lisbon joined the First Folio in the Bodleian's binding consignment to William Wildgoose in February 1624.[155] More significantly, books, including the Shakespeare First Folio, were soon exported.

Two copies vie for the status of the first exported First Folio. The recently rediscovered copy from the St-Omer Jesuit College library may have been in France by around 1650 (see Chapter 4). But just earlier—perhaps—is the date—1647—revealed on a title page of one of the Folger Folios by ultra-violet photography under the supervision of Anthony West. Put together with the name, 'Constanter', on the title page, West has identified this Folio with the Dutch diplomat and bibliophile Constantine Huygens (1596–1687), a cultured envoy at James I's court in 1622–3, who was knighted by the king.[156] Huygens, a poet, musician, and connoisseur of art, friend of Rembrandt, and correspondent of Descartes and Spinoza, clearly felt connected to England: one of his poems from 1622 describes 'the chalk-white strand of Britain...To which shores our Flemish lowlands | Were connected long ago'.[157] Some of the manuscript markings in the volume which identify preferred passages including Polonius' advice to Laertes [1.3.58–81] and Hamlet's 'To be or not to be'

[155] See also Julian Roberts, 'The Latin Trade', in John Barnard and D. F. MacKenzie, with the assistance of Maureen Bell, *The History of the Book in Britain*, Vol 4, *1557–1695* (Cambridge: Cambridge University Press, 2002), pp. 141–73.

[156] Anthony James West, 'Constantijn Huygens Owned a Shakespeare First Folio', *Notes and Queries* 55 (2008), pp. 221–2 and 'Constantijn Huygens's Shakespeare First Folio: the First to go Abroad; now at the Folger', *Notes and Queries* 60 (2013), p. 49.

[157] Quoted in Scott Oldenburg, *Alien Albion: Literature and Immigration in Early Modern England* (Toronto: University of Toronto Press, 2014), p. 176.

speech [3.1.58], seem to date from the period of his ownership. Interestingly, neither of his sons were interested in the Shakespeare volume on his death. Although it has been estimated that Constatijn—who followed his father as a diplomat and poet—and Christiaan—who became an eminent scientist—took between two and three thousand books from their father's library before sending the residue to auction, the Shakespeare book, with the remainder of Huygens' library, was sold in The Hague in 1688.[158] The ongoing project at Leiden University to identify as many of his books as possible reveals that there were a number of English language titles in the collection, by Bacon, Donne, Hobbes, Wilkins and Margaret Cavendish, although the Shakespeare is the only example of dramatic literature.[159]

The Folio passed via intermediary owners, including one who signed it 'Miss Stodart 1761', and 'Andrew Wilson M.D', the eighteenth-century Edinburgh physician who wrote a long treatise on female hysteria in 1776. (Coincidentally, around the same time another doctor with an interest in mental illness, the Bethlem physician and consultant to George III, John Monroe also acquired a First Folio at the sale of Martin Foulkes, President of the Royal Society in 1756.)[160] An eighteenth-century hand has added some lines of a contemporaneous translation of Horace on Cleopatra to the end of *Antony and Cleopatra*, beginning 'Not the Dark Palace nor the Realms below | Can Awe the Furious Purpose of her Soul'. The transcription does not exactly match any of the many printed versions I have been able to find: it was clearly a well-known poem and perhaps it was set down from memory as an analogue to Shakespeare's presentation of the Egyptian queen. At around the same period, lists of *dramatis*

---

[158] Rudolf Dekker, *Family, Culture and Society in the Diary of Constantijn Huygens Jr, Secretary to the Stadholder-King William of Orange* (Leiden; Boston: Brill, 2013), p. 96.
[159] http://www.leidenuniv.nl/fsw/verduin/constanter/ (accessed April 2015).
[160] West 30.

personae, divided between male and female characters, equivalent to those in editions of eighteenth-century dramatists, have been added to the texts of a number of the tragedies in this Folio. Eventually, it became one of Folger's last Folio acquisitions, bought from Ernest Dressel North in 1928, and given the number 75 in the Washington library.

The Huygens Folio can thus be located in seventeeth-century Holland. The St-Omer Folio takes the book to France in the same period. Another copy, complete with early annotations assessing the quality of the comedies from 'bad' (*Two Gentlemen of Verona*) to 'better in Dryden' (*The Tempest*), made its way into the Bibliothèque Nationale in Paris by the middle of the nineteenth century.[161] The first acquisition of a First Folio in Germany appears to be marked by the crossed-out signature, 'George Cook', and the date, 1746, in a copy in the Morgan Library New York.[162] A new ownership mark, 'Ex Bibliotheca J. H. Hadermanni', marks the acquisition of this book by the German, Johann Heinrich Hadermann (1710–85). Hadermann had studied in Leiden and had progressive religious views. He was Rector of the school in Schlüchtern, north east of Frankfurt in the Hessen region, and presided over the development of an impressive library, some of which is still preserved in Bergwinkelmuseum, the local history museum in Schlüchtern. As with other libraries such as the Herveys' at Ickworth, however, the most valuable of these books have been sold off. No catalogue of the Schlüchtern library exists. However, the signature in the Morgan Library can be found on early modern scientific, usually Latin, books including in the Getty Library, in Stanford, and in recent sales catalogues in the US and UK.[163] At least one other extant title with 'Ex Bibliotheca

[161] West 194.
[162] West 172. Transcription glitches in Rasmussen and West, pp. 690–1, have obscured Hadermann as a Folio owner.
[163] Other copies with the Hadermann signature include: H. Savilius, *In Taciti Historias*: http://catalogue.gazette-drouot.com/ref/lot-ventes-aux-encheres.jsp?id=

J. H. Hadermann' attests to the library's liberal educational philosophy: the 1699 English edition of the free-thinking empiricist Pierre Gassendi's *Three Discourses on Happiness*. Michael Dobson argues that during the long eighteenth century, the transformation of Shakespeare's status to 'national, indeed global, pre-eminence' served as 'one of the central cultural expressions of England's own transition from the aristocratic regime of the Stuarts to the commercial empire presided over by the Hanoverians': the circulation of First Folios across Europe is a material index to this process.[164] But Hadermann's acquisition of the First Folio was also closely contemporaneous with the early emergence of Shakespeare appreciation in Germany. The writer, philosopher, and dramaturge, Gotthold Lessing's works of criticism and commentary on Shakespeare's tragedies in the 1750s coincided with the first complete translation of Shakespeare's plays into German. In 1773, Johann Gottfried Herder expressed his wish to 'explain him, feel him as he is, use him, and—if possible—make him alive for us in Germany'.[165] At some point, the Hadermann copy left Germany and its provenance is murky until it was acquired by J. Pierpont Morgan in 1896.

Germany retains its connection with the First Folio, however. The Royal Library in Berlin holds a copy given in 1859 by William I of Prussia.[166] Much later, in 1960, as the city was reconstructed after the extensive Allied bombing raids during the Second World War, and eight years after it had twinned with Liverpool under the Council of European Muncipalities twinning movement, Köln

---

1551246 (accessed April 2015), Gassendi, *Three Discourses of Happiness* (Stanford University Library), Stockhausen, *De cultu ac usu luminum antiquo* (Getty Library), Hertoldt, *Crocologia Seu Curiosa Croci* (Cincinnati). Information on any other books from this library gratefully received.

[164] Michael Dobson, *The Making of the National Poet: Shakespeare, Adaptation and Authorship, 1660–1769* (Oxford: Oxford University Press, 1994), p. 8.
[165] Bate, p. 39.   [166] West 195.

(Cologne) University bought a First Folio.[167] Their copy had been sold in the Edwardian period by the Earl of Carysfort and had crossed the Atlantic and returned to Europe. In the same year, the State Library of Wurttemberg, part of the University of Stuttgart libraries, also bought a copy that has been digitized.[168] There are copies in Switzerland and Italy, as well as in Japan, Australia, New Zealand, and South Africa. When Senate House Library in the University of London attempted a consultation on the sale of one of their First Folios in 2012, it was revealed that they had already organized a pre-auction tour of the book to the most likely American markets—New York, Boston, Chicago and San Francisco—and to a newly likely location, the wealthy, anglophile territory of Hong Kong (no First Folio is known yet to have been acquired in any Asian country other than Japan).

Writing with characteristic contrariness in 2005, Gary Taylor asked: 'Why do theatre companies in former British colonies perform Shakespeare? They do so because English is the language of their governing classes, and by continually re-performing his works they assert their connection to a cultural legacy that makes them feel superior to other people. Why do theatre companies in Japan and Germany and Brazil perform Shakespeare? They do so in order to demonstrate that they, too, can appropriate the flagship commodity of the world's most powerful culture.'[169] Exports of Shakespeare First Folios have played an important and overlooked role in this uneasy narrative of globalization, as copies in New Zealand and in South Africa attest.

Addressing a large and enthusiastic European audience at the Theatre Royal in Auckland, in June 1883, the twice-governor of New Zealand, George Grey (1812–1898) proselytized about his lasting colonial monument: the Free Public Library, opened in 1880. The new library was for the new population of the islands,

---

[167] West 196.
[168] West 197; http://digital.wlb-stuttgart.de/start/ (accessed April 2015).
[169] *The Guardian*, 13 July 2005.

who 'have quitted their homes in England, Scotland, Ireland—
nay, Novia Scotia and distant parts of America—in France, in
Germany, in Scandinavia and Italy, all flocking to one common
centre in New Zealand' and who needed therefore to cohere
around a central linguistic and cultural focus: 'all gradually merging
into the use of that one familiar tongue—the Anglo-Saxon
language—which is to dominate the world'. A new public library,
stocked with 'a complete collection of Anglo-Saxon literature, a
complete library of the English tongue from the very earliest
periods' was the intellectual underpinning of secure, Anglocentric
colonial government. And that this library was public was a crucial
break from the mother country, where great families hoard the
nation's cultural heritage, 'all those precious documents which are
called family archives pass into the family chest and are locked up.
They are shut out from public view; great libraries are collected,
shut up for a century or two in cases defended by wire lattices, and
are exhibited on a certain day in the week to crowds of excursion-
ists.' Grey's Auckland library would be open to all, even on Sun-
days (justifiable because it would hold bibles in 'at least 120
languages or dialects').[170] As he later wrote to a New Zealand
official, in terms that seem unconsciously to echo the utopian
vision of the book-loving Gonzago for his new island dominion
in *The Tempest*, Grey toyed with a radical libertarianism: 'a new
world should be called into existence, a world freed from established churches, from great inequalities of landed possessions, and
of rank—with no standing armies, with equal political rights,
and with facilities for affording to all a complete education'.[171] In
his peroration on the new library, Grey expressed his immediate

---

[170] *Auckland Free Public Library. Address delivered by Sir George Grey, K.C.B., at
the Theatre Royal, Auckland, June 5th 1883. Reprinted from the New Zealand Herald*
(Grey Collection), pp. 7–8.

[171] Quoted in Donald Jackson Kerr, *Amassing Treasure for All Times: Sir George
Grey, Colonial Bookman and Collector* (Dunedin, NZ: Oak Knoll Press and Otago
University Press, 2006), p. 40.

aim 'to flood the Pacific with learning, and to dominate with a just and righteous supremacy—not of tyranny but of intellect'. The cornerstone, inevitably, of this ambitious cultural and ideological and colonial project, was a Shakespeare First Folio.

The Auckland Folio has a broken provenance narrative, although a signature in it indicates it belonged to Charles Grylls of Lanreath in Cornwall in the 1670s, later sheriff of Cornwall. The dates suggest that Grylls was the annotator who wrote the proverbial—but not immediately relevant—'the devill was sicke the devill a monck would bee |the deville was well the deville a monck was hee' dated 'August the 9th 1676' in the margin of *The Winter's Tale*. Perhaps he is also responsible for a line in the margin that appears to be the end of a letter: 'from you a Saturday last this convenient time shall only let you know that I am yours to command'. Someone, possibly Grylls, has written neatly at the beginning of a number of the plays, the Latin phrase 'Iam legi' (I have already read). Another signature in the book, Anne Hearle, can be identified as part of the extended Grylls family: she too has left her mark on a copy that looks to have been much in use in the first century or so of its life, with doodling and pen practice, marks of approbation by particular lines, and other corrections and smudges (see Chapter 2 for more examples and discussion of these kinds of marks of use). Grey had been in contact with that 'very Napoleon of book-sellers', the pre-eminent London Folio dealer, Bernard Quaritch, but distance made it difficult for him to send timely instructions, and he had failed to purchase at least two copies during the early 1890s.[172] It was not until 1894 that he was able to add this First Folio, bought for £85, with an additional sum for a facsimile title page. It was insured for £200 on its passage to New Zealand and to the Auckland library.

Grey's initial experience combining his colonial career with Shakespeare was not auspicious. His unpopular tenure as Governor

---

[172] Fitzgerald, p. 14.

of South Australia in the early 1840s prompted the publication of a short-lived weekly called the *Southern Star* (October 1842– February 1843), which had the 'undivided aim of attacking Governor Grey'. Each issue bore, under the title of the paper, Shakespeare's line from *Richard III*: 'Think upon Grey and let thy soul despair' [5.5.95].[173] Nevertheless, he was committed to the imperial philosophy that Shakespeare and the literary culture of Britain were an effective cultural tool of colonial government, and during his term as governor of South Africa, had laid the foundation stone for the new library in Cape Colony (now Cape Town) in 1858. The Library was opened by Prince Albert in 1860, who ceremonially placed there a copy of Charles Knight's eight-volume edition of Shakespeare's works (Knight owned a First Folio and claimed to have based his edition newly on that text, as discussed in Chapter 3). The following year, however, Grey donated his own large collection of over five thousand books and manuscripts, including a complete, tidy copy of the First Folio with some slight repairs to the page margins and a title page probably substituted from another copy.[174]

From the outset, the gift was an equivocal one, from both the British and African perspectives. The novelist Anthony Trollope, visiting South Africa in the 1870s, articulated imperial regret at the expatriation of this significant literary archive: 'It would be invidious to say that there are volumes so rare that one begrudges them to a distant Colony which might be served as well by ordinary editions as by scarce and perhaps unreadable specimens. But such is the feeling which comes up first in the mind of a lover of books when he takes out and handles some of the treasures of Sir George Grey's gift.' Trollope further intimated that this munificence may have been wasted. No doubt, he wrote, the First Folio is 'as often looked at, and as much petted and loved and cherished in the

---

[173] Kerr, p. 64.
[174] The copy is described in A. M. Lewin, *Quarterly Bulletin of the South African Library* 5 (1950), pp. 11–16.

capital of South Africa, as when it is in the possession of a British Duke', but there was not much evidence of heavy use of the Cape Colony library during his visit: 'I was told that the readers in Capetown are not very numerous. When I visited the place there were but two or three.'[175] Within months of Grey's gift, the running expenses of the library had exceeded the funds allocated for its maintenance, and the Trustees advised in a petition of January 1862 to Parliament at Westminster that 'it will be necessary to provide for the proper custody and charge of the Collection, that as the South African Public Library possesses no means out of which such provision can be made'.[176]

And the ongoing legacy of imperialism in South Africa means that the Grey Collection, still in Cape Town, and still, as Trollope observed a hundred and fifty years ago, underused and little-loved, has continued to be culturally burdensome. Post-apartheid South Africa has produced its own iconic, singular version of Shakespeare's complete works and it is not the Folio given by Grey in the nineteenth century as the cultural apotheosis of the European scramble for Africa. The substitute Shakespeare is the so-called Robben Island bible, a 1970 imprint of the popular single-volume Alexander Text of the Complete Works of Shakespeare, smuggled by ANC supporters into Robben Island prison, claimed as a religious text, and read by political prisoners, many of whom identified their favourite quotations and signed the volume. The most commonly displayed signature is that of Nelson Mandela, dated 16 December 1977—the anniversary of the end of the ANC's exclusively peaceful resistance to apartheid and the founding of its military wing in 1961—next to the lines from *Julius Caesar*: 'Cowards die many times before their deaths | The valiant never taste of death but once. | Of all the wonders that I yet have

heard, | It seems to me most strange that men should fear | Seeing
that death, a necessary end, | Will come when it will come'
[2.2.32–7].[177] The book, still in private ownership, was displayed
at an exhibition in Stratford-upon-Avon in 2006, and was the star
exhibit at the British Museum's 'Staging the World' exhibition as
part of the Cultural Olympiad in London 2012. In both contexts it
did its work in substituting the troubled legacy of colonial
dominance—the Folio itself—for the apparently radical reappro-
priation of the master-text in its counter-culture—the Robben
Island bible. The politics of the Robben Island volume have almost
entirely superseded that of Grey's First Folio in South African
literary culture; it is difficult to see how the bibliographic legacy of
colonialism can best be reconciled.

Grey's colonial philanthropy codified in book form the glorious
history of the language of Shakespeare, and set the course for its
imperial future in Africa and in Australasia. 'I have done my best to
give such an outfit for these two great outposts of civilization for
the Southern Hemisphere', he wrote to C. W. Holgate.[178] The
1865 South African Education Act made English the medium
of state-funded school education. English so dominated New
Zealand that the indigenous Maori language was not recognized
as a national language until 1987. Within these ongoing histories,
the role of colonial library collections as outposts of civilization has
been an uncomfortable one. These two colonial libraries and their
afterlives in distinct post-colonial contexts give a different slant to
old questions about Shakespeare and colonialism, often articulated
around the role of Shakespeare in Indian colonial education.[179]

[177] David Schalkwyk, *Hamlet's Dreams: The Robben Island Shakespeare* (London:
Continuum, 2012), pp. ix–x.
[178] C. W. Holgate, *An Account of the Chief Libraries of New Zealand* (London:
1886), p. 8.
[179] See, for instance, Ania Loomba, *Gender, Race, Renaissance Drama* (Manchester: Manchester University Press, 1989), and *Shakespeare, Race, and Colonialism*
(Oxford: Oxford University Press, 2002).

The material presence of these First Folios at the heart of these self-consciously imperial libraries continues to have implications for their institutions into the twenty-first century, particularly in the South African context.

From the beginning, Grey's gift was somehow unassimilable into its context: 'the Trustees recorded their unanimous opinion that, in order to comply effectually with the conditions on which this valuable gift has been bestowed, it will be necessary that the "Grey Collection" be kept wholly separate and distinct from the general Collection of Books in the Library'.[180] A century later, the previously colour-blind Cape Town library was instructed to follow government policy and create racially segregated reading rooms and book stocks. Its librarian Douglas Varley resigned, but the policy was implemented by his successor.[181] Shakespeare's own place in modern South Africa is contested. The president of the Shakespeare Society of Southern Africa struck a defensive note launching its new journal in 1987: 'Some believe this is neither the time nor the place to be founding a society to encourage the appreciation of a dramatist who was born in a foreign land over four hundred years ago, and whose works are written in an archaic form of English: South Africa has more important things to attend to.' The journal did not need to specify what: the litany of apartheid violence, the state of emergency and the whites-only general election, won by P. W. Botha's National Party and prompting Desmond Tutu to lament 'we have entered the dark ages of the history of our country'.[182] Guy Butler nevertheless continued his defence of attending to Shakespeare in South Africa: 'there are occasions when urgent matters may properly benefit from our attention to

[180] Spohr, p. 7.
[181] P. R. Coates, 'Douglas Harold Varley: A Life's Work in Librarianship, Part II', *Quarterly Bulletin of the South African Library* 55 (2001), pp. 20–30; p.23.
[182] *New York Times*, 8 May 1987.

matters of permanent importance'.[183] David Johnson's summary of
Shakespeare in South Africa is less sanguine in drawing attention
to the 'larger histories of imperial violence, in which the Bard
plays a central and deeply compromised role': small wonder that
the most recent assessment of the Grey collection suggests it has
not found a place for itself in a post-apartheid South Africa.[184]
Hedley Twidle describes how the Grey collection 'remains a
neglected and perhaps disavowed archive', echoing the South
African novelist J. M. Coetzee who, reflecting on his time in
another literary archive, wondered 'if a latter-day ark were ever
commissioned to take the best that mankind has to offer...
might we not leave Shakespeare's plays...behind to make
room for the last speaker of Dyirbal'.[185]

Further, the South African and New Zealand Shakespeare
Folios encapsulate some of the unease that attaches to Grey's
own colonial career. As Chris Gosden and Yvonne Marshall
conceptualized it in a landmark article on 'The Cultural Biography
of Objects', 'the fame of objects and the renown of people are
mutually creating, so that objects gain value through links to
powerful people and an individual's standing is enhanced through
possession of well-known objects. There is a mutual process of
value creation between people and things.'[186] 'Would the same
books be any different if they had been bequeathed by Nelson
Mandela instead?' asked one South African interlocutor in an

[183] David Johnson, *Shakespeare and South Africa* (Oxford: Clarendon Press,
1996), p. 208.
[184] Johnson, p. 214.
[185] Hedley Twidle, 'From *The Origins of Language* to a Language of Origin:
A Prologue to the Grey Collection' in Andrew van der Vlies (ed.), *Print, Text and
Book Cultures in South Africa* (Johannesburg: Wits University Press, 2012),
pp. 252–84; p. 255; J. M. Coetzee, 'Remembering Texas (1984)', in David Atwell
(ed.), *Doubling the Point: Essays and Interviews* (Cambridge, Mass.: Harvard
University Press, 1992), pp. 50–3, pp. 51–2.
[186] Chris Gosden and Yvonne Marshall, 'The Cultural Biography of Objects',
World Archaeology 31 (1999), pp. 169–78; p. 170.

inconclusive debate about the future role of the Grey Collection in national life in 2002.[187] His own answer, 'a self-evident "No"', perhaps misses the nuance of the ways in which books, especially this one, acquire the particular associations of their contexts, histories, and owners. If the prestige of the object and the person are mutually reinforcing, so too the value of the object is diminished by that of the person. Even contemporaries found Grey a 'proud, mean, overbearing man'.[188] Grey's colonial legacy is a difficult one: only as a book-collector and philologist of indigenous languages could he be entirely admired (as in Donald Kerr's account of his collecting). As one recent biography observes dispassionately, 'the humane, reserved, intellectual gentleman co-existed with a racialist and imperialist zealot'.[189]

Grey was a typical polymath Victorian intellectual, and his First Folio existed within an extensive colonial network of shared intellectual and material interests. The range of his correspondents during his time in New Zealand shows something of those interests. He wrote to Charles Darwin about the possibilities of using New Zealand to collect information about climate history, to Florence Nightingale on native schools, to the historian J. A. Froude, to the American philanthropist and library-founder Andrew Carnegie, to the directors of London Zoo, and to Millicent Fawcett on women's suffrage (her letter to him ends: 'I cannot conclude without thanking you for the splendid services you have rendered to Women's Suffrage and to the cause of justice to women wherever it has arised [*sic*]') as well as to booksellers including Joseph Lilly and Bernard

---

[187] Michael Morris, 'Report on the Great Grey Colloquium', *Quarterly Bulletin of the Library of South Africa* 57 (2003), pp. 50–2; p. 51.

[188] Thelma Gutsche, *The Bishop's Lady* (Cape Town: Howard Timmins, 1970), p. 169.

[189] James Belich, 'Grey, Sir George (1812–1898)', *Oxford Dictionary of National Biography* (Oxford: Oxford University Press, 2004) online edn., Jan 2008, http://www.oxforddnb.com/view/article/11534, accessed April 2015.

Quaritch.[190] Grey's books, sent from England, were part of a triangular trade between London, Australia, and New Zealand. London Zoo provided native British animals, including partridge, ravens, and rabbits. They even promised badgers, adding helpfully: 'in captivity we feed them on tripe (cooked), fowls necks, soaked bread and soaked biscuit. We have lately sent a pair to Australia', and requested live kiwis and cassowary in return. The Botanical Gardens in Melbourne provided exotic seeds and plants, and swapped acacia seedlings and kangaroo specimens from Grey for swans and blackbirds. Grey himself supervised the collection and export of a wide range of botanical and ethnographic material, sending to the British Museum everything from kangaroos, seagull skins, the skeleton of a sea lion, Maori texts, birds' eggs, and shells. J. Barnard Davis thanks him for 'having collected me some skulls of Bushmen'.[191] English books, including the First Folio, thus circulated within an imperial exchange system in which indigenous colonial species were transplanted to Britain as exotic curios, to be replaced with familiar British species. The large-scale structural consequences of this exchange are all too well known: from human exploitation and cultural impoverishment to habitat destruction. In his classic account of the gift in aboriginal societies, Marcel Mauss uses the Maori idea of *tonga*—forms of inalienable property—and reports on a portentous part of Grey's own ethnographic interest: 'In a proverb that happily has been recorded by Sir George Grey and C. O. Davis, the taonga are implored to destroy the individual who has accepted them.'[192] Seeing Grey's bibliographic and other gifts in this destructive context gives them a more clearly threatening aspect.

One New Zealand example may stand as a metonym of these ambivalent processes of exchange and importation. George Grey

---

[190] Sir George Grey Special Collections, Auckland City Libraries, GL G24; GL H39.
[191] Grey Collection, GL H39.   [192] Mauss, p. 13.

bought Kawau island off the north-eastern coast of Auckland for £3,700 in 1862. He established an international menagerie there around Mansion House. Since the 1980s, Kawau has been under a strenuous habitat management programme to try to eradicate numerous invasive species, particularly the possum and wallaby introduced by Grey with devastating effects on native vegetation and thus on flightless birds including the New Zealand national bird, the kiwi. Grey was by no means the only colonial resident to import alien species—and the highly mobile cultural property, Shakespeare, had already, of course, reached New Zealand independently of his book-collecting. But it is not entirely fanciful to see in the compromised ecosystem of Kawau, caused by Grey's enthusiastic importation of non-native species, a metaphor for the role of his book collection in New Zealand cultural life—or, in Mauss's anthropological terms, the *tonga* that destroys its ostensible beneficiary. Writing a history of New Zealand literature, Patrick Evans notes that the imported literary infrastructure of the nineteenth century was an efficient 'tool of colonisation' that 'for so long prevented the development of a literature that seemed to be about the places it was written in'.[193]

The First Folio was, in Auckland, an explicitly colonial text, the dominant cultural predator in an imperial ecology, and Grey's literary imports were no less damaging to the native habitat than the rabbits and redwoods he planted at Kawau. Grey's islands, both Kawau and New Zealand, combined Prospero's proto-imperial kingdom with the domesticated colonial paradise of Defoe: the historian J. A. Froude, visiting the governor, imagined himself 'a voluntary Robinson Crusoe'. Froude developed the Robinson Crusoe conceit in his *Oceana* where he imagines the cannibalistic festivals of 'Maori pirates' on Kawau beaches.[194]

---

[193] Patrick Evans, *The Penguin History of New Zealand Literature* (London and Auckland: Penguin Books, 1990), p. 18.
[194] J. A. Froude to George Grey, 7 July 1889 (Grey Collection, GL F36[9]); *Oceana, or England and her Colonies* (London: Longmans, Green, 1886), p. 319.

The New Zealand scholar Michael Neill writes of the ways Shakespeare has been not just a part of New Zealand history but 'part of the cultural apparatus by which we have learned to know that history and our place in it—for the colonizers an essential beacon of location; for the colonized, arguably, an instrument of displacement and dispossession'.[195] Neill describes a controversial late-twentieth century theatre piece called *Manama Taua/Savage Hearts* by David Geary and Willie Davis, in which a Maori chief supplicates Queen Victoria for redress over land grievances, and is made to take a company of actors to perform Shakespeare in New Zealand in return. Victoria swears to her part of the bargain on the bible, chief Tupou on the Complete Works of Shakespeare: it's a scenario in which the interpretation and cultural role of Shakespeare are suggestively interwoven with that of another Grey text, the infamous Treaty of Waitangi by which British sovereignty was imposed on the native Maori.[196] And while the Auckland Public Library has a new, well-used research centre for the Sir George Grey Special Collections, there is no equivalent in Cape Town, where, under the provocative 'The Grey Collection Up For Sale?' the chief librarian's doubt whether 'it is more than just an ikon of European values' seemed something of a rhetorical question.[197]

Writing on *Heroes and Hero-Worship* in 1840, Thomas Carlyle famously identified Shakespeare as 'the grandest thing we have yet done'. He went on, in lines particularly noted by Henry Folger in his own copy of Carlyle: 'For our honour among foreign nations, as an ornament to our English Household, what item is there that we would not surrender rather than him. Will you give up your Indian

[195] Michael Neill, 'Post-Colonial Shakespeare? Writing away from the Centre', in Ania Loomba and Martin Orkin (eds), *Post-Colonial Shakespeares* (London: Routledge, 1998), pp. 164–85, p. 172.

[196] Neill, pp. 181–3.

[197] 'Editorial: The Grey Collection Up for Sale?', *Quarterly Bulletin of the Library of South Africa* 57 (2003), pp. 51–2.

Empire or your Shakspeare?'[198] Of course, as many critics have
noted, Carlyle's choice (he opted to give up the empire, since 'we
cannot do without Shakspeare') was no choice at all: his Shakespeare was already implicated in the imperial project.[199] As Ania
Loomba and Martin Orkin put it as the starting point of their
introduction to the critical collection, *Post-Colonial Shakespeares*,
Shakespeare 'became, during the colonial period, the quintessence
of Englishness and a measure of humanity itself. Thus the meanings of Shakespeare's plays were derived from and used to establish
colonial authority.'[200] But it is with George Grey that that ideological underpinning is materialized, and it is in the problematic
presence of two imperial First Folios in differently post-colonial
contexts that we can see its equivocal legacy.

The movement of First Folio copies between individuals and
institutions during the nineteenth century is generally an index to
existing wealth and prestige. The copy that has been in the ownership of the Birmingham public library since 1881 is a distinct
exception, and is the only copy acquired specifically for a public
institution as part of a vision of working-class education. As
Birmingham grew as a centre of manufacture during the nineteenth century, the corporation took advantage of the new Public
Libraries Act of 1845 to begin to develop a municipal library
collection by the mid-1850s. The initial proposal for a specifically
Shakespeare memorial library was made in 1858 by Samuel
Timmins (1826–1902), a prominent manufacturer and amateur
Shakespearean, under the influence of the charismatic local

---

[198] See Georgianna Ziegler, 'Duty and Enjoyment: The Folgers as Shakespeare
Collectors in the Gilded Age', in Virginia Mason Vaughan and Alden T. Vaughan
(eds), *Shakespeare in American Life* (Washington DC: Folger Shakespeare Library,
2007), pp. 101–12; p. 102.

[199] Thomas Carlyle, *On Heroes, Hero-Worship, and the Heroic in History*
(London: Chapman and Hall, 1897), p. 113.

[200] 'Introduction', Ania Loomba and Martin Orkin (eds), *Post-Colonial
Shakespeares* (London: Routledge, 1998), p. 1.

non-conformist minister, George Dawson.[201] Timmins was part of a circle around Dawson committed to civic improvement and the development of working-class education, which also included Joseph Chamberlain, who, as mayor, improved Birmingham's housing, sewerage, and infrastructure and set a model for progressive local government. Timmins' published works were split evenly between works on Shakespeare and on the town, including *The Resources, products and industrial history of Birmingham and the Midland Hardware District* (1886) and *Hamlet by William Shakespeare, 1603; Hamlet by William Shakespeare, 1604: being exact reprints of the first and second editions* (1860): for Timmins, as for Birmingham, Shakespeare was a decidedly local project.

Birmingham's Shakespeare Library, then, was a manifestation of a wider ambition for the cultural and municipal life of the town, and for the betterment of its workers as it petitioned to gain city status (it became a city in 1889). Dawson's aim was 'to see founded in Birmingham a Shakespeare Library which should contain (as far as practicable) every edition and every translation of Shakespeare; all the commentators, good, bad, indifferent; in short, every book connected with the life or works of our great poet. I would add portraits of Shakespeare, and all the pictures, etc., illustrative of his works'. The collection would be part of a more general and inclusive cultural and intellectual civic life. 'A suggestion' to the local paper from 'a working man' asked that the Birmingham Shakespeare club 'should be the nucleus of a general and a public one, and that it should be incorporated, if it is not incorporated, with the Shakspere Memorial Library, and that it should be thrown open . . . Why should not Birmingham be the leader in Shaksperian literature?'

The Shakespeare collection opened in 1864 with 1,239 volumes. In April 1870, the *Daily Post* reported that 'the progress of the

---

[201] See *City of Birmingham Free Libraries Reference Department: An Index to the Shakespeare Memorial Library First Part English Editions of Shakespeare's Works, Separate Plays and Poems* (Birmingham: Percival Jones Ltd, 1900).

Shakespeare Library... is a remarkable honour to the higher literary tastes of our town' and noted 'a proposal, to purchase a splendid copy of the First folio, by donations from those who do not subscribe to the annual fund'.[202] That this was not merely a trophy, but an investment in a particular vision of Shakespeare's text, was clear: 'The time has come when mutilated and modernised editions of Shakspere must be protested against. We must have a perfect Shakspere. Let us agitate to get Shakspere pure and simple.' £200 had been raised towards a First Folio by 1873, although the committee reported that 'a proposed purchase of Mr Quaribeli's fine folio has been suspended' since it was thought that a cheaper specimen might be found (Mr Quaribeli is otherwise unknown and so is probably an exotic misapprehension for 'Quaritch'). Their delay was fortuitous, since some ninety per cent of the stock of seven thousand books in the library was destroyed by fire in January 1879. Undeterred, its supporters raised the money to buy a First Folio from 'Quaribeli' for £240 for the reopening of the library by the radical MP, John Bright in 1882, along with Shakespeare volumes in more than twenty-five languages.[203] The new library, in the distinctly civic space created in the central Chamberlain Square, with its statues of Dawson, Chamberlain, and other local worthies, was part of 'a monument to the city's municipal revival, simultaneously celebrating and memorializing it in stone'.[204] The library interior was given particular retro-treatment: 'The new home of the Shakespeare library, on which special care in decoration was lavished, is a fine room,

---

[202] This paragraph and the preceding one draw on newspaper and other papers in 'Materials for a History of the Shakespeare Memorial Library Birmingham. 1871–1930' (Birmingham City Libraries S993.2)

[203] Samuel Timmins, *Books on Shakespeare* (London: Simpkin, Marshall and Co., 1885), p. 4.

[204] Simon Gunn, *The Public Culture of the Victorian Middle Class: Ritual and Authority in the English Industrial City 1840–1914* (Manchester: Manchester University Press, 2000), p. 51.

Elizabethan in design, having enclosed book cases throughout, and enriched wherever possible with carved panelling.'

Whereas working-class access to literary culture is usually identified with the availability of cheap reprints of classic texts, here it is rather an original copy, without the accretion of commentary provided by leisured editors, that seems to have been a talisman for a library explicitly oriented towards the project of working-class education.[205] A catalogue of the collection from 1900 is headed by the First Folio, followed by various facsimiles, since, as Timmins acknowledged, the much-desired First Folio was 'intended only for general reference and far too costly for general use'.[206]

Appropriately, the dominant ownership mark on the Birmingham First Folio is the purple library stamp of the Birmingham Free Libraries Reference Department on several of its pages. Otherwise, it carries a few marks of underlining, the occasional bracket or pen-stroke, including one by Henry's exclamation about 'Taxation' [*Henry VIII* 1.2.38–41], dotted underlinings at the Player King's observation that 'The great man downe you marke his favourites flies, | The poor advanc'd, makes Friends of Enemies' (*Hamlet* 3.2.195–6), and, winningly, the faint tread of a cat's paws across a page of *Henry VI* Part 1. The book has remained in the library throughout the twentieth century. The Elizabethan panelled Shakespeare Memorial Room built for it in the nineteenth century—and quickly outgrown—was imported wholesale into a cupola on the top floor of the new £189 million futuristic Birmingham library designed by Francine Houben in 2013—although it seems somewhat forlorn without any books in it. Much like those late-Victorian landowners who were asset-rich and cash poor, and like the libraries founded by George Grey in Cape Town and by Henry Folger in Washington DC,

---

[205] On the working-class readership, see Andrew Murphy, *Shakespeare for the People: Working-class Readers, 1800–1900* (Cambridge: Cambridge University Press, 2008).

[206] Timmins, p. 6.

Birmingham Library has since found itself struggling with running costs and unable to maintain its opening hours and facilities. Whether the First Folio, always rather too expensive for its ostensible purpose, is a luxury that can be afforded in this troubled contemporary context remains to be seen.

Other transfers of First Folios to institutions register the growing importance of Shakespeare in an educational context. During the nineteenth century, the development of Shakespeare in schools, and the gradual absorption of Professorships of Rhetoric and Philology into the new university discipline of English Literature from the 1820s onwards were accompanied by the acquisition of First Folios by educational institutions.[207] The gifts of the eighteenth-century editor Edward Capell to the Wren Library at Trinity College, Cambridge, in 1779, of the keen collector, Anthony Morris Storer, to Eton College in 1799, and of the naturalist and scholar Richard Warner to Wadham College, Oxford, in 1775 are early outliers, and mostly acts of institutional piety in the wills of former students. The nineteenth century saw a pattern of gifts to, and more rarely purchases by, school and university libraries: Stonyhurst College (1837); King's College Cambridge (1850); Trinity College, Cambridge (second copy in 1863); Glasgow University Library (1874); Manchester University (1892); Cambridge University Library (1894); Winchester College (1900); Harvard University (1915); University of Pennsylvania (1932); University of Leeds (1936); and Craven Museum (1936). The British Museum acquired its copies in the century between 1818 and 1922, although it had been bequeathed its first copy in 1779. The Victoria and Albert Museum gathered its copies between 1869 and 1881.

At the time of Sidney Lee's *Census* in 1902, about one-third of copies were in public or institutional hands; a century later,

---

[207] See Neil Rhodes, *Shakespeare and the Origins of English* (Oxford: Oxford University Press, 2004), chapter 6.

according to Eric Rasmusssen and Anthony West, only around ten per cent of copies were recorded as belonging to private individuals or trusts. Recent anxiety, when sales are mooted, that First Folios will be sold to individuals and be effectively privatized have not been realized. The movement has tended rather to be from private to institutional hands, even as those institutions that have recently sold copies have come in for particular disapprobation. Gifts to public and educational institutions continued during the twentieth century and beyond. The break-up of big, often American, collections after the Great Depression meant that many private libraries were absorbed into public institutions. In 1956, the gramophone record entrepreneur, Sir Louis Sterling, gave his collection, including all four seventeenth-century Shakespeare Folios, to the University of London Library at Senate House. In 2015, it was announced that the collection of William H. Scheide, loaned to the university for decades, had been bequeathed to Princeton in its owner's will. One newspaper headline epigrammatically summarized the key collocations of value: 'Rare bibles and Shakespeare folios in $300m "wow factor" Princeton bequest'.[208]

That juxtaposition of the Bible and the Shakespeare Folio was a key manoeuvre of Victorian bardolotry. Shakespeare appreciation had gathered a distinctly and fervently religious cast by the second half of the nineteenth century, as Charles Laporte has outlined. Books with titles such as *The Poet-Priest: Shakespearian Sermons Compiled for the Use of Students and Public Readers* (1884) and *Shakespeare and the Bible: Fifty Sonnets with their Scriptural Harmonies* (1896) organized Shakespearean and biblical quotations in parallel and suggested that Shakespeare was a kind of secular scripture.[209] At the same time, Stratford-upon-Avon developed

---

[208] *The Guardian*, 17 February 2015 http://www.theguardian.com/culture/2015/feb/17/princeton-bibles-shakespeare-trove-gutenberg (accessed April 2015).

[209] Charles Laporte, 'The Bard, the Bible, and the Victorian Shakespeare Question', *English Literary History* 74 (2007), pp. 609–28.

as a site of literary pilgrimage. Since the Romantic period, such literary geographies had taken up the language, protocols and cultural space of the religious pilgrimage. Copies of the First Folio show the impact of the development of Stratford-on-Avon as a tourist destination, aided by the railway line, during the nineteenth century. An early example is found at the back of one of the Folger copies formerly belonging to William Tyssen-Amherst, the collector of antiquities, Baron Amherst of Hackney. Someone has written out, in script that might be dated to the 1620s, the epitaphs from Shakespeare's grave and his monument in Holy Trinity church, along with a third not otherwise recorded: 'Heere Shakespeare lyes whome none but Death could Shake | and heere shall ly till judgement all awake; | when the last trumpet doth unclose his eyes | the wittiest poet in the world shall rise' (Figure 1.6).[210] Another Folger copy records a late eighteenth-century 'pilgrimage to the shrine of Shakespeare on foot' by John Henderson, Isaac Reed (the Shakespeare editor associated with the Folio copy now in the Sir John Soane Museum), and John Watson Reed.[211]

The literary tourism industry that developed around Stratford was codified and elaborated in David Garrick's famous Jubilee celebrations of 1769. It developed a specifically local topography of buildings and views to visualize the dramatist's biography as a crucial point of contact with Shakespeare himself. Garrick himself owned a First Folio, and copies of the book, from Edmund Malone's onwards, were retro-fitted, like many contemporary editions, with topographical prints connecting them with the geography of Shakespeare's Stratford (see Chapter 5). After a public subscription had acquired the Shakespeare Birthplace on Henley Street in Stratford for the nation in 1847—under the threat of a purchase by the American circus magnate P. T. Barnum—the

---

[210] Robert C. Evans, '"Whome None But Death Could Shake": An Unreported Epitaph on Shakespeare', *Shakespeare Quarterly* 39 (1988), p. 60.
[211] West 68.

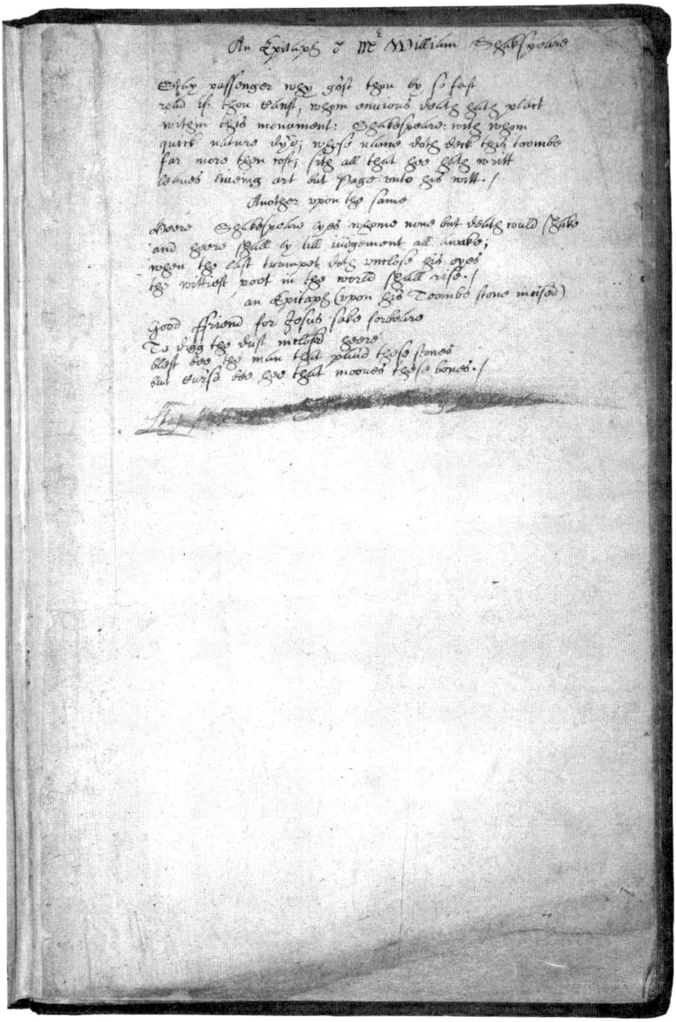

FIG. 1.6.   Epitaphs

These annotations in a Folio flyleaf reproduce the lines on Shakespeare's tomb and monument in Stratford, and an unknown additional epitaph.

Birthplace Trust was founded in 1866.[212] When Henry James
came in 1903 to write about the cult of Shakespeare as practised
at 'The Birthplace' (he never mentions Shakespeare, but the referent is nevertheless clear) he describes the place as a 'sacred'
'shrine', 'the Mecca of the English-speaking race', and uses the
religiously capitalized 'He' and 'Him' to refer to the revered author.
The caretakers acknowledge the wonder 'of treading day and night
in the footsteps He had worn, of touching the objects, or at all
events the surfaces, the substances, over which His hands had
played'.[213] Such a shrine needed a relic. Among the other dubious
items of Shakespearean furniture curated by the Birthplace as it
attempted to authenticate its own existence, only the First Folio
could escape the difficulties of provenance.[214] A resident of the
town, Anne Wheler, whose brother Robert was a notable local
historian, donated to the Trust a well-used and incomplete copy of
the First Folio in 1862 and the Trustees bought a tidier version
with a more aristocratic provenance at the sale of the Earl of
Ashburnham in 1898. Owning this iconic book was crucial to
the cultural claims of the Birthplace and to its rivalry with the
new developments of theatre performance under the patronage of
the Flower family in Stratford at the end of the nineteenth century.
Stratford-upon-Avon almost inherited a much larger collection: at
Henry Folger's funeral, the priest reported that the collector
remarked: 'I did think of placing the Shakespeare library at
Stratford, near the bones of the great man himself, but

[212] See Nicola J. Watson, 'Shakespeare on the Tourist Trail', in Robert Shaughnessy (ed.), *The Cambridge Companion to Shakespeare and Popular Culture* (Cambridge: Cambridge University Press, 2007), pp. 199–226.

[213] Henry James, 'The Birthplace', in Leon Edel (ed.), *The Complete Tales of
Henry James Volume 11 1900–1903* (London: Rupert Hart-Davis, 1964), pp.
403–65; p. 408; p. 405; p. 411.

[214] On nineteenth-century attempts to authenticate the Birthplace and its accessories, see Julia Thomas, *Shakespeare's Shrine: The Bard's Birthplace and the Invention
of Stratford-upon-Avon* (Philadelphia: University of Pennsylvania Press, 2012), pp.
91–120.

I finally concluded I would give it to Washington; *for I am an American.*'[215]

To collect may always be to sacralize. Russell Belk describes collectors as 'sacred priests able to transform an ordinary object of use into a sacred object in a collection'.[216] And while for many Folio collectors their object was already sacralized, others explicitly turned their own into quasi-religious relics by the addition of iconographic paraphernalia. One prominent example is Angela Burdett Coutts' Daniel copy, bought with such cost and publicity in 1864. When this copy was sold at auction in 1922, it included a bespoke casket (Figure 1.7). The catalogue describes the accompanying carved casket:

On a silver plate inside the flap is the following inscription: 'This Casket carved out of Herne's Oak, the tree mentioned in "The Merry Wives of Windsor," contains the First Quarto Edition of Shakspeare's Poems, published anno 1640 and the still more rare first edition of his Dramatic Works, published anno 1623. William Perry, Carver, 1866. The old tree fell down in 1863, a portion being most graciously given by Her Majesty Queen Victoria to Miss Burdett Coutts for the purpose of enclosing volumes which are not for an age but for all time.[217]

William Perry, 'wood-carver to the Queen', dedicated to Burdett Coutts his *A Treatise on the Identity of Herne's Oak* three years after the Daniel sale. Perry there explained that he had been given some timber from a tree in Windsor Park 'commonly known as 'Herne's Oak', which had fallen in 1862 and from which he made a bust of Shakespeare for Queen Victoria. Sceptics who claimed that the original Herne's Oak had actually been felled in the 1790s were 'a shock to my faith', prompting Perry to an extensive and ultimately reassuring investigation of the references to the tree in *The Merry*

[215] Cadman (1931), pp. 17–18.   [216] Belk (1995), p. 94.
[217] *Catalogue of the Valuable Library The Property of the late Baroness Burdett Coutts, Lady of Grace of the Order of St John of Jerusalem* (Sotheby, Wilkinson & Hodge, May 1922), p. 63.

FIG. 1.7. Burdett Coutts casket
Angela Burdett Coutts had this casket made for her First Folio in 1866. The silver plate explains that it was made from wood from Herne's oak tree in Windsor Park, donated by Queen Victoria.

Wives of Windsor and in historic topographies of the park. Having satisfied himself that his wood was indeed from the genuine tree, Perry then described one of the carvings made from it: 'The reader will, perhaps, be pleased to know that a Casket, designed and executed by the Author, to encase an exceedingly fine copy of the rare first folio edition of Shakespeare's Comedies, Histories, and Tragedies, and the first collected edition of his Poems, has been made from the wood of this venerable tree, for Miss Burdett Coutts.'[218] Herne's Oak, an 'overdetermined narrative and

---

[218] William Perry, *A Treatise on the Identity of Herne's Oak, shewing the maiden tree to have been the real one* (London: L. Booth, 1867), pp. ix, 56.

topographical landmark', as Adam Zucker puts it, had been included in illustrated editions such as the grangerized Folio in Eton College, and is the perfect sylvan equivalent of the mid-Victorian First Folio.[219] Further, the Shakespearean connotations of Perry's choice of term 'casket' are striking. Perhaps unconsciously, it seems to align the then unmarried heiress Folio owner, Angela Burdett Coutts, with Portia, who presides over valuable caskets set up by her father in *The Merchant of Venice*. The elaborately carved Folio casket, however, contradicts the play's moral in its casket scene: the preference for the unadorned lead casket over the rich and glistering alternatives is the distinguishing mark of the fit suitor Bassanio.

Decorative caskets were clearly high-status protective and display cladding for Victorian First Folios. Replying to Sidney Lee's *Census*, the Public Library of New South Wales reported that their First Folio, presented by Richard Tangye in 1884, was 'enclosed in a beautiful carved oak casket made from a pier of oak from the forest of Arden'. Allegedly, the casket cost more than the £750 paid for the copy of the book.[220] If these caskets, particularly in American usage of the term, had connotations that the body within was a corpse, their deathly associations were literalized in the carefully presented burnt fragments of the Folio owned by the American tragedian Edwin Forrest and destroyed by fire in 1873. These are now stored in a glass sarcophagus in the University of Pennsylvania. Even—perhaps especially, given the martyrological associations of the broken book—fragments carried the quality of the relic. 'I confidently predict', wrote bibliographer Seymour de Ricci introducing a volume containing a single genuine First Folio page, 'that the time will soon come, when the possession of a single leaf will add lustre to any library and confer on its

[219] Adam Zucker, *The Places of Wit in Early Modern English Comedy* (Cambridge: Cambridge University Press, 2011), p. 27.
[220] https://curio.artpro.net.au/exhibit/384/stories?from_collection=6&page=2 (accessed April 2015).

owner a well deserved distinction. It is with a religious emotion
that we contemplate these venerable pages through which the
spirit of Shakespeare has been for three centuries delivering the
poet's great message of beauty.'[221] Like the unfeasible quantity of
tourist curios sold in Stratford as fashioned from Shakespearean
mulberry wood, the split and fragmented Shakespeare Folio could
be endlessly monetized.

And as the Shakespeare Birthplace became a shrine, so too
collections of Shakespearana, particularly the First Folio, increasingly attracted the same vocabulary. A visitor described Horace
Howard Furness's library as 'a Shakespearean shrine'; and the
Bodleian sub-librarian, Falconer Madan, kept a list of visitors to
the returned copy under the heading 'pilgrims to the shrine'. *The
Telegraph*, praising the tercentenary exhibition at the Victoria and
Albert Museum in April 1916 amid reports of the 'the terrible
slaughter which is taking place in the various theatres of war',
picked up this same sacralizing language: the Shakespeare books
'are volumes to look upon with the reverence that a good pilgrim
manifests before some sacred shrine'.[222] Louis B. Wright, Director
of the Folger Shakespeare Library, identified on his arrival as one
of the primary tasks of the library, 'to refute the notion that we
were merely a Shakespeare shrine' (although he went on to clarify
that it is the suggestion that the library contained exclusively
Shakespeare material that was incorrect, rather than the specifically
religious language).[223]

The German philosopher Martin Heidegger, meditating on the
ontology of a jug, summarized mysteriously: 'the jug is a thing

[221] Robert M. Smith, *The Shakespeare Folios: the Forgeries of Shakespeare's Handwriting in the Lucy Packer Memorial Library of Lehigh University* (Bethlehem
Pennsylvania: Lehigh University Press, 1927), p. 25.

[222] *The Daily Telegraph*, 24 April 1916.

[223] Louis B. Wright, *The Folger Library. Two Decades of Growth: An Informal
Account* (Charlottesville: University Press of Virginia for the Folger Shakespeare
Library, 1968), p. ix.

insofar as it things'.[224] It is the irreducible philosophy of a William Carlos Williams poem. But the gestalt simplicity of the philosophical analysis of the mundane object has something to offer the analysis of a desirable and reified object. First Folios have become, over almost four hundred years, things to be read, imposed, gifted, traded, deified: thinged. Introducing to literary studies an important Heideggerian critical argument that became known as 'thing theory' in 2003, Bill Brown identified 'an imaginative possession of things that amounts to the labor of infusing manufactured objects with a metaphysical dimension'. First Folio ownership is at once possessive and imaginative: the copies discussed in this chapter instantiate some of the ways the First Folio focalized the projection and organization of a range of individual, cultural, and national desires. For Brown, the value of the thing derives ultimately from 'the material object's own excessiveness'.[225] Perhaps this hyperbolic quality, which is more often ascribed to Shakespearean content— what William Hazlitt called the playwright's habitual 'supererogation'—might be transferred to become a defining feature of the material book itself as it passes through different contexts.[226]

---

[224] Martin Heidegger, 'The Thing', in Albert Hofstader (trans. and ed.), *Poetry, Language, Thought* (New York; Evanston; San Francisco; London: Harper & Row Publishers: 1971), pp. 163–86; p. 177.

[225] Bill Brown, *A Sense of Things: The Object Matter of American Literature* (Chicago and London: University of Chicago Press, 2003), pp. 4, 14.

[226] William Hazlitt, *The Characters of Shakespear's Plays* (London: 1817), p. 54.

CHAPTER 2

Reading

A sking 'Should Collectors Read Books?' in the American periodical *The Bookman* in 1919, George H. Sargent quotes an unnamed source on the ignorance of the 'wealthy collector': 'As for a love of reading and literary taste, that is absolutely nil. None of the collectors read their books.'[1] The question of whether owners of rare and prized volumes ever actually read them is a perennial accompaniment to the history of collecting. Sargent observes drily that since neither bibliography nor literary pursuits are in themselves likely to furnish the wealth necessary to develop a serious collection, to berate collectors for not being such experts is misplaced. But if by the beginning of the twentieth century, the Folio could not be the edition of choice for the pleasure or amateur reader, this was not always so. In the first century of its life, the Folio was often intensively read and used, as extant copies can attest.

Early readers of Shakespeare's First Folio read not just a collection of stage-plays, but a material object with particular associations, organization, and reading possibilities. The particular form of the book—its size, typeface, errors and confusions; the order of the plays included; the formatting of play apparatus such as stage directions and indications of who is speaking; the prefatory

---

[1] George H. Sargent, 'Should Collectors Read Books?' *The Bookman* 49 (1919), pp. 744–9.

material known as paratexts—all shaped the encounter with the
reader. So too did contemporary reading practices. As extant
copies of Shakespeare's First Folio amply attest, early modern
reading was typically undertaken with a pen. To read a book in
this period was often simultaneously to mark it, and thus much of
our evidence for the history of Renaissance reading paradoxically
comes from writing. Shakespeare First Folios are full of such
readers' marks—some clearly purposeful, some apparently more
random. This chapter surveys a large number of types and
instances of seventeenth- and early eighteenth-century readers'
marks in copies of First Folios to try to understand both the variety
of individual encounters with this text found in specific copies, and
patterns of interaction that emerge from a larger sample.

People have left all kinds of marks in Shakespeare First Folios:
signatures, pen practice and doodling, corrections and emendations, scraps of poetry, letters, proverbs, sums and other material,
sketches, underlinings, marginalia, pointing hands and other symbols, faint or damaged text that has been inked over by hand,
round spaces in letters filled up with ink. There are also other
marks that speak eloquently of the household contexts in which
the book was open for reading: the ring marks left by drinking cups
or glasses, greasy smears that look as if food has been dropped onto
the pages, and, in at least two copies, the unmistakeable footprints
of a cat walking across the printed text (in the Birmingham City
Library copy, over the penultimate page of negotiations with the
French in *Henry VI Part 1*; in the copy belonging to the Marquess
of Northampton across *Love's Labours Lost*).[2] These suggest a
book that is not kept closed on a shelf or in a library, and one
whose contents are more important than its pristine form: less a
materially valuable object and more a household companion
amid normal domestic life.[3] Copies of the book that are now

---

[2] The two pawprint Folios are West 2 and West 33.

[3] Many recent assessments of early modern reading practices have questioned
whether 'reading' is the appropriate term for the variety of activities recorded in

unmarked tend to have been washed or heavily trimmed by later booksellers (or, to put it another way, the apparently 'clean' copy is not usually one that is unused, but rather one bearing the specific mark of a different, later intervention).

Most of these marks are effectively anonymous. Names, sometimes, but not always, identifiable as signatures, are common in First Folios, but names that can be confidently or meaningfully located in a particular place, reading context, or ownership milieu are much more rare. Only one or two copies can be identified with specific seventeenth-century contexts, and thus the copy now in Glasgow University Library is especially important.[4] This copy of the Folio bears the clear signature 'Lorenzo Cary' and thus is associated with a significant early modern intellectual circle located in Great Tew, Oxfordshire in the 1630s. Lorenzo (1613–41) was a younger son of Henry Cary, Lord Falkland and Lord Deputy of Ireland. Theirs was a family with attested connections to drama and the theatre. Henry Cary's wife, Elizabeth Cary, was a writer and translator and also a published playwright. Her closet drama, *The Tragedy of Mariam*, was published under the name of 'that learned, vertuous and truly noble ladie E.C.' in 1613. Their son, Lucius Cary (1610–43, 2nd Viscount Falkland from 1633), Lorenzo's older brother, was known to enjoy reading plays and

books. See, for example, Jennifer Richards and Fred Schurink, 'Introduction: The Textuality and Materiality of Reading in Early Modern England', *Huntington Library Quarterly* 73 (2010), pp. 345–61; Bradin Cormack and Carla Mazzio (eds), *Book Use, Book Theory: 1500–1700* (Chicago: University of Chicago Press, 2005); and William H. Sherman, *Used Books: Marking Readers in Renaissance England* (Philadelphia: University of Pennsylvania Press, 2008). The titles here indicate a preferred verb of 'use', recognizing the many purposes to which individuals put their books that exceed the definition of reading. My focus here is attentive to that wider set of practices (hence I too write about 'use'), but also keen to recover early traces of the specific activity of reading, which I understand, perhaps too permissively, as 'demonstrable attention to the printed text and some form of engagement with it'.

[4] West 11.

seeing them performed. One contemporary record has him asking for a copy of a play in manuscript in order better to enjoy it: 'if I valued it so at the single hearing, when mine eyes could not catch half the words what must I do now in the reading when I may pause upon it'.[5] Ben Jonson and Lucius Cary exchanged odes: Cary revealed a knowledge of Jonson's plays and praised his 'full Style, Strong Witt'; Jonson apostrophized the friendship between Cary and Henry Morison.[6] It has been suggested that the Folio was annotated by Henry Cary, but perhaps the bookish, sociable, and theatrically engaged Lucius is a more likely candidate.[7] If it were Lucius who marked up the First Folio associated with the Cary household, this would be one of his only literary monuments, since almost none of his personal papers or letters survive and his library was sold off by his son after the civil war.

By the mid-1630s, Lucius had built a formidable intellectual and literary circle around his home at Great Tew in Oxfordshire, including poets, philosophers, and theologians. In the aftermath of the bloody civil war which would claim Lucius Cary's life at the battle of Newbury in 1643, the Great Tew circle was romanticized as a tolerant and non-partisan society for the exchange of ideas. As one of their number, the lawyer and future royalist historian Edward Hyde, later first Earl of Clarendon, recalled it, theirs was a fellowship 'to study in a better Air, finding all the books they could desire in his Library and all the Persons together whose

[5] Andrew Gurr, *Playgoing in Shakespeare's London,* 2nd edn. (Cambridge: Cambridge University Press, 1996), p. 260.

[6] Cary's poem was published in *Jonsonus Virbius, Or The Memorie of Ben Johnson revived by his Friends the Muses* (London: 1638), pp. 1–7. The quotation is from an 'Epistle to his noble Father, Mr Johnson', published in *The Cambridge Edition of the Works of Ben Jonson Online.* Jonson's 'pindaric ode', 'To the Imortall Memorie, and Friendship of that Noble Paire, Sir Lucius Cary and Sir H. Morison', was published in *The Underwood* (London: 1641).

[7] Rasmussen and West, p. 38.

company they could wish, and not find, in any other society'.[8] Hyde's obituary for Falkland, written while in royalist exile in Jersey during the Interregnum, remembers 'a person of such prodigious parts of learning and knowledge, of that inimitable sweetness and delight in conversation, of so flowing and obliging a humanity and goodness to mankind'.[9]

Later idealizations of the Great Tew circle have made it hard to understand its true intellectual temper, and, while it is tempting to imagine the open-minded Shakespeare First Folio as a key text in a peaceable scholarly conversation, that would probably exaggerate both the role of Shakespeare and the nature of those debates.[10] Linking Cary and his circle directly with the book is difficult. A composite literary manuscript associated with Great Tew in the late 1630s and now in the Bodleian Library does not contain any Shakespearean material, focusing instead on contemporary verses by William Herbert, Francis Beaumont, John Suckling and Edmund Waller.[11] On the other hand, a later seventeenth-century discussion about Shakespeare's place in contemporary culture placed Lord Falkland at a crucial cultural debate between those Jonathan Swift would dub the 'ancients' and the 'moderns' in his satire, *The Battle of the Books* (published in 1704). Charles Gildon, writing in the 1690s, recalled Lucius Cary, flanked by other members of the Great Tew circle, including Suckling and John Hales, as a supporter of Shakespeare in 'the noble Triumph

[8] Edward Hyde, *The Life of Edward, Earl of Clarendon* (Oxford: Clarendon Press, 1759), p. 22.

[9] Edward Hyde, *The History of the Rebellion and Civil Wars in England* (Oxford: Clarendon Press, 1816), vol III, p. 178.

[10] For an idealized view, see Hugh Trevor-Roper's account of an 'esoteric graduate reading party in the country' (p. 175) in his *Catholics, Anglicans and Puritans: Seventeenth Century Essays* (London: Secker & Warburg, 1987); a more bracing view is that of J. C. Hayward, 'New Directions in the Study of the Falkland Circle', *Seventeenth Century*, 2 (1987), pp. 19–48.

[11] See *Catalogue of English Literary Manuscripts 1450–1700*: http://www.celm-ms.org.uk/repositories/bodleian-malone.html.

he [Shakespeare] gain'd over all the Ancients, by the Judgement of the ablest Critics of that time':

The matter of Fact (if my Memory fail me not) was this, Mr. Hales of Eaton, affirm'd that he wou'd shew all the Poets of Antiquity, out-done by Shakespear, in all the Topics, and common places made use of in Poetry. The enemies of Shakespear wou'd by no means yield him so much Excellence; so that it came to a Resolution of a trial of Skill upon that Subject: the place agreed on for the Dispute, was Mr Hales's Chamber at Eaton; a great many Bookes were sent down by the Enemies of this Poet, and on the appointed day, my Lord Falkland, Sir John Suckling, and all the Persons of Quality that had Wit and Learning, and interested themselves in the Quarrel, met there, and upon a thorough Disquisition of the point, the Judges chose by agreement out of this Learned and Ingenious Assembly, unanimously gave the Preference to Shakespear.[12]

The First Folio is not directly mentioned here, but it is the most likely source of Cary's Shakespearean knowledge on this occasion during the 1630s. Suckling had, of course, had his portrait painted by van Dyck with a Shakespeare Folio at around the same time (Figure I.2). It is striking, then, that the book featured in both Falkland's and Suckling's biographies at that time, and that the two of them then become key witnesses to this critical controversy about Shakespeare's reputation. In Nicholas Rowe's 1709 edition of the plays, Cary is cited as the source of a more detailed critical appreciation of Shakespeare, as one of 'three very great Men' who 'concurred ... *That* Shakespear *had not only found out a new Character in his* Caliban, *but had also devised and adapted a new manner of Language for that Character*'.[13] Certainly, Caliban's speeches are

---

[12] Charles Gildon, 'Some Reflections on Mr Rymer's Short View of Tragedy, and an Attempt at a Vindication of SHAKESPEAR, in an Essay directed to JOHN DRYDEN Esq;' in *Letters and Essays on Several Subjects* (London: 1697), pp. 85–6.

[13] Nicholas Rowe (ed.), *The Works of Mr William Shakespear; in Six Volumes. Adorn'd with Cuts. Revis'd and Corrected, with an Account of the Life and Writings of the Author* (London: 1709) vol. i, p. xxiv.

among those marked out for note and the marginal comment 'ap' (abbreviated Latin: I approve) in the Folio copy associated with Great Tew, including the lament 'I am all the Subjects that you have, | Which first was min owne King', and his 'I had peopel'd else | This Isle with *Calibans*' [1.2.343–4, 352–3].

The hand annotating the Cary copy is also distinguished by its unique attention to the list of the King's Men, headed by Shakespeare, at the beginning of the Folio (Figure 2.1). Next to the names, the reader makes various notes: the word 'know' next to Robert Benfield and Joseph Taylor, 'by report' next to the preeminent tragedian, Richard Burbage, 'by eyewitness' by John Lowin, 'hearsay' by William Ostler and 'so too' by the next names Nathan Field, Nicholas Tooley and William Ecclestone. Next to Shakespeare's name he writes 'least for making' (or, as has been suggested, 'ceased for making'), either reading suggesting that acting was known to be the lesser part of Shakespeare's work for the company. The comments can help us date the annotations. This is a reader whose playgoing definitely coincided with the long career of Lowin (a King's Men sharer from 1603 to 1642), but appears to have postdated Burbage (who died in 1619). He knows Benfield (a sharer from 1615–42) and Taylor (a sharer from 1619–1642, probably as a replacement for Burbage). He only knows by hearsay, not direct experience, of Ostler (died in 1614), Field (who left the company in 1619), Ecclestone (who was playing until 1624), and Tooley (who died in 1623), so that narrows down his playgoing experience to some time after the mid-1620s.[14] It may be relevant to note that the teenage Cary brothers returned to London at the end of their father's term of office as Lord Deputy of Ireland in 1629, having been away for most of the decade, and perhaps it is a plausible response to their exile from

---

[14] On the personnel of the King's Men, see Andrew Gurr, *The Shakespeare Company, 1594–1642* (Cambridge: Cambridge University Press, 2011).

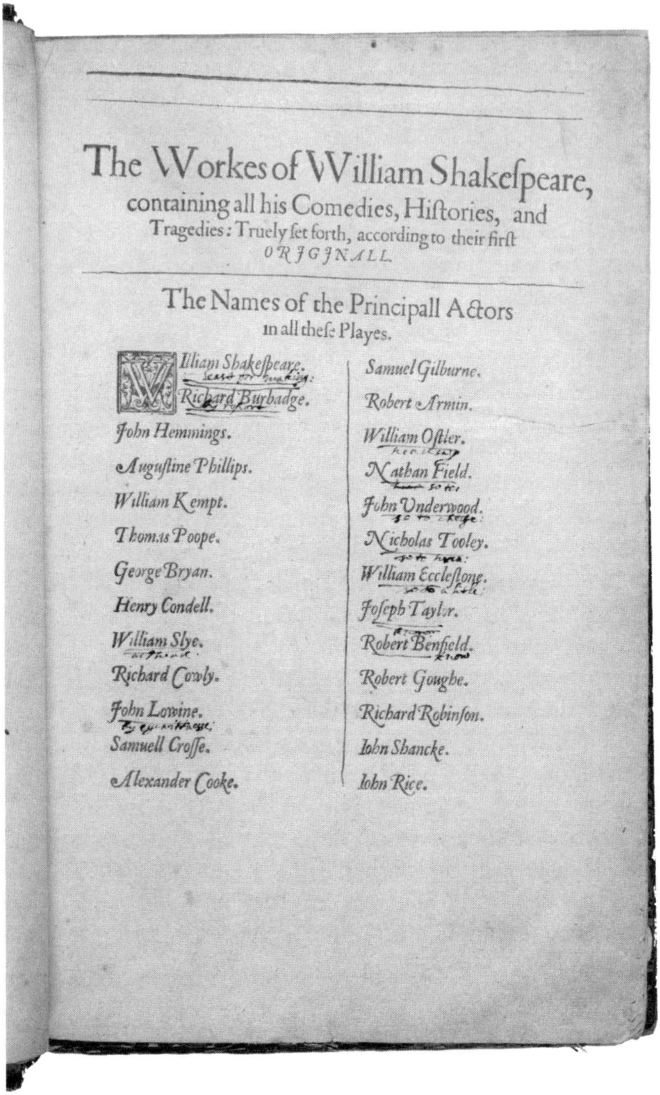

The Workes of William Shakeſpeare,
containing all his Comedies, Hiſtories, and
Tragedies: Truely ſet forth, according to their firſt
ORIGINALL

The Names of the Principall Actors
in all theſe Playes.

William Shakeſpeare.
Richard Burbadge.
John Hemmings.
Auguſtine Phillips.
William Kempt.
Thomas Poope.
George Bryan.
Henry Condell.
William Slye.
Richard Cowly.
John Lowine.
Samuell Croſſe.
Alexander Cooke.

Samuel Gilburne.
Robert Armin.
William Oſtler.
Nathan Field.
John Vnderwood.
Nicholas Tooley.
William Eccleſtone.
Joſeph Taylor.
Robert Benfield.
Robert Goughe.
Richard Robinſon.
Iohn Shancke.
Iohn Rice.

FIG. 2.1.   Glasgow actors page

An annotated list of the King's Men suggesting a reader who has some experience
of the early modern theatre in the late 1620s or early 1630s.

the metropolis to try, on their return, to connect with the temporal performance history that the list of actors documents.

The rest of the annotations can be divided into two categories. Extensive marks at the beginning of lines, particularly in the comedies, signal 'ap.' in the approved commonplacing tradition (Figure 2.2). More unusual are a few summary comments on the plays: 'pretty well' for *The Tempest*, 'starke naught' for *The Two Gentlemen of Verona*, 'very good, light' for *The Merry Wives of Windsor*, which also carries another notation 'a good jealous mans Dilemma'. Hyde wrote of Falkland that his conversion was 'enlivened and refreshed with all the Facetiousness of Wit and Good-Humour and Pleasantness of Discourse':[15] perhaps he sharpened this on Shakespeare's Folio comedies.

If the Cary copy is interesting for its suggestive connections with a well-known family and intellectual community, the most thorough seventeenth-century reader of a Shakespeare First Folio is otherwise unknown to us. His annotations are interesting precisely because they evoke his values, disposition, and habits of mind—what cultural theorists call *habitus*[16]—even as we know almost nothing else about him. The copy is now in the Kodama Shakespeare Library at Meisei University in Tokyo, and marked with the ownership mark, 'William Johnstoune his Booke'. The spelling of the name Johnstoune and of some of the annotations suggest that this reader was Scottish, part of an extensive family associated with border skirmishes over many centuries. An intriguing but faint manuscript note next to the dedicatory poem 'To the memory of my beloved, The Author Mr. William Shakespeare: And what he hath left us' by Ben Jonson appears to read 'To the memory of | My uncel | the author'. It is not impossible that Johnstoune and Jonson were related: Drummond of Hawthornden reports that the poet claimed ancestry in the

---

[15] Hyde (1759), p. 22.

[16] On *habitus*, see Pierre Bourdieu, *Distinction: A Social Critique of the Judgement of Taste* (London: Routledge, 2004), esp. p. 170.

praise womens modesty: and gaue such orderly and wel-behaued reproofe to al vncomelinesse, that I would haue sworne his disposition would haue gone to the truth of his words: but they doe no more adhere and keep place together, then the hundred Psalms to the tune of Greensleeues : What tempest (I troa) threw this Whale, (with so many Tuns of oyle in his belly) a shoare at Windsor? How shall I bee reuenged on him? I thinke the best way were, to entertaine him with hope, till the wicked fire of lust haue melted him in his owne greace: Did you e-uer heare the like?

Mis.Page. Letter for letter; but that the name of *Page* and *Ford* differs: to thy great comfort in this my-stery of ill opinions, heere's the twyn-brother of thy Let-ter : but let thine inherit first, for I protest mine neuer shall : I warrant he hath a thousand of these Letters, writ with blancke-space for different names (sure more): and these are of the second edition; hee will print them out of doubt : for he cares not what hee puts into the presse, when he would put vs two : I had rather be a Giantesse, and lye vnder Mount *Pelion*: Well; I will find you twen-tie lasciuious Turtles ere one chaste man.

Mis.Ford. Why this is the very same: the very hand: the very words: what doth he thinke of vs?

Mis.Page. Nay I know not : it makes me almost rea-die to wrangle with mine owne honesty : Ile entertaine my selfe like one that I am not acquainted withall : for sure vnlesse hee know some straine in mee, that I know not my selfe, hee would neuer haue boorded me in this furie.

Mi.Ford. Boording, call you it? Ile bee sure to keepe him aboue decke.

Mi.Page. So will I: if hee come vnder my hatches, Ile neuer to Sea againe : Let's bee reueng'd on him : let's appoint him a meeting : giue him a show of comfort in his Suit, and lead him on with a fine baited delay, till hee hath pawn'd his horses to mine Host of the Garter.

Mis.Ford. Nay, I will consent to act any villany against him, that may not sully the charinesse of our honesty : oh that my husband saw this Letter: it would giue eternall food to his iealousie.

Mis.Page. Why look where he comes; and my good man too : hee's as farre from iealousie, as I am from gi-uing him cause, and that (I hope) is an vnmeasurable di-stance.

Mis.Ford. You are the happier woman.

Mis.Page. Let's consult together against this greasie Knight : Come hither.

Ford. Well : I hope, it be not so.

Pist. Hope is a curtall-dog in some affaires:

Sir *Iohn* affects thy wife.

Ford. Why sir, my wife is not young.

Pist. He wooes both high and low, both rich & poor, both yong and old, one with another (*Ford*) he loues the Gally-mawfry (*Ford*) perpend.

Ford. Loue my wife?

Pist. With liuer, burning hot : preuent :

Or goe thou like Sir *Acteon* he, with

Ring-wood at thy heeles : O, odious is the name.

Ford. What name Sir?

Pist. The horne I say: Farewell.

Take heed, haue open eye, for theeues doe foot by night,

Take heed, ere sommer comes, or Cuckoo-birds do sing.

Away sir Corp'rall *Nim* :

Beleeue it (*Page*) he speakes sence.

Ford. I will be patient : I will find out this.

Nim. And this is true : I like not the humor of lying: hee hath wronged mee in some humors : I should haue borne the humour'd Letter to her : but I haue a sword : and it shall bite vpon my necessitie: he loues your wife; There's the short and the long : My name is Corporall *Nim*: I speak, and I auouch ; 'tis true : my name is *Nim*: and *Falstaffe* loues your wife : adieu, I loue not the hu-mour of bread and cheese : adieu.

Page. The humour of it (quoth'a?) heere's a fellow frights English out of his wits.

Ford. I will seeke out *Falstaffe*.

Page. I neuer heard such a drawling-affecting rogue.

Ford. If I doe finde it : well.

Page. I will not beleeue such a *Cataian*, though the Priest o' th'Towne commended him for a true man.

Ford. 'Twas a good sensible fellow : well.

Page. How now *Meg*?

Mis.Page. Whether goe you (*George*) harke you.

Mis Ford. How now (sweet *Frank*) why art thou me-lancholy?

Ford. I melancholy? I am not melancholy :

Get you home : goe.

Mis.Ford. Faith, thou hast some crochets in thy head, Now : will you goe, *Mistris Page*?

Mis.Page. Haue with you : you'll come to dinner *George* ? Looke who comes yonder : shee shall bee our Messenger to this paltrie Knight.

Mis Ford. Trust me, I thought on her : shee'll fit it.

Mis.Page. You are come to see my daughter *Anne* ?

Qui. Horsooth : and I pray how do's good Mistresse *Anne* ?

Mis.Page. Go in with vs and see : we haue an houres talke with you.

Page. How now Master *Ford*?

For. You heard what this knaue told me, did you not?

Page. Yes, and you heard what the other told me ?

Ford. Doe you thinke there is truth in them?

Pag. Hang 'em slaues : I doe not thinke the Knight would offer it : But these that accuse him in his intent towards our wiues, are a yoake of his discarded men: ve-ry rogues, now they be out of seruice.

Ford. Were they his men?

Page. Marry were they.

Ford. I like it neuer the beter for that, Do's he lye at the Garter?

Page. I marry do's he : if hee should intend this voy-age toward my wife, I would turne her loose to him; and what hee gets more of her, then sharpe words, let it lye on my head.

Ford. I doe not misdoubt my wife : but I would bee loath to turne them together : a man may be too confi-dent : I would haue nothing lye on my head : I cannot be thus satisfied.

Page. Looke where my ranting-Host of the Garter comes : there is eyther liquor in his pate, or mony in his purse, when hee lookes so merrily : How now mine Host?

Host. How now Bully-Rooke : thou'rt a Gentleman Caueleiro Iustice, I say.

Shal. I follow, (mine Host) I follow : Good-euen, and twenty (good Master *Page*.) Master *Page*, wil you go with vs? we haue sport in hand.

Host. Tell him Caueleiro-Iustice : tell him Bully-Rooke.

Shall. Sir, there is a fray to be fought, betweene Sir *Hugh* the Welch Priest, and *Caius* the French Doctor.

                                   Ford. Good

FIG. 2.2. Glasgow commonplacing

Underlining and the marginal mark 'apr.' are signs of commonplacing—reading to extract pithy phrases. The copy is now in Glasgow and is associated with Lucius Cary in the 1630s.

Ford. Good mine Host o'th'Garter: a word with you.

Host. What faist thou, my Bully-Rooke?

Shal. Will you goe with vs to behold it? My merry Host hath had the measuring of their weapons; and (I thinke) hath appointed them contrary places: for (beleeue mee) I heare the Parson is no Iester: harke, I will tell you what our sport shall be.

Host. Hast thou no suit against my Knight, my guest-Caualeire?

Shal. None, I protest: but Ile giue you a pottle of burn'd sacke, to giue me recourse to him, and tell him my name is *Broome*: onely for a iest.

Host. My hand, (Bully:) thou shalt haue egresse and regresse, (said I well?) and thy name shall be *Broome*. It is a merry Knight: will you goe An-heires?

Shal. Haue with you mine Host.

Page. I haue heard the French-man hath good skill in his Rapier.

Shal. Tut sir: I could haue told you more: In these times you stand on distance: your Passes, Stoccado's, and I know not what: 'tis the heart (Master *Page*) 'tis heere, 'tis heere: I haue seene the time, with my long-sword, I would haue made you fowre tall fellowes skippe like Rattes.

Host. Heere boyes, heere, heere: shall we wag?

Page. Haue with you: I had rather heare them scold, then fight.

Ford. Though *Page* be a secure foole, and stands so firmely on his wiues frailty; yet, I cannot put-off my opinion so easily: she was in his company at *Pages* house: and what they made there, I know not. Well, I will looke further into't, and I haue a disguise, to sound *Falstaffe*: if I finde her honest, I loose not my labor: if she be otherwise, 'tis labour well bestowed. *Exeunt.*

Scœna Secunda.

Enter Falstaffe, Pistoll, Robin, Quickly, Bardolfe, Ford.

Fal. I will not lend thee a penny.

Pist. Why then the world's mine Oyster, which I, with sword will open.

Fal. Not a penny: I haue beene content (Sir) you should lay my countenance to pawne: I haue grated vpon my good friends for three Repreeues for you, and your Coach-fellow *Nim*; or else you had look'd through the grate, like a Geminy of Baboones: I am damn'd in hell, for swearing to Gentlemen my friends, you were good Souldiers, and tall-fellowes. And when Mistresse *Briget* lost the handle of her Fan, I tooke't vpon mine honour thou hadst it not.

Pist. Didst not thou share? hadst thou not fifteene pence?

Fal. Reason, you rogue, reason: thinkst thou Ile endanger my soule, *gratis*? at a word, hang no more about mee, I am no gibbet for you: goe, a short knife, and a throng, to your Mannor of *Picks-batch*: goe, you'll not beare a Letter for mee you rogue? you stand vpon your honor: why, (thou vnconfinable basenesse) it is as much as I can doe to keepe the termes of my honnor precise: I, I, I my selfe sometimes, leauing the feare of heauen on

the left hand, and hiding mine honor in my necessity, am faine to shuffle: to hedge, and to lurch, and yet, you Rogue, will en-sconce your raggs; your Cat-a-Mountaine-lookes, your red-lattice phrases, and your bold-beating-oathes, vnder the shelter of your honor? you will not doe it? you?

Pist. I doe relent: what would thou more of man?

Robin. Sir, here's a woman would speake with you.

Qui. Giue your worship good morrow.

Fal. Good-morrow, good-wife.

Qui. Not so: and't please your worship.

Fal. Good maid then.

Qui. Ile be sworne,

As my mother was the first houre I was borne.

Fal. I doe beleeue the swearer; what with me?

Qui. Shall I vouch-safe your worship a word, or two?

Fal. Two thousand (faire woman) and ile vouchsafe thee the hearing.

Qui. There is one Mistresse Ford, (Sir) I pray come a little neerer this waies: I my selfe dwell with M. Doctor *Caius*.

Fal. Well, on: Mistresse *Ford*, you say.

Qui. Your worship saies very true: I pray your worship come a little neerer this waies.

Fal. I warrant thee, no-bodie heares: mine owne people, mine owne people.

Qui. Are they so? heauen-blesse them, and make them his Seruants.

Fal. Well: Mistresse *Ford*, what of her?

Qui. Why, Sir; shee's a good-creature; Lord, Lord, your Worship's a wanton: well: heauen forgiue you, and all of vs, I pray.

Fal. Mistresse *Ford*: come, Mistresse Ford.

Qui. Marry this is the short, and the long of it: you haue brought her into such a Canaries, as 'tis wonderfull: the best Courtier of them all (when the Court lay at *Windsor*) could neuer haue brought her to such a Canarie: yet there has beene Knights, and Lords, and Gentlemen, with their Coaches; I warrant you Coach after Coach, letter after letter, gift after gift, smelling so sweetly; all Muske, and so rushling, I warrant you, in silke and golde, and in such alligant termes, and in such wine and suger of the best, and the fairest, that would haue wonne any womans heart: and I warrant you, they could neuer get an eye-winke of her: I had my selfe twentie Angels giuen me this morning, but I defie all Angels (in any such sort, as they say) but in the way of honesty: and I warrant you, they could neuer get her so much as sippe on a cup with the prowdest of them all, and yet there has beene Earles: nay, (which is more) Pentioners, but I warrant you all is one with her.

Fal. But what saies shee to mee? be briefe my good shee-*Mercurie*.

Qui. Marry, she hath receiu'd your Letter: for the which she thankes you a thousand times; and she giues you to notifie, that her husband will be absence from his house, betweene ten and eleuen.

Fal. Ten, and eleuen.

Qui. I, forsooth: and then you may come and see the picture (she sayes) that you wot of: Master *Ford* her husband will be from home: alas, the sweet woman leades an ill life with him: hee's a very iealousie-man; she leades a very frampold life with him, (good hart.)

Fal. Ten, and eleuen.

Woman

border country: 'his grandfather came from Carlisle, and he thought from Annandale to it'.[17] If the 'memory' means something more than a mere echo of the title of the poem, this note at least must be dated after Jonson's death in 1637. It is not absolutely certain that the Johnstoune who wrote his name also wrote the other annotations, although in the absence of contrary information, I shall assume here that he did.[18]

Johnstoune is the one attested exception to the pattern of intermittent Folio reading found widely across other extant copies. Rather than dipping in and out of the book as his fancy took, he appears to have set himself the task of reading and annotating all the plays in the volume according to an established pattern, using the left and right hand sides of the top margin of each page to write notes on the left and right column text respectively. Occasionally he also made use of the bottom margin in the same way. He worked consistently through every play in this manner, also underlining extensively, and making use of dashes or ink slashes at the beginning of lines, perhaps to mark his progress through the text. His notes vary from plot summary to the copying out of sententiae or commonplaces, to paraphrasing of particular lines. His notes to the second scene of *Hamlet* are an indicative example (Figure 2.3). The scene depicts a black-cloaked Hamlet defending his mourning for his father against the persuasions of his mother, Gertrude, and his stepfather, King Claudius. Annotations above the left hand column read: 'most friendlie offer offers [*sic*] of court favour | entreatie to forget his fathers death | unfained and deepe sorrow for a fathers death | reasons against excessive sorrow for a fathers death'. This involves paraphrase—Johnstoune's 'unfained and deepe' is a précis of Hamlet's angry 'These indeed Seeme, | For

[17] Ian Donaldson (ed.), 'Conversations with Drummond' in *The Oxford Authors: Ben Jonson* (Oxford: Oxford University Press, 1985), p. 600.

[18] On the identity of the annotator, see Akihiro Yamada, *The First Folio of Shakespeare: A Transcript of Contemporary Marginalia in a copy in the Kodama Memorial Library of Meisei University* (Tokyo: Yushodo Press, 1988), pp. xvii–xx.

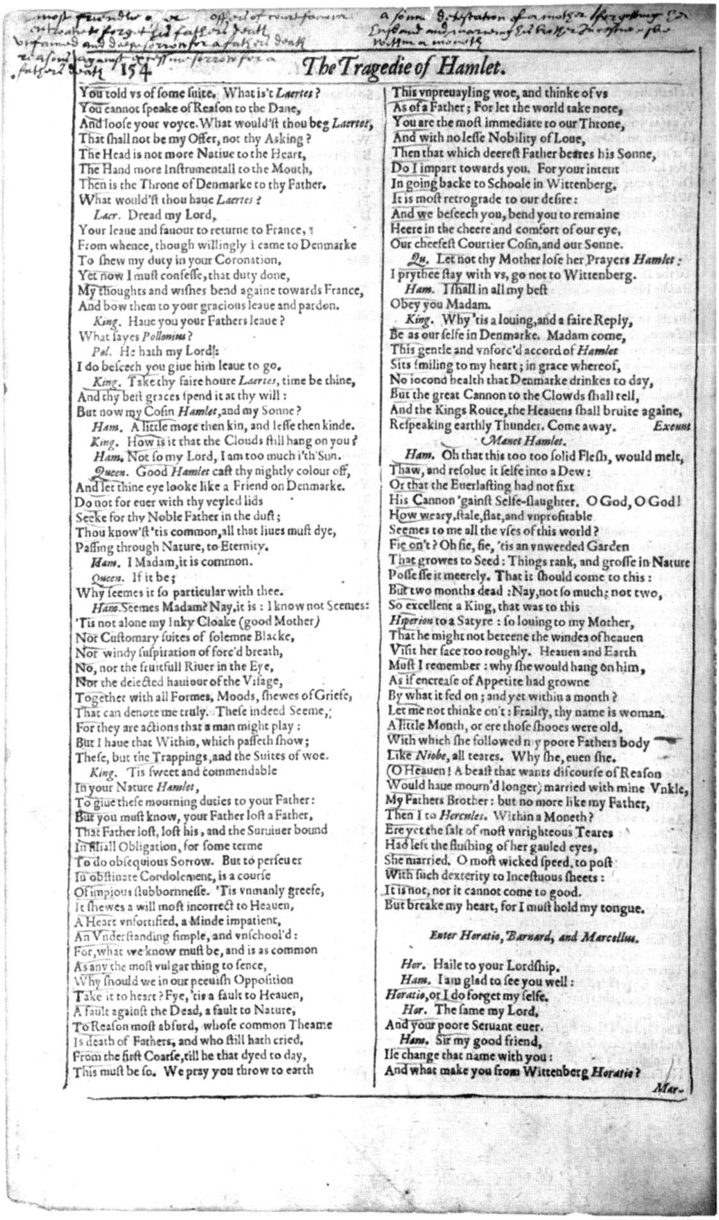
154 *The Tragedie of Hamlet.*

You told vs of some suite. What is't *Laertes*?
You cannot speake of Reason to the Dane,
And loose your voyce. What would'st thou beg *Laertes*,
That shall not be my Offer, not thy Asking?
The Head is not more Natiue to the Heart,
The Hand more Instrumentall to the Mouth,
Then is the Throne of Denmarke to thy Father.
What would'st thou haue *Laertes*?
Laer. Dread my Lord,
Your leaue and fauour to returne to France,
From whence, though willingly I came to Denmarke
To shew my duty in your Coronation,
Yet now I must confesse, that duty done,
My thoughts and wishes bend againe towards France,
And bow them to your gracious leaue and pardon.
King. Haue you your Fathers leaue?
What sayes *Pollonius*?
Pol. He hath my Lord:
I do beseech you giue him leaue to go.
King. Take thy faire houre *Laertes*, time be thine,
And thy best graces spend it at thy will:
But now my Cosin *Hamlet*, and my Sonne?
Ham. A little more then kin, and lesse then kinde.
King. How is it that the Clouds still hang on you?
Ham. Not so my Lord, I am too much i'th'Sun.
Queen. Good *Hamlet* cast thy nightly colour off,
And let thine eye looke like a Friend on Denmarke.
Do not for euer with thy veyled lids
Seeke for thy Noble Father in the dust;
Thou know'st 'tis common, all that liues must dye,
Passing through Nature, to Eternity.
Ham. I Madam, it is common.
Queen. If it be;
Why seemes it so particular with thee.
Ham. Seemes Madam? Nay, it is: I know not Seemes:
'Tis not alone my Inky Cloake (good Mother)
Nor Customary suites of solemne Blacke,
Nor windy suspiration of forc'd breath,
No, nor the fruitfull Riuer in the Eye,
Nor the deiected hauiour of the Visage,
Together with all Formes, Moods, shewes of Griefe,
That can denote me truly. These indeed Seeme,
For they are actions that a man might play:
But I haue that Within, which passeth show;
These, but the Trappings, and the Suites of woe.
King. 'Tis sweet and commendable
In your Nature *Hamlet*,
To giue these mourning duties to your Father:
But you must know, your Father lost a Father,
That Father lost, lost his, and the Suruiuer bound
In filiall Obligation, for some terme
To do obsequious Sorrow. But to perseuer
In obstinate Condolement, is a course
Of impious stubbornnesse. 'Tis vnmanly greefe,
It shewes a will most incorrect to Heauen,
A Heart vnfortified, a Minde impatient,
An Vnderstanding simple, and vnschool'd:
For, what we know must be, and is as common
As any the most vulgar thing to sence,
Why should we in our peeuish Opposition
Take it to heart? Fye, 'tis a fault to Heauen,
A fault against the Dead, a fault to Nature,
To Reason most absurd, whose common Theame
Is death of Fathers, and who still hath cried,
From the first Coarse, till he that dyed to day,
This must be so. We pray you throw to earth
This vnpreuayling woe, and thinke of vs
As of a Father; For let the world take note,
You are the most immediate to our Throne,
And with no lesse Nobility of Loue,
Then that which deerest Father beares his Sonne,
Do I impart towards you. For your intent
In going backe to Schoole in Wittenberg,
It is most retrograde to our desire:
And we beseech you, bend you to remaine
Heere in the cheere and comfort of our eye,
Our cheefest Courtier Cosin, and our Sonne.
Qu. Let not thy Mother lose her Prayers *Hamlet*:
I prythee stay with vs, go not to Wittenberg.
Ham. I shall in all my best
Obey you Madam.
King. Why 'tis a louing, and a faire Reply,
Be as our selfe in Denmarke. Madam come,
This gentle and vnforc'd accord of *Hamlet*
Sits smiling to my heart; in grace whereof,
No iocond health that Denmarke drinkes to day,
But the great Cannon to the Clowds shall tell,
And the Kings Rouce, the Heauens shall bruite againe,
Respeaking earthly Thunder. Come away. *Exeunt*
Manet Hamlet.
Ham. Oh that this too too solid Flesh, would melt,
Thaw, and resolue it selfe into a Dew:
Or that the Euerlasting had not fixt
His Cannon 'gainst Selfe-slaughter. O God, O God!
How weary, stale, flat, and vnprofitable
Seemes to me all the vses of this world?
Fie on't? Oh fie, fie, 'tis an vnweeded Garden
That growes to Seed: Things rank, and grosse in Nature
Possesse it meerely. That it should come to this:
But two months dead: Nay, not so much; not two,
So excellent a King, that was to this
Hiperion to a Satyre: so louing to my Mother,
That he might not beteene the windes of heauen
Visit her face too roughly. Heauen and Earth
Must I remember: why she would hang on him,
As if encrease of Appetite had growne
By what it fed on; and yet within a month?
Let me not thinke on't: Frailty, thy name is woman.
A little Month, or ere those shooes were old,
With which she followed my poore Fathers body
Like *Niobe*, all teares. Why she, euen she.
(O Heauen! A beast that wants discourse of Reason
Would haue mourn'd longer) married with mine Vnkle,
My Fathers Brother: but no more like my Father,
Then I to *Hercules*. Within a Moneth?
Ere yet the salt of most vnrighteous Teares
Had left the flushing of her gauled eyes,
She married. O most wicked speed, to post
With such dexterity to Incestuous sheets:
It is not, nor it cannot come to good.
But breake my heart, for I must hold my tongue.

Enter Horatio, Barnard, and Marcellus.

Hor. Haile to your Lordship.
Ham. I am glad to see you well:
Horatio, or I do forget my selfe.
Hor. The same my Lord,
And your poore Seruant euer.
Ham. Sir my good friend,
Ile change that name with you:
And what make you from Wittenberg *Horatio*?
Mar-

FIG. 2.3. William Johnstoune
The annotations to *Hamlet* by William Johnstoune, a Scottish reader of the first half of the seventeenth century, in a copy now in Meisei.

they are actions that a man might play: | But I have that Within, which passeth show' [1.2.83–6]. But it also shows a noticeable reluctance to judge the issue. Claudius's advice to Hamlet about 'unmanly greefe' [1.2.96] is glossed without comment, indicating either that Johnstoune is not concerned to judge the characters he discusses, or that he does not know at the point he annotates Claudius's pious-sounding speech how hypocritical it will come to seem as the play unfolds. (There is some evidence in other plays that Johnstoune does not know the whole shape of the plot before he begins his annotations: at the beginning of *Titus Andronicus* he suggests, as the play itself does at the same point, that Saturninus 'marries his [i.e. Titus'] doghter', and has to retract a few lines later when it becomes evident that 'Saturninus reiects lauinia and owtrages | andronicus her father': the young emperor takes the imprisoned Gothic queen Tamora as his wife instead [1.1]. Johnstoune is similarly taken in by *Measure for Measure*'s Duke, as are the onstage characters, in believing 'Lex talionis angelo executed for his iniustice': the corrupt deputy Angelo is eventually pardoned in the play's final queasy amnesties [5.1].) The next column of the same page of *Hamlet* notes: 'a sonnes detestation of a mother forgetting her | husband and marieing his brother Incestuouslie | within a moneth'. Johnstoune's annotations here identify in general terms the occasion for the speech—'a sonnes detestation of a mother'—as well as its content, echoing Hamlet's word 'Incestuous' [1.2.157] and copying exactly from his speech the phrase 'within a moneth' [1.2.145].

Different inks on some pages, however, suggest that he also returned on more than one occasion, apparently rereading the plays and augmenting the annotations. In *As You Like It*, for instance, two periods of annotation can be discerned. At his first reading of the discussion of the exiled court in the forest of Arden, Johnstoune noted 'securitie and happinesse of retired life | against cruell sport of killing Innocent deere | worldlings testaments | Error of all estates' and he seems then to have added in the observations 'miserie parts cumpanie | oppressions committed by men of all estates' and 'dyeing man for= |saken by all friends' to corroborate the account of Jacques' mournfully anthropomorphic interpretation of the dying stag 'abandoned of his velvet friend' [2.1.50]. The later annotations therefore seem to deepen and reiterate what was observed in the first pass at the text, rather than to contradict it or take early readings in new directions. Where Johnstoune has been misled by the turns of the plot, as in the examples from *Titus Andronicus* and *Measure for Measure* above, he does not return to his earlier annotations with the benefit of plot hindsight.

Johnstoune's sense of the plays is strongly teleological. He often summarizes the conclusion in clear and unambiguous terms (although he seems, like many readers since, rather to give up in bewilderment at the complicated revelations that conclude *Cymbeline*: 'Infinit questions of the circumstance of strange chances'). Not for him any lingering worry about the fate of Shylock, or whether the silenced Jessica is accepted by her new Christian society: for Johnstoune, *The Merchant of Venice* ends entirely satisfactorily: 'feares wittilie wroght and fairlie quenched | Conceived feares and losses happilie removed | Intricassies cleered and Ioyfullie ended'. Isabella's silence in the face of the Duke's unexpected marriage proposal at the end of *Measure for Measure* has been seen by modern readers as pointedly ambivalent: for Johnstoune there is no trace of the unease that would lead to the later characterization of this as a problem play. Rather, he notes, 'pleasant conclusions of the adventures' when 'The Duke takes Isabella to wife'. The use of characters' names here is intermittent in the annotations. Sometimes Johnstoune seems concerned to generalize the experience presented in the play, as in his snapshot commonplaces of *The Two Gentlemen of Verona*: 'subtile calumnies to disgrace a man to his mistres'; 'a treacherous friend'; 'womans defects'; 'wickednesse of owtlawes'. On other occasions, the specific contours of the plot are his focus, as in this gloss on *Julius Caesar*: 'a soothsaier warnes Cæsar to be worre of the Ides of March | Brutus at warre with him self excuses his sowre lookes | to his friends' [1.2.20–45].

From Johnstoune's reading, it is possible to speculate about some of the man's opinions and mental habits. He enjoys moral observation rather than comedy, and is often censorious. His judgement on one page of *The Merry Wives of Windsor*, apparently occasioned by Mistress Quickly's conversation with Falstaff about Mistress Page, seems to overlay the comic tone of the text with something more obviously sermonizing: 'hipocriticall whoore'; 'a wife trusted and left to her owne will'; 'Baudrie'; 'money makes way everie where'; 'ways to corrupt Women'. Throughout his annotations, he is particularly concerned by, and apt to discover, wanton behaviour in women. He reads the ambiguous speech of Katherine which ends *The Taming of the Shrew* [5.2.141–84] with evident satisfaction: 'husband commended for making her who | when she wes a maide and after she wes first maried | wes Intolerablie shrewd and scolding to become | loving and obedient' and 'duties of true obedience of a wife to her husband'. He is clear where blame lies in *Macbeth*: 'Macbeth furnishes to him self true reasons to | foresake his pourpose of killing the king | but his hellish wife drives him to do it' [1.7.30–82]. He takes particular care to extrapolate Iago's misogyny in his conversation with Desdemona as they wait for news of Othello: 'a woman having too much tongue puts a part | of it some times in her heart with thinking | a description of womens Imperfections and falsehoods | women rise to play and go to their beds to work | women beguile the thing the are by seeming otherwise' [2.1.100–69]. In *The Comedy of Errors*, he glosses the discussion between Adriana and Luciana [2.1.1–42]: 'women vnWilling to be controlled', and then endorses Luciana's side of the debate: 'Males masters of femels | omnes facile cum valemus'.

The Latin phrase is from Terence's comedy *Andria*, with the word order slightly inverted: in context, it is a response to advice to forget about a disappointment in love, with the phrase 'facile omnes quom valemus recta consilia aegrotis damus' ('We all find it easy to give the right advice to the sick when we are well'). The quotation must have been prompted by Adriana's reproach—'So

thou that hast no unkinde mate to greeve thee | With urging
helplesse patience would releeve me' [2.1.38–9]—but it also gives
a sideways insight into Johnstoune's other literary tastes, or perhaps his exposure to Terence at grammar school, where the plays
were a standard text. In the Induction to Jonson's play, *The
Magnetick Lady*, the young Boy completes a Latin line saying 'he
learn'd Terence i' th' third form at Westminster': the reference is
again to *Andria*. Elsewhere Johnstoune's eight Latin phrases draw
on Cicero (in a note to *3 Henry VI* and *Measure for Measure*) and
Persius, Ovid, and Juvenal (on *Measure for Measure*): all staple
grammar school authors, which might indicate the level of his
education.

Marks on the history plays may indicate a particular nationalistic interest. Johnstoune does not mention Falstaff in his annotations of *1 Henry IV*, and his summary of Hal's conduct strongly
implies that, unlike most early modern audience members, he does
not approve of him: 'dissolution of the prince robbing in the night
| and spending it In the day in drinking harlotrie | debauch and
riot with damned villaines'. He does, however, stress the play's
Scottish connections. It is the 'Battell of Holmedon where the
scots | were vanquished & their nobilitie prisoners' [1.1.67–70]
rather than the 'beastly shamelesse transformation | By those
Welshwomen done' [1.1.44–5] that catches his eye in the play's
opening scene, and three of the four annotations to the play's final
scenes focus on Douglas the Scot and what he describes as his
'Incomparable valour'. He does not, however, seem to respond to
the Scottish setting of *Macbeth*.

Johnstoune's labours on the text of Shakespeare's Folio are
unique in their extent and their consistency. Collectively, his
notes suggest a reading of the plays with a particular focus on
women's conduct, and with an attention both to the commonplace
or proverbial phrase and to running plot summary. He is not averse
to adjectival commentary to intensify his glosses. His annotations
reveal a reader who is sufficiently involved with the play's characters to judge their behaviour harshly. Sometimes, his notes seem

absorbed in the fiction of the play, as when, for instance, he identifies the words or situations of particular characters by name, while at others he is more distanced from the moment by moment unfolding of the drama and concerned instead to draw out more general or proverbial commentary. He does not show any attention to the theatrical form, to speech prefixes, or to stage directions, nor is he concerned, as other readers were, to cavil over printing errors or other presentational issues. His sparse Latin annotations connect his Folio reading to patterns of school education rather than extensive further study, and may indicate something about his other reading (no further evidence of his library has yet come to light, although it is implausible that only this book attracted his annotating attention). Like others of the readers and locations identified in this chapter, he is far from the London theatrical world, and thus, for all his exceptionalism, he also exemplifies the way this study of early Folio readers can help to rebalance certain historical biases.

Johnstoune's First Folio annotations give us a narrow window on a whole world view and allow us to build up a picture of his reading, both as practical activity and intellectual engagement. No other extant copy offers such sustained evidence. The Shakespeare Folio was a book often heavily used, particularly during its first century, and most extant copies bear witness to varieties of use, but, when looked at individually, these marks can seem too random or scattered to be meaningful. A larger-scale survey, however, reveals patterns of reading and textual hotspots of readerly attention, without tidying up all that is idiosyncratic about particular readers. Most early readers' attention to the First Folio tended to be intermittent, even distracted. It was highly focused and specific at certain textual moments and rather lax, forbearing, disinterested, or even uninterested at others. As we will see, annotations and other marks of use tend to be clustered in particular parts of the book, again suggestive of local rather than complete reading. Readings apparently aimed at self-improvement jostle with an enjoyment of bawdy; attention to the fictive world of the plays is accompanied by marks that attest to the more pressing concerns of the world of the readers; and there are occasional fleeting glimpses of now lost individual and communal lives. Most of the readers who have left their mark in Shakespeare First Folios cannot now be traced: the record of their interaction with this text is all we know of their lives.

While most marks are difficult to date precisely, the intellectual context of commonplacing to which many of them belong was particularly prominent during the seventeenth and early eighteenth centuries.[19] From Erasmus onwards, the idea of sustained reading to identify topics, examples, sayings, or commonplaces for reuse was the foundation of humanist pedagogy. Passages were to be selected as a storehouse of wisdom and virtue, both for their content and applicability within larger categories, and as expressive or rhetorical *exempla* that might be copied to enrich the reader's own vocabulary and eloquence. Thus, for example, John Hancock's manuscript commonplace book (1671–1752), now in the Houghton Library at Harvard, organizes the fruits of his reading under the alphabetical headings, 'Adam', 'Antichrist', 'Afflictions', 'Anger' and so on.[20] Edward Pudsey (1573–1612/3), who kept a commonplace book in the early seventeenth century, including a number of Shakespearean extracts, used some similar headings and also gathered as an example of 'simile': 'He knows me as the blind

[19] Many studies of manuscript annotations on early books make a similar assumption in the face of indeterminate dating. See, for instance, Sonia Massai, *Shakespeare and the Rise of the Editor* (Cambridge: Cambridge University Press, 2007), p. 14, and John Jowett, '"For Many of Your Companies": Middleton's Early Readers' in Gary Taylor and John Lavagnino (eds), *Thomas Middleton and Early Modern Textual Culture* (Oxford: Clarendon Press, 2007), pp. 286–330; p. 315. On commonplacing, see Ann Moss, *Printed Common-Place books and the Structuring of Renaissance Thought* (Oxford: Clarendon Press, 1996) and Mary Thomas Crane, *Framed Authority: Sayings, Self and Society in Sixteenth-Century England* (Princeton: Princeton University Press, 1993).
[20] Commonplace book of John Hancock: http://ocp.hul.harvard.edu/reading/vcsearch.php?cat=17+century&sub=commonplace (accessed April 2015).

man knows the cuckoo, by my bad voice' (*The Merchant of Venice* 5.1.112).[21] Commonplacing was a vital organizing principle in early modern knowledge and information retrieval systems. We can see it as the foundation of the new genre of the essay, as practised in the period by Michel de Montaigne and Francis Bacon. Montaigne's essay titles, translated by John Florio in 1603, include categories rather like John Hancock's headings, including 'Of Anger and Choler' and 'Of Friendship' and quote extensively from classical authorities. Ann Blair has described the Renaissance as a period 'of newly-invigorated info-lust that sought to gather and manage as much information as possible' which led individuals to amass 'large collections of textual information in their manuscript notes and in printed reference books':[22] reading to identify passages for potential reuse was one of the dominant hermeneutic modes of early modern England. As Thomas Fuller wrote in 1642, in a martial metaphor appropriate to the year that saw the first major military action of the civil war: 'A commonplace book contains many Notions in garison, whence the owner may draw out an army into the field on competent warning.'[23]

This commonplacing intellectual tradition has left a clear trace in many copies of the First Folio. In some copies, passages for commmonplacing are marked with the headings under which they belong, so that the reader, or some other amanuensis, might copy them into blank notebooks or printed commonplace books with ready prepared headings. Edward Dering's account book records his purchase of 'two paper books in fol. for commonplaces' for just

[21] Richard Savage (ed.), *Shakespearean Extracts from 'Edward Pudsey's booke'* (Stratford-upon-Avon: n.p., 1888), p. 6.
[22] Ann Blair, *Too Much to Know: Managing Scholarly Information Before the Modern Age* (New Haven, Conn.: Yale University Press, 2010), p. 6.
[23] Quoted in—and giving the title for—Peter Beal's 'Notions in Garrison: The Seventeenth-Century commonplace book' in W. Speed Hill (ed.), *New Ways of Looking at Old Texts: Papers of the Renaissance English Text Society, 1985–1991* (Binghamton: Medieval & Renaissance Texts Society, 1993), pp. 131–48; p. 132.

this purpose. The copy sold by Dr Williams's Library at Sotheby's in 2006 is a good example of a Folio marked up for commonplacing in this way. Five comedies are annotated in the margin with commonplace categories including 'joy', 'beuty', 'virtue', 'war', 'time', and 'wit'.[24] The war of words between the on-off lovers Beatrice and Benedick at the beginning of *Much Ado About Nothing* has a number of phrases marked in the margin as 'simile' (these are erroneous examples by modern definitions of the term—e.g. 'I would my horse had the speed of your tongue' [1.1.135]). The copy associated in the later seventeenth century with Thomas and Isabella Hervey of Ickworth in Suffolk uses underlining to identify passages of particular note.[25] On the first page of the first play, *The Tempest*, for example, Gonzalo's shipboard remonstration with the Boatswain is underlined: 'Nay, good be patient. | When the Sea is' [1.1.14]. Miranda's lamentation to her father describing the storm—'the skye it seemes would powre down stinking pitch' [1.2.3]—is marked with the word 'sky' in the margin, probably again to signal its commonplace category. Their pattern of underlining seems to be to identify notable phrases: 'which touch'd | The very vertue of compassion in thee' [1.2.26–7]; 'That this lives in thy minde?' [1.2.49]; 'Thy Mother was a peece of vertue' [1.2.56]; 'To trash for over-topping' [1.2.81]; 'the very rats | Instinctively have quit it' [1.2.147–8]. This copy appears to offer an example of readers who have confidently begun the task of commonplacing with good intentions and have worked busily on the early pages of the book. The Hervey family marks begin with a complicatedly differentiated system, sometimes using 'x', 'o' or 'ex' in the margin, but these stop after a couple of pages, perhaps because they were too laborious to continue across the hundreds of following pages.

The Herveys' commonplacing choices, as quoted above, indicate that, while commonplacing anticipates the later practice of

---

[24] West 33.   [25] West 210.

identifying memorable quotations, codified in William Dodd's *The Beauties of Shakespeare* (1752) and all the books of quotations that followed it, it does not always focus on the same textual elements. The Herveys do not seem particularly to favour purple or poetic passages, but rather to identify phrases of pleasing balance or expression that might be useful. There is no mark, for example, in the Hervey Folio against what would become for later readers the play's most significant speech, Prospero's disquisition on mutability in 'Our revels now are ended' [4.1.148], perhaps because it is just too poetically distinctive: it sounds like a quotation. At least part of the use value of the commonplace for early readers was as a textual chameleon, able to change its colour—at least hypothetically—and thus slip unnoticed into their own writing, without obviously bearing the mark of its original context. Extant examples of manuscript commonplace books that include dramatic extracts demonstrate these protocols in action. Edward Pudsey, keeping his commonplace book in London and Tewkesbury at the turn of the seventeenth century, transcribes a line from *Titus Andronicus*. In the process, he carefully changes what in the play is Tamora's dramatic and impotent plea to Titus for the life of her captive son Alarbus from a desperate question into a statement. The play has 'Wilt thou draw neere the nature of the Gods? | Draw near them then in being mercifull' [1.1.117–8], which Pudsey inverts to 'If thou wilt draw neer ye nature of ye godes, bee m[e]rciful, &c'.[26] As he transfers the commonplace from the printed text into his own manuscript compilation, Pudsey processes it to strip out the specifics. Pudsey is working from a pre-Folio text, but the principle of commonplacing remains the same throughout the century. Speaker, dramatic context, and iambic pentameter are all erased to create the reusable sententious fragment. Not all such reusable material was morally or philosophically uplifting, however. The early reader who marked up the

[26] Savage (ed.), p. 8.

suave seduction lines from the shipwrecked prince Ferdinand on meeting the deliciously unabashed Miranda in *The Tempest* may well have been hoping for the real-life opportunity to use such devastating chat-up lines as 'No, noble Mistris, 'tis fresh morning with me | When you are by at night' [3.1.33–4] or 'But you, O you, | So perfect, and so peerlesse, are created | Of everie Creatures best' [3.1.46–8], and to earn in reply 'I am your wife, if you will marrie me; | If not, Ile die your maid' [3.1.83–4]—all phrases underlined and marked with the marginal 'ap' for 'I approve'.[27]

The copy of the Folio in the possession of the Royal Shakespeare Company in Stratford-upon-Avon registers some enthusiastic marks of reading, making particular use of the drawn symbol of the pointing hand that William H. Sherman has usefully called the manicule.[28] In combination with other marks, including curly brackets around lines and the marginal quotation mark (borrowed from a convention in some early printed texts, though not the Folio itself, that uses the ' or " mark to signal quotable *sententiae*)[29] this reader indicates approval of longer passages in the plays. The marks show an enthusiasm for moments of high rhetorical passion. Marcus's famous speech in *Titus Andronicus* [2.4.11–57] when he discovers the wretched Lavinia, her hands and tongue cut out so she cannot reveal her rapists, for instance, is covered with drawn manicules. The reader's preferred mark here echoes, perhaps unconsciously, the play's own linguistic preoccupation with hands, both figurative and physical.

---

[27] West 11, now in Glasgow University Library. 'Ap' is clearly a recognized marginal mark, since it is applied by readers in a number of other copies including West 166, now in the New York Public Library, and a copy in private hands in the UK, West 229.

[28] West 39; Sherman, p. 29.

[29] On these marks in printed books, see for instance G. K. Hunter, 'The Marking of *Sententiae* in Elizabethan Printed Plays, Poems and Romances's *Library* 5th ser. 6 (1951), pp. 171–88, and Zachary Lesser and Peter Stallybrass, 'The First Literary *Hamlet* and the Commonplacing of Professional Plays's *Shakespeare Quarterly* 59 (2008), pp. 371–420.

Othello is also heavily marked up in this copy (Figure 2.4). In the scene in the Duke's war cabinet, the reader marks Brabantio's complaint at Desdemona's elopement, 'my perticlar griefe | Is of so flood-gate, and ore-eating Nature, | That it englutes' [1.3.55–7] and Othello's own defence of his professional integrity 'Let House-wives make a Skillet of my Helme' [1.3.272] and then Roderigo's intemperate, 'I will incontinently drowne my selfe' [1.3.305]. The marks identify pithy or eloquent phrases, but more importantly, they also register a broad sympathy across the play's different perspectives, and this reading continues through the rest of the tragedy. This is a reader who can enjoy both Iago's cynicism—a pointing hand identifies his misogynistic calumny on the quayside with Desdemona 'You rise to play and go to bed to worke' [2.1.18]—and what G. Wilson Knight memorably dubbed the 'Othello music', that particular, distanced poetry that characterizes Othello's beautifully orotund self-delusion: 'It gives me wonder great, as my content | To see you heere before me. | O my Soules Joy: | If after every Tempest, come such Calmes, | May the winds blow, till they have waken'd death' [2.1.184–7].[30] The reading is thus attentive and responsive to the play's divergent world views: marking up Emilia's world-weary, ''Tis not a yeare or two shewes us a man: | They are all but Stomackes, and we all but Foode, | They eate us hungerly, and when they are full | They belch us' [3.4.101–4], as well as Othello's magnificent speech of self-justification and destruction in which he casts himself as 'one, not easily Jealous, but being wrought, | Perplexed in the extreme' [5.2.354–5]. This reader's marks allow us to reconstruct an early response to this play that identifies Shakespeare's particular even-handedness and his tendency to blur moral binaries, or to make even his villains somehow compelling or sympathetic. Something more partisan seems to emerge from a different reader marking up

[30] G. Wilson Knight, *The Wheel of Fire: Interpretations of Shakespearian Tragedy* (London: Methuen, 1949), pp. 97–119.

FIG. 2.4. RSC manicule

An early reader has marked out this passage of *Othello* for particular approval using the pointing hand symbol known as a manicule.

Richard II in a copy now in the New York Public Library: his or her selection strongly suggests a sympathy with Richard's own plight, although it may be inevitable in a commonplacing age that the quotably poetic Richard would always triumph rhetorically over his more pragmatic and laconic challenger, Bullingbrooke.[31]

Humanist accounts of the purposes of commonplacing stress the personal benefit of a storehouse of moral and rhetorical wisdom. Shakespeare certainly offered readers this kind of material, but, happily, not only that. A copy now in the Morgan Library in New York shows particular enjoyment of *Merry Wives*, and of Falstaff's speeches in particular (interestingly, there are no specific marks of reading in this copy in the other Falstaff plays *Henry IV Parts 1 and 2*). This is a reader reading less for moral improvement and more for verbal play and jokes, including the French doctor Caius's suggestively accented 'What shall de honest man do in my Closset?' [1.4.68], Mistress Quickly's cheerfully malapropistic 'shee's as fartuous a civill modest wife' [2.2.96], and the satisfying alliteration of Falstaff 'in a Basket like a barrow of butchers Offall' [3.5.4–5].[32] Apparently the same reader marks other plays, more sketchily but for different reasons, commonplacing Polonius' advice to Laertes (itself a string of commonplaces) in *Hamlet* [1.2.58–80] and Iago's sententious observations that 'Good name in Man, & woman (deere my Lord) | Is the immediate Jewell of their Soules' [*Othello* 3.3.160–1]. This reader, like many others, gets pleasure and profit and reads promiscuously for jokes and amusement as well as for sagacious commonplaces.

All commonplacing involves personal selection. Readers then, as now, identified passages that corroborated their own opinions or predispositions. For example, in *The Comedy of Errors*, Adriana, wife to the errant Antipholus, complains eloquently to her sister Luciana about his neglect. One reader, in a copy now in the New

---

[31] West 166.   [32] West 171.

York Public Library, has ignored all of Adriana's remarks about the sexual double-standard and underlined instead Luciana's more orthodox statements about male authority: 'A man is Master of his libertie' [2.1.7]; 'headstrong liberty is lasht with woe' [2.1.15]; "Ere I learne love, Ile practise to obey' [2.1.29].[33] The effect is to deny the dramatic force of the conversation, and to privilege, for reasons that are presumably extra-textual and relate more to the reader's own existing opinions, one, more conservative voice above the other. The reader of *Othello* who added, in the space at the end of the play, manuscript lines from a seventeenth-century ballad, 'Fortune and nature did agree noe woman | should be fitt | for me' seems to have been channelling Iago's casual misogyny and thus to have read rather against the grain of the play's conclusion.[34]

Shakespeare's plays are complicated constructions, and many more recent readers can find the tone of particular passages difficult to judge off the page. This is a feature of early modern readings too, which are variously attentive to the interplay of Shakespearean tone. *Love's Labour's Lost* is a romantic comedy preoccupied with the use and abuse of language, and one which satirizes pretentious and affected speech. One reader has paid particular attention to this play above all others in the volume, underlining extensively and marking passages and phrases with crosses and other symbols.[35] The selection here cuts across the play's linguistic differentiation, however, marking for note laboured speeches by Holofernes and lovesick lines from the lords that seem, in the context of the play, to be set up for scorn. For example, a bombastic letter from Don Armado—a 'man of fire new words, fashion's own knight' [1.1.176] and called 'Braggart' in the Folio stage directions and speech prefixes—is marked up for

---

[33] West 166.

[34] West 42, now part of the Royal Collection, Windsor Castle. The ballad is printed as 'Loves Extasie' in *Loves Garland, or Posies for rings, hand-kerchers, and gloves* (London: 1673), sig. F5.

[35] West 211.

apparent approval. This may be a reader's enjoyment of the joke against Armado, or it may register an approval of and aspiration towards his highflown speech. Perhaps there is an ironic circularity registered in the marks of reading: the play itself strongly implies that artificial language is associated with the narcissism and pretention of reading rather than with felt experience, and in the service of this theme makes more extensive use of proverbial phrases than almost any other Shakespeare text.[36] It is a satire on commonplacing. It is thus curiously appropriate that its phrases are marked in printed copies for continued bookish recycling through commonplacing. Underlining for re-use the Boy's knowing phrase, 'They have beene at a great feast of Languages, and stolne the scraps' [5.1.36–7], suggests a kind of archness or readerly self-consciousness. Elsewhere, tone is harder to recover. A reader of this copy now in Japan marks a number of what the cynical Berowne calls 'taffeta phrases' [5.2.407] in *Love's Labours Lost* and also picks out some of the fantastical boasts of the French noblemen as they strut, overconfident, before Agincourt in *Henry V*, such as 'I soare, I am a Hawke' [3.7.15]. In context these are recognizably hyperbolic, part of the characterization of the French as complacently effete. Does the reader mark them for extraction in that spirit, or actually rather enjoy their highflown poetic aspiration?[37]

If readers mark their Folio copies to indicate what they like or feel they might profit from, they also mark them to highlight textual problems. One frequent readerly activity is that of correcting errors. This was a process that early modern books often specifically encouraged their readers to undertake. Edward Blount, for instance, one of the publishers behind the Shakespeare First Folio, wrote in a preface to a translated Spanish romance that also appeared in 1623, next to a list of errata, 'vouchsafe with your pen, the amendment of these few faults, before you begin to read the

---

[36] R. W. Dent, *Shakespeare's Proverbial Language: An Index* (Berkeley: University of California Press, 1981), pp. 3–4.

[37] West 211.

rest'.[38] There were many reasons in the transmission of texts from manuscript to printed book why thorough proof-reading might not take place, and thus readers were frequently enjoined to complete copy-editing processes that we would now understand to be pre-print. Sonia Massai has found a number of early examples of corrections in Renaissance playtexts and points out that these show 'how an early modern reader would have perfected a dramatic text, that is, what an early modern reader...would have noticed as demanding emendation'.[39] Taking the First Folio as an extended example, we can see what readers recognized as demanding emendation, as well as errors that either did not trouble them or they did not notice.

Sometimes those demands are clear, and manuscript marks work to correct an obvious misprint: the nonsense word which appears in the Folio as 'dxile' is corrected to 'exile', for example, in the copy given by Sir George Grey to the library in Auckland.[40] The same copy has underlined a mistake in Tubal's report on Jessica's Mediterranean wanderings with her lover in *The Merchant of Venice*: 'ster' instead of 'her' [3.1.76], and changed 'Mo sir' to 'No sir' in *The Taming of the Shrew* [5.1.137]. If these seem trivial examples, that's the point: they indicate finicky reading moments during which an error cannot be left uncorrected, even where its obviousness means there is no possibility of confusion (all readers, that's to say, would silently recognize 'Mo' as a misprint for 'No', so the correction is evident and therefore almost redundant). Further, there are hundreds of similar errors of the sort we would now call 'typos' in this copy, and, worse, points where misprints carry the potential for real readerly confusion, which have not been corrected. This reader's intermittent, rather than sustained, scrutiny of this text is echoed in other copies. Readers' marked corrections emerge as evidence of non-continuous forms of attention to the

---

[38] Edward Blount, 'The Printer to the Curious Reader', in Matheo Aleman, *The Rogue. Or the life of Gizman de Alfarache* (London: 1623), sig. **7v.

[39] Massai, p. 14.   [40] West 214.

printed text, showing a low tolerance for error over local passages but not continuing this corrective attention over a whole play, still less the whole book.

The resulting corrections can seem random: why these ones rather than any one of hundreds of similar ones? The answer seems to be that these are the ones their readers noticed or could not let pass. One reader corrects the misprint 'owe' to 'owne' in *The Two Gentleman of Verona*: 'That such an Asse should owe them' [5.2.28].[41] The Durham library copy changes the final letters of the strange word in *All's Well that Ends Well*, 'Impostrue', to 'or' [2.1.155].[42] The reader of one of the New York Public Library copies corrected two minor errors in *As You Like It* with a neat pen alteration, turning 'would' into 'wound' [2.4.41] and 'in beard' to 'noe beard' [3.2.365].[43] In one copy at Meisei, the last word of Oberon's 'the very time I say' has been changed to 'sawe' [2.1.155].[44] The reader of another Meisei copy has made a series of minor corrections to *The Comedy of Errors*: inserting a word into a nine-syllable line to fill out the pentameter 'And by me [too]; had not our hap beene bad' [1.1.38]; changing 'Gaze when' to 'Gaze where' [3.2.57]; and, with a nicely cloth-eared disregard for the rhetorical balance of the original phrase, turning 'what he hath scanted them in haire, he hath given them in wit' into 'what he hath scanted *men* in haire' [2.2.81-2], marking a redundant gain in sense at the expense of the sound.[45] A number of readers identify the gravedigger's claim to have been 'sixteene' in *Hamlet* as a misprint for 'sexton' and correct it accordingly [5.1.157].[46] Again, the point to note here is the localized and, in the scheme of things, inconsequential textual interventions.

[41] West 214.   [42] West 7.
[43] West 167.   [44] West 209.   [45] West 202.
[46] Copies with this correction include West 208, West 19, and West 35.

One reader's correction can be, for a later reader, itself an error for correction. A copy of the Folio in the Wren Library in Trinity College, Cambridge, apparently shows two stages of correction. Two distinct readers have tussled with Romeo's hypermetric line, which forms part of the spoken sonnet the lovers share at their first meeting. In the Folio, this reads: 'My lips to blushing Pilgrims did ready stand'. The first reader has changed 'to' to 'two' in the left hand margin and blotted out the word 'did', clarifying sense and regularizing the metre (and shaping the line as it is now most frequently printed in modern editions). A second reader, working in pencil, has had another go, under-lining the blotted word and reinstating 'did' in the right hand margin, to produce the line 'My lips two blushing Pilgrims did ready stand' [1.5.94].[47]

Another crux in the same play is worked on by a reader recorded in the Wadham College, Oxford, copy. In the scene at Juliet's balcony, the Folio prints a choppily unfamiliar version of a now well-known line: 'What? in a names that which we call a Rose' [2.1.85]. The reader tries to regularize this difficult phrasing by inserting 'is' in place of the question mark.[48] The same reader is concerned to combine sense and rhythm in a neat addition to Coriolanus' sneering exchange with the Citizens as he unwillingly wears what the stage direction calls 'a gowne of Humilitie' to seek their support to become consul. The Folio text establishes the citizens' insolent assertion of equality with the patrician military commander through syntactic parallel: '*Cor.* Mine owne desert. | *3. Cit.* Your owne desert.' The next two lines should also be metrical equivalents, as the reader realizes, and so he or she inserts the missing word: '*Corio.* I, but [not] mine owne desire. | *3 .Cit.* How not your owne desire?' [2.3.65–8]. This registers the reader's

---

sophisticated attention to linguistic patterning in the dialogue, particularly since it is the Citizen's reply that points to the error in the previous line and prompts its retrospective correction.

Other emendations may be attempts to improve the aesthetic qualities of the text. One Meisei copy changes the last word of Juliet's line 'hide me with a dead man in his grave' [4.1.85] to 'shroud', presumably to avoid the direct repetition of the previous line which also ended in 'grave'.[49] 'Shroud' is also the reading in the edition of the play published in quarto form in 1622: it may be that the reader is undertaking a comparison of the early texts, but if so, this is his or her only instance of editorial collation. Mere coincidence may be the more likely explanation. Repetitions cause momentary trouble for readers in other copies too. A copy now in the National Library of Scotland changes the first 'well' in the stuttering line 'Your Noble *Tullus Aufidius* well appears well in these Warres' to 'will' [*Coriolanus* 4.3.31–2].[50] A reader of another of the Meisei copies wants to avoid repetition in Egeus' accusation of the man he does not want his daughter to marry at the beginning of *A Midsummer Night's Dream*. The printed text has 'with faining voice, verses of faining love' [1.1.31]. The reader underlines the second use of 'faining' and proposes 'feigned' in the margin as an emendation, substituting for mere repetition a kind of witty wordplay or paronomasia, playing on 'faining' meaning 'gladsome, affectionate' (OED: 'fain' v.1)[51] and 'feigned' meaning insincere (changing 'faining' to 'feigning' in both instances here is what most modern editors opt for when rendering this line).[52] Also concerned with poetic operation of a line is the word 'free', added in the gutter of the pages of *Measure for Measure*, to begin

---

[49] West 211.   [50] West 8.

[51] '† fain, v.1'. OED Online. September 2014. Oxford University Press. http://www.oed.com/view/Entry/67667?rskey=TjMvy6&result=3&isAdvanced=false (accessed April 2015).

[52] West 206.

the line the Folio prints as 'from our faults, as faults from seeming free' [3.1.307]. This reader senses a syllable is missing, and works out an interpolation that also improves the figure of chiasmus operating across the line.[53] All these readers are identifying moments of poetic or metrical faltering as sites for intervention in the text, and proposing their own improvements at these points.

Some corrections require more obvious interpretative work with overall narrative, rather than the specific location of the problem, to identify and rectify the error. These are interesting as indications of a more plot-based or narrative attention to the whole play, rather than an eye for immediate error or quotability. For example, although there is nothing grammatically problematic about Camillo's line in *The Winter's Tale*, 'You know my Fathers temper' [4.4.467], it does not make sense in the context of the familial relationships the play has constructed (Camillo has no father, so far as we know). A reader of one of the copies in the Meisei collection has drawn on his or her familiarity with the play's fictional world and duly emended 'my' to 'your'.[54] Something similar is shown in the Durham Library copy where one aspect of the chaotic duplications of identity at the end of the subplot of *The Taming of the Shrew* is reordered by a reader: Vincentio's 'didst thou never see thy Mistris father' is amended to 'Masters' [5.1.46–7].[55] In *Henry VI Part 2*, a long speech by Queen Margaret mentions 'Elianor'—the Duchess of Gloucester—three times. Modern editors since Nicholas Rowe at the beginning of the eighteenth century have amended these to 'Margaret' in each case, recognizing that in this rant Margaret is talking about herself in the third person [3.2.73–121]. A number of early readers also anticipate this

---

[53] West 5.   [54] West 202.   [55] West 7.

editorial change, and that shows a careful attention to the details of plot and character.[56]

How might readers have understood the activity they were undertaking with these spot emendations? The evidence of all the marked-up copies of the Folio I have consulted suggests that readers rarely set out systematically to correct even a single play, let alone the whole book. Nor does any individual reader seem to have a recognizable programme of, for example, the modernization of spelling or standardization of particular words or stage directions. The foci of particular attention seem rather to register the reader's intermittent engagement with the book rather than the niggling characteristics of the Folio text itself: that's to say, correcting readers do not seem concerned to prioritize orders of error on grounds of aesthetic pleasure or comprehension, but to tinker with presenting instances as and if they notice them. Some readers want their emendations to perfect the visual appearance of the book by being as unobtrusive as possible; others so disregard the format and scale of the printed text that their annotations seem an assertion of their own authority—as in, for example, a clumsy red crayon alteration of 'thanke' to 'thinke' in a Meisei copy of *Henry VIII*.[57] And of course, we might wonder who the corrections are for. If the reader can silently emend a perceived misprint or provide an improved reading, is there any need to mark this interpretative work in the book itself?[58] Perhaps the recognition of error is more significant for asserting the literary judgement and concentration of the reader than it is for improving the imperfect printed text. The imperfect

---

[56] Including West 5 (Trinity College, Cambridge); West 33 (formerly Dr Williams's Library); West 86 (Folger Shakespeare Library).

[57] West 203.

[58] On the intended audience for manuscript annotations, see Jessica Wolfe, *Humanism and Machinery in Renaissance Literature* (Cambridge: Cambridge University Press, 2004), pp. 125–60.

text becomes a vehicle for readers to say something about their own powers of perception.

Implicit in the activity of commonplacing reading is the desirability that highlighted lines should be detachable from their immediate context, in order that they might be reused elsewhere. As we saw, Edward Pudsey stripped the deictic markers that indicate place, occasion, or speaker from his commonplacing of *Titus Andronicus*. But there are lots of examples of Folio readers whose correcting attention is directed particularly to who speaks a particular line. This suggests a different approach to reading plays—one that is more concerned for the characters in dialogue than for the omniscient voice of wisdom. Rather than stripping lines of their context to create commonplaces, some readers are concerned to identify, clarify or correct the dramatic occasion for a particular speech and, where necessary, to alter the text to conform to their interpretation. For these readers the internal coherence of the fictional dialogue is paramount.

Some examples are cued as errors in the printed text. In 2.3 of *As You Like It*, the old servant Adam warns Orlando that his brother Oliver is his enemy. The Folio text prints two consecutive speeches with the speech prefix 'Ad.' [2.3.1–20]. A number of early readers recognize this as an error—it is not how play dialogue should work—and further deduce that the last line of the first speech is in fact Orlando's question 'Why, what's the matter' [2.3.16], which cues Adam's second. They write in the speech prefix, 'Orl.' accordingly.[59] As with other corrections made to the Folio, for some readers it is clearly important to make their correction as unobtrusively as possible; for others all that matters is that an error is righted. Interestingly, the facing page of dialogue in the printed text repeats the error, but this is far less frequently corrected.

There are other examples of corrected speech prefixes where the printed text shows an obvious error: the duplication of Troilus'

---

[59] Including West 167, West 39, West 211, West 34, West 19.

speech prefixes is changed to 'Pan.' in the Wheler copy now at the
Shakespeare Birthplace Trust.[60] The same reader has corrected the
second of two consecutive Nurse speeches to 'Rom.' One reader
spots a similar error in *Twelfth Night* and changes the first speech
prefix to regularize Sir Andrew Aguecheek's inexpert flirtation
with Maria.[61] There are several examples of readers who split up
the serial speeches by Demetrius in *Titus Andronicus*, recognizing
that the reference to 'My Grandsire' makes it probable that the
lines are spoken by '*Boy*', young Lucius.[62] In the copy now in
Wadham College, Oxford, a reader notes a problem in *The Taming of the Shrew*, crosses out duplicate speech prefixes but does not
correct them; readers in both the Guildhall, London, copy and the
one now in Queen's College, Oxford are more confident on this
point and change the second speech attribution 'Hort.' to 'Luc.'.[63]
For these readers, it is important that printed dialogue works in the
approved manner with alternating speeches.

Other such emendations to the apparatus of the play are more
obviously interpretive. The RSC copy marks a change in the fourth
act of *Othello*. When Desdemona is called to her jealous husband,
who has just interrogated her maid Aemilia without result, the
reader reallocates her bewildered question 'What horrible Fancie's
this?' to Aemilia. This may be because Othello's demeaning
answer—'Some of your Function Mistris: | Leave Procreants
alone, and shut the doore'—seems more appropriately directed to
the servant than his wife [4.2.27–30]. Of course, that Othello
addresses his wife inappropriately and all women are degraded to
housewives and strumpets is key to the play's toxic misogyny.[64]
Anther example can be found in a number of copies of *Romeo and
Juliet*. There, the speech prefixes for the meeting between the

couple and the Friar as he agrees that 'holy Church incorporate two in one' are at first sight unproblematic: they alternate appropriately and give no indication of an error. However, a number of early readers realize that the speech beginning, 'Ah *Juliet*, if the measure of thy joy | Be heapt like mine, and that thy skill be more | To blazon it, then sweeten with thy breath | This neighbour ayre' [2.5.24–7] seems creepily sensual when attached, as it is in the Folio, to the speech prefix 'Fri', the Friar. They change the speech attribution to Romeo in accordance with their reading of the scene and their assessment of seemly relationships between its speakers, serving in the process to reintroduce the young man to a conversation to which he would not otherwise contribute and making him slightly more assertive in his wedding plans.[65] Clearly, reading for extractable wisdom in the commonplacing tradition would not trouble with this infelicity, since the ability to reattribute the speeches is key to their potential usefulness. However, one adjacent feature of the Folio *Romeo and Juliet* relating to appropriate speakers does not appear to have bothered early readers, or if it did, they did not mark it in their copies: the Folio prints a passage of four lines twice, allocating the speech apostrophizing 'The gray ey'd morne' first to Romeo, parting from Juliet, and then immediately again with only minor changes to the Friar [2.2.1–4]. No early reader appears to have recognized this as a problem, or at least, none has tried to correct it in an extant copy.

Many of these speech prefix emendations as inscribed by early readers have been implicitly endorsed by modern editors, but not all. The reader of a copy now in the New York Public Library wanted for some reason to move Shallow out of the conversation at the end of 2.1 of *Merry Wives of Windsor*, and reallocated his lines to Ford.[66] In a copy now in Meisei in Japan, a reader has

---

[65] Including West 210 (Meisei University); West 166 (New York Public Library); West 171 (Morgan Library New York); West 5 (Trinity College Cambridge).

[66] West 166.

reallocated speeches in 3.2 of *The Two Gentlemen of Verona*, apparently on grounds of perceived character consistency, and something similar has been done by another reader for speeches by Holofernes and Nathaniel in *Love's Labours Lost*.[67] This same reader has also changed a series of speech prefixes in *Much Ado About Nothing* from 'Mar.' to 'Bea.'.[68] Confused— appropriately, since the scene of the masked ball [2.1] is a chance for its protagonists to speak in disguise—by the opening stage direction which does not include the waiting woman Margaret, the reader allocates her speeches instead to Beatrice. By inventing this exchange as a conversation between Don Pedro and Beatrice, he or she gives a brief occasion for the unrequited relationship that is hinted at elsewhere (as when, for example, Don Pedro, perhaps in jest, asks 'Whilt thou have me, lady?' [2.1.305] later in the scene). Again, the question of what was sufficiently bothersome to attempt to correct is answered idiosyncratically by early readers: error is clearly in the eye of the beholder.

One reader's work with missing speech prefixes in *As You Like It* emboldens them to posit alternative speakers in other parts of the play too. The Queen's College, Oxford, copy spots a missing speech prefix at the prose speech beginning 'Farewell good Charles' [1.1.153], where an indentation signals that the mark 'Oli.' is missing.[69] The same hand supplies the two 'Or.' speech prefixes a couple of pages later to avoid the mistakes of two consecutive speeches by Adam. With his or her sensitivity to missing speech prefixes appropriately primed, the reader then inserts another. Rosalind, who has spent most of the play dressed as the male Ganymede to the confusion of the inhabitants of Arden, is reconciled to her father, Duke Senior, to her lover,

---

[67] West 202; West 204.   [68] West 204.   [69] West 34

Orlando, and to the rural maid, Phoebe, who has fallen in love with her. She addresses each in turn: 'Ile have no Father, if you be not he: | Ile have no Husband, if you be not he: | Nor ne're wed woman, if you be not shee' [5.4.120–2]. This reader finds an error there and reassigns the final line to Orlando, unable to contemplate a female Rosalind who is still flirting with her unfortunate rustic inamorata even at the moment when the god Hymen intervenes to solemnize heterosexual marriage. The intervention in the text works to straighten out the sexual ambiguities that the Folio text leaves very much alive at the end of the teasingly titled *As You Like It* (in Rosalind's burlesque epilogue, for instance, where she acknowledges that both women and men in the audience desire her). But before we patronize this reader's response as somehow historically limited and unable to envisage the sexual plurality that the cross-dressed comedies now tend to emphasize, we might note that most modern editions also emend the repeated pronoun to eliminate the apparent same-sex marriage Hymen conducts in the Folio (which provocatively reads 'join his hand with his' [5.4.112]). They also add to the Folio's stage directions to clarify that Rosalind is dressed as a woman at this point.[70] These editorial interventions are driven by a similar impulse to that motivating the reader of the Queen's College copy.

Stage directions are more rarely annotated, but where they are, they are particularly interesting because they suggest a specific attention to the genre of the stage play and the spatial protocols of imagined action. Missing entrance directions—as, for example, for Margaret in *Much Ado About Nothing*, as discussed above—are scarcely ever corrected, but where readers tend to be more attentive is in missing exits. We have already encountered the extensive annotator, William Johnstoune, who adds only two single stage

[70] '*Enter Hymen with Rosalind and Celia as themselves*' (edited by Alan Brissenden, Oxford: Oxford World's Classics, 1993); 'Rosalind and Celia [*both undisguised*]' (edited by Juliet Dusinberre, London: Bloomsbury Arden Shakespeare, 2006).

directions in the whole book. He clarifies at the bloody end of
Titus Andronicus that 'Sat. kils Tit., Lucius Sat.' and writes in an
exit for Hamlet to make it clear that Claudius's abortive prayer, 'O
my offence is rank' [3.3.36] is a soliloquy.[71] A reader of one of the
New York Public Library copies adds the grammatically correct
'exeunt' stage direction for Romeo and Benvolio to leave before the
scene in which Juliet's mother and the nurse talk to her about her
'dispositions to be Married' [1.3.67].[72] In the Wheler copy at the
Shakespeare Birthplace Trust, an exit is added so that Feste acts
immediately on his words to 'tell my Lady straight' [4.1.29],
leaving Toby and Andrew to manage the hot-headed Sebastian
in *Twelfth Night* as Olivia enters herself to mistake Sebastian for
her 'deere *Cesario*' [4.1.49].[73] The same copy adds exits in *Henry VI
Part 1*, *Troilus and Cressida* and *Romeo and Juliet*. The copy in the
Arundel family adds a single stage direction to *Othello*: an exit for
Desdemona when Othello dismisses her cruelly in front of the
Venetian delegation [4.2.262]. The Wadham copy also adds one
exit to *Othello* on the same opening, in this case making it clear
that Cassio exits with Bianca and does not therefore hear Iago's
malign interpretation of the scene with the purloined handkerchief
[4.1.165]. These are readers imagining a stage space as they read,
and thinking about which characters are privy to particular conversations in order to maintain the fictional coherence of the
playworld.

Elsewhere there is relatively little attention to printed stage
directions or to stage business that might be thought to be missing.
In the Auckland City Libraries copy, an emendation to the evocative description of Richard and Buckingham who enter 'in rotten
Armour, marvellous ill-favoured' [3.5] seems to replace 'rotten'
with the more literally appropriate, but less morally charged,
'rusty'.[74] The unexplained cognomen for Antipholus of Ephesus

---

[71] West 201.   [72] West 166.   [73] West 38.
[74] West 214. The annotation has been cropped by later rebinding.

as 'Sereptus' which appears only in a stage direction in *The Comedy of Errors* (and is usually omitted by modern editors as adding unnecessarily to the play's onomastic confusions) is changed by a reader of the Durham copy to 'Surreptus': it may be that this reveals the reader's knowledge of sixteenth century editions of Plautus' *Menaechmi*, which was Shakespeare's source for his play, in which the eponymous twins are known as Surreptus and Sosicles.[75] A copy in the National Library of Scotland adds 'Prince of Denm | arke' to the entrance direction for Hamlet, coming in on the King's guilty attempts at prayer [3.3].[76] One of the Meisei copies crosses out the patently erroneous stage direction in *The Taming of the Shrew*, which has the lover Hortensio as 'sister to Bianca' [1.1.47].[77] This same copy has one of the rare early examples of added stage business that goes beyond choreographing characters' forgotten exits, marking next to the line 'thou blowest for Hector' [4.6.11] in *Troilus and Cressida* the neat, but perhaps superfluous instruction 'the trumpet sounds'. Further added stage directions or other marks that seem to relate not to imaginary but to actual or intended performance are discussed in Chapter 4.

Although many of the marks in First Folio copies can be understood as part of more widespread reading practices, some are wonderfully and irreducibly personal. The reader of a Meisei University copy, who adds the word 'curre' to the end of Pistol's threatening speech to the captured French prisoner in *Henry V*, seems simply to be entering into the swaggering spirit of the scene.[78] Perhaps the annotation registers the feeling that Pistol's anodyne parting shot, 'Follow me' [4.4.62], is rather anticlimactic and unbefitting his boastful demeanour. When the reader of another

[75] West 7. On Plautus, see R. A. Foakes (ed.), *The Comedy of Errors* (London; Methuen, 1962), p. xxvi.
[76] West 9.   [77] West 209.   [78] West 202.

Meisei copy notes in pencil in the margin of *The Merry Wives of Windsor*, 'you go and hear us', s/he seems to be spelling out a potential reading of a difficult crux that would exercise later commentators: the Folio text gives us the bewildering 'will you goe Anheires?' [2.1.205–6].[79] Rather than extracting a summarizing statement, such as the repeated 'put Money in thy purse' [1.3.339], the reader of *Othello* in one Meisei copy has provided a neat précis at the end of two of Iago's long prose speeches to Roderigo: 'make money man' and 'forget not to provide money'.[80] In the copy now in Queens College, Oxford, there have been two different attempts to resolve a line that few would find as troublesome as this particular reader. As he attempts to resolve the problematic plot of *Measure for Measure* into a romantic comedy in its final scene, the Duke turns to the broken relationship between the jilted Mariana and her erstwhile fiancé Angelo. The lines in the Folio read: 'Come hither *Mariana*, | Say: was't thou ere contracted to this woman?' [5.1.371–2]. As often in Shakespearean dialogue, there is an implied change of addressee across the line break: the second line is addressed to Angelo. For some reason, this so worried the reader that he or she seems to have attempted twice to rectify it.[81] The page is smudged and scratched at the letters 'wo' as if to erase the prefix and turn the noun to 'man', thus retaining Mariana as the sole object of the two lines. Perhaps dissatisfied with this imperfect solution—or with the failure completely to obliterate the offending anomaly—the reader then crosses out 'Mariana' and writes 'Angelo' instead.

Most annotations, but not all, are in English: very occasional Latin marginalia, such as 'Iam legi' in the Auckland copy (Figure 2.5), 'hec mihi' in the Glasgow copy, or, in the classical

[79] West 203. For this crux, eighteenth-century editors gamely suggested 'on, heirs' (Warburton), 'on, hearts' (Steevens), and the more cosmopolitan 'myn-heers' (Theobald).

[80] West 209.   [81] West 34.

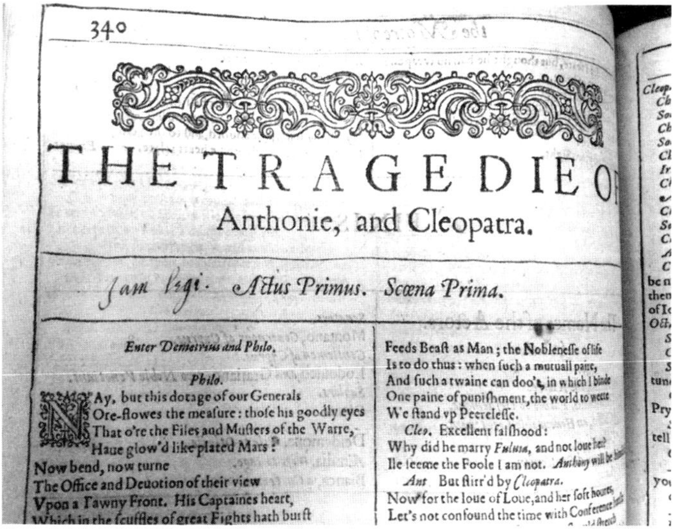
340

THE TRAGEDIE OF
Anthonie, and Cleopatra.

Iam legi. Actus Primus. Scœna Prima.

Enter Demetrius and Philo.

Philo.
Nay, but this dotage of our Generals
Ore-flowes the measure: those his goodly eyes
That o're the Files and Musters of the Warre,
Haue glow'd like plated Mars:
Now bend, now turne
The Office and Deuotion of their view
Vpon a Tawny Front. His Captaines heart,
Which in the scuffles of great Fights hath burst

Feeds Beast as Man; the Noblenesse of life
Is to do thus: when such a mutuall paire,
And such a twaine can doo't, in which I binde
One paine of punishment, the world to weete
We stand vp Peerelesse.
Cleo. Excellent falshood:
Why did he marry Fuluia, and not loue her?
Ile seeme the Foole I am not. Anthony will be
Ant. But stirr'd by Cleopatra.
Now for the loue of Loue, and her soft houres,
Let's not confound the time with Conference

FIG. 2.5. Reading *Antony and Cleopatra*
An early reader in the copy now in Auckland has marked some plays with the Latin 'Iam legi' ('I have already read').

tags in the Johnstoune copy discussed earlier in this chapter, locate the reading of the Shakespeare text within a broader and more obviously elite educational and social sphere.[82] One early copy has quoted in Latin on the death of Timon in the space around the names of the characters preceding *Timon of Athens*: the quotation is from Johann Hoffman's humanist encyclopedia, *Lexicon Universale*, first published in 1698.[83] There is little evidence in extant texts of the censoring of oaths or other offensive material: many of

[82] West 11; West 201.

[83] West 121; *Lexicon Universale* is online at http://www.uni-mannheim.de/mateo/camenaref/hofmann/hof4/Hofmann_lexicon_t4_1187_timogittia.html (accessed April 2015).

the Folio plays are printed from texts already expurgated to comply with early seventeenth-century laws against blasphemy. One reader does take exception to Launcelot Gobbo's colourful 'Be Gods sonties' [2.2.41] (an oath that modern editors tend to gloss as 'by God's saints') in *The Merchant of Venice*, and blots it out so that it is unreadable.[84] These readers exercise their own personal jurisdiction over the text in ways that register their own quirks and interests.

Some marks are less obviously interpretatively purposeful. Paper was an expensive imported luxury in the period of hand-production, and although the Shakespeare Folio crams in a lot of type in each two-columned page, there are still some white spaces around act and scene divisions, or running titles, and in margins. In many copies these spaces have been treated almost as scrap paper: for pen exercises, for doodles repeating printed words and sometimes copying their letterforms, for sketches and other marks that seem, in William H. Sherman's words to have nothing to do with their host text and therefore to be best described as 'graffiti'.[85] As Jason Scott Warren notes, crucial to graffiti in modern contexts is 'tagging', the idea of ownership, and so too readers inscribe themselves, in the form of their name, in copies of the book.[86] Early signatures, sometimes dated, provide a ghostly roll-call of Folio readers: Joseph Batailhey, Ann Bruce, James Cassall, Mary Chapman, George Cook, Godfrey Copley, Edward Duke, John ffrasere, George Gwinn, L. Hatton, James Lakin, Jacob Lendarvis, John Nash, Thomas Polewheele, Henry Sheppard. Whatever else these men and women made of its contents, they clearly wanted to chronicle their encounter with it by writing their names in the book. The signature is the visible mark of an interaction in which the

---

[84] West 204.   [85] Sherman, p. 23.

[86] Jason Scott-Warren, 'Reading Graffiti in the Early Modern Book', *Huntington Library Quarterly* 73 (2010), pp. 363–81; p. 367.

human agent is unrecoverable, but by which the book itself is forever changed.

In addition, readers' marks often situate the book firmly in their wider social or professional concerns. Thomas Madison notes down some figures relating to rents of the 'greate house' and the 'little house' and the sale of oxen in the flyleaf of the copy now in Wormsley library, dating his sums 1652—these situate the First Folio within the economy of the estate and the rhythms of the year, and, since some of the sums involved are relatively small, may hint at Madison's worries about money.[87] There are a series of similar manuscript sums in the Arundel copy.[88] The copy that once belonged to Ralph Sheldon and is now in the Folger Shakespeare Library has a note about buying 'three score pounde off sugre' on 28 November 1628.[89] A copy now in the New York Public Library has two phrases written in the spaces left at the end of *As You Like It* and *The Winter's Tale* which seem to begin 'remember', thus using the book's white space as an aide-memoire, although their unfinished state in 'remember that the' means that the notes are simultaneously records of forgetting.[90] The copy now in the University Library in Cambridge sketches a face in profile in the margin of *Richard II* alongside some pen practice copying printed letter forms for 'Scena' and 'Finis', and, coincidentally, an opportunist sketcher in the Royal Shakespeare Company copy has shaped a large blot in the central gutter of the pages into another profile in the same play.[91] One 'William Blunt' sketches a cannon firing in the space after *2 Henry IV.*[92] Elsewhere there are occasional sketches of shields or coats of arms and other pictorial doodles. One junior reader noted in a childish hand 'Elizabeth

---

[87] West 33.   [88] West 1.   [89] West 68.
[90] West 166.   [91] West 6; West 39.
[92] West 15, in the British Library.

Okell her Book 1729', and enjoyed drawing houses complete with curly plumes of smoke from the chimneys and sticklike figures standing in the doorway in the white space around the 'list of the actors' that precedes the plays (Figure 2.6).[93]

Pen practice, often apparently by juveniles, is a common use for blank space in this as in other early modern books, in an age when neither pen nor ink existed in reliable ready-made form, and paper should not be wasted.[94] There are scores of extant examples, of which these are a few indicative instances. A reader of *King John* in a copy now in London University has elaborately reproduced 'the life and death of King John' opposite the title of play; the Winchester copy has a manuscript echo of the stage direction 'Enter Gadshill' in *Henry IV Part 1*.[95] The Brotherton Library copy has 'Isa.' and 'Isabella' written in a childish hand at the beginning of *The Merchant of Venice*, and elsewhere a similarly juvenile pen seems to have added to *Henry V* a wobbly 'Enter fluellen'.[96] While these marks do not tell us much about how readers read the content of Shakespeare's plays in the Folio, they do show them interacting with the specific material form of the book: its layout and design, its typography, its dramatic architecture. And they indicate that the open spaces of the book were read as permissive: white cues for personal interaction and for bringing forward other concerns and practices.

Sometimes apparently random annotations echo strangely with the themes or metaphors of the printed text. In a copy now in the Shakespeare Birthplace Trust in Stratford-upon-Avon, a jotted arithmetical sum at the beginning of *Antony and Cleopatra* gives a curiously literal analogue to that play's ambivalence to forms of

[93] West 136, Folger Shakespeare Library.

[94] Scott-Warren, p. 368. On book annotations by juveniles, see H. J. Jackson, *Marginalia: Readers Writing in Books* (New Haven, Conn.: Yale University Press, 2001), pp. 19–22.

[95] West 22; West 41.

[96] West 12; West 204, in Meisei University Library.

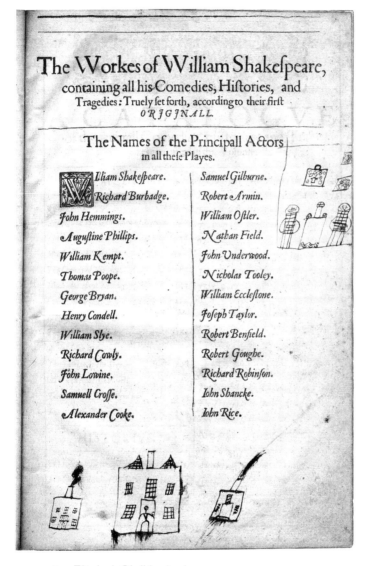

The Workes of William Shakespeare,

containing all his Comedies, Histories, and
Tragedies: Truely set forth, according to their first
ORIGINALL.

The Names of the Principall Actors
in all these Playes.

William Shakespeare.

Richard Burbadge.

John Hemmings.

Augustine Phillips.

William Kempt.

Thomas Poope.

George Bryan.

Henry Condell.

William Slye.

Richard Cowly.

John Lowine.

Samuell Crosse.

Alexander Cooke.

Samuel Gilburne.

Robert Armin.

William Ostler.

Nathan Field.

John Underwood.

Nicholas Tooley.

William Ecclestone.

Joseph Taylor.

Robert Benfield.

Robert Goughe.

Richard Robinson.

John Shancke.

John Rice.

FIG. 2.6. Elizabeth Okell her book
A young Elizabeth Okell has taken advantage of the blank paper in this copy now
at the Folger Shakespeare Library to do some drawing.

calculation: 'there's beggary in the love that can be reckoned' [1.1.15]. In the Winchester College copy, Exeter's grim soliloquy about civil dissent in *Henry VI Part 1* [3.1.191–205] is capped with two lines of incongruous miscellaneous marginal verse: 'Ten Thousand Beauties She can Spare | and yet outshine the fairest face - | Molly Fawbry'.[97] Molly Fawbry cannot be traced, but the first line of the quotation is also found in an early print miscellany, *The Merry-Thought*.[98] An early reader of *The Winter's Tale* has used the space in the right hand margin of the statue scene to record the date, 'August the 9th 1676', and a proverbial phrase: 'the devill was sicke the devill a monck would bee | the deville was well the deville a monck was hee'.[99] It seems unlikely that this is an oblique comment on Leontes' jealousy—the force of the proverb seems to be that those who are in need make promises they do not keep when their situation improves, which is scarcely applicable to Paulina's choreography of remorse, rehabilitation, and recovery in the scene. Perhaps it merely makes use of conveniently available paper. The same copy of the folio is marked with the final courtesies of a personal letter: 'from you a Saturday last this convenient time shall only let you know that I am yours to command'. Again, this has no apparent reference to the adjacent text itself— *Coriolanus*—and may again make use of blank paper, or perhaps record a mistake when a letter was being written on paper resting on the open book. The Dr Williams's copy has an intriguing cropped annotation on the last page of *Hamlet*, suggesting a more combative relationship between reader and text. It reads 'But I desier the readeres mougth to kis the wrighteres arse'.[100]

---

[97] West 41.
[98] 'From the Window of a Chamber in the Inner Temple | For dear Venilla in my Arms, | I'd scorn all other female Charms; | Ten thousand Beauties she can spare, | And still be Fairest of the Fair'. In Hurlo Thrumbo, *The Merry-Thought or, the Glass-Window and Bog-House Miscellany* (1731), Augustan Reprint Society 221–2 (Los Angeles: University of California, 1983), p. 7.
[99] West 214.   [100] West 33.

The technology of the book itself, rather than its contents, and how it might be enhanced to direct readers in how to read it, is a concern of a large class of Folio marks. Readers re-engineer the book with page numbers or correct numbering errors, provide running titles and other formatting consistency, and even emend signature marks. These interventions are attentive to the material form of the First Folio, rather than to the plays it contains: they understand the book as requiring technical tweaks to make it perform more effectively.

Some of this attention is directed to, and cued by, the book's own prefatory material. The catalogue page of the First Folio divides its contents into three genres: comedies; histories; and tragedies. A number of copies have had the title, *Troylus and Cressida* added to plays included on this catalogue page—indicating its place either before *Coriolanus* at the beginning of the tragedies, or after *Henry VIII* at the end of the histories.[101] Each play is marked by its page number, and each generic section restarts the pagination. This allows readers to identify specific plays by their title and to find them in the book, thus reading them in whatever order they choose, but it also suggests that there is a coherence within each generic section that might encourage serial reading. Clearly the plays in the histories section have been ordered and, in some cases, retitled from previous independent publications, in order to emphasize their serial nature and to encourage consecutive reading. One early reader who spotted an inconsistency by doing just that was mentioned in a letter from the librarian and antiquary Richard James, who reported, 'A young Gentle Ladie of your acquaintance, having read ye work of Shakespeare, made me this question: How Sir Jhon Falstaffe [...] could be dead in Harrie ye Fifts time, and againe live in ye time of

---

[101] Examples include West 32, West 203, West 206, and West 209.

Harrie ye sixt to be banisht for cowardize?'[102] While James
reassured this eagle-eyed reader that it was 'one of those humours
and mistakes for which Plato banisht all poets out of his com-
monwealtth', in fact this is a discontinuity invited by a combination of the form of the Folio sequencing and its indistinct
spellings of individual names. On p. 75 of the Histories, the
Hostess reports that the fat knight and companion to Prince
Hal is 'in *Arthurs* Bosome' 'for *Falstaffe* hee is dead' [*Henry V*
2.3.5–11]. Only a few pages later in the book, the messenger
delivers news of Talbot's battles in France, where he should have
triumphed '[i]f Sir *John Falstaffe* had not play'd the Coward'
[*1 Henry VI* 1.1.131]. The historical figures here are different
but their shared spelling, the shared association with cowardice,
and their close sequence in the Folio suggests they are the same
person. James's questioner reads the Folio sequentially as cued by
its careful ordering, but finds here a narrative inconsistency
through this reading method.

Not all readers seem to have read in so orderly a manner. Many
copies show that the catalogue page has been used to record
progress through the book, with some titles—perhaps those
already read—marked with a dot, tick, or dash.[103] In none of the
copies where readers appear to have checked off the play titles in
these ways does this process suggest that every play was read,
although they do tend to suggest reading in order, beginning
with the comedies. Exceptions are the Eton College copy, where
there are brown ink ticks next to the two parts of *Henry IV*,
Henry V, *Titus Andronicus*, *Timon of Athens*, *Hamlet*, *Julius Caesar*,

---

[102] A. B. Grosart (ed.), *The Poems &c of Richard James* (London: 1880), pp.
137–8. Gary Taylor has plausibly dated this letter to around 1630 in 'William
Shakespeare, Richard James and the House of Cobham', *Review of English Studies*
38 (1987), pp. 334–54.
[103] Examples include West 22 and 23; West 202; West 167.

King Lear, and *Othello* (obviously, this was a reader with little patience with the comedies) and the Glasgow University copy, where the titles of twenty four of the plays listed in the catalogue are underlined, with *Much Ado About Nothing, As You Like It, The Winter's Tale*, both parts of *Henry IV, Julius Caesar* and *Hamlet* marked with double underlining.[104] Two interesting examples show us readers with particular strategies for getting to grips with the large book. In the Auckland City Library copy, four plays are marked in the space around their titles, in a neat hand 'iam legi' (Latin: I have already read).[105] It is hard to know whether this indicates that the reader had already encountered *The Taming of the Shrew, Julius Caesar, Henry V* and *Antony and Cleopatra* in a different print form (although only *Henry V* had been published in quarto before the end of the seventeenth century), or whether they are proudly recording progress through the Folio itself. If the second, they are clearly reading in a selective order according to some now unrecoverable preference, rather than in the order set out by the book's own organization. Another copy, now in Meisei University, marks a date, presumably that of reading, at the end of a number of plays. *Two Gentlemen of Verona* is marked 'Aug 16th: 58', and greasy blots at the end of *Merry Wives of Windsor, Measure for Measure, A Midsummer Night's Dream, All's Well that Ends Well*, and *The Winter's Tale* indicate that similar notes have been messily obliterated at some later date.[106] This, then, is a reader picking through the comedies: missing out the first, *The Tempest*, and then *The Comedy of Errors, Much Ado About Nothing, Love's Labours Lost*, then another group of *The Merchant of Venice, As You Like It* and *The Taming of the Shrew*, and finally *Twelfth Night*. If this reader progressed beyond the comedies section, they had stopped recording the dates of their reading in this form. Many readers seem to have begun with good intentions, if not at the very beginning, then with the comedies, but many copies attest to the

---

[104] West 11.   [105] West 214.   [106] West 202.

scale of the task of reading all 900 pages, or the invisible pressures
of other tasks: in general, annotations and other marks tend to tail
off as the book progresses.

Readers also often correct page numbers, but usually inconsistently. Sometimes, as with other forms of correction, this has been
done carefully to minimize the visual impact on the printed page;
other times roughly without regard to the printed founts.
A number of readers begin to supply page numbers for the unpaginated *Troilus and Cressida*, but are quickly thwarted.[107] It is
impossible to make this late addition conform to the overall page
numbering design of the book: it begins with pages numbered
79–80, has twenty-five unnumbered pages, and then meets page 1
of *Coriolanus*. Where readers have corrected runs of page
numbers—as when the numbering in *Hamlet* suddenly jumps
one hundred pages—it is often possible to see the ink traces on
the facing page, suggesting the pages were turned while the page
number correction was still wet, and that therefore this was a kind
of correcting reading that did not spend any time on the text itself.
Other attempts to correct the technical apparatus of the book
include correction of the mistaken running title at the end of
Two Gentlemen of Verona. This has the preemptive title of the
next play, *The Merry Wives of Windsor*, a printing error that has no
bearing on the book's contents but nevertheless clearly troubled
several tidy-minded readers. A Meisei copy, the copy belonging at
Longleat House, and one now in the British Library record readers
who went to some trouble to copy the letter shapes of the printed
fount from one of the correct running titles.[108] Similarly, there are
examples of corrected signature marks—the alpha-numeric notation at the bottom of printed Folio pages intended as the equivalent of page numbers during the printing and binding process.[109]

---

[107] For example, West 166, West 210.
[108] West 204; West 29; West 17.
[109] West 14; West 222; West 50; West 59.

This is a kind of bibliographic pedantry, since the signature marks have no particular role in the reading experience, but some readers clearly had a low tolerance for forms of presentational disorder. Such corrections don't seem to correlate with other kinds of precise editorial work on the texts of the plays, suggesting that for certain early readers the way the book itself worked and could be improved was their focus, rather than the plays it contained. Again, this attention does not usually seem to have been sustained: if it is pedantic, it is only intermittently so. One reader of *Hamlet*, for example, clocks the page number discrepancy at the second mistaken number, and carefully corrects all the subsequent ones, but does not leaf back to find the start of the error.[110] These are readers' marks from which it is possible to suggest something about the character of particular readers and their preoccupations, their finicky focus on inconsequential detail, their low tolerance for presentational error or inconsistency.

Patterns of reading, so far as they can be deduced from legible marks in extant copies, seem to suggest that readers dipped in and out of the Folio rather than reading it from beginning to end. Reading all thirty-six plays in this heavy volume was a considerable task, and probably not often achieved. The underlinings and other non-verbal marks in the Dr Williams's copy give a relative sense of the reader's attention, and although every play has some kind of marking, their proportions vary considerably. The most attention is paid to *Henry VIII* (around 360 annotations, or one every ten lines or so); the least to *The Tempest* and *The Comedy of Errors* (only a dozen annotations, or less than one on each page).[111] These proportions do not conform to the relative positions of the plays in the volume. It is hard to generalize about particular favourites. Many copies seem to have more marked attention paid to the

---

[110] West 35.
[111] West 33. *The Shakespeare First Folio, 1623: The Dr Williams's Copy* (London: Sotheby's, 2006).

comedies, but whether this is simply because they form the first section in the book is unclear. A copy in Senate House library shows the comedies actively marked, although not the same plays that are popular in other copies, including *A Midsummer Night's Dream* or *Merry Wives of Windsor*. This copy has little evidence of reading in the histories, a rash of interest in *Coriolanus* with three small corrections, an added stage direction and two common-placed lines, and nothing else. For some, reading was organized around specific favoured plays. Another copy, again in Senate House library, has some commonplace marks only in *Much Ado About Nothing*; one Meisei copy is unusually interested in *Cymbel-ine*.[112] This patchy coverage tells us something important about early modern reading practices, and strongly suggests that this was a book enjoyed in parts rather than as a serial whole.

The evidence of use suggests that for most readers their focus on Shakespeare's works was intermittent rather than sustained. Read-ing seems not to be have been particularly ordered around the acts and scene divisions that might conventionally structure a play and that are irregularly marked in the Folio—although one copy has added manuscript divisions for acts three and four in *Hamlet*.[113] Rather, readers' interest was directed by the form of the book to a new Folio-specific unit that had not previously existed, the 250 lines or so that the folio format allowed to be viewed across the open page spread. Readers tended often to confine their marks to one particular opening, even where the sense of the speech or the scene continued overleaf. The RSC copy makes extensive under-linings across three, non-consecutive, openings of *Timon of Athens* but does not mark the rest of the play. A copy at Meisei likewise attends assiduously to the first three openings of *Love's Labour's Lost*, commonplacing it with extensive underlinings, crosses, and asterisks, but then does not mark the rest of the play at all.[114] Blots

---

[112] West 22; West 23; West 202.   [113] West 35.
[114] West 39; West 211.

and pen doodles festoon one opening of *King John* in the Winchester College copy when the other pages of the play are clean and unmarked, and there are countless examples of copies where the book, open at an apparently random page, has been doodled or catastrophically spilled on.[115] These units of attention can be traced both in evidence of reading the content of the plays and the formatting of the book. In a New York Public Library copy, for example, a reader has corrected the page number in *All's Well that Ends Well* when the opening gives '248' on the left hand verso and then '251' instead of '249' on the right hand recto, but has not turned over the page to correct '252' in the same way.[116] These, then, are readers who are easily distracted, inconsistent, or short on concentration: in these ways at least, for all else that separates us, they are much like ourselves.

Histories of print in the seventeenth century have tended, following the influential notion of the public sphere by Jürgen Habermas, to stress news publication, coffee house culture, and the polemical literary culture of London.[117] Recovering First Folio readers displaces this metropolitan and masculine focus in a number of distinct ways. Firstly, it moves literary consumption away from the city into provincial houses: Great Tew, for instance, or the Scottish home of William Johnstoune. Secondly, it challenges the common historical focus on the increasing privacy of Protestant forms of reading, on the model of the individual male scholar in his study. Johannes Amos Comenius, writing in 1659, captures this ideal reader in a description of his environment aimed at children learning vocabulary:

---

[115] West 41.   [116] West 166.

[117] Jürgen Habermas, *The Structural Transformation of the Public Sphere: An Enquiry into a Category of Bourgeois Society* (Cambridge: Polity, 1989); Alexandra Halasz, *The Marketplace of Print: Pamphlets and the Public Sphere in Early Modern England* (Cambridge: Cambridge University Press, 1997).

The *Study* is a place where a *Student*, apart from men, sitteth alone, addicted to his *Studies*, where he readeth *Books*, which being within his reach, he layeth open upon a *Desk*, and picketh all the best things out of them into his own *Manual*, or marketh them in them with a dash, or a *little star*, in the *Margent*.

The accompanying picture shows the man working alone in a room lined with bookshelves with the books placed with their pages outermost, a sloped desk with the open books and a flat surface for the student's notebook, and candles ('richer persons use a *Taper*'), for 'being to sit up late'.[118] By contrast, the evidence of serial signatures of both men and women, and records of familial and friendship groups in copies of Shakespeare's First Folio suggest something rather different: a more sociable, literal sense of community enacted on and through the medium of the book. And additionally, it is a sociability in which women are not the shrews and whores who people Johnstoune's anxious reading, but rather active agents of Shakespearean meanings: attested female readers of Shakespeare's First Folio seem more numerous than for many other early modern books.

Writing to her London friend, Mrs Lydell, from Bedfordshire in early 1639, Ann Merricke complained that she could not accompany her to the revival of Jonson's play, *The Alchemist*. Instead, she had to content herself with requests for news about court fashions and for Mrs Lydell to purchase for her some white night-time coifs, while she 'must content my selfe here, with the studie of Shackspeare, and the historie of woemen, all my countrie librarie'.[119] Reading Shakespeare here is figured as a

[118] Johannes Amos Comenius, *Orbis Sensualium Pictus* (London: 1659), pp. 200–1. Quoted in Sherman, p. 7.

[119] The latter is probably Thomas Heywood's *Gynaikeion: or, Nine Bookes of various history. Concerninge women*, of 1624. Merricke's letter is included in the *Calendar of State Papers (Domestic) 1638–9*, p. 342, and discussed in more detail in Sasha Roberts, 'Reading the Shakespeare Text in Early Modern England', *Critical Survey* 7 (1995), pp. 299–306.

poor backwater substitute for metropolitan theatre-going. In fact Merricke's pose of provincial banishment may be more arch and self-conscious: staying at Wrest Park near Silsoe she was, as her letter also hints, part of a salon of literary interests cultivated by Elizabeth Grey, including John Selden, Robert Cotton and Thomas Carew. Thomas Carew's poem in the country-house genre, 'To my Friend G.N. From Wrest', published in 1640, describes Wrest as a 'house for hospitalitie', receiving 'Noble guests' with 'more conveniencie...Then prouder Piles'.[120] Drawing attention to these cultural connections, Merricke wonders to her correspondent about the fate of 'the new playe a friend of mine sent to Sr John Sucklyng and Tom Carew (the best witts of the time)'.

We do not know whether Merricke had access to a First Folio in that library, although 'study' suggests a serious attention to the plays that might point in that direction. But there are a number of seventeenth- and early eighteenth-century women, traceable and not, who have left their marks in copies of the book. Paul Morgan assesses the number of women book owners in the period 1591–1677, as attested by signatures or other ownership marks in printed books, at around 1 per cent of the total.[121] Perhaps the Shakespeare Folio, over a slightly later period, was an exception, as a much higher percentage of ownership marks from its first century collectively suggest women's particular interest in the book. The name of Rachel Paule, probably the third wife of the seventeenth century royal chaplain and bishop of Oxford, William Paule, and who was named his executor in 1665, is found in one copy.[122] Other early women's names, occasionally dated, in extant

---

[120] Rhodes Dunlap (ed.), *The Poems of Thomas Carew* (Oxford: Clarendon Press, 1949), pp. 86–9.

[121] Paul Morgan, 'Frances Wolfreston and "Hor Bouks": A Seventeenth-Century Woman Book-Collector', *The Library*, 6th series XI (1989), pp. 197–219.

[122] West 130. Rachel Paule is mentioned in Vivienne Larminie, 'Paule , William (1599–1665)', *Oxford Dictionary of National Biography*, Oxford University Press, 2004; online edn, Jan 2008, http://www.oxforddnb.com/view/article/21607,

copies include 'Mary Wat[kin?]' (her name is cropped by later binding), who signed her name in a copy and dated it 1695; Alice Stevenson, dated 1723; Martha Primatt; and Mary Chapman.[123]

Some of the extant inscriptions directly attend to women's networks. One of the Folger copies has the domestic message on the last page of *The Merchant of Venice*: 'Dear, sistar I hoape you gaett whell too Epsom and am sorry I Colld nott', and carries the names 'William Lee | Allis | Heste' and the heartfelt message 'Wm I send for you my dear pray come'.[124] The Folger copy that records the names of Olivea Cotton, Elizabeth Hutchinson and 'Isabella' locates this book in the extended family of Lucy Hutchinson, poet, translator, and famous biographer of her parliamentarian officer and regicide husband, Colonel John Hutchinson (a late nineteenth-century family letter claims that the copy belonged to the Hutchinsons at Owthorpe).[125] Olivea was the daughter of Charles Cotton, the poet and contributor to *The Compleat Angler*, and Isabella Hutchinson and the other women were her cousins.[126] The three women's names may suggest that the cousins read together or that the Folio was passed from one to another. Their book has annotations in the comedies, including lists of *dramatis personae* that the Folio does not consistently provide, and identifications of locations including 'Scene Ephesus' (*Comedy of Errors*) and 'The Scene Verona' (perhaps unnecessarily, for *The Two Gentlemen of Verona*). It also shows a reader tagging characters in

accessed April 2015. For more on some of the women named in these copies, see Kitamura Sae, 'The role of women in the canonization of Shakespeare: from Elizabethan theatre to the Shakespeare Jubilee', unpublished PhD thesis. King's College London, 2013, esp. pp. 91–7.

---

[123] West 129; West 106; West 220; West 214.

[124] West 86.

[125] West 112. For the letter, see Rasmussen and West (eds), p. 463.

[126] The Hutchinson family tree is printed in Julius Hutchinson (ed.), *Memoirs of the Life of Colonel John Hutchinson* (London: 1808), after p. x.

the history plays to their historical counterparts: annotating the entrance for '*Buckingham and Derby*' in *Richard III* with 'Th. Stafford' and 'Tho Stanley' (although the historical Buckingham was actually Henry, not Thomas). Another Folger copy places the Folio as a token and register of familial relationships with the inscription, 'This Book is my Aunt's Elden's of Systrand to be Sent to Mr. Benj. Elden a dyer in St. Michael's of Coslany Norwich' (a Benjamin Elden who died aged sixty-two in 1759 is remembered in Thorpe Hamlet church in Norfolk and may have been the recipient of the book).[127] A sequence of other names, some clearly related by family, are also found on the front and back endpapers of the book: 'J. Brooke ex dono predicti Dni. B. Elden'; 'Robert Toomson of Stocksbey in the County of Norfolke'; 'Henery Prudence HP Henery'; and 'John Elden his Book 1714'. A Folio now in private ownership has the group inscription, 'John Love, Judith Love, Kath. Love, Herbert Love & Harry Love, Anno Domini 8th Oct. 1713', locating it at Saffron Castle in County Cork, and serving permanently to bind the book, the time and the members of the Love family.[128]

Other women have made occasional annotations that gesture fleetingly at more emotional or personal responses. Anne Hearle, who has signed her name three times in the Auckland library copy, twice in the running title of *Othello*, also copies out certain lines and it is tempting to see a pattern in her preoccupations. She echoes Hamlet's harsh confrontation of his mother after his hasty murder of Polonius behind the arras by copying out 'a bloody deed', but them smudging out the following words 'almost as', as if to protect Gertrude from the shock of his accusation: 'almost as bad, good mother | as marry with a king and kill his brother' [3.4.27–8].[129] At the top of the facing page. she copies the prince's unconvincing address to his mother, urged by the ghost who is

[127] West 100. Edmund Farrer, *The Church Heraldry of Norfolk* (Norwich: 1893), vol. III, p. 135.
[128] West 230.   [129] West 214.

invisible to her: 'How is it with you lady' [3.4.106]. Maybe these suggest nothing more than that these lines, conveniently close to the margins, suggested themselves as phrases for emphasis and pen practice. Anne's handwriting style may suggest that she was quite young, and this may give a reason for the particular appeal of this tense scene of parent–child interaction to her in particular.[130] When she copies out, 'Be patient gentle Nell forget this grief' [*2 Henry VI* 2.4.27], but changes 'this' to 'thy', is this just a mistake, or a way of reforming the text to make it more personal to her own, now entirely unrecoverable, life? Another woman signed 'Mrs Mary Lewis her booke April ye 27th 1685', and the same hand seems to have made correcting amendments to two plays, *Hamlet* and *Titus Andronicus*.[131] As Sasha Roberts points out, these annotations draw attention to two passages concerning fathers in *Hamlet*, insert stage directions and make minor amendments that show that, as for so many early readers, Mary Lewis did not encounter the Folio as a monolithic authority but rather a text to engage with, improve, and personalize.[132]

One final copy, now in the Folger Shakespeare Library, is yet more assertive. The engaged female readership indicated by the signatures of Elizabeth Brockett, dated 1695, 1702, 1712, and the emphatic 'Mary Child is the true possesor | of this booke' is accentuated by a manuscript copy on a blank binder's leaf of a twenty-four-line poem. 'To the Ladies' by Mary, Lady Chudleigh, was first published in 1703. It begins combatively: 'Wife and

---

[130] Alternatively it may be that a more mature Anne had been taught, as appears to have been common, to write in italic rather than secretary hand. Martin Billingsley noted in 1618 that italic 'is conceived to be the easiest hand that is written with Pen, and to be taught in the shortest time: Therefore it is usually taught to women', *The Pens Excellencie* (London: 1618), sig. C4r.

[131] West 109.   [132] Roberts, p. 300.

Servant are the same | But only differ in the Name', and ends with
the injunction against matrimony: 'Shun, O Shun, that wretched
state | And all the fawning Flatterer's Hate | Value your selves and
men despise | You must be proud if you'd be wise'.[133] How these
readers managed the disappointment of Shakespeare's romantic
comedies, the book does not otherwise record. The annotations in
the preliminaries of the copy, however, engage in an extended
dialogue particularly about women's role: one hand has written
'Not friends and faithful flatterer's differ more, | Than a chaste
woman and a Common whore', but this has been crossed out,
apparently in the same ink that signed 'Elizabeth Brockett her
Book 1702'. In the same copy, Mary Child appears to have
annotated the history plays with some commentary on the politics
of the interregnum, mentioning 'the marriage of my Lord Pro-
tector' 'Ireland', 'taxes' and the names of the parliamentarians,
Gilbert Pickering and [Walter] Strickland. An apparent reference
to 'to bee kinge' may fix the annotation to the period of open
discussion that Cromwell be given the royal title in the first half of
1657. The washing of this book by later owners means that Child's
annotations are difficult to piece together, but what their residue
clearly indicates is a woman reader using the Shakespeare First
Folio to pursue her active engagement with contemporary political
events.

   To read Shakespeare's First Folio in the first century of its
reception was thus always to change it: to remake and correct it,
to customize it to an individual interpretation or into a network of
interconnected readers and readings, to personalize and particu-
larize it with a signature and other personal effects. It was to sully
its white rag paper with the messy business of daily life, and to
record the various responses, disagreements, preoccupations, and
downright control-freakery of multiple readers. These are books

---

[133] West 81. Chudleigh's poem is edited by Margaret Ezell in *The Poems and
Prose of Mary Lady Chudleigh* (New York: Oxford University Press, 1993),
pp. 83–4.

that have been much used, if not, in most cases, studied in their entirety. The different copies register locations from the Scottish borders to Norfolk and mental frameworks from misogyny to feminist self-assertion. They record both individual readers and family or friendship groups, and, across a century of factionalism and civil strife, are seen billeted in both royalist and parliamentarian households. And above all, these copies capture the capacity of their readers for nuanced reading, for reconstructing plays as they wish they had been according to their own predilections. They recall the often idiosyncratic pleasure and profit to be taken from Shakespeare. In short, while these early Shakespeareans are probably the only readers for whom the First Folio has been a real reading text, they set in motion the engine of critical reception and readerly reinvention that has continued into the twenty-first century.

CHAPTER 3

Decoding

For seventeenth-century readers, Shakespeare's collected works came in folio format. Three further Folio editions were printed after the First Folio in 1623. Although none of these announced any editorial changes, each in fact took small steps to update language usage and correct obvious errors. Each also inadvertently added its own mistakes or mistranscriptions in the process of resetting the nine hundred pages of type. The third edition, in 1663, also offered 'seven Playes, never before Printed in Folio'. Of these plays, only one, *Pericles*, now generally considered a collaboration between Shakespeare and George Wilkins, has maintained its place in modern collected editions, although all seven were included in the fourth folio of 1685, and in many subsequent editions. The market for Shakespeare's works was, then, apparently satisfied by the publication of four Folio editions. In 1709, however, an edition of Shakespeare was published which dealt a fatal blow to the established folio model, and permanently recast the value of the First Folio text.

In 1709, a six-volume octavo edition of Shakespeare's plays appeared, repackaging the plays for a reading public used to the portable convenience of this format. In addition, this new edition introduced a new figure into the transmission of Shakespeare's plays: the editor. Its title foregrounds this important role: *The Works of Mr William Shakespear; in Six Volumes. Adorn'd with Cuts. Revis'd and Corrected, with an Account of the Life and Writings of the Author. By N. Rowe Esq.* Although those previous editions of Shakespeare's Folio, including the First, had involved some measure of invisible editorial labour, the agents responsible had hitherto been anonymous, hidden within the publishing operation. Nicholas Rowe (1674–1718), a trained lawyer already known as a tragic playwright of modest success, established the informed editor as the key authority in the accurate transmission of Shakespeare's text, and his own work set out the model for the work of that intermediary. Rowe prepared an introduction, including the first extended biography of Shakespeare; he developed the textual apparatus for readerly convenience, standardizing act and scene divisions which were only intermittent in the Folio; and he preceded each play with a list of its characters organized by rank and by sex titled *Dramatis personae.*

Rowe's editorial interventions had the collective effect of updating Shakespeare's plays, performing in the textual sphere a faint echo of the extensive work of retrofitting Shakespeare's plays in the contemporary theatre by adapters including William Davenant, John Dryden, and Edward Ravenscroft. His own position as a dramatist, rather than a scholar, confirmed that the edition of Shakespeare was presented to align it with contemporary theatrical and reading tastes. As Samuel Johnson would later observe, 'no man read long together with a folio on his table: —Books, said he, that you may carry to the fire, and hold readily in your hand, are the most useful after all . . . such books form the man of general and easy reading.'[1] Rowe's edition was designed to take to the fire, and to make Shakespeare familiar to modern readers, so 'that our authour's works might appear like those of his fraternity, with the appendages of a life and recommendatory preface'.[2] His lists

---

[1] George Birkbeck Hill (ed.), *Johnsonian Miscellanies* (Oxford: Clarendon Press, 1897), Vol. II, p. 2.

[2] *The Plays of William Shakespeare, in Eight Volumes, with the Corrections and Illustrations of Various Commentators; To which are added Notes by Sam. Johnson* (London: Jacob Tonson, 1765), vol. I, sig. C7.

of characters followed the pattern set by modern dramatists in print, including Dryden and William Congreve.[3] He commissioned from the French emigré artist François Boitard an illustration for each play—the advertised 'cuts' from the title page—which presented its action in a contemporary setting. Rowe's Shakespeare characters were bewigged and bedecked in the style of the early eighteenth century rather than that of their own Elizabethan period: his Romeo and Juliet die in a baroque chapel, not Shakespeare's charnel house, and Imogen's bedchamber into which Iachimo emerges from the chest in *Cymbeline* resembles nothing so much as the boudoir of Belinda, fashionable heroine of Alexander Pope's contemporary mock-epic, *The Rape of the Lock*.[4]

Rowe's editorial method thus overlays Shakespeare's non-specific dramaturgy with the visual priorities of eighteenth-century theatrical scenery and the protocols of contemporary print drama to create what Don McKenzie described, in relation to Congreve in print, as 'the hand-held theatre of the book'.[5] Some of Rowe's linguistic changes were aimed at the same modernizing effect, although he did not provide annotations or textual collations to make clear where he had intervened. Like earlier readers of Shakespeare discussed in Chapter 2, Rowe was also concerned to identify quotable passages, updating the practice of commonplacing for a new age. The second edition of his Shakespeare in 1714 advertised on its title page, 'A Table of the most Sublime Passages of this Author': the resulting 'Index of the most beautiful thoughts, descriptions, speeches &c' is organized like a seventeenth-century commonplace book with familiar headings including 'Age',

---

[3] See D. F. McKenzie, 'Typography and Meaning', in McKenzie, Peter McDonald, and Michael Suarez, *Making Meaning: 'Printers of the Mind' and Other Essays* (Amherst: University of Massachusetts Press, 2002), pp. 199–236.

[4] On Boitard's illustrations, see Stuart Sillars, *The Illustrated Shakespeare 1709–1875* (Cambridge: Cambridge University Press, 2008), pp. 31–72.

[5] McKenzie, p. 201.

'Anger', 'Despair', 'England' and 'Women'.[6] Rowe's editorial labours, therefore, elaborate, extend, and crucially, professionalize those intermittent and partial acts of correction and improvement identified in the study of Folio annotations in Chapter 2. There, early readers had added in act divisions, changed errors and made difficult passages make sense through emendation, occasionally drawing up lists of characters, and identifying for themselves the passages most worthy of particular annotation. Rowe's portable, multi-volume edition is often seen as a break with the Folio tradition, but, even as it supersedes the Folios, it develops and commodifies those reading practices established by individuals and communities of Folio users during the eight decades since 1623.

Rowe's own editorial theory did not identify any particular significance in the First Folio in establishing Shakespeare's text. In his dedication, 'To his Grace the Duke of Somerset', he admitted: 'I must not pretend to have restor'd this Work to the Exactness of the Author's Original Manuscripts: Those are lost, or at least, are gone beyond any Inquiry I could make'.[7] Instead, Rowe claimed 'to compare the several Editions, and give the true Reading as well as I could from thence'. Examples of quarto readings include the addition of the Chorus to *Romeo and Juliet*, omitted from all the Folio texts during the seventeenth century, and the scene in which Fortinbras appears with his army in *Hamlet* [4.4]. Although he prints the plays in the same order as they had appeared from 1623 onwards, there is no evidence that he had access to, or interest in, the First Folio, and the sale of his library

[6] Nicholas Rowe (ed.), *The Works of Mr William Shakespear; in eight volumes. Adorn'd with cuts. Revis'd and corrected* (London: Jacob Tonson, 1714). The table is in an unpaginated section at the end of volume VIII.

[7] Nicholas Rowe (ed.), *The Works of Mr William Shakespear; in Six Volumes. Adorn'd with Cuts. Revis'd and Corrected, with an Account of the Life and Writings of the Author* (London: Jacob Tonson, 1709), vol. I, sig. A2-v.

suggests that he owned only a Second Folio.[8] His sixth volume reprints those apocryphal plays added into the Third Folio, and his main textual reference point seems to have been the most recent edition: the 1685 Fourth Folio. It was logical: Rowe's updating priorities meant there was little reason to return to the First Folio.

For the long and often hotly contentious line of Shakespearean editors who followed Rowe, however, one vital and recurrent question in establishing the legitimacy of their own text was— and continues to be—a prior question about the status of the First Folio. The First Folio provides the only early text for half of Shakespeare's plays, as well as offering versions of the other plays that vary, in small and larger details, from their previous single-play publication. It is thus the most significant single document for the transmission of Shakespeare's plays. But, as a posthumous publication with no extant holograph or manuscript support, with a high printing error rate, evident lapses in presentational consistency, and a significant incidence of knotty or inexplicable words and phrases, the First Folio has continued to be a source of scholarly controversy as well as textual authority. If not for Rowe, then for the editorial tradition he inaugurated, the First Folio played a key role. Deciphering its text, understanding its provenance, assessing how and where it was in need of emendation: these were the crucial disciplinary manoeuvres in the fractious arena of eighteenth-century Shakespeare editing. They continue to be highly controvertible in modern editions.

In the century after Rowe's 1709 edition, there were further editions by Alexander Pope (1725), Lewis Theobald (1733), Thomas Hanmer (1744), William Warburton (1747), Samuel Johnson (1765), Edward Capell (1767–8), Johnson and George Steevens (1773), Johnson, Steevens, and Isaac Reed (1778), and Edmund Malone (1790)—as well as innumerable reissues,

---

[8] Anthony James West, 'Sales and Prices of Shakespeare First Folios: a History, 1623 to the Present', *Publications of the Bibliographical Society of America* 92 (1998), pp. 465–528.

subsequent editions and revisions, and the publication of subsets of
Shakespeare's work. All of these editions, except that by Thomas
Hanmer, were published under the imprint of Jacob Tonson at the
Shakespeare's Head. Tonson was the prestigious literary publisher
of Milton and Dryden who had bought up the majority of copyrights to Shakespeare's plays from the publishers of the Fourth
Folio of 1685.[9] Shakespeare Folios were clearly available on Grub
Street: all of these editors can be associated with specific copies of
the First Folio. A copy now in the John Rylands Library, Manchester, has the manuscript inscription on the binder's leaf, 'NB
This was the book Theobald made use of for his edition', and was
also owned by George Steevens;[10] one in Sir John Soane's museum
may have belonged to Isaac Reed;[11] Capell's copy is in Trinity
College Cambridge;[12] and Malone's at the Bodleian in Oxford.[13]
Thomas Hanmer's copy, bearing a bookplate dated 1707, is now
in the Folger Shakespeare Library.[14] No copy consulted by Pope
has been identified, but he lists the 1623 Folio among the
'Several Editions of *Shakespear's* Plays, made use of and compared in this Impression', and Steevens wrote in a letter of 1790
that 'I never knew till yesterday' that the bookseller Henderson,
without equal in reconstructing First Folios, 'had fitted up one
for Mr Pope'.[15] One copy, in particular, now in the British
Library, was owned successively by Theobald, Johnson, and

[9] Terry Balanger, 'Tonson, Wellington and the Shakespeare copyrights', in
R. W. Hunt, I. G. Philip, and R. J. Roberts (eds), *Studies in the Book Trade In
Honour of Graham Pollard* (Oxford: Oxford Bibliographical Society, 1975), pp.
195–209.

[10] West 30.   [11] West 21.   [12] West 4.

[13] West 32.   [14] West 74.

[15] Alexander Pope (ed.), *The Works of Shakespear in Six Volumes* (London: Jacob
Tonson, 1725), vol. VI, n.p.; George Steevens to Isaac Reed, October 1790, in
'George Steevens letters to I. Reed 1777–1800', Folger Shakespeare Library
(MS C.b.2).

Steevens, and, like the Shakespeare editing baton itself, was passed to these men by the publisher Jacob Tonson. This transmission of the material book embodies the dynastic succession of editorial authority bestowed serially by Tonson on the men he identified to revise the Shakespearean text and to restate his own copyright claims. A manuscript inscription in the book marks: 'G. Steevens ex dono Jacobi Tonson, Biblio: 1765'.[16]

Some of the annotations in this Tonson First Folio volume show the accretive processes of editorial labour so characteristic of the processes of contemporary editing, in which layers of notes and emendations were recorded in increasingly extensive footnote commentaries. Most eighteenth-century editors reprinted their predecessors' introductions and carried forward swathes of their commentary, and this can be seen in the Folio itself. In *A Midsummer Night's Dream*, for example, there are a number of manuscript emendations that, when read against Lewis Theobald's printed edition of 1733, are revealed as his preliminary notes towards that work. At the beginning of the play, Hermia and Lysander plan to run away from her father into the Athenian wood. The scene has been largely established as being in rhymed couplets, but Hermia's speech interrupts this aural patterning:

> And in the wood, where often you and I,
> Vpon faint Primrose beds, were wont to lye,
> Emptying our bosomes, of their counsell sweld:
> There my Lysander, and my selfe shall meete,
> And thence from Athens turne away our eyes
> To seeke new friends and strange companions [1.2.214–19].

In the Tonson Folio, a hand has corrected 'counsel sweld' to 'counsel sweet' and replaced the Folio's 'companions' with 'companies'. Theobald's printed text of 1733, reprinted in

---

[16] West 17.

1739–40, includes these emendations and offers a lengthy rationale for them:

This whole Scene is strictly in Rhyme; and that it deviates in these two Couplets, I am persuaded, is owing to the Ignorance of the first, and the Inaccuracy of the later, Editors: I have therefore ventured to restore the Rhymes, as I make no Doubt but the Poet first gave them. Sweet was easily corrupted into swell'd, because That made an Antithesis to Emptying: and strange Companions our Editors thought was plain English; but stranger Companies, a little quaint and unintelligible. It may be necessary, in Proof of my Emendation, to shew, that our Author elsewhere uses the Substantive Stranger adjectively; and Companies, to signify Companions.[17]

The Folio, therefore, records Theobald's work towards his printed edition, and shows him in the act of emending the text.

Elsewhere, too, minor emendations, shared between manuscript annotation and printed text, give us a glimpse of Theobald working out the emendations for his edition on the pages of his First Folio. In *As You Like It*, the speech prefix for Celia's line 'Your hearts desires be with you' [1.2.187] is crossed out and replaced with Orlando, reframing the line as part of his flirtation with Rosalind. The same happens, without any explanatory annotation, in Theobald's printed edition. A little later in the same play, Theobald has altered a mistake in the Folio line that reads 'To that which had too must' [2.1.49], changing 'must' to 'much'; again, this emendation appears in his edition without explanatory note.[18]

In his preface to the printed text, Theobald acknowledges the assistance of 'the Learned and ingenious Dr Thirlby of Jesus-College, there [Cambridge], who had taken great Pains with my Author, that I should have the Liberty of collating his Copy of Shakespeare, mark'd thro' in the Margin with his own Manuscript

[17] Lewis Theobald (ed.), *The works of Shakespeare: in seven volumes. Collated with the oldest copies, and corrected: with notes, explanatory and critical* (London: 1733), vol. I, pp. 85–6.

[18] Theobald (1733), vol. II, pp. 197, 207.

References and accurate Observations.[19] Thirlby is credited numerous times in Theobald's published notes. But Theobald's copy of the First Folio, passed on to later editors, also records some of those same notes in preparation for new editions. Samuel Johnson, for instance, includes a reference to Theobald and Thirlby in his 1765 edition. A note to the lines in *King John* praising the Dauphin of France: 'He is the half part of a blessed man | Left to be finished by such as shee' [2.1.438–9] reads 'Dr Thirlby prescrib'd that Reading, which I have here restored to the Text. Theobald.'[20] In the copy of the First Folio used by Johnson, there is a manuscript note to the same effect at the passage: 'Mr Theob. P. Dr Thirlby'.

Thomas Hanmer, an undistinguished Speaker of the House of Commons who also owned a First Folio, was the only eighteenth-century editor of Shakespeare to challenge Tonson's monopoly, by publishing with Oxford's Clarendon Press. His six octavo volumes were expensively illustrated with designs by Francis Hayman engraved by Hubert Gravelot. While his edition has had little lasting impact on the text of the plays, it sold well, recovering publication costs of £1,283 (including two guineas 'For the press-men to drink Sir Tho. Hanmer's health' and making a profit in its first year).[21] Hanmer's Preface promised 'a true and correct Edition of Shakespear's works cleared from the corruptions with which they have hitherto abounded', although, like his predecessors, he worked from a marked-up copy of editions by Theobald and by Pope.[22] He also made a handful of annotations in his copy of the First Folio. His manuscript annotation in the Folio text of

[19] Theobald (1733), vol. I, p. lxv.   [20] Johnson (1765), vol. III, p. 432.
[21] Harry Carter, *A History of the Oxford University Press* (Oxford: Clarendon Press, 1975), vol. I, p. 303.
[22] Thomas Hanmer (ed.), *The Works of Shakespear: in six volumes* (Oxford: Clarendon Press, 1744), vol. I, sig. A2; Andrew Murphy, *Shakespeare in Print: A History and Chronology of Shakespeare Publishing* (Cambridge: Cambridge University Press, 2003), p. 110.

Titus Andronicus as the bloodthirsty sons of Tamora kill the emperor's brother, Bassanius [2.3.117]—'stabs him'—makes its way into his edition, as do the stage directions he added to Othello's murder of Desdemona, where Hanmer's Folio is marked with 'kisses her' and 'dies', as is the scene [5.2] in his edition.[23]

Hanmer's Folio annotations suggest some of the missing stage directions he would add in his edition. In his own Folio copy, now in the Meisei Shakespeare Library in Japan, another editor pursued a different intellectual agenda. Charles Jennens, best-known as a collaborator with G. F. Handel and librettist of the oratorio, *Messiah* (1741) ('an easy task', sniffed the Shakespearean George Steevens, who was at editorial odds with Jennens, 'as it is only a selection from Scripture verses') was a bibliophile who entered into the gladiatorial arena of Shakespearean editing with five editions of individual tragedies anonymously published in the 1770s.[24] The first, *King Lear* (1770), carried a grateful dedication to himself: 'To Charles Jennens, Esq. at Gopsal, Leicestershire, under whose patronage, by access to whose library, and from whose hints and remarks, the editor hath been enabled to attempt an edition of Shakespeare.'[25] In it, Jennens established a new priority for textual scholarship in an important forerunner of the Variorum edition that would be published more than a century later. Unlike those of his predecessors, his notes to the play were not interpretative citations but rather collations—a descriptive summary of the different early editions and some of the recent editors' emendations. His copy of the First Folio shows some of the work undertaken for this project.

For example, in the opening lines of *King Lear* Jennens noted in the Folio margin next to Gloucester's line about Lear's daughters, 'for qualities are so weighed' [1.1.5], the collating note 'equalities

[23] Hanmer (1744), vol. v, p. 419; vol. vi, pp. 534, 538.
[24] West 206. Quoted in John Nichols, *Literary Anecdotes of the Eighteenth Century* (London: Nichols, Son and Bentley, 1812–16), vol. 3, p. 120.
[25] [Charles Jennens], *King Lear. A Tragedy 'Collated with the Old and Modern Editions'* (London: W. and J. Richardson, 1770).

1st 4 to', referring to the different reading in the 1608 text. By the time he produced his edition, he had opted to print the quarto reading in his text, noting in a footnote 'So the qu[arto]s; all the rest, qualities'.[26] Similarly in his copy of the Folio, Goneril's 'I do love you more than word can yield the matter' [1.1.50] has Jennens' note 'words. 1st 4to'. His edition again switches the two, opting for 'words', presumably because the plural is more appropriately hyperbolic in context, with the note 'The fo[lio]s, and R[owe] read word'.[27] Jennens' folio text thus records some, but not all, of the collating work that he then processes into the extensive textual notes in his edition. He adds in manuscript to Cordelia's outburst 'Sure I shall never marry like my sisters' [1.1.95] 'to love my father all 1st 4to', and the second line is included in his own edition in italics with the note 'The fo[lio]s and R[owe] omit these words in italic'. Sometimes there is more information in his manuscript annotations than actually transferred into the edition. When Lear curses the disobliging Cordelia for her failure to participate appropriately in his love-test, the Folio reading swears by 'the miseries of Heccat' [1.1.103]. Jennens notes next to this phrase 'mysteries. 2nd Fol.', which he presents as an emendation in his printed text without any authority: the footnote reads: 'The qu[arto]s read mistresse; the 1st f. miseries'.[28] Jennens' annotations are more numerous in the first half of his Folio of *King Lear*, and there is no sign in his own copy of the research that is reported in his editions of *Othello*, *Macbeth*, *Julius Caesar*, or *Hamlet*. There are extensive collating notes in *A Midsummer Night's Dream* with the 1600 quarto—perhaps this was to be his next project—and a few scattered acknowledgements of the eighteenth-century editorial tradition, in references to emendations of Thomas Hanmer. One account of his working practices gives a strong visual impression of the practicalities of his approach

---

[26] Jennens (1770), p. 1.   [27] Jennens (1770), p. 4.
[28] Jennens (1770), pp. 7–8.

at his editorial desk at Gopsal: 'An eminent surgeon called at his house one evening, and found him, before a long table, on which all the various editions of his Author were kept open by the weight of wooden bars. He himself was hobbling from one book to another with as much labour as Gulliver moved to and fro before the keys of the Brobdingnagian harpsichord sixty feet in length.'[29]

These examples of editors engaging with the First Folio are, however, the exceptions rather than the rules. In most cases, between Rowe's edition of 1709 and the mid-nineteenth-century editions by Folio owners, Charles and Mary Cowden Clarke, neither the copy of the First Folio, nor the edition of Shakespeare, shows much sign of the interaction. A First Folio seems to have been more an editorial talisman than a research resource: it's worth recalling that until the end of the eighteenth century no copy existed in an institutional library. Access to the book was, then, dependent on personal contacts with owners. Like Tonson's copyright monopoly, therefore, restricted access to early texts, including the First Folio, was part of the editorial, social, and literary cartel operative in the period. Nor had the book that, by the mid-nineteenth century, had established its title as the First Folio, without need of author, yet stabilized into that singularity. Rowe refers to the 'first folio edition' in 1714, and the phrase is used as a modifier of the noun 'edition' in Pope, Theobald, and Hanmer. Theobald appears to be the first to use it as a phrase in his notes, observing in *King Lear*: 'this is a reading of the first Folio, which Mr Pope very unhappily degrades'.[30] Johnson's 1765 preface refers to the 'first folio', without capitals; Capell used 'first Folio' to refer to the 1623 edition and Malone 'first folio'. Richard Farmer used 'first Folio's' in his *An Essay on the Learning of Shakespeare* of 1767 to refer, unspecifically, to more than one edition—probably all four

---

[29] Nichols (1812–16), pp. 121–2.
[30] Rowe (1714), vol. IX, p. iv; Theobald (1733), vol. V, p. 199.

seventeenth-century folios.[31] During the eighteenth century, then, the usefulness of the book had not been established by editors, and similarly the meaning of the term 'first folio' had not stabilized, nor was it exclusively identified with Shakespeare.

Rather than working from an early text, eighteenth-century editors tended to mark up a copy of their predecessor's edition, however strongly their commentary maligned this inadequate forerunner. Thus Pope worked on a Rowe base-text, and Theobald, in turn, on Pope's, and although both of them apparently had access to a First Folio, neither used it as the basis for their edition. Edward Capell's edition of 1767–8 was the first to be published under the First Folio title, *Mr William Shakespeare: his comedies, histories and tragedie*s and to provide a new collation of the texts. Capell identified the textual priority of the First Folio for all the previously unpublished plays and for a number of quarto texts: 'the first folio is follow'd; the text of which is by far the most faultless of the editions in that form; and has also the advantage in three quarto plays, in "2 Henry IV", "Othello", and "Richard III"'. But his confidence in the Folio text was limited:

the faults and errors of the quarto's are all preserved in the folio, and others added to them; and what difference there is, is generally for the worse on the side of the folio editors: which should give us but faint hopes of meeting with great accuracy in the plays which they first publish'd.[32]

Capell's own copy of the Folio, with the copies of the three subsequent seventeenth-century editions, which he also owned, is now in the Wren Library in Trinity College Cambridge.[33] A previous owner, one Edward Duke who has left his name on the dedication page to the Herbert brothers, is more visible in that

---

[31] Richard Farmer, *An Essay on the Learning of Shakespeare* (London: 1767), p. 16.
[32] Edward Capell (ed.), *Mr. William Shakespeare: his comedies, histories and tragedies* (London: D. Leach for J. and R. Tonson, 1767–8), p. 21; p. 6.
[33] West 4.

copy than Capell himself, who seems to have left no mark unless a solitary commonplacing cross in *3 Henry VI* at 'O God me thinks it were a happy life' [2.5.21] can be attributed to him. Capell's work on the First Folio was a landmark in the revaluation of its textual pre-eminence. It was, however, a critical paradigm shift that has left no trace on his copy, if not vice versa.

The eighteenth-century editor more usually associated with a textual paradigm shift is Edmond Malone, whose edition was published in 1790, even as it silently incorporated and developed many of Capell's insights. If Rowe had brought a dramatist's eye to the editorial task, and Johnson a classical one, then Malone brought the insistence on evidence and on witness statements from his own legal training. As Margreta de Grazia identifies, 'Malone's overwhelming preoccupation with objectivity marks a significant shift in the focus of Shakespeare studies from what might be termed the discursively acceptable to the factually verifiable, from accounts whose validity was assured by continued circulation to information whose accuracy was tested by documents and records.'[34] Malone's title, *The Plays and Poems of William Shakspeare, in ten volumes; collated verbatim with the most authentick copies and revised: with the corrections and illustrations of various commentators*, establishes it in relation to a century of editorial intervention since Rowe. But it also builds on Capell in identifying the First Folio—Malone owned a copy himself as part of a large library of early texts—as a particular 'authentick' copy.

Malone's edition suggested that 'the comparative value of the various ancient copies of Shakspeare's plays has never been precisely ascertained'.[35] His Preface reinterpreted the statement by Heminge and Condell, writing in a dedicatory epistle to the 1623

---

[34] Margreta de Grazia, *Shakespeare Verbatim: the Reproduction of Authenticity and the 1790 Apparatus* (Oxford: Clarendon Press, 1991), p. 5.

[35] Edmond Malone (ed.), *The Plays and Poems of William Shakspeare, in ten volumes; collated verbatim with the most authentick copies* (London: H. Baldwin for J. Rivington and Sons, 1790), vol. I, p. xi.

Folio, that previous texts were 'maimed and deformed by the frauds and stealthes of injurious imposters'. Rather than taking this entirely literally, Malone saw something of the way commercial imperatives may have shaped the presentation of the texts in the First Folio just as they did in the eighteenth-century editorial ferment: 'the players, when they mention these copies, represent them all as mutilated and imperfect; but this was merely thrown out to give an additional value to their own edition'. He noted astutely that, rather like his own eighteenth-century predecessors, 'the editors of the folio, to save labour, or from some other motive, printed the greater part of [the plays previously published in quarto format] from the very copies which they represented as maimed and imperfect'.

Malone prescribed earlier texts as, in general, more authoritative, and recognized that for those plays that are first published in the folio, that 'is the only authentick edition'.[36] He admitted that, on the advice of the critic Thomas Tyrwhitt, he had toyed with the idea of marking up a First Folio as copy text and sending it 'to the press with such corrections as the editor might think proper', but instead he presented a scholarly collation of readings from the early texts, drawing on the method established by Charles Jennens a few years previously.[37] Like his predecessors, he prints the prefaces by earlier editors after his own. By including the preface to the First Folio, signed by the King's Men actors, Heminge and Condell, he interpolated them into a line of preferred textual transmission. Although these two documents are attributed to the 'players' in his edition, a manuscript note in his copy of the Folio calls them 'editors', drawing them into the fractious genealogy of eighteenth-century editorial culture.

Malone was himself an avid book collector. While he borrowed some of his Shakespearean material from David Garrick

---

[36] Malone (1790), vol. I, pp. xii, xix.
[37] Malone (1790), vol. I. pp. xix, xlv.

and George Steevens, he also owned much of it himself, including a First Folio probably acquired in the mid-1770s and now, with many of his other early books, in the Bodleian Library.[38] Malone had his copy rebound with his monogram stamped in gold on the front, and accessorized with interleaved pictorial material, including a picture of the Globe theatre, engravings from Van Dyck's portraits of the Herbert brothers, a copy of the Chandos portrait of Shakespeare, and a facsimile of Shakespeare's signature. This practice attests both to his lawyerly interest in gathering documentary evidence and to his partiality for illustrations. One of these, an engraving of Shakespeare by the book illustrator, George Vertue, is annotated with a manuscript remark by Malone that captures his simultaneous dependence upon and denigration of, previous editors:

This Print was engraved by Vertue for Mr Pope's Edition. But Mr Pope was deceived with respect to it, for the picture from which it was engraved was not a picture of Shakespeares, but a juvenile portrait of James the First. This information I received from Mr Steevens, the last & best editor of Shakespeare, 1776 EM.

It also marks a moment of editorial harmony before Malone and Steevens quarrelled and his status as 'best editor' was decisively forfeit. Some of this same illustrative material—the signature, the Vertue engraving—was also included in Malone's own printed Shakespeare edition of 1790—as if he had retrofitted the First Folio to be more like his own edited text.[39] One illustration commissioned for the edition was a copy, by Ozias Humphry, of the so-called Chandos portrait, belonging to the Duke of Chandos. Malone was convinced that this, not the Folio's title-page

---

[38] James M. Osborn, 'Edmond Malone: Scholar-Collector', *The Library*, 19 (1964), pp. 11–37.

[39] The list of illustrations is included under a heading 'Directions to the Binder' in Malone (1790), vol. II, p. 338.

Droeshout engraving, was 'the only original Picture of our great poet Shakspeare'.[40]

Other notes in his First Folio reveal that Malone clearly did consider having the whole book rebound with margins and space for his notes—probably as part of his plan to send a marked-up Folio copy to the printers—although he did not go ahead with this, perhaps on grounds of cost. Manuscript notes at the beginning of his copy set out the number of pages in each of the three generic sections and conclude that '431 leaves wd be wanting for inlaying this work'. He has added to the list of plays in the catalogue, 'Troylus & Cressida', with a manuscript footnote in the bottom margin: 'This play seems to have been inadvertently omitted by the first Editors & afterwards printed & inserted between the Histories & Tragedies. This appears by its not being mentioned in this table (which could not have been printed until the whole work was finished) & also by its being unpaged—except only on one leaf. EM.' He changed the erroneous stage direction in *The Taming of the Shrew*, which makes Hortensio Bianca's 'sister' rather than, as he recognized, her 'suitor' [1.1.46]. There is little other evidence in Malone's copy of the First Folio of the forensic editorial intelligence he brought to bear on the text of Shakespeare in his edition of 1790, although its generally worn appearance and the existence of a ring mark from a cup or wine glass on a page of *1 Henry IV* suggests it was much referred to during the course of his work.

Editorial work by Capell and Malone by the end of the eighteenth century had, then, established the importance of the First Folio text in the transmission of Shakespeare's plays. Just as these editors worked out their theories through and on their copies of the First Folio, so other eighteenth-century owners added emendations and readings from the published commentary onto their own copies. A number of Folio copies show evidence of this

---

[40] Malone to Chandos in 1783, quoted in Martin, p. 92.

retro-fitting. The copy once owned by the Bishop of Llandaff, for example, adds a neat manuscript list of 'Dramatis Personae' in a space at the end of *Twelfth Night*, which exactly follows Nicholas Rowe's descriptions of the 'fantastical steward', Malvolio, and Olivia, 'a lady of great beauty and fortune', and also cites Theobald, Hanmer, and Warburton in manuscript commentary.[41] A copy now at the University of Indiana has been completely fitted up with the scene locations and stage directions added by Rowe to his text of *Troilus and Cressida*: 'The Grecian Camp'; 'Beating him'; 'passes over'.[42] A copy in the Victoria and Albert Museum has had a number of lists of *dramatis personae* added in manuscript, including formulations that can be dated to Rowe: 'Touchstone, a Clown attending on Celia & Rosalind'.[43] A single leaf of *Romeo and Juliet*, added at some point as a replacement into a copy bought by Henry Folger, gives a taste of some extensive eighteenth-century additions into a First Folio. Words and punctuation have been altered and stage directions added, including the note that 'Mr Pope here add's to lines from the 3rd edition'.[44] A copy now in the Library of Congress has a number of references to Rowe's edition, particularly recalling his suggestion that *Merry Wives of Windsor* was written at Queen Elizabeth's express command.[45]

The editorial role for the Folio changed relatively little during the nineteenth century, even as prices for the book escalated. John Forster, literary adviser and friend of Charles Dickens, annotated his copy with extensive red pen, proposing emendations, repunctuating, reallocating speeches, and offering commentary (of *Cymbeline*: 'Not Shakespears, any part of it') but did not produce

[41] West 128.
[42] West 147; Rowe's *Troilus and Cressida* is in vol. IV of his 1709 edition.
[43] West 25.   [44] West 68.   [45] West 142.

an edition.[46] The inveterate popularizer and leading light of the Society for the Diffusion of Useful Knowledge, Charles Knight, looking for a new serial after successful titles including the *Penny Magazine*, *Penny Cyclopedia*, *Pictorial Bible* and *Pictorial History of England*, began to prepare his Pictorial Shakespeare, which appeared in parts during 1840–1:

I diligently applied myself to a critical examination of the text to be adopted. I procured a copy of the first folio, which was read aloud to me whilst I marked upon a copy of the common *trade edition*, all the variations that presented themselves. I found that no book could be more incorrectly printed than this booksellers' stereotyped volume. I subsequently expressed my belief that the text of Shakspere had not been compared with the originals carefully and systematically for half a century. Not only had words been changed by printers, but whole lines had been omitted. The punctuation of the received text was in the most confused state.

Although he later wondered whether 'I preferred perhaps a little too exclusively the authority of the folio', he reported that numerous secret folio advocates had written to him to congratulate him, emboldened by his editorial decision.[47] Knight's Folio is currently in private hands, having the distinction of being, according to Anthony James West, 'the first First Folio to be offered [for sale] on the internet' in 2001.[48] Charles and Mary Cowden Clarke, publishing the 'People's Edition' of the plays in the 1860s, also looked anew at their First Folio, but they were less impressed by its qualities. They expressed their gratitude to Heminge and Condell:

yet it must be confessed that they were remarkably unfitted to be editors; seeing that they could never have revised (perhaps not even looked at) the proof-sheets while going through the press, that they suffered

---

[46] West 26.

[47] Charles Knight, *Passages of A Working Life During half a Century* (London: Bradbury and Evans, 1864), vol. ii, p. 285; pp. 290–1.

[48] West 217. See Rasmussen and West, p.699.

innumerable glaring errors of typography, punctuation and misplaced prefixes to pass into print uncorrected; and that they inserted one play ['Titus Andronicus'] in their collected volume which there is strong reason to believe is not Shakespeare's, while they omitted one play ('Pericles') which there is as strong reason to believe was written by him.[49]

The Clarkes had got their First Folio from their brother-in-law, the playwright and actor Thomas James Serle: he signed the first page of *The Tempest* to 'Charles & Mary V. Clarke with all good wishes for success', superimposing this record of a nineteenth century gift over an earlier, untraced ownership mark, 'Robt. Tomkins 1789'.[50] The copy has a number of annotations relating to eighteenth-century performance (discussed in Chapter 4), and is in time destined to belong to a theatre: its current owner, John Wolfson, has promised his book collection to Shakespeare's Globe in London.

The transfer of First Folio copies to the USA from the 1850s onwards also had an impact on the nascent American editorial tradition. Richard Grant White's twelve-volume edition published in Boston between 1857 and 1866 cited the Astor library copy and he had also 'had the privilege of examining the admirable copy of the first folio, now in the noble Shakespearian library of Mr Thomas P. Barton of New York'. White's Civil War text was 'founded exclusively upon that of the first folio and has been prepared, in the first instance, as if no other edition of authority had appeared since that was published'.[51] At the end of the nineteenth century, the New York Shakspere Society published parallel text editions of all the plays that had been first printed in quarto, together with their Folio counterparts (1888–1906). And in 1903, two women editors, Charlotte Porter and Helen A. Clarke, pipped Oxford University Press to the post in

[49] Charles and Mary Cowden Clarke (eds), *The Plays of William Shakespeare* (London: Cassell, Petter & Galpin, 1865–9), vol. 1; p. xxxv.

[50] West 173.   [51] Quoted in Murphy (2003), p. 154.

producing *The First Folio Edition of the Works of William Shake-speare* (New York, 1903–1913), the first edition to carry the title. The Oxford professor Walter Raleigh had proposed 'an exact reprint of the Folio, play by play, at a moderate price' as a challenge to the then dominant Shakespeare edition published by the rival press at Cambridge: '"Back to the Folio" will, I believe, be the motto of the next important edition.'[52] But seven volumes of Porter and Clarke's edition were received by the Secretary to the Delegates of the Press in early August 1905, and David Nichol Smith, recruited to the Oxford editorial team, admitted that 'the text is good—it is an accurate reprint, line for line and letter for letter, misprints and all', although he added 'I am not prepared to speak of the accuracy, nor the honesty, or the critical apparatus'.[53] Despite extensive communication between editors, including the distribution of the relevant pages of Sidney Lee's facsimile, the new 'Folio text' edition, as it is called in the correspondence, foundered, in large part because of 'these two advanced ladies'.[54] OUP did not produce a new complete Shakespeare until 1986.[55]

Porter and Clarke were clear about the progress of editorial theory: 'the English editors of Shakespeare have continuously groped backward from the most modern towards the most ancient text'. For them this was 'the First Folio [as] the text nearest to Shakespeare's stage, to Shakespeare's ownership, to Shakespeare's authority'.[56] Jeanne Addison Roberts' account of the extent to which the commentary in Porter and Clarke's Folio edition might be considered feminist reproduces a strange photograph—perhaps a symbolic commentary—pasted into one of their volumes. The picture shows the two women on bended knees,

---

[52] Shakespeare Edition Archive, Oxford University Press, 19/000039.
[53] Shakespeare Edition Archive, Oxford University Press, 19/000107.
[54] Shakespeare Edition Archive, Oxford University Press, 019/00045.
[55] Murphy (2003), pp. 165–6.
[56] C. Porter and H. A. Clarke, *The First Folio Edition: A Midsomer Nights Dream* (London: Harrup, 1903), pp. xi, ix.

reaching through some outdoor iron railings to touch the top corners of an open folio-sized book—described by Roberts as a First Folio. As Roberts notes, 'no explanation is provided': the picture captures a curious yearning for and a sense of separation—perhaps gendered, perhaps institutional—from the book.[57] It is not clear whether it is the Folio or its female editors who are behind bars. Whether the two women, who had Horace Howard Furness's patronage, had borrowed his copy of the First Folio for their editorial labours, is not recorded. Perhaps they, like White before them, had used Thomas Barton's copy, since donated with his large Shakespeare collection to Boston Public Library. Wherever they consulted the First Folio, they can claim to be the first editors to present a new First Folio text to modern readers.

Probably the last Shakespeare editors to own First Folios were Alexander Dyce, who gave his copy to the Victoria and Albert Museum, and Furness, editor of the Variorum Shakespeare and Shakespearean mentor to the Folgers: his copy is now at the University of Pennsylvania and, since 1999, available online.[58] However, the end of this tradition of editorial Folio ownership tells us less about the value of the text to editors and more about its increasing price on the one hand, and, relatedly, the gradual withdrawal of the wealthy gentleman scholar from the editorial arena on the other. Much of the textual work of late-nineteenth century and beyond was dependent on, and enabled by, the availability of a variety of facsimile reproductions (discussed in Chapter 5).

So far, then, attention to the First Folio has concentrated on arguments over its closeness to Shakespeare's lost manuscript, or his lost intentions, or his lost originals. Twentieth-century attention to the First Folio takes a different course. It can be clustered around two works that have some unexpected overlaps. Each is a

---

[57] Jeanne Addison Roberts, 'Women Edit Shakespeare', *Shakespeare Survey* 59 (2006), pp. 136–46, 137.

[58] West 24; West 180.

large, two-volume undertaking, with the first volume an outline of the argument and the second a more thorough marshalling of detailed evidence. Each works to quantify the text and to translate it into numbers. Each takes no notice of the plot or characters of Shakespeare's plays, but is concerned instead with textual specifics, such as spelling, capitalization, and the use of hyphens, which might be thought by the amateur to be unimportant. Each makes an argument of such detail and complexity that it is often hard to follow or to reproduce: the reader needs to take certain elements of the investigation on trust. Each is convinced that modern editions lose crucial evidence about how the plays were transmitted, and that there are vital clues about the provenance of the texts in those aspects of the printed book that seem accidental. And most significantly, they each investigate the First Folio itself with unparalleled seriousness and microscopic attention, more than any other previous commentators: for both, the First Folio has secrets that can be revealed by this close and painstaking work.

On the other hand, these two works could not be more different. The first, Ignatius Donnelly's 1888 book, *The Great Cryptogram: Francis Bacon's Cipher in the So-Called Shakespeare Plays*, revealed, to a rapt contemporary audience, the existence of a code inserted in the Folio by its true author, Sir Francis Bacon. Baconianism had swept the late nineteenth-century world as the Shakespearean equivalent of the religious doubt engendered by the writings of Darwin: Donnelly brought close reading of existing authorities and an electrifying clarity about the messages he found coded into the text. The other work is Charlton Hinman's study *The Printing and Proof-Reading of the First Folio of Shakespeare* (1963): 'an exercise in analytical bibliography'.[59] Hinman compared the copies of the First Folio in the Folger Shakespeare Library by means of a patent optical collating machine and substituted apparently robotic

---

[59] Charlton Hinman, *The Printing and Proof-Reading of the First Folio of Shakespeare* (Oxford: Clarendon Press, 1963), vol. 1, p. 1.

objectivity for Donnelly's fervent enthusiasms. Hinman's great contribution to the textual study of the First Folio was to shift the emphasis of editorial study away from speculating about the features and the provenance of the copies of the plays from which the book was printed, and instead, through detailed analysis, towards 'the kinds and amount of modification to which this copy was subject during the printing process itself'.[60] The two Folio analysts share, however, distinct structural and attitudinal similarities.

Donnelly's *The Great Crytogram* advertised itself as being by the author of '"Atlantis: The Antediluvian World", and "Ragnarok: The Age of Fire and Gravel"', bringing expertise in the arcane imperial and mythical geographies of the late nineteenth century to bear on the unexplored kingdom of Shakespeare (or Bacon). A progressive and energetic Minnesota congressman, Donnelly claimed no special knowledge of Shakespeare, admitting disarmingly that it was when reading, in one of his your son's books, that Francis Bacon used codes that a 'pregnant association of ideas' occurred to him, which he enumerated:

1. Lord Bacon wrote the plays.
2. Lord Bacon loved them; and could not desire to dissociate himself from them.
3. Lord Bacon knew their inestimable greatness; and
4. Lord Bacon dealt in ciphers; he invented ciphers, and ciphers of exquisite subtlety and cunning.

Then followed, like a flash, this thought:

5. Could Lord Bacon have put a cipher in the plays?[61]

---

[60] Hinman, vol. I. p. 5.

[61] Ignatius Donnelly, *The Great Crytopgram: Francis Bacon's Cipher in the So-Called Shakespeare Plays* (London: Sampson Low, Marston, Searle & Rivington. Ltd, 1888), vol. II, pp. 506–7.

Donnelly's predispositions are clear from his starting premise—
ironically quite contrary to the association of Bacon in the period
with the development of inductive and empirical rather than
anticipatory reasoning. As Walt Whitman, one of those caught
up in this exciting revelation, put it in a poem 'Shakespeare
Bacon's Cipher', published in 1887 after conversations with
Donnelly:

> I DOUBT it not; then more, immeasurably more,
> In each old song bequeathed, in every noble page or text,
> (Different, something unreck'd before, some unsuspected
>   author,)
> In every object—mountain, tree, and star—in every birth
>   and life,
> As part of each, finality of each, meaning, behind the ostent,
> The mystic cipher waits infolded.[62]

The poem's subtitle, 'A Hint to Scientists', points to Bacon's role
in 'the cultural image of science' in the nineteenth century and his
role as the forefather of modern positivism in works of contemporary philosophy such as those by G. H. Lewes and John
Herschel.[63]

The idea that Francis Bacon was the true author of the plays
attributed to Shakespeare had its nineteenth-century origins in the
work of Delia Bacon, as often rehearsed. She was an East Coast
schoolteacher who was convinced that these noble and philosophical texts could not have been written by 'a stupid, ignorant,
illiterate, third-rate play-actor'.[64] In *The Philosophy of the Plays of
Shaksper Unfolded* (1857), she elaborated an argument that Bacon
instead had the learning, breeding, and cultural capital to write the

---

[62] http://www.whitmanarchive.org/published/periodical/poems/per.00030
(accessed April 2015).

[63] Richard Yeo, 'An Idol of the Market-place: Baconianism in the Nineteenth
Century', *History of Science* 23.3 (1985), pp. 251–98; p. 253.

[64] Delia Bacon, *The Philosophy of the Plays of Shaksper Unfolded* (London:
Groombridge and Sons, 1857), p. 12.

plays as a vehicle for his new scientific philosophies, and that the context of the early modern court made it dangerous for him to admit to their authorship. Delia Bacon's theories are now routinely mocked, but they can also be seen as brave and methodologically radical in a context in which Shakespeare criticism preferred the claims of their poet's timelessness over any suggestion that the plays might have been subversive or topical.

Donnelly developed Delia Bacon's suggestions with an entirely new rigour. His instinct about the plays' authorship was, for him, satisfactorily corroborated by instances of the word 'Bacon' in Shakespeare's plays: 'When I read that phrase "On, bacons, on" [from *1 Henry IV* 2.2.77–8] I said to myself: Beyond question there is a cipher in this play.' Donnelly's first attempts with an edited edition were frustrating, until he realized that it was the First Folio itself he needed: 'I at length, July 1 1882, procured a fac-simile copy, folio size, made by photo-lithographic process, and, therefore, an exact reproduction of type, pages, punctuation and everything else.'[65] Working with Staunton's facsimile (discussed in the final chapter of this book), Donnelly noted its pagination irregularities including that there were no page numbers at all in *Troilus and Cressida*. He hit upon the idea that these were deliberate errors to signal a hidden code, and then began some elaborate systems of counting to reveal its message. His work was done by drawing lines and diagrams on First Folio facsimile pages (Figure 3.1). In fact, what Donnelly found was a string of sentences attributed to Bacon that revealed much about contemporary politics, about the biographical Shakespeare, and about the circumstances of subterfuge around the plays' authorship, many of them surprisingly explicit. The plays are 'first out abroad' 'in the name of More low [Marlowe] a woe-begone sullen fellow'; the cipher gives an account of how 'the point of his own sword stuck against his head and eye'. Later 'Seas ill [Cecil] said that More low or Shak'st

[65] Donnelly, vol. II, pp. 526, 547.

FIG. 3.1. Ignatius Donnelly, *The Great Cryptogram* (1888)
Donnelly used this page from Howard Staunton's 1864 photolithographed facsimile to work out his complicated Baconian cypher.

And take thou this (O thoughts of men accurs'd)
"*Paſt, and to Come, ſeems beſt; things Preſent worſt.*
Mow. Shall we go draw our numbers, and ſet on?
Haſt. We are Times ſubiects, and Time bids, Be gon.

Actus Secundus. Scœna Prima.

Enter Hoſteſſe, with two Officers Fang, and Snare.

Hoſteſſe. Mr. *Fang*, haue you entred the Action?
Fang. It is enter'd.
Hoſteſſe. Whers your Yeoman? Is it a luſty yeoman?
Will he ſtand to it?
Fang. Sirrah, where's *Snare?*
Hoſteſſe. I, I, good M. *Snare.*
Snare. Heere, heere.
Fang. Snare, we muſt Arreſt Sir *Iohn Falſtaffe.*
Hoſt. I good M. *Snare*, I haue enter'd him, and all.
Sn. It may chance coſt ſome of vs our liues: for hee wil ſtab.
Hoſteſſe. Alas the day: take heed of him: he ſtabd mee
in mine owne houſe, and that moſt beaſtly: he cares not
what miſcheefe he doth, if his weapon be out. Hee will
foyne like any diuell, he will ſpare neither man, woman,
nor childe.
Fang. If I can cloſe with him, I care not for his thruſt.
Hoſteſſe. No, nor I neither : Ile be at your elbow.
Fang. If I but fiſt him once : if he come but within my
Vice.
Hoſt. I am vndone with his going : I warrant he is an
infinitiue thing vpon my ſcore. Good M. *Fang* hold him
ſure : good M. *Snare* let him not ſcape, he comes continu-
antly to Py-Corner (ſauing your manhoods) to buy a ſad-
dle, and hee is indited to dinner to the Lubbars head in
Lombardſtreet, to M. *Smoothes* the Silkman. I pra'ye, ſince
my Exion is enter'd, and my Caſe ſo openly knowen to the
world, let him be brought in to his anſwer: A ſoo Marke
is a long one, for a poore lone woman to beare: & I haue
borne, and borne, and borne, and haue bin fub'd off, and
fub'd off, from this day to that day, that it is a ſhame to
be thought on. There is no honeſty in ſuch dealing, vnles
a woman ſhould be made an Aſſe and a Beaſt, to beare e-
uery Knaues wrong.

Enter Falſtaffe and Bardolfe.

Yonder he comes, and that arrant Malmeſey-Noſe *Bar-*
dolfe with him. Do your Offices, do your offices: M. *Fang,*
& M. *Snare*, do me, do me, do me your Offices.
Fal. How now? whoſe Mare's dead? what's the matter?
Fang. Sir *Iohn*, I arreſt you, at the ſuit of Miſt. *Quickly.*
Falſt. Away Varlets, draw *Bardolfe* : Cut me off the
Villaines head : throw the Queane in the Channel.
Hoſt. Throw me in the channell? Ile throw thee there.
Wilt thou? wilt thou? thou baſtardly rogue. Murder, mur-
der, O thou Hony-ſuckle villaine, wilt thou kill Gods of-
ficers, and the Kings? O thou hony-ſeed Rogue, thou art
a hony-ſeed: a Man-queller, and a woman-queller.
Falſt. Keepe them off, *Bardolfe.*
Fang. A reſcu, a reſcu.
Hoſt. Good people bring a reſcu. Thou wilt not thou
wilt not? Do, do thou Rogue: Do thou Hempſeed.
Page. Away you Scullion, you Rampallian, you Fuſtil-
lirian : Ile tucke your Catſtropbe.

Enter Ch. Iuſtice.

Iuſt. What's the matter? Keepe the Peace here, hoa.
Hoſt. Good my Lord be good to mee. I beſeech you
ſtand to me.
Ch. Iuſt. How now ſir *Iohn*? What are you brauling here?
Doth this become your place, your time, and buſineſſe?
You ſhould haue bene well on your way to Yorke.
Stand from him Fellow; wherefore hang'ſt vpon him?

Hoſt. Oh my moſt worſhipfull Lord, and't pleaſe your
Grace, I am a poore widdow of Eaſtcheap, and he is arre-
ſted at my ſuit.
Ch. Iuſt. For what ſumme?
Hoſt. It is more then for ſome (my Lord) it is for all : all
I haue, he hath eaten me out of houſe and home ; he hath
put all my ſubſtance into that fat belly of his ; but I will
haue ſome of it out againe, or I will ride thee o'Nights,
like the Mare.
Falſt. I thinke I am as like to ride the Mare, if I haue
any vantage of ground, to get vp.
Ch.Iuſt. How comes this, Sir *Iohn*? Fy, what a man of
good temper would endure this tempeſt of exclamation?
Are you not aſham'd to inforce a poore Widdowe to ſo
rough a courſe, to come by her owne?
Falſt. What is the groſſe ſumme that I owe thee?
Hoſt. Marry (if thou wer't an honeſt man) thy ſelfe, &
the mony too. Thou didſt ſweare to mee vpon a parcell
guilt Goblet, ſitting in my Dolphin-chamber at the round
table, by a ſea-cole fire, on Wedneſday in Whitſon weeke,
when the Prince broke thy head for lik'ning him to a ſin-
ging man of Windſor; Thou didſt ſweare to me then (as I
was waſhing thy wound) to marry me, and make mee my
Lady thy wife. Canſt y deny it? Did not goodwife *Keech*
the Butchers wife come in then, and call me goſſip *Quickly?*
comming in to borrow a meſſe of Vinegar : telling
vs, ſhe had a good diſh of Prawnes : whereby y didſt deſire
to eate ſome : whereby I told thee they were too hot, a
wound? And didſt not thou (when ſhe was gone downe
ſtaires) deſire me to be no more ſo familiar with ſuch poore
people, ſaying, that ere long they ſhould call me Madam?
And did'ſt thou not kiſſe me, and bid mee fetch thee 30s.
I put thee now to thy Book-oath, deny it if thou canſt.
Fal. My Lord, this is a poore mad ſoule : and ſhe ſayes
vp & downe the town, that her eldeſt ſon is like you. She
hath bin in good caſe, & the truth is, pouerty hath diſtra-
cted her. But for theſe fooliſh Officers, I beſeech you, I
may haue redreſſe againſt them.
Iuſt. Sir *Iohn*, ſir *Iohn*, I am well acquainted with your
maner of wrenching the true cauſe, the falſe way. It is not
a confident brow, nor the throng of wordes, that come
with ſuch (more then impudent) ſawcines from you, can
thruſt me from a leuell conſideration, I know you'ha pra-
ctis'd vpon the eaſie-yeelding ſpirit of this woman.
Hoſt. Yes in troth my Lord.
Iuſt. Prethee peace : pay her the debt you owe her, and
vnpay the villany you haue done her : the one you may do
with ſterling mony, & the other with currant repentance.
Fal. My Lord, I will not vndergo this ſneape without
reply. You call honorable Boldnes, impudent Sawcineſſe :
If a man will curt'ſie, and ſay nothing, he is vertuous : No,
my Lord (your humble dutie remembred) I will not be your
ſutor. I ſay to you, I deſire deliu'rance from theſe Officers
being vpon haſty employment in the Kings Affaires.
Iuſt. You ſpeake, as hauing power to do wrong : But
anſwer in the effect of your Reputation, and ſatisfie the
poore woman.
Falſt. Come hither Hoſteſſe.

Enter M. Gower.

Ch. Iuſt. Now Maſter *Gower*; What newes?
Gow. The King (my Lord) and *Henrie* Prince of Wales
Are neere at hand : The reſt the Paper telles.
Falſt. As I am a Gentleman.
Hoſt. Nay, you ſaid ſo before.
Fal. As I am a Gentleman. Come, no more words of it.
Hoſt. By this Heauenly ground I tread on, I muſt be
faine to pawne both my Plate, and the Tapiſtry of my dy-
ning Chambers.

spur never writ a word of them', and 'the son of a poor peasant who yet followed the trade of glove making' certainly did not either. Shakespeare's marriage to Anne 'eldest by seven years' is figured, the Queen sends troops to find him. The narrative revealed by the code is both detailed and clear, and utterly baffling. Donnelly defends himself against the incredulity of his readers: 'I should not dare to utter these opinions save in the presence of so many marvelous proofs. But there is no imagination in the multiplication table; no self-deception can invade the precincts of addition and subtraction; two and two are four, everywhere, to the end of the chapter.'[66] Donnelly asserted that Bacon had placed the ciphers into the Folio text and that therefore where plays had been printed prior to the Folio, these texts could be used to focus cryptographic attention onto the additional material added in 1623. For Donnelly, the question was clear-cut:

Is there or is there not a Cipher in the Plays? A vast gulf separates these two conclusions. Are the Plays simply what they are given out to be by Heminge and Condell, untutored outpourings of a great rustic genius; or are they a marvelously complicated padding around a wonderful internal narrative? I am sorry to see that some persons seem to think that this whole question merely concerns myself, and that it is to be answered by sneers and personal abuse. I am the least part, the most insignificant part, of this whole matter. The question is really this: Is the voice of Francis Bacon again speaking in the world? Has the tongue, which has been stilled for two hundred and sixty years, again been loosened, and is it about to fill the astonished globe with eloquence and melody?[67]

This method, postulating an elaborate spatio-verbal schema devised by Bacon in which every letter and word was in a pre-set square on the page, was entirely dependent on Donnelly's complete ignorance about early modern printing practices. It is hard to imagine any way in which the transmission of manuscript copy

---

[66] Donnelly, vol. II, pp. 690–1; pp. 718–19, 729, 840–1, 865.
[67] Donnelly, vol. II. p. 639.

into printed text could have been prosecuted with the degree of precision, detail, and authorial control he imagined: Donnelly did not know that the Folio was set and printed in sixes, or which pages were part of the same printed sheet, or the freedom that individual compositors exercised over matters such as spelling and punctuation. All of these contextual factors were the stock in trade of Charlton Hinman in his own two-volume work, *The Printing and Proof-Reading of the First Folio of Shakespeare* (1963). Like Donnelly, Hinman was interested in irregularities, layout, type, and errors and like him he had little space amid his extensive calculations for any appreciation of the plays as literary dramas. Unlike Donnelly, Hinman saw these examples of spelling and other niggles or unconformities in the Folio text as extrinsic to the author (almost whoever that might be) and attributable instead to the working practices of the printing shop, the exigencies of workflow, and the availability of copy, the distinctive individual preferences of experienced and less experienced pressmen and apprentices working in William Jaggard's printshop in London's Barbican, as well as to the nature of the copy from which the printers were working. Or, to put it another way, both Donnelly and Hinman found significant examples of spelling, capitalization, hyphenation, layout, and pagination in the First Folio that they attributed not to Shakespeare but, in Donnelly's case, to Bacon instead, and in Hinman's, to a previously undifferentiated team of printshop workers now designated Compositor A, B, C, D, and E. History has been sure that Hinman was right, and that Donnelly was wrong; perhaps what is more interesting is the similarity of their approach to the First Folio.

Hinman's work collating the copies of the Folio in the Folger library deployed analytical bibliography as retrospective academic justification for Folger's Folio stockpile. Folger had himself planned to undertake a comparison of his copies in retirement—a fantasy of proximity to his multiple purchases that, during his lifetime, were all crated up in secure storage—but never did so. He did claim in 1914 that 'every one of the 47 copies seems to have an excuse for its presence', but at that point, there was no sustained corroboration of this defence, no confirmation that indeed there was any intellectual advantage to be gained from this Folio hoard.[68] That is to say, if Folger's extravagant collection of First Folios enabled Hinman's work, it also needed it. In completing this unfinished founder's task, Hinman effectively inaugurated the Folger Shakespeare Library as a place of sustained and serious scholarship, even if the mechanical labours of his collating machine rather underlined the inhuman scale of the collection. His methodology was influenced by his wartime service as a Naval cryptanalyst whose code-breaking unit in Washington DC included eminent bibliographers Fredson Bowers and Giles Dawson (the Folger's postwar curator of books and manuscripts). One of their abortive military techniques, the comparative analysis of pre- and post-strike aerial photographs, underpinned the principles of the mechanical collation machine Hinman would develop after the war.[69]

Hinman's exhaustive labours on the First Folio texts built on earlier compositorial studies by Thomas Satchell and Edwin Eliott Willoughby (the Folger's chief bibliographer from 1935–58).[70] He identified from the printed Folio distinctive individual pieces of type and printers' ornaments or other furniture and traced their gradual wear and tear over their recurrence in the book. He also spotted places where the skeleton of the page—the running title, page numbers, and ruled lines, which did not always need to be entirely changed for each page of the book—revealed something about the order of printing. Together, this evidence established a

---

[68] Grant, p. 97.

[69] See Steven Escar Smith, '"The Eternal Verities Verified": Charlton Hinman and the Roots of Mechanical Collation', *Studies in Bibliography* 53 (2003), pp. 129–61.

[70] Thomas Satchell, 'The Spelling of the First Folio: A Letter to the Editor', *Times Literary Supplement* 959 (3 June 1920), p. 352; Edwin Eliott Willoughby, *The Printing of the First Folio of Shakespeare*. Supplements to the Bibliographical Society's Transactions, 8. (Oxford: Oxford University Press for the Bibliographical Society, 1932).

new chronology of its printing over a two-year period from November 1621 to November 1623, interrupted by other work going through Jaggard's presses at the same time. This showed that the comedies, then the histories, and then the tragedies were printed, not in order but in formes—a sheet of paper with two printed pages side by side on the front and another two on the reverse—which were then bound mostly in quires of six leaves or twelve pages. For the printing shop, it was the technical configuration of the forme and then the quire, not the individual play that was the major unit of production. Finally, the preliminary material, and then the belated inclusion, *Troilus and Cressida*, were completed. These discoveries, although significant, did not really require multiple copies: they did not provide the scholarly justification for Folger's collection.

By comparing multiple copies, however, Hinman did add new evidence to his findings about print-house practices. He identified some five hundred variants or press-corrections: errors that had been picked up from printed sheets while the press continued to work, which were then corrected for the remainder of the run, and from which copies were bound up with random arrangements of corrected and uncorrected sheets. Some pages were corrected more than once, where the correction of errors introduced new mistakes or failed to rectify those that were noted for action. Disappointingly, not one of the corrections made a material difference to the interpretation of the text: most were errors of a similar order to those corrected by early readers and discussed in Chapter 2. Reviewing these conclusions, Peter Blayney, Hinman's successor as chief Folio expert, noted sympathetically: 'while it is immensely valuable to know that the Folio contains few variants of any textual significance, Hinman must have found that result a disappointing reward for several years of hard work'.[71] Hinman and Folger both:

[71] Peter W. M. Blayney, 'Introduction to the Second Edition', *The Norton Facsimile: The First Folio of Shakespeare*, prepared by Charlton Hinman, second edition (New York and London: W.W. Norton and Company, 1996), p. xxxii.

the discoveries were a derisory scholarly payoff for the expensive effort of decades in buying up First Folios for this comparative exercise, as well as for the work of that exercise.

Donnelly's analysis of the Folio had enlivened it with hidden characters and cross-currents of dialogue encoded in its irregularities. Hinman, too, found a cast of characters hidden beneath the Folio's surface. He traced the particular spelling and punctuation preferences of a range of distinct compositors: compositor A, who preferred spellings including *doe*, *goe*, *young*, and *here* over his colleague, compositor B's, preference for *do*, *go*, *yong*, and *heare*. So sure was he of these spelling patterns that a page in *Macbeth*, where Banquo speculates darkly about the elevation of his old comrade-in-arms [3.1], in which these preferences changed halfway through took on its own workplace choreography. Hinman explained this with a little scenario in which 'Compositor B was called away' and his workmate A 'finished the page for him *at case y*': '(in other words, A filled in for B standing at B's own workstation)'.[72] The other compositors were less distinctive. Compositor C combined some of the existing spelling features into a new profile, whereas the short-winded Compositor D preferred shorter spellings wherever possible. These men exist only as curious back-projections from a cluster of orthographic predilections (and the occasional hair that has been caught in the ink, or black fingerprint visible on the margins of Folio copies). But Hinman's fifth man, Compositor E, takes on some more distinctly human characteristics. His work, confined to parts of the tragedies section of the Folio, 'teem[s] with mistakes'. 'Not', said Hinman kindly, 'to be sure, that he was *utterly* incapable of setting manuscript copy', but even E's co-workers expected him to make a lot of mistakes: his 'deficiencies were evidently well-known to his superiors, and all that he did was subject to more or less systematic review'.[73] It must

[72] Hinman, vol. 1, p. 217.   [73] Hinman, vol. 1, pp. 219–20.

have seemed somewhat unfair to the hapless E that his work was so scrutinized, since errors by his fellow pressmen were apparently subject to many fewer spot corrections, but Hinman does not speculate so far into his feelings. He does, however, identify that this supervised, inaccurate worker is likely to be an apprentice, and, further, that he is most probably therefore John Leason, a Hampshire youth apprenticed to Jaggard in November of 1622 and about whom nothing further is known, in or out of the printing trade.

Hinman's work is rightly identified as a landmark of descriptive bibliography, based on tireless, eye-straining work on the Folger Shakespeare Library's archive of First Folios. Donnelly's now— and to many at the time too—looks like the work of an excitable crank. But there are some notable similarities. Both approaches identify the main interest of the First Folio in its apparently accidental, even chaotic, features of type and layout, and for both, these random-seeming elements rearrange themselves into meaningful, human patterns. Both, in Jeffrey Masten's lovely phrase, 'convert characters into characters—spellings into an individual constituted as a range of (ortho)graphic behaviors'.[74] Both Donnelly and Hinman superimpose their own human dramas onto the pages of the First Folio, replacing Shakespeare's own plays and speakers with their own complicated dialogues of character, causation and effect. They each pursue their own oblique version of the character criticism dominant in Shakespeare studies over the period of their work.

Psychologists have explored a willingness to believe conspiracy theories—such as that the works of Shakespeare were in fact written by Bacon—as a kind of 'fundamental attribution error', in which the individual is particularly predisposed towards 'dispositional' understandings of causation—those that identify

---

[74] Jeffrey Masten, 'Pressing Subjects; Or, The Secret Lives of Shakespeare's Compositors', in Jeffrey Masten, Peter Stallybrass, and Nancy Vickers (eds), *Language Machines: Technologies of Literary and Cultural Production* (London and New York: Routledge, 1997), pp. 75–107; p. 84.

humans as the most prominent agents. 'In most cases', writes Steve Clark, 'the conventionally accepted non-conspiratorial alternative to a conspiracy theory is a situational one', where 'situational' explanations recognize contextual and environmental factors as crucial to any theory of causation.[75] Interestingly, according to this analysis, Hinman's findings are also deeply dispositional in their tendency. His patented optical collator, described by one local newspaper as a 'a bulky, box-like metal monster about six feet tall with a row of toggle switches, flashing lights and a generally sinister appearance', a 'new creature' to Hinman's 'Frankenstein Redivivus', may appear futuristic and scientific.[76] But as the reference to Frankenstein hints, Hinman's labours were directed towards something human: the recovery, or invention, of the five compositors whose work he decodes from the orthography and typesetting of the folio. Even as Hinman acknowledges that spelling was not standardized, he hypothesizes a number of pressmen whose spelling preferences were so recognizable and unchanging that he can actually identify the place in *Macbeth* where they swap working stations for a moment. Hinman even allows himself the 'pleasant' speculation that one 'John Shakespeare, son of a Warwickshire butcher' who had been apprenticed to Jaggard from 1610–1617, might have been Compositor B.[77] These are indeed pleasant conjectures, but in their desire to identify human agents for the detailed appearance of the First Folio, they move closer to the dispositional epistemology discredited in Donnelly and his adherents.

[75] Steve Clark, 'Conspiracy Theories and Conspiracy Theorizing', in David Coady (ed.), *Conspiracy Theories: The Philosophical Debate* (Aldershot: Ashgate, 2006), pp. 81–98; p. 81.

[76] David L. Vander Meulen, 'A History of the Bibliographical Society of the University of Virginia: The First Fifty Years', in David L Vander Meulen (ed.), *The Bibliographical Society of the University of Virginia: The First Fifty Years* (Charlottesville: Bibliographical Society of the University of Virginia, 1998), pp. 1–81; p. 24.

[77] Hinman, vol. II, p. 513.

Hinman's work set the agenda for mid-twentieth-century bibli-ography. Many editors working on other authors made use of his collating machine, in studies including *The Scarlet Letter* and *Alice in Wonderland*. The Hinman collator was patented and more than fifty units were sold to libraries across Europe and North America. It even had some commercial success proofreading prescription labels in the pharmaceutical industry.[78] But significant though Hinman was in his field, this penetration is dwarfed by that of Donnelly and his adherents. It is hard to convey the scale of the excitement and cultural saturation of Baconian theories in the early decades of the twentieth century. And this sceptical discourse had deep and wide connections with First Folio ownership. Bacon loyalist, Sir Edwin Durning-Lawrence owned a First Folio along with a large collec-tion of Bacon material now in Senate House Library. Adolph Sutro pasted a review of Donnelly's book into the end papers of his copy in San Francisco. A copy now in Texas has an accom-panying folder of cuttings relating to Folio codes. Replying to Sidney Lee's request for information about First Folios for his census in 1902, the Revd R. H. Roberts of Gorleston near Great Yarmouth, who had inherited his copy from his father, answered that question that Lee had never asked: 'My father was not a convert to the Bacon theory but considered that the Baconians had made out a strong case, so much concerning Shakespeare being conjecture only.'[79] Now at the Folger Library, this copy includes an 1889 letter enthusing about Donnelly's work uncover-ing 'a great & wonderful cipher-system running through the whole of the Shakespeare Folio of 1623' from Mrs Henry Pott, author of numerous works on Bacon's authorship, including *Did Francis Bacon write 'Shakespeare'? Thirty-two Reasons for Believing that he*

<hr/>

[78] See Steven Escar Smith, '"Armadillos of Invention": A Census of Mechanical Collators', *Studies in Bibliography* 55 (2002), pp. 133–70.
[79] West 23; West 51; West 185; Shakespeare Birthplace Trust ER85/6/1/ Returns 21–40.

Did (1884).[80] John Davis Batchelder, who donated his large collection of books, manuscripts, coins, and other material to the Library of Congress in 1936, seems to have spelled out some of the initial ciphers in his copy of the Folio, marking 'bacon?' in the margin of the first page of *The Tempest*.[81] Batchelder also collected Baconian material, including Bacon's signature.

Baconianism comes closer to the Folio heartlands, too. The year before he died, Henry Folger wrote to his British book dealer, Broadbent, that 'I . . . am coming towards the end of my interest in Bacon; for all the books I have seen, read by him, tend to prove that he could not have been in any way responsible for the Shakespeare plays.'[82] The sentence suggests that Baconian authorship was by no means unthinkable to Folger during the time when he was amassing his Folios. It is striking, given the almost exclusive concentration of his collecting on Shakespearean texts, that he was so assiduous in collecting material by and about Bacon, and about the authorship controversy. There were almost no other contemporary authors represented in Folger's collection except those acknowledged as Shakespeare's sources, and the Folger Library only later acquired its impressively wide early modern collection by buying up the thousands of volumes in the Harmsworth collection on the eve of the Second World War. A. S. W. Rosenbach's eulogy at Henry Clay Folger's funeral in 1930 felt the need to confirm that the great collector was 'not a believer in the Baconian theory', even as he acknowledged that 'Mr Folger formed an almost complete library on this subject, including many manuscripts and autograph letters'.[83] Any suggestion of author scepticism in its founder would be an embarrassment for the Folger, which was burned by adverse publicity in 1948 when a supporter of the Earl of Oxford's claim to the authorship of Shakespeare's works sued its

---

[80] West 91.   [81] West 142.
[82] Grant, p. 78.   [83] Cadman, p. 103.

curator Giles Dawson over the claims made about contentious X-ray evidence in an early modern painting bought by Emily Folger after her husband's death.[84] Whereas in the twenty-first century professional academics tend to ignore the claims of different authorship candidates, early twentieth-century scholars felt a need to engage more fully with these arguments. The bibliographer, A. W. Pollard, for instance, included an account of the use of printers' ornaments in his account of *Shakespeare Folios and Quartos* (1909) 'in view of attempts made to discover secret meanings in everything connected with Shakespeare'.[85]

The great period of author scepticism in the last decade of the nineteenth and first two decades of the twentieth century focused on coded readings of the Folio thus also coincided with an unprecedented level of sales of the book and a huge increase in its price at auction. More Folios changed hands in these decades than at any time before or since, and over the thirty-year period the record high price for a First Folio rose from £750 in 1888 to more than £10,000 in 1922.[86] To collect and study First Folios in the period was perforce to engage with the spectre of Bacon's authorship. Paradoxically, cryptographic interest in the secrets of the First Folio text played a significant part in the ramping up of prices. The period of the First Folio's increasing desirability was also, and not entirely unconnectedly, the period when the idea that it was not by Shakespeare had most cultural permeation.

In 1920, however, one Thomas Looney published a book that would permanently redirect the authorship question away from Francis Bacon, and also, away from a close attention on the Folio text. Looney's identification of the Earl of Oxford, Edward de

---

[84] The contested painting is discussed in William L. Pressly, 'The Ashbourne Portrait of Shakespeare: Through the Looking Glass', *Shakespeare Quarterly* 44 (1993), pp. 54–72.

[85] A. W. Pollard, *Shakespeare's Folios and Quartos: a Study in the Bibliography of Shakespeare's Plays, 1594–1685* (London: Methuen, 1909), p. 132.

[86] See West (2001), vol. 1, pp. 56, 62.

Vere, as the literary contemporary whose life and experiences most convincingly mapped onto the Shakespeare canon, was taken up by an age increasingly interested in authorial biography. The celebrity endorsements that had previously appeared to validate Baconian theories now attached themselves to Oxford's candidacy. Sigmund Freud, for instance, was an admirer of Looney's work, and mentioned his adherence to the Oxfordian view when he accepted the award of the Goethe prize in 1930.[87] The methods of argumentation of the Oxfordians were also different. Cecil Palmer, who published Looney's book, marketed it as a complete break from the cryptographic methods that had dominated Baconian theories since Donnelly's *Great Cryptogram*: its main selling point was that it contained 'no cipher, cryptography or hidden message'.[88] As such, it had no interest in the text of the First Folio either. Looney's focus on parallels between the plays and the life history of Oxford meant that his theories could work with any one of the popular texts available in the bookshops: for such a strongly aristocratic theory, its argumentative premise was widely democratic. The days of Shakespearean cryptography were waning, although Alfred Dodd published a series of books championing the so-called Prince Tudor theory (that Bacon was the son of Queen Elizabeth) alongside the authorship question, throwing in another esoteric factor for good measure: 'Even a cursory examination of the Shakespeare Plays showed that the Folio, whatever else it was as pure literature—history, poetry, encyclopaedic knowledge—was undoubtedly the greatest Masonic book in the world. It was saturated with Masonic thought. It reeked with Masonic phraseology.' Having identified in a Folio page from *Richard II* the injunction, 'Swear too! Know you embrace! know this! Know too the grand geometrician, Jachin! Know Boas! Bacon's the name: and I be a freemason!', Dodd felt that perhaps

---

[87] James Shapiro, *Contested Will: Who Wrote Shakespeare?* (London: Faber, 2010), p. 212.

[88] Quoted in Shapiro, p. 222.

this code was too secret to be fully explicated: 'After all, this peculiar esoteric knowledge must be sought for personally. It cannot very well be shouted from the house-tops. It is the secret path for the savants and scholars of the Quatuor Coronati to explore, and for the Masonic Research Associations to examine . . . not the general public.'[89]

But if cryptography did not leave a lasting mark on the First Folio, the Folio did leave its imprint on cryptography. From the very beginning, scepticism about Shakespeare's authorship of the plays attributed to him had intersected with contemporary developments in coding. Delia Bacon had originally been prompted to investigate Francis Bacon's authorship by her friend Samuel Morse's interest in concealed and coded communication. Donnelly's *Great Cryptogram* and its scores of imitators and followers developed the paradigm, focusing ingenious attention on the variants and non-standard forms, particularly in the First Folio, but also in other texts, particularly early editions of Shakespeare's sonnets. At the end of the nineteenth century, a high school principal named Elizabeth Wells Gallup extended the sophistication and complexity of Baconian cryptography by her application of a cipher described by Bacon himself in his *De Augmentis* (1624). Her mentor Dr Orville Ward Owen, a fervent Baconian physician who had developed an elaborate mechanical deciphering wheel to reveal secret authorial messages, had also interpreted the First Folio: following a tip-off that Jonson's poem on the Droeshout engraving could be anagrammatized to read the helpful instruction 'Seek, sir, a true angle at Chepstow— F', he launched an expedition to the Welsh borders to find documents that would finally prove Bacon's authorship. It was

[89] Alfred Dodd, *The Secret Shake-speare: Being the missing chapter from 'Shake-speare, Creator of Freemasonry' in which the identity of Shake-speare is plainly declared together with Many Curious Secret Messages of profound interest to all lovers of literature, to Elizabethan Students and Freemasons in particular* (London: Rider & Co, 1941), p. 20; p. 57; p. 20.

unsuccessful, and a broken Owen eventually advised anyone who would listen: 'Never go into this Baconian controversy, for you will only reap disappointment.'[90]

Undeterred, his one-time assistant, Gallup, developed her own techniques. In *The Bi-Literal Cypher of Sir Francis Bacon discovered in his works and deciphered by Mrs Elizabeth Wells Gallup* (Detroit, Michigan, 1899), Gallup made a minute study of different letter forms and concluded that these variant founts were the heart of an extensive cryptographic system, revealing, *inter alia*, that 'The proofs are overwhelming and irresistible that Bacon was the author of the delightful lines attributed to Spenser,—the fantastic conceits of Peele and Green,—the historical romances of Marlowe,— the immortal plays and poems put forth in Shakespeare's name, as well as the Anatomy of Melancholy of Burton.'[91] Gallup's findings were extensively reported and queried. The reviewer in *The Times*, who had consulted a First Folio in the British Museum as well as a range of other seventeenth-century books, quibbled with some of her counting but also suggested, more substantively, that the typographical variants she had found were not specially placed as a code in these secretly connected literary works, but rather were a commonplace in books of the period; even the Bacon society was unconvinced and announced itself 'unable to give any support or countenance to the alleged discovery'.[92]

But support was forthcoming. Colonel George Fabyan was a wealthy eccentric, whose Riverbank Laboratories in Geneva, Illinois, were dedicated to experimentation in biodynamic agriculture, the genetics of fruit flies, cures for foot and mouth disease in cattle, and the development of new energy sources. He was also a

---

[90] Samuel Schoenbaum, *Shakespeare's Lives*, new edn. (Oxford: Clarendon Press, 1991), pp. 414–15.

[91] Elizabeth Wells Gallup, *The Bi-Literal Cypher of Sir Francis Bacon discovered in his works and deciphered by Mrs Elizabeth Wells Gallup* (Detroit, Michigan: Howard Publishing Co., 1899), p. iii.

[92] *The Times*, 26 December 1901; Schoenbaum, p. 416.

Baconian, who had supported Orville Ward Owen's work. He offered Elizabeth Wells Gallup a research base and a staff at Riverbank to continue her cryptographic work. Among the young recruits to the decoding project was a young graduate called William Friedman, born Wolfe Friedman in Moldova, part of the Russian Empire. Together with a clever English Literature graduate, Elizebeth Smith, whom he was later to marry, Friedman worked as Gallup's assistant in 1915–16. It was an exciting time. The filmmaker, William N. Selig, had secured a blocking injunction against Fabyan preventing him from publishing his demonstration of Bacon's authorship, since it would damage the reception of Shakespearean films designed to capture the tercentenary of Shakespeare's death in 1916. Judge Richard S. Tuthill of Cook County Circuit Court found in favour of Fabyan and Bacon, pronouncing the court convinced that 'Francis Bacon is the author' and awarded the colonel damages of $5,000, later overturned on appeal.[93]

Reviewing their Riverbank work some fifty years later, Mrs Friedman recalled, with clear-sighted affection for their employer:

I can state categorically that neither I nor any other one of the industrious research workers at Riverbank ever succeeded in extracting a single long sentence of a hidden message; nor did one of us so much as reproduce, independently, a single complete sentence which Mrs Gallup had already deciphered and published. It is fitting here to point out once more that in any true cryptogram any given number of decipherers must and will arrive at the same solution.[94]

Nevertheless, Gallup and Riverbank played an important role in the development of military cryptography. As one historian notes,

[93] Quoted in Frank W. Wadsworth, *The Poacher from Stratford: A Partial Account of the Controversy over the Authorship of Shakespeare's Plays* (Berkeley: University of California Press, 1958), p. 75.
[94] William F. Friedman and Elizebeth S. Friedman, *The Shakespearean Ciphers Examined: An Analysis of Cryptographic Systems Used as Evidence that Some Author other than William Shakespeare wrote the Plays Commonly Attributed to him* (Cambridge: Cambridge University Press, 1957), p. 205.

America entered the First World War in 1917 in an 'extraordinary
state of cryptographic unreadiness. Early in 1917, neither the army
nor the navy had any organization for intercepting enemy communications, let alone for studying or deciphering them': official
cryptographers were sent to Riverbank to work on decryption
under William Friedman's direction.[95] A photograph from 1918
of these trainees on the steps of the Riverbank's accommodation at
the Aurora Hotel in Illinois visualizes a human version of the bi-
literal cipher (the subjects face in different directions as anthropo-
morphized fount variants) to spell out—almost—the Baconian
dictum 'knowledge is power'. Bacon and Shakespeare are thus god-
parents at the birth of modern military cryptography. Friedman himself became the head of the US military's Signal Intelligence Service,
the nascent National Security Authority. He became known after the
Second World War, in the title of his biography, as *The Man Who
Broke Purple*, the important Japanese diplomatic code.

Baconian theories based on an encoded First Folio thus stimulated the development of a national military decoding unit. The
Friedmans never lost touch with their Shakespearean beginnings,
moving to Capitol Hill in Washington DC to be close to the First
Folio resources of the Folger Shakespeare Library in 1952 where
they overlapped with Hinman and his optical collator, and finally
publishing in 1957 the fruits of their longtime project 'to present a
full-scale appraisal of the cryptographic arguments from the point
of view of the professional cryptanalyst... The preparation of the
study has been delayed by our professional duties during and since
the Second World War.'[96] Even the launch of this academic book,
published by Cambridge University Press, offered Friedman a

---

[95] Ronald W. Clark, *The Man Who Broke Purple: The Life of the World's Greatest
Cryptologist Colonel William F. Friedman* (London: Weidenfield & Nicolson,
1977), p. 20.
[96] Friedman and Friedman, p. vii. They mention Hinman: 'Letter by letter,
these copies [of Folios in Folger] are being collated by Prof. Charlton Hinman, of
Johns Hopkins University, aided by a grant from the Old Dominion Foundation

cover for a clandestine visit to GCHQ, the UK Government's intelligence hub, as part of the attempt, post-Suez, to patch up the relationship of the Anglo-American intelligence services by sharing new understandings of encryption in the computer age.[97]

The Friedmans' analysis of the cryptographic turn in authorship studies was brisk, informed, and unsparing: Donnelly, Ward, Gallup and their adherents were all found to be covering inconsistent, unverifiable, or downright illogical methods under the mask of pseudo-mathematical science. This, for example, is their coolly devastating account of their encounter with Walter Conrad Arensberg, who claimed to have found repeated acrostic declarations of Bacon's authorship in the First Folio:

Taking the first play in the First Folio, The Tempest, and beginning with the first line of Act 1 Sc.1, he told us that he had produced, by the method of anagrammatic acrostics, the message 'The author was Francis Bacon' seven consecutive times. He was disappointed at our calm reception of the news, and sceptical of our contention that the method was so flexible that anyone could, with patience, produce equally impressive but quite different results. We met him again the next afternoon, and had by then produced seven consecutive times, using his own methods and his own book as a text, the message 'The author was William F. Friedman'. We began, as he did, at the beginning, starting from the first line of Chapter 1; and for good measure our message was four letters longer than the one derived by Arensberg from The Tempest. We were hesitant of showing him our findings; we found that we need not have been. He rallied splendidly from the shock, and his reply showed that blend of incurable optimism and illogicality which characterized his work: he admitted that we had made good our contention, and added 'But you know, and I know, that I wrote The Cryptography of Shakespeare and not you, so I am not particularly disturbed by that. All the same, what you have done does not

and an ingenious electrical collating machine of his own design. The aim is to ascertain the measure of similarity and the extent of the differences' (p. 227).

[97] Clark, p. 181.

disprove the presence of the sentence 'The author was Francis Bacon' which I found in The Tempest.[98]

None of the purported ciphers survived their scrutiny.

Shakespeare, then, marked the beginning of Friedman's enormously successful and influential cryptanalytical career. And he looped back to this early form, reflecting on his work when addressing the American Philosophical Society in Philadelphia in 1962 on the subject 'Shakespeare, Secret Intelligence and Statecraft'. His talk demonstrated that, unlike many of those whose cryptographic explorations he reviewed, he retained an abiding interest in the content, not just the form, of Shakespeare's plays. In reviewing his own career, Shakespeare would be his judge:

Did Shakespeare have any private views concerning the ethics of interception, the collection of secret intelligence, and its use in the conduct of public business? I wonder. Did he recognise that it is difficult to reconcile such activities with the democratic ideals of a free and open society that would prefer its government to conduct all its internal or domestic affairs openly, so far as possible, and also to conduct all its external or foreign affairs in the same manner? How far is open conduct of public affairs compatible with the national security of a democracy? What about its conduct in dealing with a closed society? I wonder what Shakespeare's answers to questions such as these might be?[99]

Appropriately enough for a man who had worked so extensively on supposedly pseudonymous publications, this article was attributed simply to a 'Reader' at the Folger library when it was published.[100] No answers about Shakespeare's own views on his profession were forthcoming for Friedman, who had learned his cryptographic craft working with Baconian theories about the authorship of the First Folio and used this training to lead the development of a

---

[98] Friedman and Friedman, pp. 150–1.   [99] Clark, p. 201.
[100] Shawn James Rosenheim, *The Cryptographic Imagination: Secret Writing from Edgar Poe to the Internet* (Baltimore: Johns Hopkins University Press, 1997), p. 154.

military superpower. According to the official account from the NSA, 'when asked how he happened to become the father of American cryptology, William F. Friedman smiled and said, 'I was seduced': the siren song was those secrets Elizabeth Gallup thought could be found in the pages of Shakespeare's First Folio.[101]

The cryptographic attention reviewed so sceptically by the Friedmans tended to focus on a few particular Folio hermeneutic hotspots: the prefatory material, especially the two poems by Ben Jonson, the book's opening play *The Tempest* and its depiction of the bookishly Baconian magus Prospero, aberrant page numbering, the nonce word 'Honorificabilitudinatibus' [5.1.41] in *Love's Labours Lost*, and the significance of the differences between the first printed editions of *1 Henry IV* (porcine references were, inevitably, a particular fascination), and that which appeared in the 1623 text. One further point of particular interpretative interest was the title page's engraved portrait by Martin Droeshout of a balding Shakespeare with a high forehead and an awkwardly stiff ruff over a soberly decorated dark doublet.

By the mid-nineteenth century, it had been established that the portrait existed in at least two states. The first state survived in only a handful of copies. J. O. Halliwell-Phillips, associated with at least three copies of the First Folio, boasted in 1884 that 'the gem of my collection is the engraving of Shakespeare by Droeshout, 1623, *in its original state before it was altered by an inferior hand into the vitiated form in which it has been so long familiar to the public*'.[102] The majority of extant copies included second-state examples of the portrait, which had added some shading around the neck and chin to improve its awkward three-dimensionality. It was unusual in early seventeenth-century publishing to make a portrait of the

---

[101] https://www.nsa.gov/about/cryptologic_heritage/center_crypt_history/almanac/index.shtml#article2 (accessed April 2015).

[102] J. O. Halliwell-Phillips, *A Hand-list of the Drawings and Engravings Illustrative of The Life of Shakespeare Preserved at Hollingbury Copse, Near Brighton* (Brighton: private printing, 1884), p. 7.

writer so prominent a feature of the book's presentation, and authorship sceptics during the nineteenth century made much of the portrait's artistic deficiencies. Generally, the anti-Stratfordians preferred to see these problems as a code that the author-figure was a sham rather than as Droeshout's own failures of execution.

The Jesuit, George O'Neill, addressed a meeting in Dublin on 'The Clouds Around Shakespeare', claiming his consultation of a local First Folio in support of his interpretation:

What has become evident to an increasingly large number of those who scrutinize the picture, what I have studied myself in the original Folio which is treasured in the library of the Jesuit Fathers at Milltown Park, what I invite you to judge for yourselves in any clear and complete (not truncated) copy of it, is this—that here we have no representation of any human face whatsoever, but the portrait of a mere mask.[103]

The pre-eminent English Baconian, Sir Edwin Durning-Lawrence (1837–1914), went one better. Durning-Lawrence was a wealthy parliamentarian whose greatest contribution to the House of Commons, according to his obituary in *The Times*, was the distinction of wearing the most expensive silk hats. He was convinced of Bacon's authorship by reading Donnelly's *Great Cryptogram*, and followed Donnelly's cryptographic methods, using the First Folio he bought himself around 1890 as part of an extensive Shakespearean and Baconian library.[104] He was an indefatigable lecturer and contributor to the international press on this topic, and often reproduced from his First Folio the Droeshout portrait that was part of his rallying cry:

England is now declining any longer to dishonour and defame the greatest Genius of all time by continuing to identify him with the mean, drunken,

[103] George O'Neill, SJ, *The Clouds Around Shakespeare: A Lecture Delivered before the Royal Dublin Society, February 22 1911* (Dublin: E. Ponsonby Ltd, 1911), p. 8. It has not been possible to trace O'Neill's 'original Folio' from these details.

[104] K. E. Attar, 'Sir Edwin Durning-Lawrence: A Baconian and his Books', *The Library* 5 (2003), pp. 294–315; West 23.

ignorant, and absolutely unlettered, rustic of Stratford who never in his life wrote so much as his own name and in all probability was totally unable to read one single line of print.[105]

As always in the authorship debate, there was more at stake than Shakespeare for this baronet-sceptic. In his decisively-named book *Bacon is Shakespeare* (1910), Durning-Lawrence focused in particular on the portrait, finding it 'a cunningly drawn cryptographic picture, shewing two left arms and a mask', which, together with his decoding of the Jonson poem that glosses it, showed 'that the real author is writing left-handedly, that means secretly, in shadow, with his face hidden behind a mask or pseudonym'.[106] Professional corroboration swiftly followed. Durning-Lawrence reported in a penny pamphlet that the *Tailor and Cutter* newspaper agreed that the figure in the Folio portrait 'was undoubtedly clothed in an impossible coat composed of the back and front of the same left arm'. The *Gentleman's Tailor Magazine* also took up this 'Problem for the Trade', and printed as evidence 'the two halves of the coat put tailor fashion, shoulder to shoulder', observing that 'it is passing strange that something like three centuries should have been allowed to elapse before the tailor's handiwork should have been appealed to in this particular manner'.[107] Hundreds of pamphlets, arguing for and against Durning-Lawrence's position, were published in the Edwardian period. One stands out: W. Grimshaw's investigation into the Folio's verses 'To the Reader'. His repeated title *Droeshout's Fronispiece* [sic] *1623 and Verses to the Reader* (1922) somewhat compromised the care and accuracy of his scholarship: this was precisely the kind of error that conspiracy cryptographers fell on as an indication of disguised authorship.

[105] Edwin Durning-Lawrence, *Bacon is Shakespeare* (London: Gay & Hancock Ltd, 1910), p. 82.

[106] Durning-Lawrence, pp. 23, 27.

[107] Edwin Durning-Lawrence, *The Shakespeare Myth* (London: Gay & Hancock, 1912), p. 6.

The testimony of expert tailors was not enough to convince everyone. Writing in 1911, William Stone Booth used some of the new forensic techniques to give an air of scientific discovery to his assertion that 'the characteristics of a face constitute a definite linear pattern precisely as do the lines of finger and thumb prints, and my method of identification is like that which is pursued by the police authorities in their use of fingerprints or Bertillon measurements in the identification of criminals'. His book created collages of the Droeshout portrait and a portrait of Francis Bacon, illustrating the argument through Pythonesque mash-up images with added tall hat or a beard:

(1) We have established a suspicion of identity between the poet known as William Shakespeare and Francis Bacon. (2) This suspicion is corroborated by the discovery of a structural signature of Francis Bacon in the works of the poet. (3) We see that the portrait of the poet, used as a frontispiece to the plays in which Bacon's structural signature is found, is anatomically identical with the portrait of the man bearing the name so signed.[108]

Booth made use of photographic expertise, thanking 'Mr Octave Henri Bourdon of the Notman Photographic Company of Boston', and his language of modern criminal investigation (Bertillon's work on identifying criminals through measurements known as anthopometry had been introduced to the US in the late 1880s) suggested that only now could a historical mystery be solved.[109]

This application of new technology is a perennial theme in analyses of the portrait. In 1995, Lillian Schwartz, an artist and

[108] William Stone Booth, *The Droeshout Portrait of William Shakespeare: An Experiment in Identification* (Boston: W. A. Butterfield, 1911), pp. 3–5.

[109] Carlo Ginzburg discusses Bertillon's method and the 'elusive quality of individuality' in 'Clues: Morelli, Freud, and Sherlock Holmes', in Umberto Eco and Thomas A. Sebeok (eds), *The Sign of Three: Dupin, Holmes, Peirce* (Bloomington: Indiana University Press, 1983), pp. 81–118; p. 106.

expert in computer-generated art, published an article in *Scientific American* about the findings from new image-manipulation software 'that can flip, scale and juxtapose pictures': a digital version of Booth's analogue montage processes. The subtitle for the piece was 'Riddles posed by ancient works of art fall to historical analyses and electronic explorations'.[110] Schwartz's targets were predictably recognizable ones: she juxtaposed Leonardo's face with that of the Mona Lisa, developed a computer-generated recolouring of a Piero fresco, and, 'in 1990 I started to compare portraits of Shakespeare with those of his contemporaries in the hope of establishing the bard's identity'. Comparisons with 'the Earl of Oxford and many other notables' reached a 'stalemate', until a eureka moment in the National Portrait Gallery in front of George Gower's portrait of Elizabeth I: 'the very same eyes I had been scrutinising for weeks'.[111] She argued that the jowly effect of a double chin on the right of Shakespeare's portrait was in fact the artist compensating for the narrower contours of Elizabeth's face. Although Schwartz was coy about the authorship implications of these visualizations, newspaper and television coverage leapt on the idea that Queen Elizabeth might have written the plays: one literal manifestation of the persistent historical 'desire to bring Shakespeare and Elizabeth together'.[112] Others followed in her footsteps: the inveterate Shakespeare portrait detective, Hildegard Hammerschmidt-Hummel, used various computerized techniques borrowed from the German Federal Bureau of Criminal Investigation to compare the Droeshout with other portraits of Shakespeare and discover *The True Face of William Shakespeare* (2006).

[110] Lillian Schwartz, 'The Art Historian's Computer', *Scientific American* (April 1995), pp. 106–11.
[111] Schwartz, p. 111.
[112] Helen Hackett, *Shakespeare and Elizabeth: The Meeting of Two Myths* (Princeton and Oxford: Princeton University Press, 2009), p. 3.

Seeing similarities between the Droeshout engraving and a portrait of a preferred candidate has become a familiar trope of authorship studies. Thomas J. Looney saw 'the same facial proportions, the same arching of the eyebrows, the identical pose (three-quarter face), the same direction of gaze' such that 'when the two could be brought together, a very strong case might be made out for Droeshout having worked from this portrait of Edward de Vere'.[113] Visualizing this overlay in a composite illustration splicing the Folio engraving to a different portrait gave the sceptics their standard iconography. In 1911, Basil Brown suggested that an image from a 1642 pamphlet by John Taylor, the water-poet, was a caricature of the Droeshout engraving, although it is an index of the uncertain tone of authorship challenges that it is hard to be entirely sure whether this privately printed squib is a spoof or not.[114] Definitely serious was Calvin Hoffman's quest to prove that Marlowe had written the plays attributed to Shakespeare. In 1955, Hoffman published the fruits of his investigation into Christopher Marlowe as the author of the plays under the title, *The Man Who Was Shakespeare*. The dust jacket carried the Droeshout engraving and a reproduction of a portrait of am Elizabethan young man recently discovered during renovation works at Corpus Christi College, Cambridge together with the question 'Two men... or one?'. Hoffman was enthusiastically convinced that the Corpus find was a portrait of Marlowe, but in a curious loop of logic, his main grounds for believing so were 'its strong likeness to the First Folio engraving by Martin Droeshout of the genuine author of the First Folio plays'. Because Marlowe wrote Shakespeare, the new portrait could be confidently identified. 'Not trusting to my judgment at the time', Hoffman added, 'I showed both pictures to portrait specialists. To a man

[113] Thomas J. Looney, *'Shakespeare' Identified in Edward de Vere, the Seventeenth Earl of Oxford* (London: C. Palmer, 1920), p. 534.

[114] Basil Brown, *Supposed Caricature of the Droeshout Portrait of Shakespeare* (New York: privately printed, 1911).

they said the two were portraits of the same individual, the only difference being one of age.'[115] Charlton Ogburn's argument that the Earl of Oxford wrote the plays also had a cover bisecting the Droeshout portrait with one of Edward de Vere (*The Mysterious William Shakespeare: The Myth and the Reality*); and the same design concept shaped the jacket of Graham Philips' *The Shakespeare Conspiracy* and, cartoonishly tongue-in-cheek, for James Shapiro's scholarly account of the controversy in *Contested Will*. Boosted by some high-profile supporters in the theatre industry, including Derek Jacobi and Mark Rylance, a federation of authorship sceptics launched an online campaign to encourage signatories to a 'Declaration of Reasonable doubt about the Identity of William Shakespeare'. Their logo was, inevitably, a version of the familiar engraving, this time with the features replaced by a large question mark.[116] The significance of the portrait to authorship debates continues: a circular email headed 'Shakespeare First Folio' I received in 2014 from shakespeareauthorship.co.uk read: 'It is with the utmost pleasure we write to announce the Martin Droeshout engraving and Stratford Monument have been decoded' (the answer was a hidden cryptogram pointing to Lady Jane Grey).

Even those who were not concerned to revise the identity of the portrait's subject were still interested in what it might reveal about the author. William Blake claimed to have discussed the Droeshout engraving with Shakespeare himself on the beach at Felpham, and reported that 'he is exactly like the old engraving which is said to be a bad one. I think it very good.'[117] In his *Shakespeare's Portraits Phrenologically Considered*, E. T. Craig was reassured

[115] Calvin Hoffman, *The Man Who Was Shakespeare* (London: Max Parrish, 1955), p. 67.
[116] http://doubtaboutwill.org (accessed April 2015).
[117] M. H. Speilmann, *The Title-Page of the First Folio of Shakespeare's Plays: A Comparative Study of the Droeshout Portrait and the Stratford Monument* (London: Oxford University Press, 1924), p. 51.

that his analysis of the Droeshout engraving revealed Shakespeare's 'large benevolence, veneration and ideality, and his small
destructiveness and acquisitiveness leading to his control over
his feelings and generous sympathy for others': although Craig
did not mention it, this judgement was particularly useful
in countering some of the negative biographical claims about
Shakespeare's personality.[118] Writing in the *Book of Homage to
Shakespeare* in 1916 for the tercentenary of Shakespeare's death,
M. H. Speilmann praised the 'frank young English face—the calm
placidity of its observant gaze, the delicate firmness of features and
expression, the characteristic aspect of large sympathy held in
control by critical judgement, the strong reserve of individuality'
in its lineaments, suggesting that 'we have here, then, the
Shakespeare of the Sonnets and of *Love's Labour's Lost* rather
than the Shakespeare of the Tragedies': just right for the middle
of the war.[119] In 1996, *The Times* reported that German surgeons
had diagnosed Mikulicz's syndrome, a cancer of the tear duct,
from a swelling evident in the left eye of the portrait, and this
pathology joins other diagnoses from the portrait including various explanations—tumour, fatty prolapse, or lymphoma—for a
perceived lump over the eyebrow. Research into the Droeshout
engraving alongside other portraits has discovered 'a series of
signs pointing to a long-term systemic illness from which the
poet was suffering'.[120] Everyone, from gentlemen's tailors to
physicians to criminologists, has had something to interpret
from the Droeshout engraving.

[118] Marjorie Garber, 'Looking the Part', in Stephanie Nolen et al. (eds), *Shakespeare's Face* (London: Piatkus, 2003), pp. 156–77; p. 162.

[119] Israel Gollancz, *A Book of Homage to Shakespeare* (London: Oxford University
Press, 1916), pp. 6–7.

[120] *The Times*, 24 April 1996; Hildegard Hammerschmidt-Hummel, *The True
Face of William Shakespeare: The Poet's Death Mask and Likenesses from Three Periods
of His Life* (London: Chaucer, 2006), pp. 68, 131.

The interest in forensic technologies and the conspiratorial quality of authorship theories made J. L. Carroll's best-selling thriller *The Shakespeare Secret* (2007) an inevitable, but belated, supplement. Watching as a second research library goes up in flames, the young American Shakespearean scholar, Kate Stanley, faces a serial killer whose target is First Folios. The dangerous Foliocide warns her to keep out via one of its torn-out pages— from the misogynistically violent *Titus Andronicus*. She realizes that 'the bastard responsible was willing to kill, to burn whole buildings, just to destroy Folios'—in order to erase their secretly coded evidence about their authorship. At the Jesuit College in Valladolid, Stanley encounters a copy (imaginary) of the First Folio marked with a chimerical beast, a composite of the crests of Derby, Pembroke, Bacon and Oxford. The proof of the theory of collaborative aristocratic authorship is inscribed, like so many of the other interpretations discussed in this chapter, on the copy of the Folio itself. The mastermind turns out to be a knight of the realm whose crazed confession is that Shakespeare's reputation must be protected from the claims of aristocratic pretenders because 'the Stratford boy's story illustrates a point that matters a great deal: genius can strike anywhere . . . Shakespeare once helped me pull myself up from the gutter'.[121] But the book draws back from its own genocidal conceit of Folio destruction. The thespian psychopath turns out to have preserved the priceless Folios in his own library, encapsulating the story's love–hate relationship with the book. Carroll's mystery revives the Baconian biliteral cypher of Elizabeth Gallup alongside more recent interest in Shakespeare's Catholicism and the identity of 'Cardenio' or 'Cardenno', a now-lost play by Shakespeare and John Fletcher based on *Don Quixote*. As it shuttles between university libraries and eccentric private collectors and between detailed scholarship and equally detailed fancy, *The Shakespeare Secret* is murderously fascinated by the First

---

[121] J. L. Carroll, *The Shakespeare Secret* (London: Sphere, 2008), pp. 93, 444.

Folio as a kind of Shakespearean grail quest, just as its detective hero entertains ambivalent feelings towards her own academic training. This enjoyably earnest thriller thus epitomizes some of the many ways the First Folio has been deployed, valued, and decoded, inside the academy and without.

CHAPTER 4

Performing

Early editions of Shakespeare's plays published during his life-time in the single-play quarto form tended to serve as a kind of advertisement for their playing company. So, for example, the 1608 text of *King Lear* boasted that it had been performed 'before the Kings Majesty at White-Hall' and that commoners might also experience 'his Majesties servants performing usually at the Globe on the Bank-side'. As part of its more aspirational presentation, however, the Folio edition appears to have minimized the theatrical origins of its contents. Nowhere does the book mention the King's Men, who were still one of the predominant playing companies in London in 1623, and, instead, the repeated emphasis, in a dedicatory letter 'To the Great Variety of Readers', is 'reade him therefore; and againe, and againe'. Only a couple of allusions to performance in the dedicatory material and a list of 'principal actors', headed by Shakespeare's name, acknowledge the plays' life in the early modern playhouses including the Theatre, the Globe, and Blackfriars. To be canonical, lasting, and significant, and to find a place in libraries and important book collections, these plays apparently needed to shed the topicality and ephemerality of performance. The hefty Folio was presented as Shakespeare's 'monument', a format designed for the study rather than the stage. Nevertheless, the relation of the Folio to the theatre, the extent to which its texts have been valued because of their perceived proximity to the plays' first performances, or the instructions they include for future productions, has been a constant theme, and the book's ownership, use and idolization by generations of actors and theatre professionals, is the topic of this chapter.

Many early readers, as already discussed in Chapter 2, display their attention to the plays as drama on the pages of the Folio by emending errant speech prefixes or correcting serial speeches into dramatically appropriate to-and-fro conversations. Occasionally these readers use their knowledge of what is characterologically plausible to reassign speeches, as in the example of the Friar complimenting Juliet in *Romeo and Juliet*, or, more individually, the decorous reallocation of Rosalind's polymorphously flirtatious address to her husband-to-be, Orlando, in *As You Like It*. In a handful of cases discussed in the same chapter, readers have addressed themselves to inadequate, missing, or otherwise problematic stage directions. All these annotations would be irrelevant if the primary focus of readerly engagement was towards commonplacing. Several readers from the late seventeenth century onwards add lists of *dramatis personae*, as in Constanter Huygens' copy, where such a list is written into the space at the end of *Romeo and Juliet*.[1] All these forms of reading engage with the specifically dramatic apparatus of the text, and thus show a particular generic awareness of theatre and its possible realizations on a real or imagined stage. Readers of First Folios in the seventeenth century were, then, variously alert to the plays' theatrical qualities. In correcting the specifically dramatic apparatus of the plays, such as speech prefixes and stage directions, even armchair readers showed an attention to the works as theatre.

Other Folio copies, however, record more active theatre-making practices. The first recorded purchaser of a First Folio, the Kentish gentleman and courtier, Sir Edward Dering, was keen

---

[1] West 133. There are a number of character lists in other copies including West 90 and 112.

on amateur performance with family and friends at his manor in Surrenden. He bought playbooks and costumes, and may well have organized scribal copies of scripts for performance. One of these, apparently his own conflation of the two parts of Shakespeare's *Henry IV* prepared in the early 1620s, survives in the Folger Shakespeare Library.[2] It is not possible to identify decisively whether either of Dering's two First Folio copies is still extant, although it has been suggested that a copy now in the University of Padua that has been marked up for early performance might be associated with Surrenden.[3] In this case, the book provided the base-text on which a theatrically-minded reader could build their own particular dramatic script for performance, noting the actors, props, blocking, and cuts necessary for a specific staging or occasion now lost to us. The Padua Folio probably offers the earliest extant examples of performance scripts superimposed in manuscript on the Folio text. *Macbeth*, *Measure for Measure*, and *The Winter's Tale* have all been marked up in handwriting and style consistent with the conventions of the pre-Restoration theatrescape.

A manuscript note for a 'Senett' at the beginning of *Macbeth* 4.4 suggests such an early date, since the OED's references to this theatrical sound are all Elizabethan or Jacobean. In 1960, presenting a collotype facsimile of the Padua Folio, G. Blakemore Evans made a case that the names of actors overlapped with names found in theatrical and other documents associated with Sir Edward Dering, although a later publication retracted this speculation.[4] The reshapings for performance involve cutting elements

---

[2] See G. Blakemore Evans, 'The "Dering MS" of Shakespeare's "Henry IV" and Sir Edward Dering', *Journal of English and Germanic Philology* 54 (1955), pp. 498–503.

[3] G. Blakemore Evans (ed.), *Shakespearean Prompt-books of the Seventeenth Century* (Charlottesville, Virginia: Bibliographical Society of Virginia, 1960), vol. I, pp. 7–8.

[4] Evans (1960), pp. 7–8; G. Blakemore Evans, 'New Evidence on the Provenance of the Padua Prompt-books of Shakespeare's *Macbeth*, *Measure for Measure*, and *The Winter's Tale*', *Studies in Bibliography* 20 (1967), pp. 239–42.

unpalatable to mid-seventeenth-century audiences, including the bawdy prose of the Porter who grumbles as he replies to the knocking on the castle gate in *Macbeth* [2.3] for instance, or certain profanities or examples of loose talk in *Measure for Measure*. Other cuts seem designed to reduce the length of Macbeth's part, perhaps so as to be less onerous for an amateur actor—or at least, one less experienced than the chief King's Men tragedian Richard Burbage. Thus the interview between Macbeth and the murderers he has commissioned to assassinate Banquo and his son is cut [3.1]. The long scene in which Malcolm tests Macduff by convincingly listing his imagined faults has often been found unsettling in performance, and it is here substantially trimmed [4.3]. Some manuscript notes call for emblematic props: a 'Cauldorne' for the witches, and a 'Treade' to indicate horses' hooves, are evocative but probably manageable within the everyday inventory of an amateur performance context.[5] At some points, the annotator has written in a larger, more visible hand entrance directions that are already in the Folio (for example 'Chardge. Flourish. K: Malcolm, Donalbain, Lenox, Captaine' in the space around the 'Scena Seconda' heading on the play's first folio page). This, and many similar examples, often marked off by horizontal lines, suggests that the Folio, with its relatively small fount and cramped layout was itself used in the theatrical environment. Highlighting stage business amid its close type was a practical necessity. In the Padua text of *Measure for Measure*, there are a couple of so-called anticipatory entries, including the imperatives to the grimly named prison hangman, 'Bee ready Abhorson' and 'Bee ready' [4.2 and 4.3]. These are apparently practical reminders since in the first case a number of intervening lines have been cut, and in the second the entry comes soon after the turned page. The absence of elaborate stage directions and props and the apparent intent to trim large speaking roles all point to amateur performance, by a company

---

[5] Evans (1960), p. 29.

including Mr K., Mr Carlile, T. S., Mr G., E. H. and Mr H., all names or initials used in the manuscript some time in the early decades after the book was published. It is worth remembering that none of these three plays existed in any more portable printed format at this period in the seventeenth century: any putative performance would therefore need to be based on the Folio.

If the copy now in Padua gives us the earliest known performance First Folio, the so called Nursery Prompt-books of *The Comedy of Errors* and *A Midsummer Night's Dream* amassed by the inveterate book collector James Orchard Halliwell-Phillips (1820–1889), and now in the University of Edinburgh, probably come chronologically next. These two plays have been separated from the larger volume and bound individually to make them into manageable theatrical scripts. The names written in by the prompter or other theatre professional are recognizable as members of one of the two theatre companies licensed by Charles II on his restoration to the monarchy. Mr Biggs (who played Antipholus of Ephesus) and Mr Disney (his Syracusan twin), Mrs Cooke, who played Luciana, and Mr and Mrs Coysh (Dromio of Ephesus and Adriana) were all members of Thomas Killigrew's King's Company performing at Drury Lane in London in the 1660s and 1670s. It is probable that the texts were used by an offshoot of the King's Company, the Nursery Company of younger players, either in Hatton Garden or possibly for touring, in Norwich and elsewhere.[6] The speech prefixes in the First Folio identify the Antipholus twins in an inconsistent and sometimes confusing way. Interestingly, no other extant copy suggest that this was a problem to early readers: it only emerges as an ambiguity when using the Folio as a performance text. The Nursery annotator has standardized these to make it clear how the speeches divide

---

[6] See entries in Philip H. Highfell Jr, Kalman A. Burnim, and Edward A. Laghans, *A Biographical Dictionary of Actors, Actresses, Musicians, Dancers, Managers & Other Stage Personnel in London, 1660–1800* (Carbondale and Edwardsville: Southern Illinois University Press, 1975).

between the actors. This already short play has been cut by about one-fifth, with particular attention to trimming very long speeches. There are directions for added songs and dances (the play is unique among the comedies in having no scripted music in the First Folio). The other play, *A Midsummer Night's Dream*, may show pre-preparation for performance: it has been marked up for cutting, but has no other annotations or casting decisions. Of these five First Folio plays marked up for seventeenth century performance that are now in Padua and in Edinburgh, *A Midsummer Night's Dream* is the only play that was also potentially available to theatre companies in the single-work quarto format (editions were published in 1600 and 1619). Some further marked-up pages from *Hamlet* originally from the same Folio form part of two composite copies at the Folger Shakespeare library.[7]

Other copies show signs of localized mark-up with performance, probably amateur, in mind. The copy now in Wadham College, Oxford, seems to have its text of *1 Henry IV* adapted for performance, perhaps in the later eighteenth century (Figure 4.1).[8] This preparation includes cutting substantial portions of the text, apparently for dramaturgical reasons, and reshaping the scenic organization. There is a note, for example, after the end of Walter Blount's ineffective parley with the rebel Hotspur, 'Act ends here' [4.3], and the final scene of Act 4 is cut. The character of the Vintner who appears only in one tavern scene is crossed out and replaced with 'Hostess', probably to save an actor in a busy scene that already demands eight actors. Cuts in this copy are marked on the page with a freehand ink box around the deleted lines. Other more local excisions seem to be designed to take out unpalatable material, such as the line 'where the gluttons dogs licked his sores' [4.3.25–6]. No other play in this copy bears any similar performance-oriented annotation.

---

[7] West 139 and West 140.   [8] West 35.

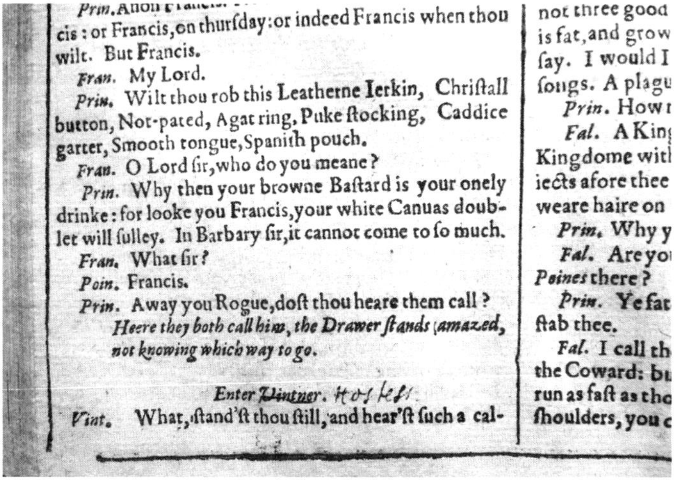

FIG. 4.1. Wadham copy *Henry IV*

These annotations mark up the text of *I Henry IV* for amateur performance.

Coincidentally, the St-Omer copy, discovered in the library of a former English Jesuit College in France in 2014, is also marked up for performance of *1 Henry IV*. Drama was an important pedagogical tool in Jesuit educational practice for teaching boys Latin and rhetoric, as well as a range of other skills: memory, confidence, musical accomplishment, and even dancing and deportment.[9] A majority of plays for the Jesuit theatre were tragedies on historical themes, drawing out typologies or didactic messages: Shakespeare plays were apt for adaptation in this context.[10] G. Blakemore Evans has found a number of play transcripts for use at the college at Douai at the end of the seventeenth century

[9] Jan Graffius, 'A Gift from Poetry', *Times Literary Supplement*, 4 February 2015.

[10] Alison Shell, *Catholicism, Controversy, and the English Literary Imagination, 1558–1660* (Cambridge: Cambridge University Press, 1999), chapter 6.

and demonstrated that a Second Folio was the source.[11] St-Omer produced large numbers of plays and declamation exercises for both internal and external audiences of civic or ecclesiastical dignitaries. By the end of the seventeenth century, the college could boast 'a Wardrobe for the Stage, Music-schools, a Great Theatre, a Little Theatre and a Common Magazine of the two Theatres in addition to a substantial drama library'. Stage directions in extant Latin tragedies by the seventeenth century St-Omer playwright, Joseph Simons, suggest a well-equipped performance space with a forestage and curtained discovery spaces or alcoves upstage.[12] Even before the rediscovery of the St-Omer Folio, Martin Wiggins had made a convincing case that at least one of the dramatists associated with the Jesuit college had access to an early copy of Shakespeare's collected plays. The author of the St-Omer Latin historical play 'Innocentia Purpurata' about the end of the reign of Henry VI, had used a number of elements unique to Folio texts of Shakespeare's *Henry 3 VI*, *King John*, and *All's Well that Ends Well*: Wiggins argues that 'evidently the dramatist had his Folio open before him as he wrote'.[13] The dramatist is recorded as Father Clarke, most probably the Francis Clarke who was St-Omer's Professor of Humanities in the 1650s.

Wiggins' analysis shows how the St-Omer First Folio was used and cannibalized for new historical plays in the seventeenth century. The annotations on the copy of the First Folio itself date from a later period but show some continuities with these uses. The text of *1 Henry IV* is cut, excising unsuitable material: the 'beastly shamelesse transformation | by those Welshwomen done' in the account of the battle [1.1.44–5], and the 'tongues of Bawdes'

---

[11] G. Blakemore Evans, 'The Douai Manuscript: Six Shakespearean Transcripts (1694–5), *Philological Quarterly* 41 (1962), pp. 158–63.

[12] William H. McCabe, *An Introduction to the Jesuit Theater: a posthumous work* (St Louis: Institute of Jesuit Sources, 1983), p. 126.

[13] Martin Wiggins, 'Shakespeare Jesuited: The Plagiarisms of "Pater Clarcus"' *The Seventeenth Century* 20 (2005), pp. 1–21; p. 15.

and 'Wench in Flame-coloured Taffeta' [1.2.8–11] that Prince
Hal bandies with Falstaff are all marked for deletion in the first
page opening. A—probably—nineteenth-century hand has added
'Exit' and 'Exeunt omnes' stage directions in the Gad's Hill scene,
changed Peto's speeches to 'Poins', and marked the scene with
Hotspur's wife Kate (2.4) 'left out'. The Hostess has been changed
into 'Host' throughout, and all references to Mistress Quickly
excised. Jesuit plays did not include female roles, and clearly
Henry IV 1 has been cut to omit them. One added stage direction,
when the Sheriff demands entrance to the tavern, follows mid-
nineteenth-century editions in its phrasing: 'Knocking is heard,
exeunt Bardolph and Host'.[14] In the text of *Henry V*, shorter
scenes, perhaps for set-piece performance or declamation, have
been identified in pencil note: the King's 'Call in the Messengers'
reads 'Begin', and the note 'end' is added just before the Chorus's
speech [1.2.221–310]. Another scenelet is marked similarly
between the Dauphin's address to 'My most redoubted Father' to
the end of the act [2.4.14–146]; a third shapes out Mountjoy's
interaction with the King after the capture of Harfleur
[3.6.115–70]; and a fourth focuses on the famous St Crispin's
day speech [4.3.20–130].

The so-called 'Nursery copy' named actors who were associated
with Thomas Killigrew (1612–83), the playwright and theatre
manager who returned from exile with Charles II in 1660, and,
together with William Davenant, was granted a royal duopoly on
dramatic performance. Killigrew's particular advantage for his
King's Company was the exclusive right to the plays of Ben
Jonson, but the rights to Shakespeare were divided between the
two companies. After a protracted legal dispute with his father,
Charles Killigrew (1655–1724/5) took over the company together
with Thomas's post of Master of the Revels. He ran the Theatre

---

[14] Samuel Burdett Hemingway, *A New Variorum Edition of Shakespeare: Henry
the Fourth Part I* (Philadelphia and London: J. B. Lippincott Company, 1936),
p. 167.

Royal, Drury Lane, rather ineffectually, and was accused of inconsistently conducting his office of licensing plays. He was officially reprimanded for insufficient attention to his duties in 1699, and later was criticized by Colley Cibber for his 'zealous Severity' as Master of the Revels. Cibber remarked that 'he would strike out whole scenes of a vicious or immoral character', including the entire first act of Cibber's adaptation of *Richard III* because it 'might put Weak people too much in mind of King *James*, then living in *France*'.[15] Killigrew owned a copy of the First Folio with which he did not deal in such a censorious way. His well-used and grubby book, now in Meisei University in Tokyo, seems to have been an early issue of the Folio since it does not include *Troilus and Cressida*.[16] The copy bears his large signature on the title page and again at the foot of the list of actors, as well as a rough sketch of a dog, perhaps a hunting breed, curled into a circle. The majority of the marks of reading in this copy are commonplacing marks, underlinings and stars by lines and passages of particular note: it has no obviously theatrical annotation. Another copy, which used also to be identified with Killigrew and is now in the Folger, has the beginnings of a list of characters for *The Winter's Tale* and the name 'T.Killig.'.[17] It is possible this has something to do with a planned production of *The Winter's Tale*, one of the plays to which Killigrew was granted the performance rights by Charles II in 1669, but for which no records of early Restoration performance survive.

Killigrew's library was extensive: a sale in December 1725 contained 'several Thousand Volumes of the most Valuable Books in Greek, Latin, English, French, Italian and Spanish',

---

[15] Judith Milhous and Robert D. Hume, 'Charles Killigrew's Petition about the Master of the Revels' Power as Censor (1715)', *Theatre Notebook* 41 (1987), pp. 74–9; p. 79; Colley Cibber, *An Apology for the Life of Mr Colley Cibber* (London: printed by John Watts for the author, 1740), p. 160.
[16] West 211.   [17] West 131.

but no English drama and no Shakespeare First Folio.[18] Apparently the volume had passed to the dramatist, William Congreve (1670–1729): it is not clear whether it was a gift or purchase from Killigrew. The Shakespearean publisher, Jacob Tonson, described Congreve's library as 'genteel & well-chosen', and, urged his nephew to buy at the sale after Congreve's death, adding that his books included 'several notes of his own of corrections & everything from him will be very valuable'.[19] To his First Folio, Congreve added only a handful of such notes. Two in particular in the margin to *As You Like It* connect the book to the contemporary theatre world. Next to the exiled Lord's description of Jacques and the deer [2.1.52], Congreve has written 'Anthony in all for Love by Dryden': the character Anthony in Dryden's reworking of *Antony and Cleopatra* imagines himself in 'a shady forest's sylvan scene' where a herd of deer pass. This passage has no equivalent in Shakespeare's play of Roman and Egyptian lovers but it does echo *As You Like It* here. Similarly, the phrase about the panting and wounded stag whose sides are 'almost to bursting' [2.1.38] with effort on the same page in the Folio has the annotation 'Spanish fryer' in the margin. This is the title of another play by Dryden, but it is not so clear what the specific reference is, if any.

Dryden was the pre-eminent Shakespearean of the Restoration, through his reworkings of Shakespeare's plays for the stage, and his influential critical statements defending Shakespeare against Francophile neoclassicism: he 'need[ed] not the spectacles of Books to read Nature; he look'd inwards, and found her there'. In his *An Essay of Dramatick Poesie* (1668) he compared Jonson with Shakespeare: 'I admire him, but I love Shakespeare'.[20]

---

[18] *Catalogus Librorum in omni fere scientia & facultate prasetantium; ex bibliothecis Caroli Killigrew* (London: Gyles Fletcher, 1725).
[19] Quoted in John C. Hodges, *The Library of William Congreve* (New York: New York Public Library, 1955), p. 9.
[20] John Dryden, *An Essay of Dramatick Poesie*, in Samuel Holt Monk (ed.), *The Works of John Dryden: Prose 1668–1691. An Essay of Dramatick Poesie and Shorter*

Dryden is cited in several other First Folios: two copies now in the
Folger library have passages from Dryden on Shakespeare on the
front flyleaf, and another copy now in Paris has the comment
'better in Dryden' against *The Tempest* (along with the approba-
tions 'pretty good' and 'good' against other comedies).[21] Dryden,
together with Davenant, had rewritten *The Tempest* as *The
Enchanted Island* in 1667, with new characters, and a Prologue
alluding to the absence of Shakespeare from the stage which
began: 'As when a Tree's cut down the secret root | Lives under
ground, and thence new Branches shoot | So, from old Shake-
spear's honour'd dust, this day | Springs up and buds a new
reviving Play'.[22] The copy associated with the parliamentarian
household of Colonel Hutchinson has annotations alluding to
Dryden, including a version of his observation 'But Shakespeare's
magic could not copied be; | Within that circle none durst walk
but he' next to lines from *Macbeth*.[23] The unattributed eighteenth-
century manuscript verse in the beginning of the Bodleian's Folio
also asserts Shakespeare's superiority, claiming 'the great Effort |
In Dryden and the rest, has since fell short'.[24] These Folios
participate in an explicit comparison between Shakespeare and
more contemporary writers and are updated to take account of
later critical and literary history. They also register a particular
moment in critical history in the later seventeenth century, when
Dryden was the predominant reference point for Shakespearean
appreciation and analysis.

Works (Berkeley; Los Angeles; London: University of California Press, 1971),
pp. 55, 58.

   [21] West 71 and West 129; West 194.
   [22] John Dryden, *The Tempest or The Enchanted Island*, in Maximillian E. Novak
(ed.), *The Works of John Dryden. Plays. The Tempest. Tyrannick Love. An Evening's
Love* (Berkeley; Los Angeles; London: University of California Press, 1970), p. 6.
   [23] West 112.   [24] West 32.

The Killigrew First Folio that passed to Congreve was handed on in turn to his natural daughter, Mary, via her mother, Henrietta, Lady Godolphin. A satirical squib at Henrietta's death in 1733 recorded lewdly that 'the Works of *Congravino* gave her the greatest satisfaction'.[25] Henrietta's will left to Mary 'Al Mr Congreves Personal Estate that he Left Me'. Mary married Thomas Osborne, the 4th Duke of Leeds and the First Folio passed to Mary's son, Francis, an amateur playwright. The book remained in the possession of the Leeds family at Hornby Castle in Yorkshire until a sale in 1930.[26] At some point it suffered an interesting wound: in reply to Sidney Lee's request for information on copies for his 1902 *Census*, Stuart P. Reid filled in the information about the Duke of Leeds' copy: 'apparently the first half of the volume was dinted by a bullet, but it has been skilfully repaired and the injury is now almost invisible'.[27]

If Dryden shaped Shakespeare's reputation in the seventeenth century, then his 'self-proclaimed representative on earth' in the eighteenth was the actor David Garrick (1717–79).[28] Garrick collected a large library of plays, including a First Folio. He made these available to many late-eighteenth-century scholars, among them the editors, Edward Capell and George Steevens, the antiquarian, Bishop Thomas Percy, and the Oxford Professor of Poetry, Thomas Warton. Steevens suggested that Garrick had paid £1 16s to the bookseller, Thomas Payne, for the book around 1760.[29] Garrick left 'all my Collection of old English plays' to the

---

[25] Anon, *The Court Parrot: A New Miscellany in Prose and Verse* (London: 1733), sig. C2.

[26] C. Y. Ferdinand, D. F. McKenzie, 'Congreve, William (1670–1729)', *Oxford Dictionary of National Biography*, Oxford University Press, 2004; online edn, Jan 2008, http://www.oxforddnb.com/view/article/6069, accessed April 2015.

[27] Shakespeare Birthplace Trust: ER85/6/1.

[28] Jonathan Bate, *Shakespearean Constitutions: Politics, Theatre, Criticism* (Oxford: Clarendon Press, 1989), p. 30.

[29] George Steevens and Samuel Johnson (eds), *The Plays of William Shakspere, in Fifteen Volumes* (London: 1793), vol. 1, p. 446.

British Museum on his death in 1779, but the Trustees were concerned on visiting Garrick's house in Adelphi Terrace that the copy of 'Shakespeare's Works in Folio' was not among the books ready for transfer to the Museum.[30] Further approaches to Garrick's nephew, Carrington Garrick, to whom the rest of the library had been bequeathed, and to his widow apparently went unanswered, and the Folio was never received by the British Museum. Steevens wrote that 'after the death of our Roscius, it should have accompanied his collection of old plays to the British Museum; but had been taken out of his library, and has not been heard of since'.[31] Two years later, on the death of Garrick's wife, Eva Maria, the book appeared as lot 2405 at the sale of his books and other items, where it was acquired by the bookseller, Thomas Thorpe, for £34 2s 6d, sold on to Thomas Jolley and then again in his sale in 1844.[32]

Garrick's own fame continued to inspire later collectors, and his relics were commonly intermingled with Shakespeare's in important collections. Both Angela Burdett Coutts and Henry Folger specialized in Garrick letters and other memorabilia alongside their First Folio purchases, and Horace Howard Furness kept a pair of gloves given to him by Fanny Kemble in gratitude for his work on the New Variorum, that claimed a Shakespearean provenance but had more immediate theatrical associations. Furness wrote: 'That they are veritably Shakespeare's Gloves, I hope; that they belonged to Garrick, Mrs. Siddons & Mrs. Kemble, I know, and with that I am satisfied.'[33] The Garrick Folio is now in

---

[30] George M. Kahrl and Dorothy Anderson, *The Garrick Collection of Old English Plays* (London: British Library, 1982), pp. 47–8; Steevens (1793), vol. 1, p. 446.

[31] Steevens (1793), p. 446.

[32] *A Catalogue of the Library, Splendid Books of Prints, Political and Historical Tracts of David Garrick Esq* (London: Saunders, 1823), p. 81.

[33] James M. Gibson, 'Horace Howard Furness: Book Collector and Library Builder', in Georgianna Ziegler (ed.), *Shakespeare Study Today: The Howard Horace Furness Memorial Lectures* (New York: AMS Press, 1986), pp. 169–89; p. 176.

Queen's College, Oxford, who bought it in 1850; it bears the inscription 'Coll.Reg. Oxon. Munificentia Robert Mason', marking the gift of a former student with which the college acquired the book. The book carries the actor's bookplate: an engraved cartouche with his name, topped with a bust of Shakespeare, and a French motto from the popular table talk of the French philosopher, Gilles Ménage.

But the absence of any other distinctive markers of his ownership in the book attests to Garrick's ambivalent relationship with the early texts of Shakespeare. Garrick's prominent contemporary reputation for reintroducing the texts of Shakespeare was recorded in his monument in Westminster Abbey: 'Though sunk in death the forms the poet drew, the actor's genius bade them breathe anew; though, like the Bard himself, in night they lay, immortal Garrick call'd them back to day.' The idea that Garrick had newly restored Shakespeare's plays to the stage was much-repeated. But in fact, Garrick's play texts were always heavily cut and reworked to suit contemporary tastes and performance structures. His abridgements of *Winter's Tale* as *Florizel and Perdita*, or *Taming of the Shrew* as *Catharine and Petruchio* were only the most extreme examples of 'his astuteness as Shakespeare's dramaturge'.[34] One eighteenth-century addition to his Folio just may relate to one of his theatrical innovations: a new production of *Coriolanus* at Drury Lane in 1754, cut by more than a third, and with the Irish actor, Henry Mossop, in the title role (Garrick knew he was too physically slight to be a convincing military general). Garrick's *Coriolanus* was a commercial attempt to rival Thomas Sheridan's popular reworked version at Covent Garden, but it ran for only a few performances. A flowing pencil hand in Garrick's First Folio has begun to use the blank page adjacent to the opening of Coriolanus to produce a list of 'Actors' (copying the Folio's word for such a

---

[34] Michael Caines, *Shakespeare and the Eighteenth Century* (Oxford: Oxford University Press, 2013), p. 88.

list, although it is more properly a record of characters), but it has given up after the first three named characters to enter the play-world. One study of Garrick identifies his period as one 'before editors and actors went their separate ways', and Garrick's scant attention to his First Folio certainly corresponds with that of many contemporary editors.[35] Garrick's approach to the text of Shakespeare both in the study and in the theatre was less attentive than might be expected from the persistent myth that he had restored Shakespeare to the stage. His First Folio, more or less unmarked save for his bookplate, is thus the bibliographic equivalent of his elaborate Shakespeare Jubilee at Stratford in 1769, which famously included none of Shakespeare's plays.

Garrick's presence is actually more keenly felt elsewhere in First Folio copies. There are numerous modern annotations among an assemblage of pages from different copies, bought by Folger in 1920, which cite the actor. These include notes in *1 Henry IV* that 'Garrick acted Hotspur 1746' and 'Restored by Theobald and here by Garrick'.[36] One other copy links Garrick to a particular role—the jealous king, Leontes, in *The Winter's Tale*, alongside Hannah Pritchard as Hermione—a role she first played in 1756. Although there is no acknowledgement of this in the copy of the First Folio, the play as printed must have seemed very different from Garrick's adaptation of it as *Florizel and Perdita*, cut to form half of a double-bill performance. Its prologue, spoken by Garrick himself, stated "Tis my chief Wish, my Joy, my only Plan | To lose no Drop of that immortal man' while acknowledging the original 'five long acts, from which our three are taken', and confining itself entirely to Bohemia and to the adulthood of Perdita.[37] A series of other lists—alongside *All's Well that Ends Well*, *Twelfth Night*,

[35] Vanessa Cunningham, *Shakespeare and Garrick* (Cambridge: Cambridge University Press, 2008), p. 13.

[36] West 139.

[37] David Garrick, *Florizel and Perdita: A Dramatic Pastoral in Three Acts* (London: J. and R. Tonson, 1758), 'Prologue' (n.p.).

Hamlet and *Timon of Athens*—also link these plays to specific late-eighteenth-century productions. *Twelfth Night* carries two separate accounts: the space to the right of the closing ornament identifies performers including Packer, Palmer, O'Brien, Yates, Love, and Vernon, who all played in a Drury Lane production in 1763–4. The adjacent list is dated 'Dec. 10 1771', the opening night of the Drury Lane production, a revival of Garrick's 1751 production with a cast headed by Thomas King as Malvolio.[38] *All's Well* lists the cast who performed at Drury Lane on October 23 1762. The list for *Timon* adds Edmund 'Kean' in the title role, Henry 'Bengough' as Apemantus, Henry 'Wallack' as Alcibiades' and 'Holland' as Flavius, and refers to a later production, an adaptation by George Lamb at Drury Lane in October 1816. The playbill for the production promised 'appropriate splendour', an 'incidental ballet' and Miss Tree, Mrs Vedy and Miss Hart as 'Amazons'.[39] Clearly this Folio is connected with the Drury Lane theatre in the later eighteenth century, although it has not been possible to trace the 'Robt Tomkins' who signed his name on the volume in 1789.[40]

Drury Lane theatre is cited in another Folger volume assembled from leaves originally belonging to different copies. Next to *As You Like It*, an annotation updates the play with reference to *Love in a Forest*, the adaptation by 'Dr Cha. Johnson in the year 1723'; the same reader has also written in a reference to John Lacy's *Sauny the Scot*, an adaptation of *The Taming of the Shrew*, first performed in 1667.[41] Both comparisons set a distinctly different stage adaptation as a reference point for the Folio text, and like these other First Folio references to Restoration adaptations, embody what

[38] Charles Beecher Hogan, *Shakespeare in the Theatre 1701–1800* (Oxford: Clarendon Press, 1957), vol. ii, pp. 659–61.
[39] Playbill reproduced at the Victoria and Albert Museum Theatre Collection: http://collections.vam.ac.uk/item/O1169422/eddison-collection-album-kean-edmund (accessed April 2015).
[40] West 176.   [41] West 103.

Michael Dobson has identified as the apparent paradox of 'the urge to enshrine Shakespeare's texts as national treasures with the desire to alter their content'. These annotations are miniature examples of those 'mutually reinforcing' processes of canonization and adaptation in the period.[42] A copy now in the Victoria and Albert Museum in London has a manuscript list of late seventeenth-and early-eighteenth-century plays, presumably either read or seen in the theatre by an early owner. This includes works by Beaumont and Fletcher, Dryden, Nahum Tate, John Crowne, Margaret Cavendish and Thomas Otway, and serves to situate Shakespeare's plays within a wider contemporary theatrical context.[43] Only one extant Folio records early modern Shakespeare performances. The Cary copy associated with Great Tew in Oxfordshire in the 1630s and now at the University of Glasgow, as discussed in Chapter 2, has a particular eye to the theatrical past. Someone, perhaps the enthusiastic playgoer, Lucius Cary, has marked the list of actors with notes including 'eye-witness', 'by report', by hearsay'. This reader obviously wants to record his playgoing experience in the pages of the book, capturing the moment of personal overlap with the book's receding point of theatrical origin.[44]

Other actors who, following Garrick, owned First Folios include Edmund Kean (1789–1833): a sale of 'a unique selection of valuables' belonging to Kean was held in Covent Garden in 1834, and included a snuff box presented by Byron and a First Folio 'presented by Stephen Price Esq., at New York'.[45] Price was the owner of the Park Theatre and had brought Kean over to America in the autumn of 1820 to perform Richard III before packed audiences. It's not known where he got the Shakespeare

---

[42] Dobson, pp. 4–5.   [43] West 103.   [44] West 25.
[45] Edmund Kean, in James Fullarton Arnotte (ed.), *Sale Catalogues of Eminent Persons Volume 12: Actors* (London: Mansell, with Sotheby Parke Bernet Publications, 1975), pp. 367–78; p. 367; p. 374.

book from, but his gift to Kean is clearly an early exception to the standard direction of transatlantic Folio travel. John Philip Kemble (1757–1823), whose copy, now in the Sir John Soane Museum, was extensively washed, trimmed, and relaid onto new paper at the end of the eighteenth century, as part of 'a theatrical library which, as combining selectness and extent, is perhaps the finest in the kingdom'. The copy was not in the catalogue of Kemble's library sale, and was bought by James Boswell the Younger. One early memoir of Kemble praised him for instituting appropriate historical costume in his productions: 'every character henceforward assumed its proper habit; and taste and judgement were no longer offended by the most incongruous absurdities, and the violation of all historical authority'.[46] Thomas Dibdin's contemporaneous verdict on Kemble's costuming of his First Folio offers an enjoyable juxtaposition: 'The inlaying was on large paper, with blank leaves at the beginning and end: and the book, having been sumptuously bound in morocco by Mackinlay, and enclosed in a case of calf leather, cost its late owner exclusively of the first price, threescore guineas. As a specimen of genuine and tasteful restitution, it was a failure.'[47] Kemble's attitude to the material and theatrical Shakespeare clearly diverged. His Folio appears to have been bound into three separate volumes, although they have been amalgamated at some date since then: James Boaden noted that the book had been 'purified from stains, inlaid, bound into three volumes then into one. Thus sumptuously equipped, it was deposited in a neat case with a lock and key.'[48]

[46] John Ambrose Williams, *Memoirs of John Philip Kemble, Esq.* (London: John Bowley Wood, 1817), pp. 58, 22.

[47] T. F. Dibdin, *The Library Companion; or The Young Man's Guide and The Old Man's Comfort in the Choice of a Library* (London: Harding, Triphook and Lepard, 1825), p. 412.

[48] James Boaden, *An Inquiry into the Authenticity of Various Pictures and Prints, Which... have been offered to the public as portraits of Shakespeare* (London: Robert Triphook, 1824), p. 7.

The American tragedian, Edwin Forrest (1806–1872), bought copies of all four Shakespeare folios in the 1860 sale of the library of William E. Burton, the actor-manager, magazine publisher, and Shakespeare-lover (he called his son William Shakespeare Burton). The total cost was $775. Forrest had just returned to the stage in the role of Hamlet at Niblo's Garden in New York: it seems the Shakespeare Folio was just the symbol and talisman for this new venture. Forrest was known as 'a great lover of books', and kept the Folio on display at his house in Philadelphia.[49] In January 1873, only weeks after his death, Forrest's library was destroyed by fire. There may be an element of *schadenfreude* in the reference to the loss in a copy now in Trinity College Library: pasted in to the end-papers is a newspaper clipping recounting the destruction by fire of 'the most valuable portion' of Forrest's library, 'the Shakespearian part, which was very extensive, and contained many rare and valuable volumes'. The loss of a First Folio 'reduces the number of copies of this edition known to exist to thirty-nine'.[50] The charred pages of Forrest's Folio are kept in the Kislak Center for Special Collections at the University of Pennslyvania (Figure 4.2), although they are not catalogued and do not reach the minimum standard to be identified as a First Folio in the modern taxonomy developed by Anthony James West.[51]

Just as for most of the eighteenth century editors of Shakespeare who owned a First Folio it seems to have been a talisman rather than a work of professional reference, so too the actors and theatre managers who owned a copy before the twentieth century do not seem to have made any active use of it in their work. Augustin Daly's 'exceedingly good copy' of the First Folio was sold at

[49] Lawrence Barrett, *Edwin Forrest* (Boston, Mass.: 1881), p. 155.

[50] West 5.

[51] Anthony James West, 'A Model for Describing Shakespeare First Folios, With Descriptions of Selected Copies', *The Library* 21 (1999), pp. 1–49.

FIG. 4.2. Edwin Forrest's First Folio
The burnt remains of Forrest's First Folio, kept in a glass sarcophagus.

auction in 1900, along with copies of second, third and fourth folios.[52] Daly's successful theatre in New York had made Shakespearean comedy a central plank of its repertoire. In 1886, he accompanied a revival of *The Merry Wives of Windsor* with a publication combining the production's promptbook with a photo-lithographed facsimile of the first quarto publication (1602). Textual differences were again foregrounded the following

---

[52] *Auction Catalogue of the Library of Augustin Daly* (New York: 1900), p. 308.

year when his production of *The Taming of the Shrew* reintroduced the Folio's 'Induction' scene, which had been cut in the standard performance text since at least Garrick.[53] A letter to Daly from his company in cod-Elizabethan to mark the one hundredth performance of *Taming of the Shrew* had as the spoof postscript: 'Baconne, who never yet did care for ye "Taming of ye Shrew," nowe claimes its authorshippe.'[54] In 1888, Daly acquired copies of the four seventeenth-century Shakespeare Folios and a range of other valuable books—the First Folio had been imported to New York after the sale of the library of woollen merchant and fine-art collector Samuel Addington at Sotheby's in 1886. Writing in his *Plays for Puritans* of 1901, George Bernard Shaw observed that Daly 'thought no price too extravagant for an addition to his collection of Shakespear relics; but in arranging Shakespear's plays for the stage, he proceeded on the assumption that Shakespear was a botcher and he an artist'.[55] One recent editor acknowledges that for Daly 'fidelity and purity...were slippery terms' and describes his production as 'a proto-musical, proto-Cecil B. DeMille *Shrew*'.[56] Earlier editors were also interested in Daly's dramaturgical labours. As they put on *Merchant of Venice* in 1895, Horace Howard Furness wrote to Daly suggesting that 'the interpretation of one who has cogitated as much on the play as I have, is not altogether valueless'; he had mentioned Daly's production in the Variorum volume of *As You Like It* in one of the earliest references to a modern stage interpretation in

[53] Joseph Francis Daly, *The Life of Augustin Daly* (New York: 1917), pp. 395, 426.

[54] Daly, p. 431.

[55] George Bernard Shaw, *Plays for Puritans*, in *The Works of Bernard Shaw* (London: Constable, 1930–2), vol. IX, p. xxxiv.

[56] Barbara Hodgdon (ed.), *The Taming of the Shrew* (London: The Arden Shakespeare, 2010), p. 86.

editorial commentary.[57] Unsuprisingly, for a man whose professional success rested on his ability to marry words and images, Daly had a particular interest in extra-illustrated books.

Also keenly connected with American performance is the copy now in the Scheide Library at Princeton and recently given to the university.[58] The veteran Massachusetts politician, Edward Everett, has written on the flyleaf: 'It is said that the manuscript of the Pandects at Florence used to be exhibited with lighted tapers, as a sacred relic. I should be more inclined to pay that honour to a copy of the First Folio of Shakespeare', and signed it on the two hundredth anniversary of Shakespeare's death in Boston, April 1864.[59] The dated autographs of contemporary actors including Adelaide Ristori, Fanny Janauschek (both women were known for their performances of Lady Macbeth) and Edwin Booth (acclaimed for his Hamlet), follow: the latest is dated February 1880. Clearly, by the second half of the nineteenth century in East Coast America, Shakespeare's text had its most divine embodiment in contemporary actors.

This was some shift. The role of actors in the transmission of Shakespeare's plays into the First Folio had long been considered a regrettable one. Alexander Pope had described the actors as 'stage-editors' and explained the crux in *Henry V* when the dying Falstaff's 'Nose was a sharpe as a Pen, and a Table of greene fields' [2.3.16–7] as 'nonsense brought in by a mistake of the stage-editors, who printed from the common piecemeal-written Parts in the Play-house'. Pope elaborated inventively: 'A Table was here directed to be brought in, (it being a scene in a tavern where they drink at parting) and this direction crept into the text from the margin. Greenfield was the name of the Property man in that time who furnish'd implements &c. for the actors.'[60] Pope's

---

[57] Daly, p. 631.   [58] West 159.
[59] West 159.   [60] Pope (1725), vol. III, p. 422.

ingenious gloss explained the garbled line with reference both to the mechanics of theatrical performance and the exigencies of theatrical transmission: the players were thus doubly responsible. Lewis Theobald described the process by which corrupted texts had been printed: 'When the Players took upon them to publish his Works intire, every Theatre was ransack'd to supply the Copy; and Parts collected which had gone thro' as many Changes as Performers, either from Mutilations or Additions made to them. Hence we derive many Chasms and Incoherences in the Sense and Matter.'[61] In his proposal for his edition of 1756, Samuel Johnson noted that the labour of editing corrupt texts was amplified in the case of Shakespeare's plays because he 'sold them not to be printed, but to be played'. Thus they were subject to deleterious emendation 'by the affectation of the player'.[62] The full title of Edward Capell's 1767–8 edition made a clear distinction between texts that he judged had the authority of Shakespeare himself and those that were transmitted by actors: *Mr William Shakespeare his comedies histories and tragedies: set out by himself in quarto, or by the players his fellows in folio.*

Summarizing recent Shakespeare editions in 1845, the *Edinburgh Review* observed that two agents were generally blamed for errors in Shakespeare's texts: the printers and the players, who 'are said to have corrupted them by changes, chiefly of interpolation, calculated to fit the plays better for a coarse and uninstructed audience'.[63] Romantic readers of Shakespeare simultaneously extolled his poetic virtues while denigrating performance. Charles Lamb summarized this prevailing anti-theatricalism: 'the Lear of Shakespeare cannot be acted'. The implicit answer to the title of

---

[61] Theobald (1733), vol. I, p. xxxviii.

[62] Samuel Johnson, *Proposals for Printing, by Subscription, the Dramatick Works of William Shakespeare* (London: 1756), p. 3.

[63] *Edinburgh Review* on recent editions of Shakespeare (1845), quoted in Murphy (2003), p. 337.

his essay 'On the Tragedies of Shakspeare, Considered with Reference to their Fitness for Stage Representation' was 'not very'.[64] Sidney Lee, heir to the pre-twentieth century editorial tradition in many of his assumptions including this one, deplored the lack of 'genuine respect' accorded to the author's words once they reached the playhouse.[65] Anything unsatisfactory in the Folio texts was thus attributed to the lamentable intervention of theatrical exigencies in general and actors in particular. That Shakespeare's plays, including the First Folio, had had anything to do with actors and the theatre had come to be a matter of textual regret.

By the end of the nineteenth century, however, a new sense of gratitude to the two actors John Heminge and Henry Condell for their invaluable act of preservation was discernable. The rehabilitation of Heminge and Condell drew on, and reinforced, a changing sense of the authenticity and relative accuracy of the First Folio they presented to the public in 1623, as well as a new value for contemporary actors in the transmission of Shakespeare's plays. The Shakespearean actor, Henry Irving, became the first theatrical knight in 1895 (Gladstone had wanted to present the honour in 1883, but was then persuaded that Irving's liaison with Ellen Terry might make for embarrassing publicity). A year later Sir Henry was a guest of honour when a monument to Heminge and Condell was unveiled before the Lord Mayor and Sheriffs of the City of London and the American ambassador. While there is no evidence of Shakespeare ever attending a London church, both his fellow King's Men had been active parishioners of St Mary Aldermanbury, and as churchgoers and 'industrious, careful men', they emerged from this celebration as the unassuming, salt-of-the-earth

---

[64] Charles Lamb, 'On the Tragedies of Shakspeare, Considered with Reference to their Fitness for Stage Representation', in E.V. Lucas (ed.), *Miscellaneous Prose by Charles and Mary Lamb* (London: Methuen & Co. Ltd, 1912), pp. 112–29; p. 124.

[65] Sidney Lee (ed.), *Shakespeares comedies, histories, & tragedies: being a reproduction in facsimile of the first folio edition, 1623, from the Chatsworth copy in the possession of the Duke of Devonshire, K.G.* (Oxford: Clarendon Press, 1902), p. xviii.

heroes of the Shakespearean story.[66] Their own claim in the prefatory material to the Folio that they had prepared the volume without 'ambition either of selfe-profit or fame' was amplified. Irving spoke, to cheers from the assembled company, of the 'happy and blessed inspiration' of 'these two players who lived in affectionate friendship with a fellow-player, a playwright and a player, William Shakespeare'.[67] Alluding to the Baconian controversies, a pamphlet written as a souvenir of the occasion suggested that the real mystery about Shakespeare's plays was not how they were written but how they came to be preserved through Heminge and Condell's 'beautiful instance of unselfishness, singular love of Shakespeare, and unaffected modesty'.

Since no likeness of Heminge and Condell survived, their monument was in the form of the First Folio. The souvenir pamphlet described a sculpture 'of Aberdeen red granite, polished, with an open book of the lightest gray granite representing the famous First Folio; one leaf has its quaint title page, and on the opposite leaf the exquisite extract from the old players' own preface'. Atop this pedestal was a bust of Shakespeare, modelled on the Droeshout engraving (Figure 4.3). Charles Clement Walker, an amateur astronomer and wealthy gas engineer, who commissioned and paid for the monument, believed—without any evidence—that 'there is the highest degree of probability that the First Folio was produced in the small parish of St Mary Aldermanbury; for wherever the manuscript plays were kept, the collectors would most probably arrange them for publication at their homes, as they lived so near each other'.[68] This sculptural image of Shakespeare as a three-dimensional pop-up from the pages of his most famous book is quite distinct from the contemporaneous memorial

---

[66] Charles Clement Walker, *John Heminge and Henry Condell. Friends and Fellow-Actors of Shakespeare and What the World Owes to Them* (London: C. J. Clay and Sons, 1896), p.18.

[67] *The Times*, 16 July 1896.   [68] Walker, pp. 4, 25, 21.

FIG. 4.3. First Folio monument
The monument at St Mary's Aldermanbury to Heminge and Condell and the First Folio.

by Lord Ronald Gower in Stratford (1888), which encapsulated
Shakespeare via his most famous theatrical characters, prioritiz-
ing theatre over reading. And it is different again from the
Scheemakers statue in Poet's Corner (1740), where William
Kent had pictured the playwright leaning his elbow on a pile of
untitled books—perhaps his sources—but pointing to words
from *The Tempest* handwritten on a scroll, privileging the lost
authenticity of authorial manuscript over the mechanical production
of print. This is a memorial to Shakespeare as the First Folio, and
vice versa; a memorial to a book that itself was presented as a
memorial.[69]

Walker's monument to the decency and far-sightedness of
Shakespeare's fellow actors soon had its intellectual counterpart.
Alfred W. Pollard, then assistant keeper at the British Museum
and secretary of the Bibliographical Society, published in 1909 his
folio-format study, *Shakespeare Folios and Quartos*, as a riposte to
what he saw as the 'bibliographical pessimists', chief among them
Sir Sidney Lee, who were mordantly preoccupied with dishonest
publishers and pirated texts, particularly the 'deplorable' text of the
First Folio. Heminge and Condell were clearly, for Pollard, the
conduit for playhouse manuscripts in the possession of the King's
Men, and he argued strongly that 'the whole of the copy for the
First Folio was derived either immediately or ultimately from
the players'.[70] Pollard's friend W. W. Greg confirmed the view of
the theatrical provenance of the Folio, suggesting that, given their
busy lives as theatre professionals, Heminge and Condell could not
have undertaken the preparation of the texts for publication in the
Folio. Greg unearthed one Edward Knight, the book-keeper for

[69] See Laurie E. Maguire, 'Composition/Decomposition: Singular Shakespeare
and the Death of the Author', in Andrew Murphy (ed.), *The Renaissance Text:
Theory, Editing, Textuality* (Manchester: Manchester University Press, 2000),
pp. 135–53.
[70] A. W. Pollard, *Shakespeare Folios and Quartos: A Study in the Bibliography of
Shakespeare's Plays* (London: Methuen & Co., 1909), pp. v, 123.

the King's Men, proposed him as the actors' deputy in this matter, and crowned him 'a person of hitherto unsuspected importance in the history of English literature'. Greg argued that while this editorial trio did not apply modern methods of textual criticism, their text was of 'very considerable, if not always of the very highest, authority', and that 'we should not exaggerate the merits of their edition, but neither should we yield to the fashionable belief that [the First Folio] is in any profound manner corrupt or misrepresentative of what Shakespeare really wrote or intended his public to hear'.[71] His marked-up copy of Lee's *Census*, which was prefaced with Lee's own account of the Folio's provenance and publication history, is peppered with contentious marginalia: 'rubbish', 'rot', 'ass' and 'idiot'.[72] The editorial guard was changing, and, as Joseph Loewenstein has observed, the New Bibliography and the contemporary rare-book market, especially in First Folios, were mutually reinforcing.[73] The opportunity of the Folio's Tercentenary in 1923, with numerous First Folio copies on display in celebratory exhibitions, was the occasion for, as well as a reflection of, a new appreciation of the Folio text.

John Dover Wilson, writing in a volume to celebrate that three hundredth anniversary of the publication of the First Folio, noted that nowhere did Heminge and Condell claim to be editors of the plays they introduced, and thus lifted from them the unreasonable burden of having to provide texts to a modern editorial standard. 'It is safer', Dover Wilson concluded, 'to assume that the Folio gives us an unedited text.' 'Heminge and Condell's prefaces are the title-deeds of our greatest national possession; and our views upon the integrity of the Folio texts depend in a large measure upon the views which we believe Heminge and Condell themselves took of their own responsibilities.' Most of the texts supplied to the

---

[71] W. W. Greg, *The Shakespeare First Folio: Its Bibliographical and Textual History* (Oxford: Clarendon Press, 1955), pp. 79, 89.
[72] Quoted by West, vol. 1, p. 41.
[73] Loewenstein, in Maguire and Berger (1998), p. 37.

printers were 'prompt-books from the theatre'. Trusting to Heminge and Condell was less, Dover Wilson concluded, a matter of bibliographic investigation and more an ethical point: 'If I were to say how the new criticism chiefly differs from the old', 'I should single out something much simpler and more fundamental. It is the belief in the essential integrity of ordinary human nature which, like the English law, regards a man innocent until he has been proved guilty.' Heminge and Condell were neither 'knaves in league with Jaggard to hoodwink a gullible public' nor 'fools who did not know how to pen a preface'.[74] Rather they were decent men of high standards and disinterested motives: those pillars of St Mary Aldermanbury church.

If the reputation of the actor-editors John Heminge and Henry Condell was revamped by changing bibliographic narratives about the provenance and authority of their texts, so too was the First Folio being reassessed as an actors' Shakespeare. In 1919, a bookseller's catalogue claimed that a copy of the Folio with the name 'Samuel Gilborne' written out next to the printed name in 'The Names of the Principal Actors in all these Playes', probably belonged to the actor himself. We know almost nothing of Gilborne beyond his listing in the King's Men, and it is much more likely that the 'signature' is merely the copying out of the words by another, unrelated hand, but the idea that early actor provenance would be a selling point attests to a new status for actors in conceptions of the Folio.[75] Folger acquired another Folio with a possible early actor's signature, the 'J. Tonstall' which may register James Tonstall, a friend of Edward Alleyn.[76] As we have already seen, the format of this large book does not easily lend itself to active use in the rehearsal room, but nevertheless, claims that its

---

[74] John Dover Wilson, 'The Task of Heminge and Condell, 1623–1923, *Studies in the First Folio Written for the Shakespeare Association* (London: Oxford University Press, 1924), pp. 53–77; p. 55; pp. 61–2; pp. 76–7.
[75] West 70.   [76] West 125.

specific orthography, punctuation, and layout were a purposeful aid to the theatrical presentation of Shakespeare's plays began to be heard in the second half of the nineteenth century and were amplified in the twentieth.

In 1877, Allan Park Paton published a pamphlet on the use of capital letters in the Folio text of *Macbeth*, which asserted that the 'frequent and invariably intelligent employment of Capital Letters ... is the Key to the way in which he read his own Works, and in which they ought to be read by others'.[77] The archival discoveries of material about the Elizabethan theatre, particularly the de Witt drawing of the Swan, prompted a new interest in early theatrical practices at the end of Victoria's reign. An early adopter of this new discourse was William Poel, the pioneer of original staging practices. At the end of the nineteenth century he constructed a maquette of a reconstructed Globe theatre as part of a proposal for a new Elizabethan National Theatre, at the same time as his Elizabethan Staging Company performed a number of Shakespeare plays in early modern costume, with minimal scaffold-type staging, and with period music. Poel's textual experiments included a harshly-judged performance of the first published edition of *Hamlet* (1603), after being in correspondence with its editor, the Shakespere Society President, H. J. Furnivall. Nevertheless, he was vocal in the pages of the *Times Literary Supplement* in 1921 that the punctuation of the early texts, including the First Folio, represented authentically authorial pointing of the plays. Poel suggested that the apparently random scattering of capital letters in the Folio was sometimes a purposeful deployment of 'genuine emphasis-capitals', citing as examples Malvolio's emphatically luxurious 'branch'd Velvet gowne' in *Twelfth Night* [2.5.45–6] or Hamlet's portentous declaration of his secret interiority, 'I have

---

[77] Allan Park Paton, *The Tragedy of Macbeth: According to the First Folio* (Edinburgh: Edmonston and Co, 1877), p. 1.

that Within, which passeth show' [1.2.85].[78] Poel's interlocutor in
the newspaper letters pages was George Bernard Shaw, a playwright
known for his own extensive stage directions, which tried in print to
communicate to actors the author's intentions about the performance of his texts. Shaw expressed himself as 'a publishing playwright',
asserting that it was impossible to use a printed play to indicate how
the actor should speak his lines, and he dismissed Poel's suggestions
with a topical flourish: 'To cherish Shakespear's punctuation, or
pretend to greater authenticity for it than for the colons of Rowe or
Dr Johnson or Pope or Malone or the Cowden Clarkes or Q or any
modern editor is next door to Baconian cipher hunting.'[79]

   Poel's instinct, however, gathered a small but fervent following.
The excitement about all matters First Folio around the tercentenary in 1923 had as one of its results a limited edition series of
'The Players' Shakespeare' with introductions by Harley Granville-
Barker. The publishers' announcement set out its distinctive editorial stance: 'an edition of Shakespeare's dramatic works printed
litteratim from the First Folio of 1623 (save that the long s is
replaced by s and the forms I, J, V, i, j, u, v etc., are made to accord
with modern use)'. Granville-Barker encouraged a return to the
Folio text as a kind of alienation-effect for the 'too accustomed
eye': 'This printing of the plays, with its modest nomenclature,
scanty directions and ignoring of all scenic impediments—
compare it with our modern elaborations! —does much to give
us Shakespeare as Shakespeare was.'[80] The texts retained capitalization, spelling, and punctuation as in the Folio, thus appearing to
endorse Poel's suggestions. Theatrical and bibliographical work
was thus beginning to converge in speculating that beneath the

[78] William Poel, 'Shakespeare's "Prompt Copies": A Plea for the Early Texts',
Times Literary Supplement, 3 February 1921.
[79] George Bernard Shaw, 'Shakespeare: A Standard Text', *Times Literary Supplement*, 17 March 1921.
[80] Harley Granville Barker (ed.), *The Player's Shakespeare: Macbeth* (London:
E. Benn, 1923), p. xxiv.

printed texts of the Folio lay Shakespeare's own autograph manuscript, described evocatively in the scholarly literature as 'foul papers'.

In 1948, Richard Flatter published a study called *Shakespeare's Producing Hand* with the subtitle 'A Study of His Marks of Expression to be found in the First Folio', in which he argued that most of Shakespeare's perceived 'irregularities' 'amount to stage-directions, wrought into the text itself'. He argued against the standardization of half-lines, irregular metre, and punctuation, ending with the plea: 'Let the actor find those broken-off lines, those gaps and pauses, and he will know how to fill them—with his own feelings' and claimed Shakespeare himself as 'a greater actor than Burbadge and his entire company and legions and generations of players, all rolled into one'.[81] Influenced by Flatter, Patrick Tucker, director for stage and television, and founder of the Original Shakespeare Company in the 1990s, has become one of the most prolific modern advocates of acting from the First Folio. His books of audition speeches for men and women actors, using First Folio spelling, punctuation and capitalization, have been sponsored by the prestigious British acting school LAMDA.

Tucker draws on his own practical experience: 'my observation is that all the Shakespeare pieces I have worked on over the years— whether they are in full length productions, in selected scenes, or in individual speeches—come over better, and are easier to act, when the original text and all its punctuation and capitals are strictly adhered to', noting that 'once some things are "edited" to become more "correct", then the flood-gates are opened and literally thousands of changes are foisted upon Shakespeare's priceless Folio lines'. Taking as an example Ferdinand's speech in *Love's Labours Lost* as he reads Armado's intercepted letter [1.1.227–50]: 'where the same word is printed either with or without an extra "e",

---

[81] Richard Flatter, *Shakespeare's Producing Hand: A Study of his Marks of Expression to be Found in the First Folio* (London: W. Heinemann, 1948), pp. 10, 170, 53.

then that is an indication of an extra choice or stress on that word. This means that the word "mee" is not the same as "me"—it is an additional piece of information to the actor as to how to perform it.'[82] In his longer analysis, published as *Secrets of Acting Shakespeare*, Tucker gives the example of the capitalization of the words 'Honourable' and 'Ambitious' in Mark Antony's clever funeral oration over the body of Caesar, which famously begins 'Friends, Romans, Countrymen' [3.2.74–106] as evidence, *pace* Poel, that capital letters 'could reflect an actor's intonation and stress', and suggests that the Folio's question mark should be retained at the end of Malvolio's final 'Ile be reveng'd on the whole pack of you' [5.1.374] in *Twelfth Night*: 'I find that the real support for the Folio punctuation comes from performance, where Malvolio starts his exit with a threat, realizes he is outnumbered, and leaves us laughing at the deflation of his pomposity.'[83] Even Tucker had to acknowledge that sometimes a cigar is just a cigar and sometimes irregularities just are mistakes: citing Berowne's speech on love in *Love's Labour's Lost* [3.1.169–200] he notes that 'The Folio prints "German cloake"—this has reluctantly been changed to "German Clocke" because of the sense.'[84]

The logical development of Tucker's project, as promulgated through his publications and an extensive programme of actor workshops across the UK, USA and Australia (detailed on his winningly titled website friendlyfolio.com) was the Applause series of texts, based on the First Folio and intended for actors. Tucker's championing of the Folio text needed a material counterpart, to allow actors to take practical advantage of his method. In 1995, Doug Moston acknowledged Tucker's formative influence as he prepared a reduced-size Folio facsimile in paperback. At $45 and

---

[82] Patrick Tucker, *First Folio Speeches for Men* (London: Oberon Books, 2004), pp. 11–12, 19.

[83] Patrick Tucker, *Secrets of Acting Shakespeare: the Original Approach* (London, New York: Routledge, 2002), pp. 232–3, 244.

[84] Tucker (2004), p. 35.

later £32.50 this was probably the cheapest First Folio facsimile ever produced, and the only one that could hope for a wide readership. Moston took as his epigraph Alexander Pope's observation that 'most of our Author's faults are less to be ascribed to his wrong judgment as a Poet, than to his right judgment as a Player'. The Applause facsimile was in fact a collation of facsimiles, reproducing 'the most fully corrected pages' from the Norton and Yale facsimile editions (see Chapter 5) as well as pages from copies in the New York Public Library, harmonized by the use of 'a slightly darker setting on the computer for uniformity'. Because it includes 'clues to playing that are omitted or "regularized" by modern editors', 'having recourse to the First Folio is becoming more important to actors today than ever before'.[85]

Moston's account of matters of punctuation and pauses was indebted to Flatter, and his interpretation of the importance of capitalization to Tucker. His account of an actor's new encounter with the opening speech of Folio *Richard III*, in which 'Winter', 'Discontent', 'Summer', 'Son', and 'Ocean' are capitalized described a dramatic epiphany: 'A powerful character arose from within him immediately...His portrayal was thorough, quickly done, and powerful to witness'. Moston organized the facsimile around the Through Line Numbering system developed by Charlton Hinman for his facsimile 'with permission', but it seems that something miscarried and there was some copyright dispute over this element of the text.[86] Moston produced a further facsimile, published by Routledge, but this time based on Halliwell-Phillips' nineteenth-century edition and less useful because less clearly reproduced. A series of 'Applause First Folio Editions' of individual plays prepared and annotated by Neil Freeman was published in Canada in the 1990s. These portable and convenient paperback books could conceivably be used in the rehearsal room,

[85] Doug Moston (ed.), *The First Folio of Shakespeare 1623* (New York and London: Applause Books 1995), pp. 891, xliii, xiii.

[86] Moston, p. xlvi; p. xxiii.

and were presented as 'scripts' for actors' use. Freeman set out his method: 'In the body of the play-text that follows, the words (including spellings and capitalizations), the punctuation (no matter how ungrammatical), the structure of the lines (including those moments of peculiar verse or unusual prose), the stage directions, the act and scene divisions, and (for the most part) the prefixes used for each character will be as set in the First Folio.'

Implicit in the project was a rejection of the theories of Hinman and the New Bibliographers about the contingencies of printshop working practices, and of scholarly ideas about the role of scribes, compositors and other agents intervening between Shakespeare and the posthumously printed text (discussed in Chapter 3). Something of Moston's citational difficulties still pertained to the Folio project. Explaining how his typeset texts could be keyed to a facsimile of the First Folio, Freeman praised Charlton Hinman's 'brilliantly simple line-numbering system' (the only part of Hinman's labours that was remotely compatible with the precepts of Freeman's authorially-intentionalist editorial stance), but lamented that 'the current holders of the rights to the TLN withheld permission for the system to be used in conjunction with this series of Folio texts': instead the numbering of the Riverside Shakespeare was used.[87] Photographic technology had made the 1623 book easily and cheaply reproducible, but copyright meant that the bibliographic technology necessary for writing about it was restricted to the Norton company.

The influence of these theories on classical Shakespearean theatre is clear. Peter Hall, founder of the Royal Shakespeare Company and later director at the National Theatre, asserted that 'the purity of the Folio text, naive though it can be, also reveals clues for the actor, who can, with practice, "hear" the shape of the original play in a way that is impossible with the over-punctuated texts of

---

[87] Neil Freeman (ed.), *Measure for Measure* (New York and London: Applause, 1998), pp. vii, xlvi, xxvii.

later editors'. His much-reprinted *Shakespeare's Advice to the Players* reassured any actor who approaches the plays 'armed with a facsimile of the Folio' that they could have 'the confidence that they will be understood'.[88] Both Hall and his successor at the RSC, Adrian Noble, wrote appreciative blurbs to the 'Shakespeare Folios' advertised as 'the definitive edition...more often than not the closest we can now get to what Shakespeare actually wrote', and edited by Nick de Somogyi in 2001–3.[89] These directors influenced generations of actors. Writing, for instance, of his work to prepare the character of Prospero for the RSC season in 2000–1, Philip Voss repeated the importance of Folio punctuation and capitalization in lines such as 'The Cloud-capped Towers, the gorgeous Palaces, | The solemn Temples, the great Globe itself' [4.1.152–3], concluding: 'look at the way Shakespeare writes and he'll tell you what he wants'.[90] Alan Dessen reports on two American productions of the 1990s that were so Folio purist as not to correct 'obvious' errors: retaining the excremental sense of the Folio's 'pood pasture' (always emended to 'good') in *As You Like It* and the error 'Butonio' for 'Antonio' in *The Taming of the Shrew*.[91] The Oregon Shakespeare Festival has been accompanied in recent years by the display of a First Folio loaned from the Microsoft millionaire and philanthropist, Paul G. Allen.[92]

But the anti-Folio backlash is a strong one. Patrick Tucker acknowledges that 'For reasons that I am not completely sure of, putting the Folio forward as a valid text seems to make some

[88] Peter Hall, *Shakespeare's Advice to the Players* (London: Oberon Books, 2003), pp. 22, 14.
[89] Quoted by Abigail Rokison, *Shakespearean Verse-Speaking: Text and Theatre Practice* (Cambridge: Cambridge University Press, 2009), p. 55.
[90] Philip Voss, 'Prospero', in Robert Smallwood (ed.), *Players of Shakespeare 5* (Cambridge: Cambridge University Press, 2003), pp. 15–28; p. 18.
[91] Alan C. Dessen, *Rescripting Shakespeare: The Text, The Director, and Modern Productions* (Cambridge: Cambridge University Press, 2002), pp. 11–12.
[92] West 145.

people very angry—shouting, even, that I am completely wrong, and that the Folio is riddled with errors and not an authentic text to work from.' The rebuilt Globe in London, committed to the exploration of original practices, also published a set of Folio facsimiles (discussed in Chapter 5) but was anxious to be clear that the books were not to offer 'implied support for First Folio fundamentalists who argue that the Folio's very commas, upper cases and transmitted spellings came directly from Shakespeare's mind or hand'.[93] The most measured and informed scholarly critique of some of the Folio-centric working methods advocated in the late-twentieth-century theatre is by Abigail Rokison: she is clear that the desire to read Shakepeare's theatrical intentions has ossified attitudes to spelling and lineation, and paradoxically made verse-speaking more rigid and less immediate.[94] But the association of the Folio with the theatre remains a popular one. A text that eighteenth-century editors deplored for its proximity to the corruptions of actors has found its literal way into the theatres, where actors themselves have tended to be deeply invested in its secrets.

Perhaps inevitably, therefore, the only modern edition of Shake-speare's plays to present itself as an edition of the First Folio, Jonathan Bate and Eric Rasmussen's *Complete Works* published in 2007, has as its alternative title, *The RSC Shakespeare*. Edmond Malone had briefly considered sending to the press a marked up copy of the First Folio as the basis for his 1790 edition, but he thought better of it, deciding instead to provide a collation of early texts, drawing on 'a table which I had formed of the variations between the quarto and the folio'.[95] This synthetic editorial prac-tice, albeit with a varying sense of the relative merits of quarto and folio texts, has been dominant in Shakespeare publishing for much

---

[93] Patrick Spottiswoode (ed.), *Globe Education Facsimiles* (London: Globe Edu-cation and British Library), p. 5.
[94] Rokison, chapter 1.   [95] Malone (1790), vol. II, pp. xliv–xlv.

of the time since. But Bate and Rasmussen held their nerve: 'the polemical proposition behind the project is that the Shakespeare First Folio is the most important book in the history of world drama and yet no-one has edited it'. As one reviewer of their edition put it, with a kind of horrified admiration: 'it has had the courage (or "nerve", if you dislike the results) to cut the Gordian knot of Shakespearean textual studies in spectacular fashion. Instead of agonising over the relationship between the quarto and the folio texts of any given play, Bate and Rasmussen simply favour the readings provided in the First Folio where they can be shown to make any sense at all.'[96]

In a polemical piece not included as part of the edition but instead published online, the 'Case for the Folio', Bate established the rationale for a First Folio edition, channelling Heminge and Condell's 1623 dismissal of earlier editions as 'stolne and surreptitious copies, maimed and deformed' in his fierce description of texts such as the quarto *King Lear* (1608) as 'an often flawed text, highly variant in comparison with that in the Folio'. After a spirited account of variant texts as registering the fluid states of composition and performance, Bate nevertheless plumps for the folio as 'the best that Shakespeare's friends and fellow-actors could do in the way of preparing a text': 'we can be confident that the First Folio of 1623 represents the first authorized "complete works"'. As well as a working hardback copy with yellow covers, the edition also came in a Limited Collector's edition, boxed and leather bound, in homage to the material form of the First Folio itself by the early twentieth century.

'In asking what would be the best text for the RSC today,' Bate wrote in the online 'Case for the Folio', 'the obvious answer was the text of the original royal Shakespeare company—his own company, the King's Men.'[97] Although there is no evidence that the

---

[96] Michael Dobson, 'For his nose was as sharp as a Pen, and a Table of greene fields', *London Review of Books*, 10 May 2007.

[97] http://www.rscshakespeare.co.uk/first.html (accessed April 2015).

RSC edition was indeed 'for' the theatre company in any practical sense, since it suffers from the same problems in the rehearsal room as the unwieldy Folio format has always done, the rhetoric taps into a powerful association. The Royal Shakespeare Company owns a copy of the First Folio, currently at the Shakespeare Birthplace Trust Library and, at the time of writing, it is planned to put it on permanent display in new galleries in the Swan wing from 2016.[98]

Perhaps the zenith of the over-identification of the First Folio with performance on the one hand and with a kind of sacred materiality on the other is the RSC's anecdote about taking their copy of the book to the Vatican in 1964. The First Folio had been given to the fledgling company by Charles Edward Flower, member of the local brewing dynasty, who spearheaded the development of the Shakespeare Memorial Theatre in Stratford in 1879. Along with the so-called 'Droeshout original', a seventeenth-century portrait given to the Shakespeare Memorial Gallery in 1895, the First Folio donated by the Flower family was part of an active local re-creation myth perpetuated in partnership between the new theatre, the Shakespeare Birthplace Trust, and the developing tourist industry. During the second half of the nineteenth century, both institutions worked, together and competitively, belatedly to construct as ineluctable Shakespeare's biographical and creative ties to Stratford. Flower's First Folio is heavily marked with commonplace crosses, and in particular with enthusiastically-drawn manicules, ink hands pointing out particularly fine passages. These include Othello's preparation for the murder of Desdemona [5.2.1–22], Marcus's speech over the mutilated Lavinia in *Titus Andronicus* [2.4.11–57] and, in less bloodthirsty mode, Dromio's hyperbolic description of the hemispheric kitchen maid in *The Comedy of Errors* [3.2.110–52] and Oberon's description of the mermaid in *A Midsummer Night's Dream*

[2.1.148–54]. These may well be the work of Samuel Madden (1686–1765) who has signed his name and the date 1705 on a blank page facing the opening of *Romeo and Juliet*. Madden was a student at Trinity College Dublin at the time he wrote his name in this copy of the First Folio: he went on to write his own successful tragedy, *Themistocles, the Lover of his Country*, which was performed at London's Theatre Royal. He was also a friend of Jonathan Swift, and founded the Royal Dublin Society. At his death, his books were donated to his university; but not this one, which was eventually acquired by James Orchard Halliwell-Phillips, who transferred its portrait into another copy. It may well have been the 'gem' of his collection boasted of in 1884 (see Chapter 3). This copy, denuded of all its preliminary leaves, was bought by Flower at Halliwell-Phillips' sale for 130 guineas in 1889. Its endpapers record both the gift from Flower and, in a pasted cutting, the story of the papal visit, although the typed statement 'After the recital Dorothy Tutin presented this Folio to Pope Paul VI who blessed it' has been crossed out.

Tony Church, one of the RSC's founder associate members in 1960, with fellow actors Derek Godfrey and Dorothy Tutin, took part in an Anglo-Italian Shakespeare programme. As Church recalled in his autobiography:

I asked if we could borrow [the RSC First Folio] because I'd planned that each of us should read a sonnet at the end of the performance and it would be a splendidly theatrical touch to do it from what was virtually a contemporary text of Shakespeare's. With great to-do-ment, the volume was produced and the insurance company put £25,000 as a price on it with the stipulation that it travel by sea rather than by air because if it were lost at sea it could be salvaged. The Folio was carried to Rome by the press officer in a locked briefcase chained to the courier's wrist.[99]

Of course, the Folio does not include Shakespeare's sonnets, but instead the reduced company used the book's dedication to the

---

[99] Tony Church, *A Stage for a Kingdom* (n.p.: Oneiro Press, 2013), p. 142.

Herbert brothers as an introduction to their elevated papal
audience. The Vatican-printed programme noted 'Read from an
original of the Edition, in the possession of the Royal Shakespeare
Theatre Library'.[100] The stress throughout the recital was on
Shakespeare as a Christian writer, ending with Wolsey's pious
exit 'my hopes in heaven dwell' [*Henry VIII* 3.2.460]. One of the
extracts chosen was described as 'the drama of the victory of mercy
over the pitiless injustice' (or, as it might otherwise be summarized,
the dramatization of how a Jew and a Christian are different under
the law of Venice), the trial scene from Act 4 of *The Merchant of
Venice*. It is interesting to wonder how this intersected with the
day-to-day business of the Second Vatican Council: Church
recalls that when they went to dinner that night with the English
bishops, '[Cardinal] Heenan said how appropriate the Shylock
scene had been and described how, with some difficulty, he had
persuaded the conference to amend that ancient edict which had
condemned all Jews perpetually for the crucifixion of Christ'.[101]
One of the three Declarations of Vatican II was indeed *Nostra
Aetate*, credited with inaugurating a new, more tolerant theology of
religious difference for the Catholic church. It speaks loudly of the
RSC's commitment to a positive and benign Shakespeare that the
supercessionism of the Venice court room, like the story of Henry
VIII's split with the pope, is here repurposed, just as the possibility
that the Folio received a papal blessing is both recorded and
retracted in the pages of the book.

It is highly unlikely that any copy of the First Folio found its
way into an early modern playhouse. But it has been a relatively
frequent visitor to theatres in recent years. Amid the numerous
celebrations of the Folio tercentenary in 1923 was one at the Old
Vic theatre, where under the auspices of the director Lilian Baylis,

---

[100] *IV Centenario della nascita di William Shakespeare Auditorium Palazzo Pio
Roma 12 Novembre 1964* (Vatican Press, 1984), Royal Shakespeare Company
archives at the Shakespeare Birthplace Trust SMT/PROG/1964/46.
[101] Church, pp. 143–4.

a copy held by a private individual was displayed.[102] This exhibition concluded a period of programming during which every one of the First Folio plays was in repertory at the Old Vic, culminating in a production of *Troilus and Cressida* which opened on 7 November 1923, 'the 300th anniversary of the entering of the First Folio of Shakespeare's plays at Stationer's Hall'. After the production, the cast celebrated with a party including a speech on the First Folio, flowers presented to Baylis, and a chorus of the National Anthem.[103] As a publicity stunt for a Christie's auction of a First Folio in 2001, two actors read from the book on the wooden stage of the rebuilt Globe, before the book was sold for \$5.6 million.[104] The actor Vanessa Redgrave was the celebrity champion for the Bodleian's fund-raising campaign to digitize its First Folio in 2012, and was pictured in the press turning its tatty pages. Sir Patrick Stewart was chosen by the Craven Museum to front a video about their newly-identified First Folio; Simon Russell Beale fronted a BBC documentary about the 'secret life' of the book in 2014; and in February 2015, in an inversion of the usual pilgrimage-trail *to* a First Folio, the recently-discovered St-Omer Folio visited London.

At a press conference at the Globe, actor Mark Rylance and other members of the Globe staff were photographed with a book dubbed 'magical'. Rylance, a prominent authorship-sceptic, had previously endorsed Neil Freeman's series of Folio acting texts as 'the greatest thing to happen for Shakespearean actors at the end of this century, an annotated, unedited original text, spelling mistakes and all'.[105] To welcome the St-Omer Folio, Globe actors Olivia Ross and James Parker performed scenes from *Henry V*, not

[102] West 28.

[103] Doris Westwood, *These Players: A Diary of the 'Old Vic'* (London: Heath Cranton Ltd, 1926), p. 73.

[104] West 145.

[105] Jacket endorsement for Neil Freeman (ed.), *The Applause Shakespeare* (New York: Applause Theater and Cinema Books, 1997–2001).

an entirely happy Shakespearean image of the entente cordiale, but ended with the wooing scene between Henry and the French princess Katherine, and the St-Omer Folio's own official Twitter feed announced 'Live from @TheGlobe—a historic moment, the First Folio is back to its roots!' If the monument to Heminge and Condell at the end of the nineteenth century was an index of a new respect for actors as able and authentic communicators of Shakespeare's works, then the garlanded visit of the St-Omer Folio to the Globe in 2015 marked the apogee of the book as celebrity poster-child of 'original practices' theatre. A book that tried hard to cut any obvious ties with the theatre on its first publication had been brought back there by generations of playgoers, actors, theatre professionals, and spin-doctors.

CHAPTER 5

Perfecting

The title page of the First Folio includes the apparently paradoxical statement that it was 'published according to the True Originall Copies'. The claim mobilizes a number of concepts about authenticity and reproducibility that echo through its subsequent history. The First Folio reproduced a canon of plays many of which had been previously printed, and further, was itself a reproduced object—estimates of the original print run vary, but it is likely to have been produced in around 750 copies.[1] Even the name that came to be given to this book by the end of theeighteenth century, the 'First' Folio, suggests at once primacy and reproducibility: it is the original for its implied successors, the Second, Third and Fourth Folios during the seventeenth century, which, with the hundreds of editions since, attest to one aspect of its replicability. This chapter considers the many ways in which this product of the early modern technology of mechanical reproduction housed in William Jaggard's print shop in the Barbican has itself been reproduced, in whole and in part, by a range of technologies producing an assortment of copies variously categorized as forgeries, fakes, and facsimiles. The motivations for copying the First Folio are similarly various, from improving a damaged copy to testing out the detailed capacities of new technologies, and from providing a practical or affordable surrogate for

---

[1] Blayney (1991), p. 2.

a valuable original to increasing the value of extant part-copies. Perfecting the First Folio has always involved a negotiation between the claims of the original and the copy in the realms of aesthetic, historic, and commercial value. The continuous work to reproduce and perfect this book also simultaneously reifies the idea of the original.

As the market value of First Folios escalated during the nineteenth century, collectors began to fetishize the individuality of particular copies.[2] Simply owning a First Folio was no longer sufficiently distinctive; the specific and unique qualities of the particular copy needed to be asserted—or invented. A First Folio that was part of the collection of James Lenox that inaugurated the New York Public Library has had a title page inserted from another copy, skilfully altered to give the apparently unique publication date of 1622. A pencil note on the reverse says, hopefully, 'I think this is genuine'.[3] The famous forger, William Henry Ireland, boasted that he had reproduced in another volume Ben Jonson's signature 'which I had copied from his handwriting affixed to the first edition in folio of Shakespeare's plays, which I had purchased of White, in Fleet Street, for thirty guineas, at which high price it was sold because conceived to be (and I have no doubt that it really was) the presentation copy from the editors of Shakspeare's plays to Ben Jonson': the syntax obscures the likely fact that Ireland either forged the inscription or made up the existence of the copy.[4]

Numerous First Folios carry manuscript notes by their owners on blank binders' leaves, which record the passage of other copies through the auction room. Prices, provenance, and, increasingly, the dimensions of copies down to the last sixteenth of an inch,

---

[2] On nineteenth-century prices at auction, see West (2001), vol. 1, p. 100.

[3] West 167.

[4] William-Henry Ireland, *The Confessions of William Henry Ireland Containing the Particulars of his Fabrication of the Shakespeare Manuscripts* (London: 1805), p. 193.

were marked, while others registered the printing variants—caused by stop-press correction during the printing process—of the particular copy. There is, that's to say, a sustained collective attempt by Folio owners and sellers to distinguish and individuate specific copies, to name them according to noteworthy aspects of their provenance, and to identify their specific features. Two major scholarly projects served to corroborate and retrospectively to confirm this movement towards individuation. The first was the cataloguing of extant copies that took its organizational coordinates from the gossipy bibliographer and founder of the Roxburghe Club for wealthy book-collectors, Thomas Frognall Dibdin. In *The Library Companion* of 1825, Dibdin boasted: 'I am about to make mention of THIRTY COPIES (described in a manner more or less circumstantial) of the *first folio* of 1623', noting that 'it is a bold, and perhaps a fearful thing, to class the copies of the several Owners according to their supposed merits: but I will venture upon the following arrangement'.[5] It was a taxonomy imported into a more substantial catalogue, Sidney Lee's *Census* of copies in 1902, published as a supplement to a facsimile of the First Folio. Most recently, modern bibliographic research methods (and global air travel) have made possible the even more extensive list in Eric Rasmussen and Anthony James West's *The Shakespeare First Folios: A Descriptive Catalogue* (2012). By listing all the copies they could identify, Dibdin, Lee, and West and Rasmussen confirmed the value not of the edition as a whole but as inhering in each individual copy and, by extension, its owner.

The second confirmation of this singularity of the First Folio copy were the scholarly conclusions of Charlton Hinman. Hinman's work collating First Folio variants in the Folger collection in the mid-twentieth century, discussed in more detail in Chapter 3, discovered that the notion of the singular or ideal Folio is itself is 'an abstraction'. His research demonstrated that 'no two copies of

---

[5] Dibdin (1825), p. 409.

the First Folio selected at random should ever be supposed textually identical throughout' and 'no single copy is likely to preserve
anything that can properly be considered "*the* First Folio text"'.[6]
Now it is commonplace to adduce the uniqueness and irreproducibility of each individual copy—as in the outcry, for instance,
when the University of London Senate House Library proposed
to sell one of their two copies in 2012. The Bibliographical Society
launched an online petition pointing out that the argument that
'the folios are "duplicates"... is bibliographically unsound' and
stressing the importance of variants in books of the handpress
era as well as later 'copy-specific features of the book'.[7] When
H. R. Woudhuysen wrote condemning this abortive sale in *Standpoint* magazine (stated aim: 'to defend and celebrate Western
civilisation') he expressed surprise at needing 'to explain to professional librarians and others that there is no such thing as a "duplicate" of this kind'.[8]

    The same cataloguing and collating information that revealed
the relative commonness of First Folio survivals relative to other
early modern books was thus redeployed to emphasize the irreducible value of each individual copy. Works produced by a print
technology that might appear to mass-produce identical products
have undergone a series of scholarly investigations and adjustments
that revalue them as unique artefacts, conceptually (and commercially) closer to Van Gogh's series of variant sunflower paintings
than to the machine-made print commodity. In 1950, the *Book*

    [6] Charlton Hinman, 'Variant Readings in the First Folio of Shakespeare',
Shakespeare Quarterly 4 (1953), pp. 279–88, p. 281; p. 283.
    [7] Petition: Senate House Library, University of London: Reconsider the
proposed sale of its first four Shakespeare Folios, https://www.change.org/p/sen
ate-house-library-university-of-london-reconsider-the-proposed-sale-of-its-first-
four-shakespeare-folios (accessed September 2013).
    [8] Daniel Johnson, http://www.standpointmag.co.uk/manchester-square-june;
H. R. Woudhuysen, http://standpointmag.co.uk/critique-november-13-lessons-
for-librarians-of-londons-folio-fiasco-h-r-woudhuysen-libraries-senate-house
(accessed April 2015).

Handbook, 'for all who delight in old books', even published a do-it-yourself Folio collation table by Reginald Horrox.[9] In part this individuating process redirects the useful observation Freud called 'the narcissism of minor differences': writing in *Civilization and its Discontents*, Freud identified that insignificant cultural variants were used to justify aggression between neighbouring and similar peoples.[10] A bibliographic manifestation of this narcissism makes minor differences between copies a source of personal validation for their owners, of enhanced significance for the objects, and of increased value within the marketplace. Connoisseurship, both amateur and scholarly, has made Folio 'copies' (the products of the print shop) into 'originals' (in the hands of their owners): back to the title page paradox of 'True Originall Copies'.

Addressing readers of the First Folio about those texts of Shakespeare's plays that had already reached the bookstalls of St Paul's, Heminge and Condell asserted the superiority of the versions they themselves were providing: 'even those are offer'd to your view cur'd, and perfect of their limbes'. Since a keen play reader in 1623 might well already have bought half the plays in individual copies, their assertion has more to do with persuading potential customers to buy the collection than describing its provenance. But the Folio's own claims to textual and corporeal perfection have haunted its subsequent history. The fantasy of the 'perfect' copy has been a persistent bibliographic hallucination in libraries and auction rooms for centuries.

One of the earliest references to a First Folio purchase is in the accounts of John Buxton (1608–1660), a young Norfolk gentleman, who, after being admitted to Gray's Inn in 1626, married and set up home in 1627. Buxton would later become High Sheriff and MP for Norfolk. Buxton's youthful account books reveal that, not

[9] Reginald Horrox, 'Table for the Collation of the First Folio', *Book Handbook* 9 (1950), pp. 129–38.
[10] Sigmund Freud, *Civilization and its Discontents*, trans. David McLintock (London: Penguin, 2005), p. 64.

unlike his contemporary, Sir Edward Dering, with whom this study began, he enjoyed playgoing and fancy clothes. Buxton was also keen on the fashionable vice of tobacco. Amid a quantity of other domestic purchases associated with his new household, he spent a modest average of £3 per annum on books at the end of the 1620s. In 1627 he records a payment of six shillings 'for the changing of Shak-spheares works for on that is perfect'.[11] It is difficult to be sure what 'perfect' might mean in this context. Perhaps Buxton's copy had become somehow damaged or marked in the four years since its publication in ways that made it less desirable, although since he was only nineteen years old in 1627, it may not have been in his hands that the damage occurred. Perhaps he had acquired a copy without *Troilus and Cressida*, which, as discussed earlier, was printed belatedly and out of sequence because of problems obtaining the rights: at least one otherwise complete extant copy does not have the play included.[12] There are other questions too: presumably the book could still be bought new at Paul's Churchyard, four years after its publication (it would be another five years before the first edition had sold out and a second was published), but does Buxton's account suggest he was able to hand in his original copy, pay a supplement, and take home a new copy? These questions, and the precise bibliographic definition of 'perfect', are in any case less important than this early indication that a premium might be paid—more than a quarter of the original cost of the Folio at £1 bound—for a copy that was believed by its owner to be superior in some way to another one. Buxton thus anticipates the many later Folio owners who swapped or improved their book-collections to acquire a copy deemed preferable according to some particular personal criterion. And his wish for a

---

[11] David McKitterick, '"Ovid with a Littleton": The Cost of English Books in the Early Seventeenth Century', *Transactions of the Cambridge Bibliographical Society* 11 (1997), pp. 184–234; p. 215.

[12] West 211, owned by Charles Killigrew and William Congreve and discussed in Chapter 4.

'perfect' copy antedates a whole range of methods adopted in the subsequent centuries to 'perfect' Folios. That long record reveals that the notion of bibliographic perfection is a highly subjective and historically contingent one.

For the nineteenth-century book-trade, 'perfect' was a term that pulled in two directions. In its adjectival form the word had the connotations of 'pure', 'flawless', 'completely formed' and 'unadulterated': for a book, this would appear to imply a copy that was preserved in its original and complete state.[13] One early American collector, Thomas Barton of Boston, directed the book-dealer, Thomas Rodd, to seek out only an 'arch-perfect' copy, for which he was willing to pay more than a hundred guineas in 1845: the ceiling was insufficient.[14] Quaritch advertised a Folio from the collection of William Borlase in 1887: 'to people who know in a superficial way that the first folio Shakspeare is a comparatively common book, the price of a fine copy may seem surprisingly large, but not to those who are aware that this is probably THE ONLY COPY, UNDOCTORED, GENUINE, SOUND AND FINE, WHICH CAN COME INTO THE MARKET FOR PROBABLY ANOTHER QUARTER OF A CENTURY'. The price was £785 for a copy in 'splendid original condition, untouched by the hand of any modern renovator'.[15] The Rosenbach Company advertised a copy that was 'untouched, unwashed, and perfect throughout', bought by the Swiss bibliophile, Martin Bodmer, thus presenting perfection as the absence of later interventions.[16] For W. Carew Hazlitt, 'the

---

[13] 'perfect, adj., n., and adv.'. OED Online. Oxford University Press, http://www.oed.com/view/Entry/140704?rskey=6Pr66K&result=1&isAdvanced=false (accessed April 2015).

[14] Robert M. Smith, 'The Formation of Shakespeare Libraries in America', *The Shakespeare Association Bulletin* 4 (1929), pp. 65–73; p. 67.

[15] Bernard Quaritch, *Catalogue* 81 (London: 1887), p. 71.

[16] [The Rosenbach Company], *William Shakespeare: A Collection of First and Early Editions of his Works* (Philadelphia: Rosenbach Company, 1951), p. 1. The Bodmer copy is West 216.

purest copy of the first folio Shakespeare we ever saw was Miss Napier's, in the original calf, but wanting the verses': here original binding is the crucial authenticating factor.[17]

Variant bindings meant that Hinman's discovery that there was no singular object called a First Folio had always been literally true. Differences between Folios are materially evident even before opening its variously calf, vellum, morocco, Russia, or goatskin covers. Most copies of the First Folio were probably sold at Edward Blount's print shop in St Paul's Churchyard unbound. Owners could opt for various binding options, of which dark brown calf on boards with optional decoration was the most common.[18] A number of copies exist in some version of seventeenth-century binding, sometimes restored later, including the Bridgewater copy now at the Huntington Library, a tattered calfskin copy in the Folger bearing the signature of Walter Hacket, dated 1650, the original Bodleian library copy discussed in Chapter 1, and the Getty copy now in Wormsley.[19] These last two copies also show the distinctive deckled edges of the paper, marking their original trimming with a binding knife. Binders often used waste printed paper as part of the binding: the Bodleian copy uses pages from a fifteenth century edition of Cicero. On at least one early occasion, waste pages from the First Folio were in turn used to stiffen a binding of a later title: William Proctor Williams found in the library of the University of Kansas a sheet from *Coriolanus*—the scene in Act 4 when the servants of Aufidius marvel at the Roman general's defection to their cause—torn unceremoniously into strips to protect the stitching on the inside binding of George Hakewill's *An Apologie or Declaration of the*

[17] W. Carew Hazlitt, *The Book-Collector: A General Survey of the Pursuit and of those who have Engaged in it at Home and Abroad from the Earliest Period to the Present Time* (London: G. Redway, 1904), p. 233.

[18] Blayney (1991), p. 29.   [19] West 56; West 88; West 31; West 33.

Power and Providence of God (Oxford, 1627).[20] Williams speculates that this paper waste was cleared out of Isaac Jaggard's print shop when it was sold on his death in 1627 and sold on to a binder as scrap. West 200, now in Japan, has early manuscript instructions to binders about where to put *Troilus and Cressida*, added belatedly to the volume after the catalogue page of its contents had already been printed, and extant copies include this play in different places, just as they often bind the preliminary leaves in varying sequence. Some cryptic early annotations in another copy, for example 'looke two leaues forward & there the next side comes in right', may also be connected to binding.[21]

Early bindings are sometimes marked with gilt armorial plates—such as the Sheldon copy at the Folger discussed in Chapter 1. Later readers tended to use engraved bookplates inside the cover or endpapers. One copy in Meisei, for instance, has the bookplates of the Earl of Aylesford, John William Pease, and Howard Peace on the inside cover, tracing the serial ownership of the book during the nineteenth century.[22] Other owners marked their copies with manuscript signatures, with monogramming on the binding (EM for Edmond Malone, is one example), or with crests and other ornamentation, such as the coat of arms of the Newdigate family on a copy now in Austin, Texas, the armorial stamp of the Prince Regent on the copy in the Royal Library, or the new baronial coat of arms created for the Newport colliery owner Thomas Watson.[23] These are all paradigmatic instances of Jason Scott-Warren's discussion of graffiti: 'a person, a place, and the documentation of a relationship between them', or, more demotically, 'I was here'.[24]

---

[20] William Proctor Williams, 'F1 *Coriolanus* Fragment Found in 17th Century Binding', *Shakespeare Newsletter* 16 (1966), p. 12.

[21] West 204.   [22] West 68; West 202.

[23] West 32; West 185; West 42; West 225.

[24] Scott-Warren (2010), p. 366.

Just as the book's first binding was an act of customization to the buyer's specifications, so subsequent Folio owners, at least until the mid-twentieth century, tended to have scruffy copies rebound as a mark of their new ownership: unsurprisingly, the vast majority of extant copies are in bindings dating from the mid-nineteenth century to the 1920s, the period of greatest churn in the Folio market. Many collectors had sets of the seventeenth-century folios bound in matching style. Book-binding has always tended to be conservative in style, but Folios generally made even more of a retro-statement. Bernard Quaritch advertised in 1888 'a genuine, sound, fine, and very large copy (13 1/8 inches in height) bound in red morocco super extra, in the Veneto-English style of Queen Elizabeth's time, by Bedford 1623' at £1,200.[25] Such retrospective designs, often in red morocco with gilt tooling, were the stock in trade of the pre-eminent nineteenth-century bookbinders Robert Riviere (1808–82) and Francis Bedford (1799–1883), whose names are associated with a considerable number of Folio copies. Their predecessor, Roger Payne (1738–97), had created the most desirable bindings of the late eighteenth century, and his detailed and animated descriptions on his bills made him famous. Joseph Lilly advertised a copy 'elegantly bound in russia, the back and sides appropriately tooled, with Shakspeare's arms inlaid on the side, inside joints, gilt edges, by Roger Payne, in his very neat and peculiar style'.[26] Selling on the same copy fifty years later, Quaritch described that 'exquisite taste which distinguished the work of that genius' and included Payne's description of his binding work in a Folio in his 1913 catalogue:

Finished in the Taste I thought suitable to the Book. The Top of the Pane with (Herne the Hunters Hornes Wives of Wind.) & Laurels the Arms of Shakespere studded d'Or The Half Moon Midds. N Dream. The Insides

---

[25] Bernard Quaritch, *Catalogue 93* (1888), p. 177.
[26] Joseph Lilly, *Catalogue* (1867), p. 92; West 69.

Finished with the Lyne. The Greatist care hath been taken of the Margins. The Binding in the very best M(anner) 3: 8: o.[27]

The book, with Payne's bill and an 1800 engraving of him in his workshop tipped into the copy, was bought by Henry Folger the following year (Figure 5.1). Another copy has the note 'Bound by R. Payne £10' on an end paper.[28] Payne's fame made it relatively common to claim him for a particular binding. One copy not now attributed to Payne had 'bound by Roger Payne' pencilled into the binder's leaf, perhaps after it left the Thorold family at the famous Syston Park sale in 1884; another Folger copy has a similar attribution.[29] And the desirability of a Payne binding made it inevitable that there would be imitations, even fakes: a copy owned since 1887 by Lehigh University, Pensylvannia, carries the catalogue note, 'bound by Clarke in the style of Roger Payne'.[30] Joseph Lilly advertised one book 'very elegantly bound in russia extra, with insides and joints, gilt edges, in the manner of Roger Payne, by Clarke and Bedford' and another 'in the best style of Roger Payne, by Bedford, in his very best manner'.[31] Later bindings aspired to an idealized antiqued form which early bindings never actually possessed, characterized by deep colours, gold-tooled decoration, particular attention to the banding and decoration of the spine, and solander or other bespoke cases for storage.

A few copies have been broken—or collected—into separately bound subsets. The copy at Dulwich College exists in two volumes of Comedies and Histories, and although the provenance of this Folio is murky, it seems to have been in this multiple binding since at least 1734 when the catalogue recalls 'two old playbooks of Shakespear'.[32] Dibdin describes Isaac Reed's grangerized copy

---

[27] Bernard Quaritch, *Catalogue*, May 1913, p. 273.
[28] West 69; West 185.   [29] West 65; West 71.
[30] West 176.   [31] Joseph Lilly, *Catalogue* (1852), p. 67; (1860), p. 73.
[32] West 18.

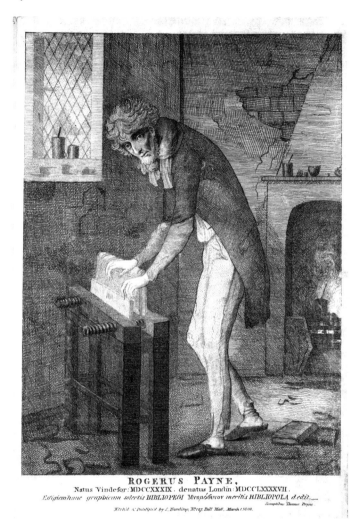

ROGERUS PAYNE,
Natus Vindefor: MDCCXXXIX. denatus Londin: MDCCLXXXXVII.
Effigiem hanc graphicam solertis BIBLIOPEGI Μνημόσυνον *meritis* BIBLIOPOLA *dedit.*

Sumptibus Thomæ Payne.

Etch'd & Publish'd by J. Harding, N.º 127, Pall Mall, March 1, 1800.

FIG. 5.1.   Roger Payne
One copy, now in the Folger library, bound by the famous binder Roger Payne, carried this engraved picture of him in his workshop.

'bound in three vols. elegant in russia, and beautifully inlaid by the late Mr Henderson, with additional portraits'.[33] Henry Folger's collection included a number of aggregate copies (West 139 is bound in sixteen volumes, West 140 is bound in thirteen). But if most copies of the First Folio retained their integrity in single volumes, the book effectively became part of a multi-volume work in the twentieth century, when packages of all four seventeenth-century editions were the norm at auctions, and sometimes even larger sets were produced by including facsimile editions in matching livery. Joseph Lilly, for instance, advertised seven volumes, including a copy of the 1807 facsimile edition, in a catalogue in 1859: 'most splendidly and elegantly bound in red morocco super extra, the backs very richly tooled with gold, with gold tooling on the sides, gilt edges, in the best style of Roger Payne'.[34]

Rebinding a First Folio almost always involved losing the provenance and historical information of the old binding and its end papers, and often included processes of washing, resizing, or trimming the pages or replacing torn or missing pages with equivalents from other copies or in facsimile. When Gladwyn Turbutt brought a copy of the First Folio to the Bodleian Library in 1905 it was to ask advice about rebinding and 'the restoration of a copy of the First Folio of Shakespeare': the fact that it had not been rebound enabled the librarian to identify its provenance.[35] Many copies carry pencil numbers in the inside gutters, particularly on the unpaginated preliminary leaves to aid reassembly; others have early annotations or other marks cropped during rebinding. Cropping was a standard part of rebinding, so the book that had not been excessively trimmed took on additional rarity value. The Shakespearean forger (and Oedipal wreck) William-Henry Ireland had confessed himself 'tormented' by a rash promise to his father that he could supply 'two copies in folio

---

[33] Dibdin (1825), p. 412. This copy has recently been found in the Buto Collection at Mount Stuart House.

[34] Joseph Lilly, *Catalogue* (1859), p. 70.

[35] Bodleian Library Records, b.862/8vo.

of Shakspeare's works with uncut leaves'.[36] Ireland's forgeries are an index of objects of scholarly Shakespeare-lust in the period: as editors and antiquarians found gaps in the biographical and historical record, Ireland filled them in, supplying reassuring documentation of Queen Elizabeth's enjoyment of Shakespeare's plays, the playwright's declaration of his Protestant faith, and his sincere love for Anne Hathaway. It is not therefore surprising to find this ultimate bibliographic treasure on his list. But, the man who overreached himself in a thrilling and orthographically comic account of how one of his own ancestors had saved Shakespeare from drowning in the Thames, no thanks to a careless boatman 'much toe merrye throughe lyquorre', jibbed at presenting such an epitome of perfection as an uncut Folio.[37] Ireland could not, or could not bring himself to, forge this object. The Folio that had not had its margins trimmed was a holy grail of book collectors, and, like all true quests, always tantalizingly just beyond reach.

Some bibliographic voices were, inevitably, raised against the depradations of improvements as destructions. Thomas Frognall Dibdin passed on one horror story in his characteristically lively prose: 'Mr Grenville informs me that an ancestor of Sir Watkin Williams Wynn had a copy of the first folio Shakspeare UNCUT. It was lying on the table in that condition when, in a luckless moment, a Stationer (in the neighbourhood of Wynnstay) came in. The book was given to him to be bound: and OFF went, not only the edges, but half of the margins!! O unprecedented act of bibliopegistic barbarity.'[38] Williams Wynn was the owner of the Payne Folio decorated with Herne the Hunter described above: he is not associated with any other copy so far as we know, and so it seems unlikely that he would have trusted a local stationer with work on a valuable book. The source of the anecdote, Grenville himself, however, was, according to Dibdin, the owner of a fine

---

[36] Ireland, p. 202.   [37] Ireland, p. 234.
[38] Dibdin (1825), pp. 410–11.

copy now bound in red morocco that he had bought in its 'old ragged binding—apparently original': perhaps the story displaced his guilt at his own 'bibliopegistic barbarity'.[39] The bibliographer William Carew Hazlitt believed that 'a copy of the first folio Shakespeare ... in unblemished primitive clothing, could not be re-attired with out making the party convicted of the act liable to capital punishment', and argued that changing an original binding was 'not merely sacrilege, but absolute surrender of value'.[40] Modern conservation, particularly in institutions, considers rebinding or restoration an anathema, but Rasmussen and West identify at least one copy in private ownership which is still being being renovated with additional leaves.[41]

Relatedly, size began to matter in First Folio description, particularly in the early twentieth century. As wealthy industrialists competed to build the tallest skyscrapers in New York (one Folio owner, Darwin P. Kingsley, supervised the construction of the New York Life Building in 1926–8), so the dimensions of the book their plutocratic peers often bought to show off their disposable income were boasted in book-catalogues and flyleaves.[42] The New York auction catalogue of the library of Robert Hoe in 1911 described his First Folio as 'a very fine tall copy, believed to be the second largest known, with some rough and uncut edges, measuring 13 3/8 × 8 1/2 inches'; two years later Bernard Quaritch advertised a copy for sale as 'perfectly sound, exceptionally large (13 × 8 3/4 in)'; a copy in the Morgan Library in New York includes a manuscript list on a flyleaf of recent sales and their dimensions in square inches, thus bypassing the difficulty of assessing whether a taller or a wider copy is preferable.[43] The

[39] Dibdin (1825), p. 410.   [40] Carew Hazlitt (1904), p. 233.
[41] West 229.   [42] West 182.
[43] *Catalogue of the Library of Robert Hoe of New York* (New York: Anderson Auction Company, 1911), p. 505; Bernard Quaritch, *Catalogue* (May 1913), p. 273; West 171.

note was perhaps intended as proof of something alleged of this copy in *The Times* in July 1896: 'it is the largest and most desirable example in existence'.[44] In 1923, amid heightened attention to the First Folio in its tercentenary year, the *Times Literary Supplement* reported that a previously unrecorded copy had been found in the Library of the Thomason Engineering College at Roorkee in North India: no details were given except that, mouthwateringly, it seemed to be two inches by one inch larger than any other extant copy.[45] Nothing was heard of this gargantuan rarity again. A pencil note in a copy in Meisei University that apparently belonged to Lord Astor claims, 'Repaired in several places but enjoying the indisputable honour of being the tallest copy now extant'. The copy in Stuttgart bears the inscription 'One of the Ten Largest and Perfect Copies known!' on a binder's leaf.[46]

Like those analysts of the irregularities of the Droeshout engraving discussed in Chapter 3, Sidney Lee recorded the Folio's own version of the forensic system of identification pioneered by contemporary criminologist Alphonse Bertillon. These measurements formed part of the social and bibliographic identikit of each copy in Lee's 1902 census, which organized the entries according to his own hierarchy of perfection. His categories were 'Class I (Perfect Copies)', 'Class II (Imperfect)', and 'Class III (Defective)'.[47] As he informed the owners to whom he wrote seeking details of their books, 'I shall, naturally, give chief prominence in the published results of the census to copies that are perfect at all points; but I hope to mention all copies, even those that are imperfect, about which information is furnished me.'[48] Lee's classification, however, was somewhat optimistic. Even his Class

[44] *The Times*, 16 July 1896.
[45] *The Times Literary Supplement*, 5 July 1923.
[46] West 209; West 197.   [47] Lee (1902), p. 7.
[48] Sidney Lee, 'Letter to the Editor', *The Times*, 15 March 1901. This letter was also printed in Lee's questionnaire to owners.

I examples included copies that had been variously improved, relaid, washed, rebound, and otherwise tampered with. And, given the anthropomorphic drift of the use of a term for assessing human not bibliographic populations, his census slipped uneasily into a judgement on the owners themselves. Most of Lee's information came from these owners, who were the immediate distinguishing feature of each copy in his list, and who had provided their own analysis of their copy by filling in Lee's questionnaire— sometimes rather grumblingly, as Francis Jenkinson from the University Library in Cambridge: 'I never collated a First Folio before; & (apart from the dulness) I keep wondering what points you want noted & what not.'[49] Lee's update on his census, published in *The Library* in 1906, records some copies he missed in his first catalogue, and registers other changes of ownership over the intervening years. It also reveals how some owners tried to haggle over his judgement. Lee was forced to admit that the copy owned by Levi Ziegler Leiter, owner of Marshall Field's Department Store in Chicago, should, following correspondence from his widow, be 'numbered in the class of forty-three perfect exemplars instead of in the first division of the second class of eighty imperfect exemplary, to which to my regret I located it'.[50] Perhaps he had been persuaded by the cheerful slogan of the Leiter retail empire: 'Give the lady what she wants'. The Leiter copy, now in Meisei, is better known by the name one of its earlier owners, William Johnstoune, discussed in Chapter 2.[51]

Asserting the unique perfection of a specific First Folio became a competitive trope of booksellers and collectors. Size, condition, and provenance were all possible sources of this ideal authenticity. Writing of the Bodleian's copy, returned to the library in 1905, the librarian, Falconer Madan, asserted that this First Folio was 'the

---

[49] Shakespeare Birthplace Trust, ER85/6/1.
[50] Sidney Lee, *Notes & Additions to the Census of Copies of the Shakespeare First Folio* (London: Oxford University Press, 1906), p. 6.
[51] West 201.

only one which can be regarded as a standard exemplar. It was the copy selected by the publisher for permanent preservation at a time when it was seen to be an advantage that some one copy, such as this, should be accessible in the future for purposes of reprinting.'[52] The idea of the Bodleian as a repository for the very best copy of each printed book has no evidential basis. Madan's assessment of the newly rediscovered book, like many of the other claims about the superiority of various copies, exemplified the psychoanalytic notion of idealization, being developed by Freud in contemporary Vienna. Freud identified the phenomenon of 'sexual [read biblio-graphic?] overvaluation—the fact that the loved object enjoys a certain amount of freedom from criticism, and that all its charac-teristics are valued more highly than those of people who are not loved, *or than its own were at a time when it itself was not loved*'.[53] Madan's description—his book-love—can easily be read as over-compensation for the Bodleian's previous lack of love in the carelessness of letting go of the First Folio in the seventeenth century.

While contemporary collectors haggled over the superiority of different First Folio copies, later analyses emphasized the import-ance of individual copies, in what Joseph Loewenstein has explored as the mutual economics of the rare book market and the rise of the New Bibliography.[54] In his lecture on 'The Dupli-city of Duplicates' in 1911, Madan encouraged his audience: 'let us suppose we are all Pierpont Morgans, and possess two copies each of the First Folio of Shakespeare'. Further, let us suppose we dispose of one as a duplicate, keeping 'the better and taller and cleaner', but neglecting the all-important fact that the sold-on copy 'had the Droeshout engraving in its first state'. The audience of bibliographers and bibliophiles must have enjoyed their

---

[52] Madan and Turbutt, p. 6.
[53] Sigmund Freud, *Mass Psychology and Other Writings*, trans. J. A. Underwood; intro. Jacqueline Rose (London: Penguin, 2004), p. 65 (italics added).
[54] Loewenstein, in Maguire and Berger (eds), p. 37.

hypothetical besting of Pierpont Morgan: 'when you have found that the copy you retained is ordinary and the one you parted with is extraordinary in this respect, you begin to believe in the Duplicity of Duplicates'.[55] Or, perhaps, as Madan did not say, when you have given away a First Folio in place of a Third (the language of deaccession in the seventeenth-century Bodleian library was precisely the language of 'duplicates'). The 'perfect' copy was the Platonic ideal of a Folio, therefore, not any one of those now, or perhaps ever, extant; no single or exemplary copy could begin to embody the variations increasingly seen as intrinsic to the First Folio object.

While the adjectival form of 'perfect' waned into impossibility, the verb form waxed into view. 'To perfect' suggested an active process of improvement and modification by which a copy could achieve perfection: in the OED's terms, to 'improve', 'complete or finish successfully', 'to bring to perfection' or 'in a weaker sense, "to bring near to perfection, to improve"'.[56] Just as money could buy a First Folio in the first place, so more money could make it better. But the meanings are in tension between the unspoilt and the worked-upon. When the bookseller, Joseph Lilly, elaborated on 'a perfect copy', which has the Jonson verses supplied 'in most accurate facsimile', we can see the strain of the terminology: perfecting the book cannot, by definition, make it perfect.[57] On the other hand, many owners were—and continue to be—keen to customize their First Folio to their own particular tastes. Chapter 3, for example, identified a number of examples of editorial retrofitting, adding in manuscript new readings, commentary, or emendations by the editorial tradition into the pages of the book. Others

---

[55] Falconer Madan, 'The Duplicity of Duplicates', *Transactions of the Bibliographical Society* 12 (1914), pp. 15–24; p. 16.
[56] 'perfect, v.'. OED Online, Oxford University Press. http://www.oed.com/view/Entry/140705?rskey=INnWzJ&result=2&isAdvanced=false (accessed April 2015).
[57] Joseph Lilly, *Catalogue* (London: 1863), p. 112.

undertook a similar kind of reverse-engineering, adding pictures and other material to the First Folio to align it with more modern editions.

A copy from the family of the parliamentarian, Colonel John Hutchinson, has a later, probably nineteenth-century, manuscript disparagement of the Droeshout as 'but a course [*sic*] performance'. The volume improved on this unsatisfactory image by tipping in a reproduction of the portrait by Cornelius Jansen: 'This portrait is from the Portrait by Jansen, 1610, supposed to be the best, most authentic portrait of the great Bard.'[58] Jansen's portrait was first circulated by Charles Jennens in his edition of *King Lear* in 1770, who added a mezzotint of the painting from his own collection as a frontispiece. Its smooth skin, deep dark eyes, neat beard, and sparkling ruff were widely appreciated as a more suitable representation of the poet than Droeshout. Folger bought the portrait in 1932, but in the following decades scholars identified Sir Thomas Overbury as a more likely sitter.[59] But adding pictures to make a Folio look more like a more recent edition was a widespread practice.

Adding illustrations, in the practice known as 'grangerizing', after James Granger, a prominent eighteenth-century print collector, was, as Lori Anne Ferrell observes, a means for owners to transform 'a mass-produced text into a one-of-a-kind, handcrafted, luxury object. It was based upon the premise that published books ... could be refashioned into a connoisseur's private cabinet.'[60] Not everyone agreed. 'A passion for books illustrated, or adorned with numerous Prints representing characters, or

[58] West 112.

[59] Tarnya Cooper, with essays by Marcia Pointon, James Shapiro, and Stanley Wells, *Searching for Shakespeare* (London: National Portrait Gallery, 2006), pp. 68–9.

[60] Lori Anne Ferrell, 'Extra-illustrating Shakespeare', *Shakespearean Configurations: Early Modern Literary Studies*, special issue 21 (2013): http://extra.shu.ac.uk/emls/si-21/08-Ferrell_ExtraIllustratingShakespeare.htm (accessed April 2015).

circumstances, mentioned in the work', wrote Thomas Dibdin, 'is a very general and violent symptom of the Bibliomania.' A later commentator was more critical of this 'morbid and biblioclastic' behaviour, in which 'the patient is a sort of literary Attila or Genghis Khan, who has spread terror and ruin around him'.[61] In his *Imperfect Hints Towards a New Edition of Shakespeare* of 1787, Samuel Felton did for illustrations in the age of Granger what the mid-eighteenth-century editorial tradition had done for commentary and annotation: he chose his preferred portraits and vignettes, in modern style, for a proposed new edition. This turned the Shakespeare First Folio into a handheld version of John Boydell's Shakespeare Gallery in Pall Mall that was then in planning and would open two years later.

Most extra-illustrated versions of Shakespeare were themselves based on later and cheaper editions, including the 1807 Wright facsimile, amplified in a copy at Warwick Castle including one hundred and twenty seven plate illustrations.[62] At least one copy of a grangerized First Folio is, however, extant. Some hand-drawn rubrication on the title page of Anthony Morris Storer's bequest to Eton College at the end of the eighteenth century hints at its decorative theme. This otherwise unmarked Folio is bound with ninety illustrations at the back of the volume, ranging from topographical engravings of places such as 'Dunsinane' or the Tower of London mentioned in Shakespeare's plays, portraits of historical characters including Sir Thomas Erpingham, who lends Henry V a cloak on the evening before Agincourt, or the Cleopatra who 'beggared all description' [2.2.205], plus miscellaneous pictures from Shakespeare's life and times.[63] Edmond Malone's copy now

[61] Dibdin, *Bibliomania*, p. 496; Holbrook Jackson, *The Anatomy of Bibliomania* (London: Soncino Press, 1932), p. 736.

[62] William Jaggard, *Shakespeare Bibliography: A Dictionary of Every Known Issue of the Writings of our National Poet and of Recorded Opinion Thereon in the English Language* (Stratford-upon-Avon: The Shakespeare Press, 1911), p. 510.

[63] West 10.

in the Bodleian Library has also been bound with extra preliminary leaves to carry various illustrations, including a portrait of Philip Earl of Pembroke based on a van Dyck engraving, a drawing of New Place in Stratford-upon-Avon, colour pictures of King James and Charles I, an engraving of *Romeo and Juliet* 3.7, and a version of the Chandos portrait of Shakespeare.[64] While full-scale extra-illustration is rare, many extant copies have additional prefatory material particularly in the form of portraits, or tipped-in cuttings from auction catalogues or newspapers.

A copy of the Shakespeare First Folio was, however, less likely to be the recipient of grangerizing material than its unwilling donor. Many—perhaps even most—copies have had some part removed. Discussing the Droeshout engraving in 1824, James Boaden noted that copies of the First Folio were 'usually found divested of their original title' because 'it has been torn out, to afford an illustration to some fanciful assemblage of English portraits'. Boaden himself is associated with a fine and complete copy of the First Folio now in the Martin Bodmer Foundation Library in Geneva.[65] With an eye to the antiquarian gothic that the bibliographer, medievalist and ghost story writer M. R. James would make his own, Andrew Lang anatomized 'the Book-Ghoul' 'who prowls furtively among public and private libraries' and 'combines the larceny of the biblioklept with the abominable wickedness of breaking up and mutilating the volumes from which he steals. He is a collector of title-pages, frontispieces, illustrations, and book-plates brooding "over the fragments of the mighty dead".'[66] One such mutilated copy was sold in 2002 by Dr Williams's Library, where it had been for two centuries: suspicion falls in at least one account of the

---

[64] West 33.

[65] James Boaden, *An inquiry into the authenticity of various pictures and prints, which . . . have been offered to the public as portraits of Shakespeare* (London: Robert Triphook, 1824), p. 6; West 216.

[66] Lang, p. 56.

library on the 'two gentlemen to examine Shakespeare folio entered in the Visitors' book on February 27th, 1864'.[67]

The movement towards the individual description of every extant copy was accompanied by a different contemporaneous impulse: to reproduce, in facsimile form, the first edition—singular—of Shakespeare's plays. From early in the nineteenth century, facsimiles began the process of fixing and marketing ideal copies. The ideal copy from which a facsimile should be taken was of course influenced by the contested notions of perfection already discussed. Facsimiles might draw on the provenance and therefore the intrinsic social value of their original. Sidney Lee's facsimile (1902), for example, bore on its title page its aristocratic lineage 'from the Chatsworth copy in the possession of the Duke of Devonshire, KG'. Rather as the 1623 First Folio had addressed itself to its noble dedicatees, William and Philip Herbert, even as it operated not within the economics of patronage but of the marketplace (its second dedicatory letter is 'To the Great Variety of Readers', urging them to buy the book), so Lee's modern photographic facsimile was constructed both as democratizing and as reassuringly elite. It reproduced the work—making it more available—but it simultaneously restricted that availability. Limited to a print-run of one thousand copies, each individually numbered and signed, Lee's facsimile was at once mass-produced and individual. Appropriately, its first three numbered copies were presented, aspirationally, to Edward VII, to the German Emperor, and the US President.[68] Lee's description of the Duke of Devonshire's copy as 'the cleanest and freshest examplar in existence' is typical of the impulse to reproduce books that show as little sign of wear, use, or reading, as possible.

For England at the turn of the twentieth century, it is easy to see that the ideal copy might well belong to an aristocrat. For 1960s

---

[67] [Dr Williams's Library], *A Short Account of the Charity & Library Established under the Will of the Late Rev. Daniel Williams, D.D.* (London: 1917), p. 72.

[68] Murphy (2003), p. 215.

America, the platonic essence of First Folio was in the unreal perfection of a composite copy. Charlton Hinman's Norton facsimile of 1968 materialized his intellectual labour in collating the Folger collection of Folios in Washington DC (discussed in Chapter 3) by picking leaves from thirty different copies of the text for reproduction. Thus he produced an ideal compound Folio with each page in its corrected state, and all chosen for their cleanness, clarity and amenability to photographic reproduction. His First Folio facsimile copied a book that never existed, since no extant copy combined all these perfect leaves. Hinman's publishers trumpeted this hyperreality, asserting in their advertisement not that the copy equalled the original but that it exceeded and improved on it. As the publicity material noted, 'the Norton Facsimile is without question superior to any Folio facsimile hitherto produced. It is even closer to the original publisher's intention than any extant original Folio, and it is as a whole better and more cleanly printed than any extant original Folio.'[69] The facsimile exceeds the original: reproducing the First Folio allowed the fantasy of recuperating an old book, blemished by compositorial errors and the bleed-through of ink from one page to its reverse, marked with annotations and blots from use, into a pristine form.

For the late eighteenth century, the general grubbiness of First Folio copies was axiomatic. George Steevens' amusing vignettes about the 'effect of gravy' and the 'thin flakes of piecrust between the leaves of our author' that 'communicated their grease to several pages deep' were much repeated. Steevens imagined an open First Folio at the breakfast table: 'how aunt Bridget's mastication might be disordered at the sudden entry of the Ghost into the Queen's closet' or 'the half-chewed morsel dropped out of the gaping 'Squire's mouth when the visionary Banquo seated himself in the chair of Macbeth'.[70] Percy Fitzgerald confirmed that 'this work is

---

[69] Quoted by David Bevington, 'First Folio of Shakespeare by Charlton Hinman', Modern Philology 68 (1970), pp. 98–100; p. 100.

[70] Steevens (1793), vol. 1, p. 446.

usually found frayed, maimed, soiled, smeared, imperfect, leaves and sheets torn out in the middle, the beginning and end', and the assessment was much repeated in bibliographic and popular accounts of the book.[71] By contrast, the prevalence of Hinman's invaluable facsimile in Shakespeare scholarship, in its 1968 edition and the second edition of 1996, has perpetuated a dominant image of the perfect, legible, and complete book that is far from the reality of the varyingly partial, mended, and stained copies in existence, even as it has almost entirely superseded any scholarly recourse to those original copies. Umberto Eco, writing of the allure of the pastiche and the status of the reproduction in American popular culture, suggested that 'perhaps the fetishistic desire for the original is forgotten, these copies are perfect' and added 'this is not an attempt to absolve the shrines of the Fake, but to call the European sanctuaries of the Genuine to assume their share of guilt': the suggestion is that such reproductions service the original's own complicated duplicity.[72]

Just as eighteenth-century editors tended to acquire First Folios even as their own editions worked to supersede them, so too, the directors of facsimile editions in the nineteenth and early twentieth century can be linked with individual copies. Howard Staunton is associated with a copy, now in Brown Library, which includes on a flyleaf his own otherwise unknown (and rather overwrought) manuscript poem 'On the First Folio' ('Find me some nook in Dream-land'). Ironically, the personalized, unique quality of this copy means that it is thereby unsuitable for the kind of anonymized facsimile. Staunton chose the copy then owned by the Dryden family of Canons Ashby (now owned by a co-founder of Microsoft).[73] Halliwell-Phillips is associated with a number of

---

[71] Fitzgerald, p. 255.
[72] Umberto Eco, 'Travels in Hyperreality', in *Faith in Fakes: Essays*, trans. William Weaver (London: Secker and Warburg, 1986), pp. 1–58; p. 39.
[73] West 184; West 145.

Folio copies, some of which bear his inscription.[74] A letter of 1856 described the enclosed Folio, sent to a purchaser in Glasgow, as 'my second best', and added 'my other although wanting title and all the preliminary leaves is as useful to me for working purposes as the best, and indeed in some respects more as it is not such great consequence if it gets an ink blot.'[75] Halliwell-Phillips' publishers, however, acquired a copy specifically for the purpose of reproduction, although for some reason they used this for only half the facsimile and then reverted to Staunton's facsimile.[76] Duncan C. Dallas, who produced a small number of individual plays in facsimile in 1895 in his patent Dallastype, also owned a Folio: like Staunton, he preferred another copy, one held by the British Library, perhaps because his own copy, now in private ownership in Tokyo, had a distinctive pink damp stain in the top right hand corner.[77]

Early reproductions of the First Folio were type-facsimiles: the text was entirely reset in a fount approximating to the original, following the spelling, punctuation, and layout of the 1623 text. E. and J. Wright published a type-facsimile in 1807 with a reproduction title page, and without any introductory or other material. This was presented to the public as a surrogate for the book, not an introduction to it, and in some cases was apparently mistaken for an original. A catalogue of books at Eaton Hall, the seat of the Grosvenor family, at the end of the nineteenth century, was ambiguous about whether the library contained a First Folio or the Wright facsimile, and the Duke of Westminster maintained that his original had been stolen by a woman later killed by a bomb

---

[74] West 11.   [75] West (2001), vol. 1, p. 31.

[76] Charlton Hinman. 'The Halliwell-Phillips Facsimile of the First Folio of Shakespeare', *Shakespeare Quarterly* 5 (1954), pp. 395–401.

[77] West 213.

in the Blitz.[78] The text used by the Wrights is not known. Edmond Malone was unimpressed, spiking as unrealistic a current fad—championed by John Horne Tooke in particular—for the text stripped of its commentary:

The new folio facsimile I have just looked at. How far it is correct, or *faithful in its incorrectness*, I know not, nor does any body, I suppose; but it is boasted that great pains have been taken to make it resemble its prototype in every respect. But who are to be the buyers after all? Nobody that knows anything of the matter will rely on it; and what have the idle gentlemen of the town to do with first folios or any folio of Shakspeare?—It is very pleasant, however, to hear some of them talk upon the subject:— 'Ay, now we shall have the true thing, and perfectly understand this great author, without being bewildered by the commentators'.—I should like to see a paraphrase by some of these gentlemen, on six pages of the first folio, having been shut up for 12 hours in a room with this volume, and without any other book. It would probably be a very curious performance.[79]

Another reader answered Malone's question about reliability. A correspondent to *Notes and Queries* in 1853 described a collation by William Upcott of Wright's edition. Upcott had spent 'four months and twenty-three days' at the London Institution 'comparing the *pretended* reprinted facsimile *first* Edition of Shakspeare with the original' and noted 368 typographical errors. For his pains he was rewarded with 'a single copy of the reprint [presumably complete with its errors] published at five guineas'.[80]

Sixty years later, in the same year that Angela Burdett Coutts set Folio hearts aflutter with the record price paid at the Daniel sale, Lionel Booth produced another type-facsimile. It emerged into an excited market. As Umberto Eco observed, 'for the

---

[78] Leslie A. Morris, *Rosenbach Redux: Further Book Adventures in England and Ireland* (Philadelphia: Rosenbach Museum and Library, 1989), p. 65.

[79] Arthur Tillotson (ed.), *The Correspondence of Thomas Percy and Edmond Malone* (Baton Rouge: Louisiana State University Press, 1908), p. 242.

[80] F.C.B., 'The Reprint, in 1808, of the First Folio Edition of Shakespeare', *Notes and Queries* 167 (1853), p. 47.

reproduction to be desired, the original has to be idolized'.[81] *The Times* reported that Booth had had a 'new clean-cut type' cut 'specially for the purpose', and noted that he had tended to prefer corrected states of the text rather than following, errors and all, any one specific copy.[82] As was common in nineteenth-century publishing, Booth's edition was sold in several formats targeting different purses, ranging in price from the limited-run Folio size (only a hundred copies printed at 5 guineas each) to the small paper at 31s 6d. His title page included a postage-stamp sized reproduction of the Droeshout engraving, and his own publishers' mark at the foot of the page: 'Shakespeare as put forth in 1623. | A Reprint of Mr. William Shakespeares Comedies, Histories, & Tragedies. | Published according to the True Originall Copies. | London. Printed by Isaac Jaggard, and Ed. Blount, 1623; | and Re-Printed for | Lionel Booth, 307 Regent Street. 1864.' The title page enacts the direct, unmediated succession from 1623 to 1864, and many reviewers appreciated the absence of intervening commentary. 'What he has done', wrote the *The Press* in January 1862, when one instalment of the work was released, 'is for general readers of the poet, worth more than all the criticism and illustration, and commentary which the two and a half centuries since Shakespeare died have produced.' *The Daily Telegraph* elaborated that this was 'the most commendable act performed of late years in Shakespearology' because it placed 'in the hands of the public a simple reproduction of the folio of 1623. That rare edition has always been the fountain-head of authority, though somewhat choked by weeds of errors. In plucking these away, emendators have too often "plucked out brain and all", their improvements frequently serving to destroy the most Shakespearean of Shakespeare's fancies.'[83] Again, Horne Tooke's idea that access to

---

[81] Eco, p. 19.   [82] *The Times*, 20 January 1864.

[83] Press comments from a publisher's flier included with Booth's edition of *Pericles* printed in 1807 and bound with the First Folio facsimile in the English Faculty Library, Oxford, Stack 2: H70.

Shakespeare needed to be refreshed by returning to the original unedited volume resurfaced.

Despite its accuracy, Booth's facsimile was not a financial success. Booth was reported twenty years later saying he did not know why he had ever undertaken it. His edition was immediately overtaken by a new technology. Howard Staunton's photo-lithograph version was serially published in 1864–5, like novels of the same year, including Trollope's *Can You Forgive Her?* and Dickens' *Our Mutual Friend*. But if the publishing schedule was orthodox, the technology of printing certainly was not. Staunton's facsimile developed the curious partnership between Shakespeare and new technology that grew up in the Victorian period, when Shakespeare's works were often used to provide the legitimating 'launch material' for the demonstration of innovative machines. This was true of the spoken word, in, for example, early wax cylinder recordings from 1889 of Edwin Booth delivering speeches from *Hamlet* and *Othello* or Alexander Graham Bell declaiming, 'To be or not to be' to demonstrate telephony at the Philadelphia exhibition in 1876.[84] But it was also sustainedly true of developments in print technology, and Staunton's facsimile was an important example. In 1860, the Ordnance Survey published a booklet to advertise the ability of a new process, photo-zincography, to 'produce authentic copies of any of the numerous rare manuscripts which are carefully preserved in different parts of the world, and print any number of copies of them that may be required at a cost which will not exceed one penny for a folio-sized sheet'. The examples of this artful reproduction were iconic national and cultural documents and illustrations: a page of the Domesday book, engravings of Raphael and

[84] Katherine Rowe, 'Shakespeare and Media History', in Margreta de Grazia and Stanley Wells (eds), *The New Cambridge Companion to Shakespeare* (Cambridge: Cambridge University Press, 2010), pp. 303–45; p. 306.

Piranesi, and a page from the First Folio.[85] The page chosen, the first of *King John*, is itself a scene preoccupied with reproduction and the relation of offspring and parent. Philip Faulconbridge, the play's Bastard, asks the King to judge whether 'I be as true begot or no' [1.1.75] and invites the explicit comparison of the sons as copies of the father: 'Compare our faces, and be Iudge yourself | If old Sir *Robert* did beget vs both' [1.1.79–80].[86] Ordnance Survey continued to develop photo-zincography by photographing the Dryden family copy of the First Folio, but only published the preliminaries and the first eight comedies of the planned facsimile volume. Handsomely bound copies of this part facsimile were 'distributed by the Secretary of State for War to members of the Government in 1862', presumably to show off the Ordnance Survey's technological advancement.[87]

The project to reproduce the First Folio in its entirety was left to the chess-master-turned-Shakespearean Howard Staunton. Staunton's previous experience with facsimile technology was that, having licensed his name to a manufacturer of chess pieces, he authenticated the most expensive ivory sets with his manuscript signature while standard sets bore only a facsimile.[88] Staunton took up this new technology with the first photo-lithographed facsimile of an early printed book, a quarto of *Shakespeare's Comedy of Much Ado About Nothing*, 'photo-lithographed, by press permission and under the superintendence of, Mr H. Staunton from the matchless original of 1600, in the library of the Earl of Ellesmere'. The same year, 1864, in celebration of the three hundredth anniversary of

[85] Colonel Sir Henry James, *Photo-Zincography* (Southampton: Forbes and Bennett, 1860), pp. iii–iv.

[86] Alan Galey, *The Shakespearean Archive: Experiments in New Media from the Renaissance to Postmodernity* (Cambridge: Cambridge University Press, 2014), pp. 148–9.

[87] A. W. Pollard et al., '"Facsimile" Reprints of Old Books', *The Library* 4 (1926), pp. 305–28; p. 314.

[88] David Hooper and Ken Whyld (eds), *The Oxford Companion to Chess* (second edition, Oxford: Oxford University Press, 1992), p. 392.

Shakespeare's birth, he published a folio format volume, *Memorials of Shakespeare*, including a photo-lithographed Droeshout (from Ellesmere's copy), and boasting 'the most perfect reproductions of Shakespeare's Will that [have] ever appeared', plus signatures and the deeds of conveyance and mortgage on his Blackfriars property.[89] He then turned to the progress already made by Ordnance Survey, to produce his own complete facsimile edition of the First Folio in 1866. Reviewers were delighted by the application of new methods: 'as rumours have gone abroad that the appearance of such a facsimile by means of photo-lithography would be an impossibility, it is pleasant now to see the best contradiction of such a report in the actual appearance of the work'.[90]

A rival process tried to capture the market with a similar photographic technique. Duncan C. Dallas used a facsimile publication of the First Folio preliminaries and *The Tempest* to advertise the technical merits of his new patented 'Dallastype Process of Photographic Engraving': 'Dallastype reproduces type work in clear and accurate facsimile, and is much superior to, and more reliable, in this class of work, than photo-lithography, photo-zincography, or photo-zincotype, which require numerous erasures and corrections. The Dallastype is the pure and untouched reproduction of the original text.'[91] Launching with the First Folio was also a feature of later technological developments. In 1997 the Arden Shakespeare produced an expensive CD-ROM including a facsimile of the First Folio along with a number of quartos and other significant reference works. In 2001, Octavo released a CD-ROM with a digital facsimile of the Daniel copy at the attention-grabbing price of $16.23.[92] In 2010, the University of

---

[89] Howard Staunton, *Memorials of Shakespeare* (London: Day, 1864), sig. b.
[90] *The Times*, 20 January 1864.
[91] Duncan C. Dallas, *The Dallas type Shakespeare: A Reduced Facsimile of the First Folio, 1623* (London: 1893).
[92] Murphy (2003), p. 267.

Oxford launched a free download of transcribed First Folio texts to mark its entry into a new digital publication sphere: 'Shakespeare's entire First Folio, including original spelling, is being made available to download for free, as Oxford University becomes one of the first universities to add ePubs to iTunesU, a dedicated area within the iTunes store.' Armadillo Productions, working with the British Library, advertised in the Apple AppStore 'eBook treasures', a mobile app including a facsimile of Shakespeare's First Folio, advertised under the banner headline 'These are the original handwritten books and manuscripts from Leonardo da Vinci, Jane Austen, William Shakespeare and many others; the ones that shaped art, science, faith and the world around us.'

New technologies, however, did not always live up to their promise of cheaper and more accurate reproductions. Halliwell-Phillips introduced his facsimile edition in 1876, in a format reduced to eye-wateringly small type. 'It is scarcely necessary', wrote Halliwell-Phillips in his preface, 'to say that the volume has been for generations the most exclusive property of wealthy collectors, and a sealed book to the generality of readers and students. By the aid of modern science it is now placed in a conveniently reduced form within the reach of all.'[93] It was, wrote one enthusiast, 'the best piece of fortune which has yet befallen the Shakesperian student, and we cannot conceive a better laid out half-guinea, than that through which he can obtain possession of this marvellous reproduction'. Presumably, the transcribed First Folio text of *Macbeth* that followed these remarks was taken from the facsimile volume.[94] But Halliwell-Phillips' facsimile was a curious pantomime horse of an edition. Chatto and Windus, Halliwell-Phillips' publishers, had acquired a copy of the First Folio for the purpose of reproduction. This copy was then sold

[93] *The First Edition of Shakespeare. The Works of William Shakespeare in reduced facsimile from the Famous First Folio edition of 1623 with an introduction by J. O. Halliwell-Phillips* (London: Chatto and Windus 1876), p. xi.
[94] Allan Paton, p. vii.

on to the Revd Robert Roberts of Boston, Lincolnshire (the Bacon-curious owner discussed in Chapter 3) and thence inexorably to Henry Folger who bought it in 1903. But, as Charlton Hinman observed, the second half of Halliwell-Phillips' facsimile reproduces Staunton's facsimile. Half of its pages are copies of a copy, facsimiles of a facsimile. And Staunton's facsimile was itself drawn from two different copies in the British Museum and in the collection of the Bridgewater family. Further, as Hinman noted with evident pleasure, the very process of stop-press correction that has produced the variant readings in original Folios was itself reproduced in the preparation of Halliwell-Phillips' volume, which itself existed in different uncorrected and corrected forms, resulting in a 'handy but untrustworthy little facsimile'.[95]

There were other forms of desirable authenticity than the textual, however. A type-facsimile in three large volumes, called *The National Shakespeare*, was published in Edinburgh in 1888: the publishers' advertisement promised particular attention to the material properties of the original: 'It will be printed in a *special antique type*, such as was actually employed in the "First Folio," upon *hand-made paper*, with rough edges, specially manufactured for this work, to maintain the antique character of the edition.'[96] It was not revealed what original was being reproduced in this edition. But facsimile reproductions using retrograde technology have tended to be found wanting: David Bevington described how the 'less expensive unscreened or lined-photo-offset method of reproduction (in lieu of screened offset or collotype) resulted in various disadvantages, blots, and illegibilities in the Yale facsimile undertaken by Helge Kökeritz in 1954.[97] Reviewing the Yale

---

[95] Hinman (1954), pp. 400–1.

[96] Sir Joseph Paton (ed.), *The National Shakespeare: A Facsimile of the text of the First Folio of 1623* (London and Edinburgh: Mackenzie, 1888), publishers' advert attached to Bod Dunston B 36/1.

[97] Helge Kökeritz (ed.), *Mr William Shakespeares Comedies, Histories and Tragedies* (New Haven; London: Yale University Press, 1954); Bevington, p. 98.

facsimile of a copy in the Elizabethan Club that had belonged to A. H. Huth, bibliographer Fredson Bowers suggested that the compromise on facsimile quality in order to produce a volume for 'ordinary teachers and students of Shakespeare' was a serious misjudgement: 'it is a sad fact . . . that the present Folio facsimile, as far as accuracy of reproduction is concerned, appears to be the second faultiest ever offered for sale', pointing out in particular the widespread 'altering or expunging of line-ending punctuation' during the reproduction process.[98] A pasted-in Errata slip in many copies acknowledged some of these difficulties. Part of Bowers' dismay seems to be the fear that a photographic facsimile is often seen as a seamless substitute for the original, rather than as a specific and autonomous product of a particular technology. That facsimiles might be dangerously close to the original while not being identical with it was an early and ongoing concern. Describing in 1925 what the literary student might need from the new reproductive technologies, A. W. Pollard prescribed as ideal 'a photographic facsimile made by a process which reduces the risk of well-meaning faking to a minimum'.[99]

When Sidney Lee publicized his plans for his 1902 facsimile, there was an assumption that the market was already cornered. A. E. Dryden wrote back discouragingly: 'you are no doubt aware that in 1866 a Photographic reproduction of the first Folio was brought out'. He continued: 'I suppose the Chatsworth copy is more perfect than any other—otherwise it seems rather futile to bring out a second photographic copy, when there is such a fine one in existence.'[100] But as their plans for a new edited text of Shakespeare foundered, Oxford University Press prepared plans for a new facsimile in the early 1920s. Kenneth Sisam wrote asking, 'Why don't you do another Shakespeare First Folio in facsimile?'

[98] Fredson Bowers, 'The Yale Folio Facsimile and Scholarship', *Modern Philology* 53 (1955), pp. 50–7; p. 51.

[99] Pollard (1926), p. 307.

[100] Shakespeare Birthplace Trust, ER/85/6/1.

adding 'Your previous issue has been very scarce and dear for a long time, & there must be room for another' and there was discussion in the Press about a new facsimile over the next few years.[101] 'Will you press [A.W.] Pollard again to name a good, clean, interesting copy, which we might get permission to use?'[102] No facsimile was produced.

That facsimiles democratize the First Folio, as the inevitable corollary of the impossible prices of the original, has been a perennial theme. W. Carew Hazlitt, detailing early editions of Shakespeare in his *Hand-Book to Early English Literature* (1867) abbreviated the entry for the First Folio, since 'space would be wasted in describing a book which, through facsimiles, has become so accessible to all who care about such matters'.[103] In 1811, Thomas Dibdin anatomized a Victorian malady he called 'Bibliomania, or Book-Madness' and suggested that 'the re-printing of scarce and intrinsically valuable works is another means of preventing the propagation of this disorder'.[104] But many early facsimiles were themselves produced in limited quantities, and thus it was always possible for a new edition to state that previous facsimiles were themselves now rarities. Explaining their decision to publish a 'compact' facsimile of the book in 1985 to commemorate twenty years of Meisei University, the director, Mitsuo Kodama, suggested that existing facsimiles 'are difficult to obtain for the scholars and readers of today, and being reproduced at actual size are far from easy to handle and carry'.[105] Thus facsimiles came to replace previous facsimiles rather than any notion of an original.

[101] Oxford University Press Archives, OUP 18/000168,
[102] Oxford University Press Archives, OUP 18/000026.
[103] W. Carew Hazlitt, *Hand-book to the Popular, Poetical and Dramatic Literature of Great Britain: From the Inventing of Printing to the Restoration* (London: J. R. Smith, 1867), p. 547.
[104] T. F. Dibdin, *Bibliomania: Or Book Madness. A Bibliographical Romance* (London: Henry G. Bohn, 1842), p. 58.
[105] Mitsuo Kodama (ed.), *William Shakespeare: The First Folio 1623* (Tokyo: Meisei University Press, 1985), p. xii.

Kodama's 1985 facsimile was reproduced, like the Hinman, from an ideal unidentified selection of the Meisei copies, although a note identified the portrait and 'To the Reader' as being from the Houghton copy. It is a mark of what has changed in what is valued about Folio copies that the facsimile they reproduced for their fiftieth anniversary was the heavily annotated seventeenth-century copy complete with William Johnstoune's often disobliging commentary, discussed in Chapter 2.

Often fascimiles were envisioned as complements to valuable original copies, both in private and institutional hands. The Birmingham Shakespeare Library, the only British public library to hold a First Folio during the nineteenth century, listed it first in its catalogue, followed by the Wright, Booth, Staunton, Halliwell-Phillips and National facsimiles, and a similar organizational hierarchy can be seen in scores of booksellers' catalogues in the period. The Burdett Coutts library sale in 1922 included the Lee and Halliwell-Phillips facsimiles as well as the two original copies bought by A. W. S. Rosenbach en route to Henry Folger. Folger himself cited the acquisition of the 1887 American issue of Halliwell-Phillips' facsimile for $1.25 shortly after his marriage as the beginning of his Folio quest; in June 1903 he bought the Roberts copy that had been (partly) reproduced in this volume.[106] Mitsuo Kodama, reflecting on the origins of the unexpected Shakespeare collection, now including twelve copies of the First Folio at Meisei University in Tokyo, attributed their zeal to acquire this book to the early purchase of a Norton facsimile in 1968. The Revd Robert Roberts of Boston, Lincolnshire, wrote in the flyleaf of the First Folio copy, previously acquired by Chatto and Windus for the purposes of facsimile reproduction: 'Collated with Staunton's Photo-litho Facs. And found to be correct.'[107] At least one Folio owner asserted the irreproducible value of their

---

[106] George E. Dimock, 'Biographical Sketch', in Cadman (ed.), p. 25.
[107] West 91.

original in an age of facsimiles. The copy now in Winchester College has about twenty per cent of its leaves missing as a pencil note on the flyleaf acknowledges: 'almost a fifth or sixth wanting. "Half a loaf" & c' (referring to the proverb 'half a loaf is better than no bread'). Half a loaf is also clearly better than a facsimile loaf: the annotator continues, referring to the Halliwell-Phillips copy: 'in the "reduced fac-simile" 1876 | "kis" is converted to "'tis"| So much for "fac-simile"'. The Earl of Carysfort recorded in the inside leaf of his First Folio that he had 'Compared with Oxford facs. of Devonshire copy', found two examples of corrected states, and observed with evident satisfaction 'The portrait is <u>less worn</u> than in the Devonshire copy'.[108]

Many of the subscribers to Lee's 1902 facsimile were also those owners of original copies who were listed in the accompanying census, including Bernard Macgeorge of Glasgow, William White of Brooklyn, and William Phelps of Gloucestershire. Visiting the Free Library in New South Wales in 1886, the Cornish engineering magnate Richard Tangye (himself a Lee subscriber whose library included that and the Halliwell-Phillips facsimile) noted with approval that his founding gift of a First Folio had a practical supplement: 'I saw the librarian, Mr R.C. Walker, who was very pleased to meet me, and gave the whole morning in showing me over the building. He is delighted to have possession of the Shakespeare, and has had a copy of the Staunton photo-lithographed copy of the First folio placed outside the case for students to examine, as he very rightly keeps the original close and untouched, except upon very rare occasions, when he has permitted scholars to compare it with Staunton's facsimile'.[109] There was no mention of the fact that at least two leaves in the New South Wales original were themselves facsimiles. Similar security

[108] West 41; West 196.
[109] William Downing (comp.), *My Library Catalogue: Coombe Bank, Kingston-on Thames Richard Tangye* (London: 1904); Richard Tangye, *Notes of my Fourth Voyage to the Australian Colonies* (Birmingham: White and Pike, 1886), p. 51.

concerns about the value of the original have often been mitigated by placing a facsimile on public display, although the copy held by the University of Manchester that was stolen in 1972 remains unrecovered after thieves targeted one of the rare occasions when it was the original, not the copy, that was on display. The police issued an unconvincing description of the missing book that was the very opposite of the careful differentiation undertaken by bibliographers and owners over the previous century: they were looking for a red leather-bound volume with 'Shakespeare' on the spine and the last page incorrectly numbered 993.[110]

In 1954, individual plays were published as 'a facsimile of the First Folio text' taken from the Grenville copy in the British Library, each with an introduction by J. Dover Wilson.[111] Launching a series of paperback individual play facsimiles published by Globe Education, Patrick Spottiswood stated that 'the aim of Globe Folios is to provide students, actors, and the general reader with portable and affordable facsimiles of individual plays taken from the First Folio of Shakespeare's plays', although he added hastily, 'these facsimiles should complement and not replace good modern editions.'[112] The shadow of the connection between the Folio and non-scholarly dogma that had its expression in the Baconian theories discussed in Chapter 3 is still present. The Globe editions exercised an interesting selection of the Folio preliminaries with which to precede each individual play, leaving out the dedicatory epistle to the Herberts and the poems by lesser writers than Jonson. Even as it partially reproduces the First Folio, therefore, this choice has the useful modernizing effect of presenting Shakespeare as free from aristocratic patronage and endorsed by a still-canonical contemporary in poetic terms: 'not for an age but for all time'.

---

[110] *The Times*, 29 July 1972.

[111] The edition was published by Chiswick Press for Faber and Faber.

[112] The edition was published by Globe Education and the British Library. Spottiswoode's manifesto is on p. 5 of each play.

These twentieth-century facsimile editions clearly circulate in entirely different ways from original First Folio copies, and could never be mistaken for those 'True Originall' books. But much of the development in facsimile reproduction from the hand-written pen facsimiles of the eighteenth century onwards was motivated by the desire to fill out missing leaves in First Folio copies. By 1793, George Steevens noted:

Every possible adulteration, has of late years been practised in fitting up copies of this book for sale. When leaves are wanting they have been reprinted with battered types, and foisted into vacancies, without notice of such defects and the remedies applied to them. When the title has been lost, a spurious one has been fabricated, with a blank space left for the head of Shakespeare, afterwards added for the second, third or fourth impressions. To conceal these frauds, thick vermilion lines have been usually drawn over the edges of the engraving and discoloured with tobacco-water till it had assumed the true jaune antique. Sometimes leaves have been inserted from the second folio, and in a known instance, the entire play of Cymbeline, the genuine date being altered.[113]

Steevens was himself a major player in the activity he called 'vampment', writing to a correspondent in 1790 of his aim to 'retain, if possible, my own copy, changing only such leaves in it as had been blotted, greased or scribbled on by Dr Johnson'. He clearly undertook this for others, too. Dibdin reported that 'Lord Spencer's copy had every leaf picked by the experienced hands of the late George Steevens', and if he is talking about the copy now in the Folger, a note records a number of facsimile and repaired leaves: 'The first nine leaves & last leaf in facsimile' plus more than two dozen 'Leaves made up & mended'.[114] Percy Fitzgerald observed that 'almost every copy, save two or three that can be named, is "made up"—that is, the defects of one are supplemented

---

[113] Steevens (1793) vol. I, p. 445.
[114] Dibdin (1825), p. 411. West 96.

from others'.[115] The detailed analyses by Rasmussen and West in their catalogue prove the truth of this judgement. Almost every copy has added facsimile leaves, inlaid leaves, missing leaves, or leaves imported from other copies of this, or later, Folios.

Facsimile reproduction was an important aspect of this drive for perfection. The publisher Charles Knight recalled in his autobiography how an encounter with a battered First Folio had been a foundation for his printing, and literary, career. Given a 'sadly defective' copy of the First Folio as a young man he 'devised a plan for making the rare volume perfect'. This involved purchasing Wright's type-facsimile, assembling an old type fount 'which exactly resembled that of the folio of 1623', and deploying 'abundant fly-leaves of seventeenth-century books which matched the paper on which this edition was printed'. 'I set myself', recalled Knight, 'the task of composing every page that was wholly wanting, or was torn and sullied. When the book was handsomely bound I was in raptures at my handiwork. I was to have the copy for myself; but one of the Eton private-tutors, to whom my father showed the volume, offered a tempting price for it and my treasure passed from me.'[116] This facsimile of a facsimile pre-empted Knight's later acquisition of a First Folio to produce his pictorial serial edition of Shakespeare.

The preliminary leaves and the final pages of *Cymbeline* were particularly susceptible to damage or removal. The copy in Wadham College has a late-eighteenth-century pen facsimile page, carefully patterned on the original typed layout and clearly copied from a Second Folio since it follows the spellings and corrects the page number to 339 (it is misprinted as 993 in the First Folio) (Figure 5.2). Sidney Lee estimated in his census that at the beginning of the twentieth century 'only one in every fifteen copies possesses the last leaf and title-page uninjured', and these were

---

[115] Fitzgerald, p. 254.
[116] Charles Knight, *Passages of A Working Life During Half a Century* (London: Bradbury and Evans, 1864), vol. I, p. 80.

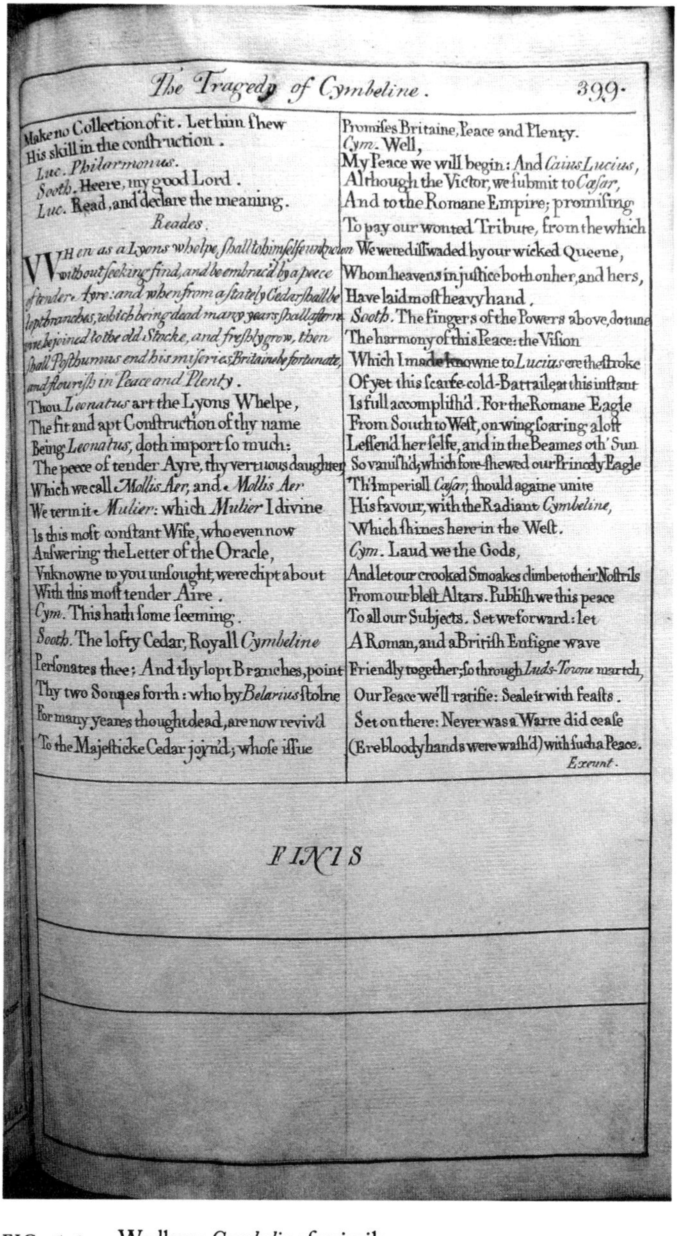

The Tragedy of Cymbeline. 399.

Make no Collection of it. Let him shew
His skill in the construction.
Luc. Philarmonus.
Sooth. Heere, my good Lord.
Luc. Read, and declare the meaning.
Reades.

WHen as a Lyons whelpe, shall to himselfe unknowne,
without seeking find, and be embrac'd by a peece
of tender Ayre: and when from a stately Cedar shall be
lopt branches, which being dead many yeares, shall after
one be joyned to the old Stocke, and freshly grow, then
shall Posthumus end his miseries, Britaine be fortunate,
and flourish in Peace and Plenty.

Thou *Leonatus* art the Lyons Whelpe,
The fit and apt Construction of thy name
Being *Leonatus*, doth import so much:
The peece of tender Ayre, thy vertuous daughter
Which we call *Mollis Aer*, and *Mollis Aer*
We terme it *Mulier*: which *Mulier* I divine
Is this most constant Wife, who even now
Answering the Letter of the Oracle,
Vnknowne to you unsought, were clipt about
With this most tender Aire.
Cym. This hath some seeming.
Sooth. The lofty Cedar, Royall *Cymbeline*
Personates thee: And thy lopt Branches, point
Thy two Sonnes forth: who by *Belarius* stolne
For many yeares thought dead, are now reviv'd
To the Majesticke Cedar joyn'd; whose issue

Promises Britaine, Peace and Plenty.
Cym. Well,
My Peace we will begin: And *Caius Lucius,*
Although the Victor, we submit to *Cæsar,*
And to the Romane Empire; promising
To pay our wonted Tribute, from the which
We were disswaded by our wicked Queene,
Whom heavens in justice both on her, and hers,
Have laid most heavy hand.
Sooth. The fingers of the Powers above, do tune
The harmony of this Peace: the Vision
Which I made knowne to *Lucius*, ere the stroke
Of yet this scarce-cold-Battaile, at this instant
Is full accomplish'd. For the Romane Eagle
From South to West, on wing soaring aloft
Lessen'd her selfe, and in the Beames oth' Sun
So vanish'd; which fore-shew'd our Princely Eagle
Th'Imperiall *Cæsar,* should againe unite
His favour, with the Radiant *Cymbeline,*
Which shines heere in the West.
Cym. Laud we the Gods,
And let our crooked Smoakes climbe to their Nostrils
From our blest Altars. Publish we this peace
To all our Subjects. Set we forward: let
A Roman, and a Britith Ensigne wave
Friendly together: so through *Luds-Towne* march,
Our Peace wee'll ratifie: Seale it with feasts.
Set on there: Never was a Warre did cease
(Ere bloody hands were wash'd) with such a Peace.
Exeunt.

FINIS

FIG. 5.2. Wadham *Cymbeline* facsimile
The final page of this Folio has been supplied in pen facsimile, copied from the
Second Folio.

often supplied from cannibalized or copied Second Folio pages.[117] By the nineteenth century, facsimiles tended to be printed. Often—but not always—the borrowing was clearly stated, as in the leaves from 'Day's Photographic Facsimile' (the edition superintended by Howard Staunton) reported in the manuscript notes on the copy dated 1870.[118] The Bodleian Library's copy of Staunton's facsimile, otherwise in fine condition, has a very badly damaged, possibly replaced, title page—perhaps taken out of the facsimile as a souvenir or to provide a replacement in another copy.[119]

Original, facsimile, and blended copies of First Folios circulated in many of the same outlets and to many of the same clients. George Grey, purchasing a First Folio to crown the collection he would give to Auckland Free Public Library, was offered by Bernard Quaritch 'a Facsimile Title Page with Portrait to First Folio Shakespeare 1623' (no price) to complete his purchase.[120] A week later, on July 4 1894, Ellis and Elvey booksellers wrote 'to inform you that the leaves are now inserted in your copy of the First Folio Shakespeare and that they very much improve your book'.[121] A look at the stock of the London bookseller Joseph Lilly in the decade from 1859 offers a snapshot of the capacious and overlapping market for improved, facsimile or perfected copies. In 1859, Lilly offered for sale as a single lot a multi-volume Folio set in matching bindings of 'red morocco super extra, the backs very richly tooled with gold, with gold tooling on the sides, gilt edges', including both a First Folio and a copy of the 'reprint', presumably Wright's 1807 publication. Lilly's 1860 *A Catalogue of a Very Choice, Valuable and Interesting Collection of Rare, Curious and Useful Books* (an annotator of the copy in the Bodleian library has

[117] Lee (1902), p. 10.   [118] West 112.   [119] Bod M10 L00021.
[120] Sir George Grey Special Collections, GL:Q1(12).
[121] Sir George Grey Special Collections, GL:E15.

inserted the observation 'exorbitantly dear' after 'very') offers a
Folio described 'with the whole of the genuine title-page having
a very fine clear impression of the portrait by Droeshout in the
centre: remarkably fine copy, entirely free from stains and dirt: but
the verses by Ben Jonson are by Harris'; another is a 'very clean,
sound, and entirely perfect copy, except Ben Jonson's verses
opposite the title are in facsimile by Harris... the portrait by
Droueshout [*sic*] in the centre of the title-page is very clear and
brilliant'; in 1866, the catalogue emphatically offers 'A perfect and
most desirable copy of this precious volume. The only exception is
that the top and bottom of the title, in the centre of which is
A REMARKABLY FINE IMPRESSION OF THE PORTRAIT BY DROESHOUT,
is supplied in most perfect facsimile by Mr. Harris.'

Lilly's sale catalogues resonate with one name synonymous with
nineteenth-century First Folio perfecting and facsimiles: Harris.
In 1863, Lilly had six First Folios for sale, and all of them had at
least some work by Harris, usually around the Jonson verse on the
verso facing the title page, or on the title page itself. John Harris
(1791–1873) was thus the preeminent supplier of supplementary
or perfecting material for First Folios and other valuable books and
manuscripts in the nineteenth century, and was employed by a
number of private collectors as well as the British Museum. In an
1854 account of his artist father, also John Harris, he described
himself as 'an Artist following a variety of branches connected
with the Fine Arts, but priding himself more particularly
upon executing fac-simile Leaves for perfecting rare old
books'.[122] His own advertisement in the 1850s offered 'Fac-similes
of the early Wood and other Engravers, also of Block and other
early Printing, after Faust, Schoeffer, Wynkin de Worde,

---

[122] Philip J. Weimerkirsch, 'John Harris, Sr., 1767–1832. Memoir by his son,
John Harris, Jr., 1791–1873', in *The Book Collector* 42 (1993) pp. 245–52; p. 251.

B. Pynson and others, to supply deficiencies in imperfect Books'.[123] Harris was the commercial artist of the drive to perfect books, especially the First Folio. One of his noble references came from the Duke of Sussex, describing him as 'a very ingenious man, who repairs manuscripts and imitates old books in a way quite surprising, so as to make it impossible to observe them from the original'. Recollecting his work at the British Museum, Robert Cowtan recalled how the library's experts examined a book and were forced to summon Harris to identify his facsimile: 'it was only after some considerable search that the artist was able to detect his own handiwork'. It was thereupon agreed that all facsimiles would be marked 'to prevent the possibility of subsequent librarians being imposed upon'. Cowtan observed, with marked understatement: 'a complete list of all the books completed by Mr. Harris in facsimile would be a curious and valuable document'.[124]

Numerous copies of the First Folio include leaves unobtrusively signed by Harris, tucking his initials in the bottom of the gutter. But almost certainly, the extent of Harris's facsimile work in First Folio copies has been underestimated, and a good deal of it is probably undetected. Lee acknowledged that Harris's 'magical skill increases the need of wariness in dogmatizing about the perfect state of almost any extant First Folio'.[125] The facsimilist wrote an account of his working practices for the report on the Great Exhibition, which documents the ways in which new and old technologies collaborated in his practice:

Formerly I made an accurate tracing from the original leaf, and afterwards retraced it on to the inlaid leaf by means of a paper blacked on one side; this produced an outline lettered page, which by being gone over carefully

---

[123] Quoted from a copy in Reading University Library in David McKitterick, *Print, Manuscript and the Search for Order 1450–1830* (Cambridge: Cambridge University Press, 2003), p. 145.

[124] Robert Cowtan, *Memories of the British Museum* (London: R. Bentley and Son, 1872), pp. 336–7; p. 335; p. 335.

[125] Lee (1923), p. 84.

and imitating the original, produced the desired leaf. This process was found to take up much time, and was consequently expensive, but it was the method I adopted while employed by Mr Whittaker [John Whittaker, of Westminster, bookbinder]; and he, to carry out the deception still further, had two sets of tools cut of the large and small letters generally used by Caxton, with which he has often been at the trouble to go over the pages after my work was done, to give the appearance of the indentation of the type. The process afterwards adopted by me was to make the tracing in a soft ink, to transfer the same to a thin paper, and to re-transfer on to the intended leaf: by this means I saved one-third, or one tracing of the work, which was a great saving in both time and expense. I pursued this process for some years; but I have within the last 10 or 12 years had recourse to lithography, producing the tracing on to the stone, and finishing up the letters on the same: this has been beneficial, particularly when more than one copy was wanted; but I occasionally find even this process irksome and uncertain, and frequently at this present time have recourse to my own, or the second method described, and execute fac-similes by manuscript process.[126]

Harris won an 'honourable mention' from the judges for 'his imitations of ancient typography'.

How far these facsimiles were intended to deceive is unclear, although the language of trickery hovers around their descriptions. Harris himself mentions 'deception' above; Lilly's habitual epithet of 'clever' shifts in one case to 'so cleverly done as to defy detection'. Harris's work circulates and has value within a Folio economy of perfected copies. Two examples from Lilly's 1863 catalogue reveal the bibliography of various kinds of vampment: 'Ben Jonson's verses are by Harris, the title and portrait are printed in facsimile, 3 of the preliminary leaves are in facsimile by Harris, and the last leaf is by Harris, the most accurate facsimile on old paper'; 'Ben Jonson's verses are by Harris; the title and portrait are the facsimile

---

[126] Exhibition of the Works of Industry of All Nations 1851, *Reports by the Juries on the Subjects in the Thirty Classes into which the Exhibition was Divided* (London: 1852), p. 405.

reprint, the preliminary leaves are from the second edition, and the last two leaves are in facsimile by Harris.'[127] Facsimile, Harris facsimile, old paper, reprint—the terms establish a hierarchy of simulation, in which Harris's work here is of the highest value. Even as he is producing facsimiles, his own name is the guarantee of their quality. Harris's exacting work cost him his eyesight, and he saw out his days in the Royal Masonic Benevolent Institution for Aged Freemasons and their Widows in Croydon. His son continued his work for some years.

Lilly's catalogue makes clear that particular facsimile attention was required for the Droeshout engraving, at once the most iconic and desirable marker of the First Folio and also the leaf least likely to be present in its original form. The portrait had always been subject to numerous reproductions and re-engravings, beginning with the reverse portrait by William Marshall that accompanied John Benson's 1640 edition of Shakespeare's *Poems*. It was copied again by E. A. Ashbee for the Bathurst edition of 1773 and for Isaac Reed's 1785 edition, and re-engraved again by William Sherwin and printed in 1790.[128] Such reproductions circulated widely. For example, Joseph Lilly offered in 1862 'the celebrated Portrait of Shakspeare as engraved by Droeshout, for the first collected Edition of his Works published in 1623, supposed to be after the Chandos portrait, very finely re-engraved by H. Robinson, together with a facsimile of his autograph'. Many Shakespeare collections, including at the Victoria and Albert Museum and at the Folger Shakespeare library, hold free-floating title-page facsimiles, which clearly circulated as spares or substitutes. The New York Public Library has a copy, once owned by James Lenox, which he describes in a pencil note on the binder's leaf: 'Since it came into my possession I have added the genuine

---

[127] Joseph Lilly, *Lilly's Catalogue of Rare, Curious, valuable and useful books* (1863), p. 112.
[128] J. Parker Norris, *The Portraits of Shakespeare* (Philadelphia: Robert M. Lindsay, 1885), pp. 58–66.

[title page] in a leaf, a condition very rarely seen and the title with the date 1622: the title belonging to it having the date 1623 and an impression of "Harris" fac simile portrait.'[129]

The line between authentic title pages cut from First Folios and imitations made by different means was not always clear. In 1913, Arthur Reader had sent Henry Folger a Shakespeare portrait on approval. Folger wrote back: 'I am afraid someone has taken advantage of you in stating that it is an original. It is not from the original plate, nor is the water-mark in the paper like any of the watermarks in the First Folio.'[130] New technologies produced not just copies of the Droeshout, but improvements on it. In 1882, Walter Rogers Furness did for the title page portrait what his editor father had done for the text of Shakespeare in the Variorum edition: collected and juxtaposed all the variants, making use of Staunton's facsimile. The effect of the composite 'Photograving by the Typographic Etching Company' portraits is eerily three-dimensional, or, as Furness senior reported in a letter to the Cambridge Shakesepearean, W. Aldis Wright: 'to me the first composite, made of all the selected portraits, has a more lifelike look than any single one of the lot. And moreover, there is a touch of humour in the face that justifies the comedies.'[131] But deficiencies in some title pages were supplied with less skill or technical ingenuity. Figure 5.3 shows a page amateurishly patched up by its pre-Folger owners.[132]

Publishing partial facsimiles, of preliminary material or a single play, was an intermittent part of commemorative culture in the twentieth century. As if to flatter the form of the Folio, celebratory

---

[129] West 167.   [130] Grant, p. 117.
[131] Walter Rogers Furness, *Composite Photography Applied to the Portraits of Shakespeare* (Philadelphia: Robert M. Lindsay, 1885); H. H. Furness Jr (ed.), *The Letters of Horace Howard Furness* (Boston and New York: Houghton Mifflin, 1922), vol. I, p. 235.
[132] West 100.

FIG 5.3. Title page, West 100
We are used to facsimiles and reproductions of perfect First Folios: this wonky title page is more representative of their general state of repair.

volumes were often constructed as pastiche or imitation: the letter-press folio format of Lee's *Census*, for example, printed in antique fount, to accompany his facsimile in 1902; or the account of the missing Bodleian Folio published by sub-librarian Falconer Madan and hand-press printed at the University Press three years later. When the Bodleian launched a fund-raising campaign to digitize the same copy it had bought back in 1905, it offered as an incentive a prize draw: 'Paul W. Nash, the Bodleian's printing specialist, will produce a specially commissioned letterpress keep-sake, in the form of a folio bifolium of English hand-made paper, printed in the Bodleian's Hand-Printing Workshop, with Leonard Digges' encomium to Shakespeare, taken from the pre-liminary matter of the First Folio.'[133] The three hundredth anni-versary of the publication of the First Folio saw a number of homages to the typography and layout of the book. The London Shakespeare League published a sixpenny pamphlet to celebrate the Folio, with particular stress on John Heminge and Henry Condell as the powers behind the book. Sidney Lee remarked that to them 'the supreme glory of the enterprise must belong', and suggested that 'in the name of just sentiment and of sound history, it would be well, from this Tercentenary year onwards, for every editor of Shakespeare's collected works to honour the names of Heminge and Condell and to follow their example by prefixing to the edition a reprint of the First Folio's prefatory pages'. The pamphlet reproduced the title-page from the Grenville copy in the British Museum via photographic intermediary: 'The plate has been electrotyped from that in the illustrated edition of Sir Sidney Lee's "Life of Shakespeare" by permission of the publisher, Mr John Murray.' The other prefatory pages were presented in type facsimile.[134] Another similar publication was produced by a

---

[133] http://shakespeare.bodleian.ox.ac.uk/the-project/prize-draw/ (accessed April 2015).

[134] The London Shakespeare League, *Tercentenary of the Publication of the First Folio of Shakespeare's Works* (London: 1923), n.p.

different organization with a rival scholar at the head: *In Commemoration of the First Folio Centenary* with an introduction by Sir Israel Gollancz. This prestige volume, designed to showcase the ongoing skill of the Stationers' Company, used a new fount designed to copy that of the First Folio: 'great care has been taken in giving a faithful rendering of the type arrangement, as regards size, justification, and spacing. The headpieces and initials have been engraved on wood, and, except for their reduced size, are exact facsimiles. The title-page, also reduced, has been photographically reproduced by the line process of engraving on zinc.'[135] This mixed medium—letter-press typography and photo-zincography—has a faint echo of the production in 1623, where the Droeshout engraving, which required a rolling press, may well have been outsourced by the Jaggard printing business to a specialist workshop, perhaps belonging to the engraver himself.

This facsimile was designed to accompany an exhibition at Stationers' Hall in which the publisher, John Murray's, copy of the First Folio was on display: according to Lee's census, that copy itself included two facsimile leaves and a handful of imports from the Second Folio. Something similar happened in the 1923 exhibition at Cardiff, where the colliery owner, Thomas Watson, loaned his copy, with all the preliminaries, fourteen other leaves, and the last eight leaves supplied in facsimile. The Elizabethan Club copy in Yale that was used for Kökeritz's facsimile also had the initial verses in facsimile and a number of other leaves from other copies.[136] The Duke of Devonshire's copy, which was picked out by Lee for his facsimile, had an inlaid portrait and a number of leaves supplied from a shorter copy, with margins added to even out the pages. Even the apparently authentic object, that is to say,

---

[135] Israel Gollancz (ed.), *In Commemoration of the First Folio Centenary. A Resetting of the Preliminary Matter of the First Folio, with a Catalogue of Shakespeariana Exhibited in the Hall of The Worshipful Company of Stationers* (London: Oxford University Press for the Shakespeare Association, 1923), p. 29.

[136] West 108.

was itself usually an artefact combining early modern and modern technologies of reproduction, and many facsimiles were facsimiles of partial or whole facsimiles.

There was also an active market in part-copies of Folios that could be reused to complete better copies, although this rarely surfaces in trade catalogues. One exception is found in Bernard Quaritch's 1869 catalogue, which, in addition to 'a fine sound, and very cheap copy' of the First Folio (£165), offers at £25 'a fragment, which measures 12 7/8 inches by 8, will be found useful as a specimen copy of the first Shakespeare, or for supplying leaves wanting in other copies'. In 1889, the American collector, Adolph Sutro, acquired a part-Folio bound in twelve volumes comprising nine complete plays and volumes entitled 'Imperfect First Folio edition of Henry the Fourth', 'Imperfect copies of Henry the Fifth and Henry the Sixth 1623' and 'Fragments of the First Folio Shakespeare'.[137] In spring of 1911, Henry Folger informed a London bookseller of his interest in securing 'any parts' of a First Folio but he later rejected an offer from Maggs Bros for First Folio *Julius Caesar* leaves because the price, £63, was too high.[138] This particular Roman fragment seems to have been doing the rounds: it was the only part of an original First Folio on display at the 1923 Shakespeare First Folio Tercentenary exhibition at Southwark Library, 'lent by Messrs Maggs Bros'. The other Folios on display were the Wright reprints of 1807 and the Staunton, Halliwell-Philips, National, Lee, and Methuen facsimiles.[139] For those who could never afford a complete volume, individual leaves came to have a unique value, bound up in new books with accompanying explanatory material. Seymour de Ricci published *A Noble Fragment, Being a Leaf of the Original First Folio of William*

[137] West 52. [138] Grant, p. 101, 103.
[139] London Borough of Southwark, *Shakespeare 1st Folio Tercentenary, 1623–1923: Southwark Commemmoration Exhibition Catalogue* (Southwark: 1923), n.p.

Shakespeare's Plays Printed in 1623 (1926) which included one original leaf and a facsimile of the title page, and the Grabhorn Press of New York published in 1935 a volume—or a number of unique copies—of *Original Leaves from the First Four Folios of Shakespeare's Plays*. There were similar publishing projects for leaves of the Gutenberg bible.[140] There were ontological questions posed by this fragmentation and recollection, however. Sidney Lee, reviewing his census in 1923, described a Washington correspondent who had gathered 'by dint of persistent search in all parts of the world, eight hundred and ninety-eight out of the nine hundred and eight leaves of which the perfect volume originally consisted'. Would Lee accept this 'shapeless conglomeration of scraps' into a new edition of his census? 'I am not sure about my answer.'[141] What counts as a copy continues to be debated. Anthony James West persuaded the Folger to add another three copies to their tally by redesignating three composite, multi-volume editions as numbers 80, 81 and 82. His criteria were based on a complicated tally of number of original leaves, provenance, and location ultimately aimed at 'admit[ting] all Folios scholars might want to know'.[142]

One effect of the proliferation of facsimile Folios was to reemphasize the significance of detailed attention to the orthography, typography, and presentation of the edition. One review identified that chief among the advantages of Staunton's facsimile over Booth's reprint was that 'in all the extremest minutiae the photographic copy is pre-eminent': 'extremest minutiae' had become the Folio's major selling point.[143] Introducing his own facsimile in 1876, James Halliwell-Phillips repeated that the First Folio's

[140] Adam   G.   Hooks,   http://www.adamghooks.net/2012/06/breaking-shakespeare-apart.html (accessed April 2015).   [141] Lee (1924), p. 82.

[142] Anthony James West, 'How Many First Folios Does the Folger Hold?' *Shakespeare Quarterly* 47 (1996), pp. 190–4; p. 190.

[143] *The Times*, 20 January 1864.

'value increases every day, for day by day it is more clearly ascertained that many of the subtler meanings of passages in the works of Shakespeare depend upon minute indications and peculiarities which are alone to be traced in the original printed text'.[144] Duncan Dallas advertised his own facsimile on similar grounds: 'Such an exact verisimilitude has never before been attempted or attained. Every peculiarity in the original is facsimiled, even to the errors in pagination, and other points, which distinguish the First Folio from all other editions.'[145]

Many readers paying particular attention to these 'minute indications and peculiarities' developed their own theories about the First Folio with reference to readily available facsimile editions. Struggling to find the Baconian code he knew must be present, in Shakespeare, Ignatius Donnelly's epiphany was textual: 'I at length, July 1 1882, procured a fac-simile copy, folio size, made by photo-lithographic process, and, therefore, an exact reproduction of type, pages, punctuation and everything else. It is one of those "executed under the superintendence of H. Staunton," and published in 1866 by Day & Son, London.'[146] A facsimile designed for and marketed at Baconians was already in the wings. The publishers' advertisement for *The National Shakespeare* type facsimile of 1888 alluded to the 'remarkable theory' of 'an elaborate cypher by means of which the plays convey, besides their obvious meaning, a second or hidden narrative bearing upon the vexed question of their authorship'. While not confirming this view, the advertisement continued: 'every lover of Shakespeare naturally desires to have the means of forming his own opinion in the controversy'.[147] Edward D. Johnson prefaced his

---

[144] Halliwell-Phillips, p. v.
[145] Publisher's advertisement bound with the Bodleian copy: M.adds.88 c.2.
[146] Donnelly, vol. ii, p. 547.
[147] Publisher's advertisement bound with the Bodleian copy: Dunston B 36/1.

calculations about Bacon's authorship with an unexpected 'Chartered Accountant's Certificate' in which Bertram C. Ottey of Birmingham declares: 'I hereby certify that I have personally checked the counts and numbers contained in the following work with the Facsimile of the First Folio produced to me by Mr Edward D. Johnson and that the same are correct.'[148] It appears from Johnson's account that the facsimile in question is that of Sidney Lee, also preferred by Walter Conrad Arensberg in his *The Cryptography of Shakespeare* (1922). Some nifty work with tracing paper and the 1954 Yale facsimile enabled Olive Wagner Driver to discover in the Droeshout engraving a reversed inscription that was ANT—which, with HONY found down the margin, confirmed 'Anthony Bacon' as the author.[149] But not all readers of facsimiles were concerned with coded authorship. Keats owned a copy of the 1807 type-facsimile by J. Wright, and when, in the title of his famous poem, he sat down to read *King Lear* again it was most probably in this edition. Geoffrey Grigson's poem from the early 1970s, 'The First Folio', addresses, with some trepidation about what unfamiliar readings it may provide in place of much-loved phrases, a cased Shakespeare facsimile, almost certainly a copy of the Norton edition of 1968.[150]

Most extant Folios are thus a combination of facsimiles, imported leaves, and original leaves. Facsimile Folios have served to substitute for, to supplement, to perfect, and to validate the original: they have contributed to its increasing reification even as they threaten to undermine that singularity. There are so many facsimile pages and elements to supposedly original First Folios

[148] Edward D. Johnston, *The First Folio of Shake-speare* (London: Cecil Palmer, 1932), n.p.
[149] Garber (2003), p. 13.
[150] Geoffrey Grigson, *Collected Poems 1963–1980* (London: Allison & Busby, 1982), p. 149.

that the distinction between original and copy is unsustainable: practically obscured and theoretically opaque. Most 'First Folios' are constructed post-hoc as hybridized or blended artefacts operating within a misleading rhetoric of authenticity that works to obscure the labour of their simulation.

The blurring between original and facsimile reaches an extreme in the most recent forms of digital reproduction online. At least a dozen facsimile editions are now available online. Three of the Folger's copies, copies from Stuttgart, New South Wales, the Bodleian Library, the Kodama Memorial library at Meisei, the Universities of Pennsylvania, Leeds, Miami and Brandeis have all been digitized.[151] To digitize a First Folio is now so routine a reflex that the St-Omer copy was made available online within weeks of its recent rediscovery. These different digitizations tend to preserve the technologies of their construction—the earliest, at Penn, dates from the mid-1990s—and thus also to prescribe the ways in which they can be read. Placing the large double-columned pages on a computer screen, on a tablet or other device, for instance, means that it is often impossible to see the entire page-layout in a size that also allows the print to be read. The sense of the opening that was so important to early readers is hard to reproduce in these new versions, and so too are any of the forms of active engagement marked in ink, pencil, mud, grease and wine on pages of First Folio copies (see Chapter 2). Finding a way through the facsimile is not always easy: assessing where we are in the book at any one point is one of the easy physical experiences of reading a book that the digital experience finds difficult to reproduce. As David McKitterick emphasizes, 'the two-dimensional screen cannot illustrate adequately a three-dimensional object that constantly

---

[151] Sarah Werner posts a list of these resources on the Folger's Collation blog: http://collation.folger.edu/2013/04/first-folios-online and asks 'What do we want from online facsimiles of Shakespeare?' in a user's guide on her personal site: http://sarahwerner.net/blog/2013/05/what-do-we-want-from-online-facsimiles-of-shakespeare/ (accessed April 2015).

changes shape as its leaves are turned'.[152] The Bodleian Library
version has a searchable transcription of the text alongside the
digital images, and also uses a page-turning software to simulate
the experience of handling the leaves of the book. Many of the
Folger copies in Luna, their digital image repository, exist as
separate high-quality images that need to be opened individually.
Both the Bodleian and the Folger have made their images available
under creative commons licences that encourage reuse.

The idea that digital facsimiles somehow augur the end of the
codex, as proclaimed by Robert Coover in 1992 and many others
before and since, has been so frequently proclaimed that we all now
know it is not true.[153] Many commentators have remarked that
one consequence of digital access to content has been to encourage
interest in the book as object and paradoxically to revive what
Jessica Pressman has called 'an aesthetic of bookishness'.[154] The
period of Folio digitization has also been a period where many
museums and collections globally have moved to a permanent
display of the book itself. Facsimiles are still seen as supplements,
not substitutes, for First Folio copies. Amid the outcry when
Senate House Library attempted to sell one of their First Folios,
the consensus that this was cultural vandalism was barely chal-
lenged. Even Jerry Brotton's slightly angular piece for *The Guardian*, which reminded readers that 'the play's the thing: the Bard's
online too', did not quite have the courage of its convictions.
Citing the crisis in library and humanities funding, the growing

---

[152] David McKitterick, *Old Books, New Technologies: the Representation, Conservation and Transformation of Books Since 1700* (Cambridge: Cambridge University
Press, 2013), p. 4.

[153] Robert Coover, 'The End of Books', *The New York Times*, 21 June 1992:
http://www.nytimes.com/books/98/09/27/specials/coover-end.html   (accessed
April 2015). In riposte, see, for example, Leah Price, 'Dead Again', *The New York
Times*, 10 August 2012.

[154] Jessica Pressman, 'The Aesthetics of Bookishness in Twenty-First-Century
Literature', *Michigan Quarterly Review* 48 (2009), pp. 465–82.

use of tablets and laptops in the classroom, and the fact that few of the protestors, or the London university students for whom they presumed to speak, had ever accessed a valuable book like the First Folio, it seemed clear where Brotton's argument was heading. 'It is now possible', he wrote, 'to produce digital facsimiles of the four folios that the library proposes to sell at a high enough resolution to see every correction, revision and blot, even down to the nature of the paper stock and its watermarks (issues which are crucial in providing clues to the book's creation, and hence its potential meaning).' The logical conclusion—digitize, then sell the Folio, and use the online surrogate to reach a wider public and the sale money to prop up the library. Simple. But Brotton stopped short, urging Senate House to stop the sale, to digitize the First Folio, and to plan a commemorative exhibition displaying material and digital versions.[155] Getting rid of the book itself still seemed unthinkable.

[155] Jerry Brotton, 5 September 2013, http://www.theguardian.com/commentisfree/2013/sep/05/save-shakespeare-folios-senate-house (accessed April 2015).

Conclusion

Owning, or even hosting, a First Folio can be a headache. Soliciting US state institutions to receive a visiting exhibition for 2016 initially called 'Shakespeare and his First Folio' and gussied up to the more emphatic 'First Folio! The book that gave us Shakespeare', the Folger Shakespeare Library set out very specific environmental and security requirements, not to mention firm rules about any advertising that might compete with selected tour sponsors. Lighting, temperature and relative humidity parameters were all specified; security for the courier between the airport and the venue and professional guards at all times the exhibition was opened were the responsibility of the host institution.[1] It was a snapshot of the onerous requirements for the public display of a First Folio in the twenty-first century.

The Craven Museum in Skipton, a small market town in North Yorkshire, experienced this new world when an old book in its collection, owned by a local cotton and tobacco manufacturer turned amateur entomologist and donated in 1936, was redescribed by Anthony West in 2003. It had always been classified as a Second Folio, but West's examination identified almost sixty per cent original First Folio leaves. A new exhibition, with considerable security, a case in which the book could be on permanent display, and a video introduction by the Yorkshire-born actor Sir

---

[1] https://apply.ala.org/shakespeare/guidelines (accessed April 2015).

Patrick Stewart, was opened in 2011. It is hard to please everyone, however: the book is judged too fragile to be accessible to scholars, and there was disagreement in the local press in 2014 when it was lent to the Yorkshire Museum in York in 2014 in return for two Iron Age gold bracelets. In the county museum it would, explained a council spokesman, 'take the place of Richard III's head in the Medieval Gallery and become the museum's main marketing attraction for the spring/summer season'.[2] Here the newly identi-fied First Folio has increased exchange value in a provincial econ-omy of museum objects, including decorative jewellery from the Brigantes tribe and the head of Richard III—a replica commis-sioned by the Richard III Society from a CT scan of the skull found under a Leicester car park in 2013, but it has had to sacrifice another form of accessibility.

Sometimes the exacting requirements of holding a First Folio have become so burdensome as to be no longer worthwhile. In 2006, the Chairman and Director of Dr Williams's Trust, the Dissenting library which had had a First Folio as part of its collection since the eighteenth century, wrote to the Friends of the organization outlining the finances of this single object. It cost the library £3,000 a year in insurance for the First Folio alone. As Peter Lindenbaum wrote in the *Times Literary Supplement* in defence of the controversial sale:

the volume itself has been at best a mixed blessing for the institution (hence its imminent sale). The Library's space restrictions, shortage of staff and limited insurance coverage were such that the volume could not be left in a display case or accessed easily (the theft of a copy of the First Folio from Durham University Library in 1998 haunts smaller, under-funded libraries such as this one). The volume was kept in a strongroom and could be viewed only in the immediate presence of the Library's Director, who would have to take time off from other duties when the

---

[2] *Craven Herald*, 14 February 2014.

occasional visitor (such as myself) requested (in writing, in advance, with good reasons) to examine the book.[3]

If some have wanted to divest themselves of this book, for others it has been an enticing lure. Eric Rasmussen's book, *The Shakespeare Thefts*, focuses on criminal acquisitions of a 'coveted First Folio', and tells the wonderful story of a bungled attempt to steal the copy from Williams College in 1940. A shoe clerk down on his luck was dressed up by crooks as a scholar—'an ill-fitting suit and a pair of old-fashioned eyeglasses' and his hair greyed with powder—and sent with a forged letter of introduction to steal the book. Later, however, he gave himself up to the police, claiming that he had read 'how Hitler and Goebbels collect rare books and send their agents to foreign countries to buy old editions' and the book was returned.[4]

Rasmussen's other example of a prominent recent theft has become a much more troubling parable of Folio value. In June 2008, a man who looked not at all like a scholar but rather in beach clothing (his sockless loafers seem to have been a source of particular distress to the librarian) claiming to have flown in from Cuba, turned up unannounced at the Folger Shakespeare Library, carrying a book he wanted to have authenticated. Their bibliographic expertise identified that Raymond Scott had brought the First Folio that had been missing for a decade from the Cosin Library in Durham.[5] The theologian, John Cosin, had bought the book in the 1620s. During the interregnum, when he was exiled from his post as Master of Peterhouse at Cambridge University, the book joined the college's library. But at the Restoration, Cosin reclaimed it and, as the new Bishop of Durham, took the First

---

[3] Peter Lindenbaum, 'Dispatches from the Archives', *Times Literary Supplement*, 2 June 2006.

[4] Eric Rasmussen, *The Shakespeare Thefts: In Search of the First Folios* (Basingstoke: Palgrave Macmillan, 2011), pp.132–3, 140.

[5] West 7.

Folio as part of a foundational collection in the new public library next to the cathedral. It remained there until it was stolen, along with medieval manuscripts, in 1998. Arrested for the theft of the book, Scott's expensive lifestyle and eccentric habits were widely publicized: 'Suspect in Folio Theft Is Something of a Character', remarked the *Washington Post* headline drily.[6]

The return of the Durham First Folio to its library is the most recent transfer of a copy of the book at the time of writing, and I had intended to end my book with the account of Scott's highly theatrical trial. Its—in retrospect—unsettlingly garish combination of Shakespeare and louche showmanship promised the perfect counterbalance to Sir Edward Dering's acquisitions of the 1620s. Dering enjoyed dandy clothing and jewels; Scott, on arriving at court, 'took time to detail his Valentino sunglasses, Versace silver crocodile-skin shoes and rings, Cartier watch and Louis Vuitton bum-bag to bystanders'.[7] Where Dering sought preferment through an advantageous marriage and his indulged son little Anthony, Scott, the newspapers reported, 'hoped to pay off £90,000 in debts and bring 23-year-old Heidy Rios, a raven-haired exotic dancer he met on holiday in Cuba, to Britain'.[8] Dering and Scott bookending this study, each using a First Folio as part of an elaborate and public strategy of self-fashioning through luxury props: you can see how it might have looked.

At Scott's trial, bibliography's flirtation with its investigative contemporary, criminology, was consummated. Anthony James West was the Expert Witness for the Crown Prosecution Service,

---

[6] *The Washington Post*, 17 July 2008.

[7] http://www.theguardian.com/uk/2010/jun/17/shakespeare-first-folio-trial (accessed April 2015).

[8] http://www.dailymail.co.uk/news/article-1299635/Conman-Raymond-Scott-tried-sell-stolen-Shakespeare-manuscript-2m.html#ixzz3YFExYPcQ   (accessed April 2015).

proving beyond doubt that the copy belonged in Durham.[9] Raymond Scott was sentenced to eight years in prison for handling stolen goods and removing stolen property from the UK. Eighteen months later he became one of the sixty-one deaths by suicide in jails in England and Wales in 2012.[10] He had cut his throat. The ombudsman investigating Scott's death reported in 2014 that the prisoner had 'become fixated with his sentence and appeal and the remainder of his time in custody seemed insurmountable', ruling that there had been 'a number of deficiencies in the operation of the suicide and self-harm monitoring'. There was worldwide publicity for Scott's original trial; only the local paper reported the findings of the inquest.[11]

Raymond Scott's final interview had touched on his motives: '[the First Folio] wasn't kept in a bank vault—it was openly kept on a book shelf and lovingly cherished. Then maybe the person fell in love and thought it's time to realise an asset. Perhaps this person decided to live one day as a lion rather than spend his days as a lamb. To live life to the full in Havana, London, Paris. You can't do this without money, without a lot of money. This is just a fairy story, of course.'[12] In its sad and conflicted conjunction of cultural, emotional, and economic value, Scott's statement stands as a coda to this book's over-determined history.

The fact of Scott's suicide casts the questions of value, equivalence and context with which this book has been concerned in a much darker light. It would clearly be unethical—just wrong—to annex what is publicly known of his story to the narratives of symbolic density I have been tracing in this book, but so too it seems an evasion to ignore Scott's story and its ending. The

---

[9] Anthony James West, 'Proving the Identity of the Stolen Durham First Folio', *The Library* 14 (2013), pp. 428–40.

[10] http://www.inquest.org.uk/statistics/deaths-in-prison (accessed April 2015).

[11] *Northern Echo*, 24 September 2014.

[12] http://www.theguardian.com/culture/2012/mar/14/shakespeare-folio-dealer-dead-scott (accessed April 2015).

investment in the individuality of First Folio copies, the forensic bibliographic expertise located in and identified with the Folger Shakespeare Library, the enormous price of First Folios, the public interest in their transfer, the rhetoric of eccentricity and extreme wealth that hovers around their acquisition: all these stories, established over centuries as outlined in this book, converge to make Scott's irruption on the Folio scene its almost inevitable epilogue. Durham University Library calls their now-returned book 'the physical embodiment of the human experience': in the context, the cliché is deeply uncomfortable.[13] Much of this study has been about the kinds of value—literary, cultural, national, dramatic, personal as well as economic—that First Folio copies have accrued, at different times and in different places for different individuals. But if it were not already evident throughout my account, this final First Folio shows that it is quite possible to over-value this most valuable of books.

---

[13] https://www.dur.ac.uk/news/shakespeare_folio/background/ (accessed April 2015).

Bibliography

UNPUBLISHED MATERIAL

Auckland City Libraries, Sir George Grey Special Collections.

Birmingham City Libraries—'Materials for a History of the Shakespeare Memorial Library Birmingham. 1871–1930'. S993.2.

Bodleian Library Records—Shakespeare First Folio 1905–6 b.862, b.863, and c.1220.

British Film Institute—'The National Lottery Live: The First Draw Broadcast 19 November 1994'. BFI ref. 433428.

Folger Shakespeare Library—'George Steevens letters to I. Reed 1777–1800', MS C.b.2.

Houghton Library, Harvard, commonplace book of John Hancock http://ocp.hul.harvard.edu/reading/vcsearch.php?cat=17+century&sub=commonplace.

Oxford University Press Archives—Shakespeare Edition CP1/18–19.

Shakespeare Birthplace Trust—Papers relating to Sidney Lee's *Census* ER85/6/1.

PUBLISHED MATERIAL

Adams, John and Charles Francis Adams. *The Works of John Adams, Second President of the United States*, 10 volumes (Boston: Little, Brown, 1850–6).

Aleman, Matheo. *The Rogue. Or the life of Gizman de Alfarache* (London: 1623).

Anonymous. *Jonsonus Virbius, Or The Memorie of Ben Johnson revived by his Friends the Muses* (London: 1638).

Anonymous. *Loves Garland, or Posies for rings, hand-kerchers, and gloves* (London: 1673).

Anonymous. *The Court Parrot: A New Miscellany in Prose and Verse* (London, 1733).

Anonymous [The Talk of the Town], *The New Yorker*, 7 July 1986, pp. 19–20.

Appadurai, Arjun. 'Introduction: Commodities and the Politics of Value'. In *The Social Life of Things: Commodities in Cultural Perspective*, edited by Arjun Appardurai (Cambridge: Cambridge University Press, 1986), pp. 3–63.

Appardurai, Arjun, editor. *The Social Life of Things: Commodities in Cultural Perspective* (Cambridge: Cambridge University Press, 1986).

Ardizzoni, Heidi. *An Illuminated Life: Belle de Costa Greene's Journey from Prejudice to Privilege* (New York and London: W. W. Norton, 2007).

Askegaard, Søren, editor. *Collecting, Luxury and the Production of Consumer Desire* (Los Angeles: SAGE, 2014).

Attar, K. E. 'Sir Edwin Durning-Lawrence: A Baconian and his Books'. *The Library* 5 (2003): pp. 294–315.

Aubrey, John. *Aubrey's Brief Lives*. Edited by Andrew Clark, 2 volumes (Oxford: Clarendon Press, 1898).

Bacon, Delia. *The Philosophy of the Plays of Shaksper Unfolded* (London: Groombridge and Sons, 1857).

Balanger, Terry. 'Tonson, Wellington and the Shakespeare copyrights'. In *Studies in the Book Trade In Honour of Graham Pollard*, edited by R. W. Hunt, I. G. Philip and R. J. Roberts (Oxford: Oxford Bibliographical Society, 1975), pp. 195–209.

Barber, Giles. 'Libraries'. In *The History of the University of Oxford*: Volume VIII, *The Twentieth Century*, edited by Brian Harrison (Oxford: Clarendon Press, 1994).

Barker, Harley Granville (ed.). *The Player's Shakespeare: Macbeth* (London: E. Benn, 1923).

Barker, Nicholas and Simon Jervis. *Treasures from the Libraries of National Trust Country Houses* (New York: Royal Oak Foundation and The Grolier Club, 1999).

Barnard, John and D. F. MacKenzie with the assistance of Maureen Bell, editors. *The History of the Book in Britain, volume IV, 1557–1695* (Cambridge: Cambridge University Press, 2002).

Barrett, Lawrence. *Edwin Forrest* (Boston, Mass.: 1881).

Barthes, Roland. *Image–Music–Text*, translated by Stephen Heath (London: Fontana, 1977).

Bartlett, H. C. and A. W. Pollard. *A Census of Shakespeare's Plays in Quarto 1594–1709* (New Haven: Yale University Press; London: Oxford University Press, 1916).

Bate, Jonathan. *Shakespearean Constitutions: Politics, Theatre, Criticism* (Oxford: Clarendon Press, 1989).

Bate, Jonathan, editor. *The Romantics on Shakespeare* (London: Penguin, 1992).

Bate, Jonathan, et al., editors. *William Shakespeare and Others: Collaborative Plays* (Basingstoke: Palgrave Macmillan, 2014).

Baugh, Albert. 'A Seventeenth-Century Play List'. *Modern Language Review* 13 (1918): pp. 401–11.

Beal, Peter. 'Notions in Garrison: The Seventeenth-Century Commonplace Book'. In *New Ways of Looking at Old Texts: Papers of the Renaissance English Text Society, 1985–1991*, edited by W. Speed Hill (Binghamton: Medieval & Renaissance Texts Society, 1993), pp. 131–48.

Belk, Russell. *Collecting in a Consumer Society* (London: Routledge, 1995).

Belk, Russell. 'Collectors and Collecting'. In *Collecting, Luxury and the Production of Consumer Desire*, edited by Soren Askegaard (Los Angeles: SAGE, 2014), pp. 13–30.

Benjamin, Walter. *Illuminations*, translated by Harry Zohn (London: Fontana Press, 1992).

Bevington, David. 'First Folio of Shakespeare by Charlton Hinman'. *Modern Philology* 68 (1970): pp. 98–100.

Billingsley, Martin. *The Pens Excellencie* (London, 1618).

Birmingham, Kevin. *The Most Dangerous Book: The Battle for James Joyce's 'Ulysses'* (London: Head of Zeus, 2014).

[Birmingham Free Libraries]. *City of Birmingham Free Libraries Reference Department: An Index to the Shakespeare Memorial Library First Part English Editions of Shakespeare's Works, Separate Plays and Poems* (Birmingham: Percival Jones Ltd, 1900).

Blair, Ann. *Too Much to Know: Managing Scholarly Information Before the Modern Age* (New Haven, Conn.: Yale University Press, 2010).

Blayney, Peter W. M. *The First Folio of Shakespeare* (Washington DC: Folger Library Publications, 1991).

Boaden, James. *An Inquiry into the Authenticity of Various Pictures and Prints, which . . . have been Offered to the Public as Portraits of Shakespeare* (London: Robert Triphook, 1824).

Booth, William Stone. *The Droeshout Portrait of William Shakespeare: An Experiment in Identification* (Boston: W. A. Butterfield, 1911).

Bourdieu, Pierre. *Distinction: A Social Critique of the Judgement of Taste* (London: Routledge, 2004).

Bowers, Fredson. 'The Yale Folio Facsimile and Scholarship'. *Modern Philology* 53 (1955): pp. 50–7.

Brissenden, Alan, editor. *As You Like It* (Oxford: Oxford University Press, 1993).

Brock, M. G., and M. C. Curthoys, editors. *The History of the University of Oxford*, Volume 7: *Nineteenth Century Oxford Part 2* (Oxford: Oxford University Press, 2000).

Brotton, Jerry, *The Guardian*, 5 September 2013, http://www.theguardian.com/commentisfree/2013/sep/05/save-shakespeare-folios-senate-house

Brown, Basil. *Supposed Caricature of the Droeshout Portrait of Shakespeare* (New York: privately printed, 1911).

Brown, Bill. *A Sense of Things: The Object Matter of American Literature* (Chicago and London: University of Chicago Press, 2003).

Bruce, John, editor. *Calendar of State Papers Domestic Series in the Reign of Charles I*, vol. 13: 1638–9 *(London: Longman, 1871)*.

[Brydges, Grey]. *Horae Subsecivae. Observations and Discourses* (London: E. Blount, 1620).

[Burdett Coutts, Baroness]. *Catalogue of the Valuable Library The Property of the late Baroness Burdett Coutts, Lady of Grace of the Order of St John of Jerusalem* (London: Sotheby Wilkinson and Hodge, May 1922).

Cadman, S. Parkes. *Henry C. Folger 18 June 1857–11 June 1930* (New Haven, CT: Privately Printed, 1931).

Caines, Michael. *Shakespeare and the Eighteenth Century* (Oxford: Oxford University Press, 2013).

Cannadine, David. *The Decline and Fall of the British Aristocracy* (New Haven CT; London: Yale University Press, 1990).

Cannon, Carl L. *American Book Collectors and Collecting From Colonial Times to the Present* (New York: H. W. Wilson Company, 1941).

Capell, Edward, editor. *Mr. William Shakespeare: his comedies, histories and tragedies*, 10 volumes (London: D. Leach for J. and R. Tonson, 1767–8).

Carlyle, Thomas. *On Heroes, Hero-Worship, and the Heroic in History* (London: Chapman and Hall, 1897).

Carnegie, Andrew. 'Wealth'. *North American Review* 148 (June 1889): pp.653–64.

Carrier, James G. *Gifts and Commodities: Exchange and Western Capitalism since 1700* (London: Routledge, 1995).

Carroll, J. L. *The Shakespeare Secret* (London: Sphere, 2008).

Carter, Harry. *A History of the Oxford University Press* (Oxford: Clarendon Press, 1975).

Carter, John. *Taste and Technique in Book-Collecting: A Study of Recent Developments in Great Britain and the United States* (Cambridge: Cambridge University Press, 1948).

[Chamberlain John]. *The Letters of John Chamberlain*, edited by N. E. McClure, 2 volumes (Philadelphia: The American Philosophical Society, 1939).

Chartier, Roger. 'Laborers and Voyagers: From the Text to the Reader', translated by J. A. Gonzalez. *Diacritics* 22 (1992): pp. 49–61.

Chernow, Ron. *The House of Morgan* (London: Simon and Schuster, 1990).

Church, Tony. *A Stage for a Kingdom* (n.p.: Oneiro Press, 2013).

Cibber, Colley. *An Apology for the Life of Mr Colley Cibber* (London: printed by John Watts for the author, 1740).

Clark, Andrew, editor. *The Life and Times of Anthony Wood, antiquary, of Oxford, 1632–1695*, 5 volumes (Oxford: Oxford Historical Society at the Clarendon Press, 1891–1900).

Clark, Beverly Lyon. *The Afterlife of 'Little Women'* (Baltimore: Johns Hopkins University Press, 2014).

Clark, Ronald W. *The Man Who Broke Purple: The Life of the World's Greatest Cryptologist Colonel William F. Friedman* (London: Weidenfield & Nicolson, 1977).

Clark, Steve. 'Conspiracy Theories and Conspiracy Theorizing'. In *Conspiracy Theories: The Philosophical Debate*, edited by David Coady (Aldershot: Ashgate, 2006), pp. 81–98.

Clarke, Charles and Mary Cowden, editors. *The Plays of William Shakespeare*, 3 volumes (London: Cassell, Petter and Galpin, 1865–9).

Clennell, William. 'The Bodleian Declaration: A History'. *The Bodleian Library Record* 20 (2007): pp. 47–60.

Cliffe, J. T. *The World of the Country House in Seventeenth-Century England* (New Haven, Conn.; London: Yale University Press, 1999).

Coady, David, editor. *Conspiracy Theories: The Philosophical Debate* (Aldershot: Ashgate, 2006).

Coates, P. R. 'Douglas Harold Varley: A Life's Work in Librarianship, Part II'. *Quarterly Bulletin of the South African Library* 55 (2001): pp. 20–30.

Coetzee, J. M. *Doubling the Point: Essays and Interviews*, edited by David Attwell (Cambridge Mass.; London: Harvard University Press, 1992).

Comenius, Johannes Amos. *Orbis Sensualium Pictus* (London, 1659).

Cooper, Tarnya, with essays by Marcia Pointon, James Shapiro, and Stanley Wells. *Searching for Shakespeare* (London: National Portrait Gallery, 2006).

Coover, Robert. 'The End of Books'. *The New York Times*, 21 June 1992.

Cormack, Bradin and Carla Mazzio, editors. *Book Use, Book Theory: 1500–1700* (Chicago: University of Chicago Press, 2005).

Cowtan, Robert. *Memories of the British Museum* (London: R. Bentley and Son, 1872).

Crane, Mary Thomas. *Framed Authority: Sayings, Self and Society in Sixteenth-Century England* (Princeton: Princeton University Press, 1993).

Cresswell, Tim. 'Value, Gleaning, and the Archive at Maxwell Street, Chicago', *Transactions of the British Geographical Society* 37 (2012): pp. 164–76.

Cunningham, Vanessa. *Shakespeare and Garrick* (Cambridge: Cambridge University Press, 2008).

Dallas, Duncan C. *The Dallas Type Shakespeare: A Reduced Facsimile of the First Folio, 1623* (London, 1893).

[Daly, Augustin]. *Auction Catalogue of the Library of Augustin Daly* (New York, 1900).

Daly, Joseph Francis. *The Life of Augustin Daly* (New York, 1917).

Dekker, Rudolf. *Family, Culture and Society in the Diary of Constantijn Huygens Jr, Secretary to the Stadholder-King William of Orange* (Leiden; Boston: Brill, 2013).

de Certeau, Michel. *The Practice of Everyday Life*, translated by Steven Rendell (Berkeley CA and London: University of California Press, 1988).

de Grazia, Margreta. *Shakespeare Verbatim: the Reproduction of Authenticity and the 1790 Apparatus* (Oxford: Clarendon Press, 1991).

de Grazia, Margreta and Stanley Wells, editors. *The New Cambridge Companion to Shakespeare* (Cambridge: Cambridge University Press, 2010).

Dent, R. W. *Shakespeare's Proverbial Language: An Index* (Berkeley: University of California Press, 1981).

Dessen, Alan C. *Rescripting Shakespeare: The Text, The Director, and Modern Productions* (Cambridge: Cambridge University Press, 2002).

Dibdin, T. F. *The Library Companion; or The Young Man's Guide and The Old Man's Comfort in the Choice of a Library* (London: Harding, Triphook and Lepard, 1825).

Dibdin, T. F. *Bibliomania: or Book Madness. A Bibliographical Romance* (London: Henry G. Bohn, 1842).

DiPietro, Cary, editor. *Bradley, Greg, Folger* (London: Continuum, 2011).

Disraeli, Benjamin. *Endymion* (London: Longmans, Green, 1881).

Dobson, Michael. *The Making of the National Poet: Shakespeare, Adaptation and Authorship, 1660–1769* (Oxford: Oxford University Press, 1994).

Dobson, Michael. 'For his nose was as sharp as a Pen, and a Table of greene fields'. *London Review of Books*, 10 May 2007.

Dodd, Alfred. *The Secret Shake-speare: Being the Missing Chapter from 'Shakespeare, Creator of Freemasonry' in which the Identity of Shake-speare is Plainly Declared together with Many Curious Secret Messages of Profound Interest to all Lovers of Literature, to Elizabethan Students and Freemasons in Particular* (London: Rider and Co, 1941).

Donaldson, Ian, editor. *The Oxford Authors: Ben Jonson* (Oxford: Oxford University Press, 1985).

Donnelly, Ignatius. *The Great Crytopgram: Francis Bacon's Cipher in the So-Called Shakespeare Plays*, 2 volumes (London: Sampson Low, Marston, Searle and Rivington Ltd, 1888).

Downing, William, editor. *My Library Catalogue: Coombe Bank, Kingston-on Thames. Richard Tangye* (London: 1904).

Dryden, John. *The Tempest or The Enchanted Island*. In *The Works of John Dryden. Plays. The Tempest. Tyrannick Love. An Evening's Love*, edited by Maximillian E. Novak (Berkeley; Los Angeles; London: University of California Press, 1970).

Dryden, John. *An Essay of Dramatick Poesie*. In *The Works of John Dryden: Prose 1668–1691. An Essay of Dramatick Poesie and Shorter Works*, edited by Samuel Holt Monk (Berkeley; Los Angeles; London: University of California Press, 1971).

Dunlap, Rhodes, editor. *The Poems of Thomas Carew* (Oxford: Clarendon Press, 1949).

Durning-Lawrence, Edwin. *Bacon is Shakespeare* (London: Gay and Hancock Ltd, 1910).

Durning-Lawrence, Edwin. *The Shakespeare Myth* (London: Gay and Hancock, 1912).

Dusinberre, Juliet, editor. *As You Like It* (London: Arden Shakespeare, 2006).

Eco, Umberto. *Faith in Fakes: Essays*, translated by William Weaver (London: Secker and Warburg, 1986).

Eco, Umberto and Thomas A. Sebeok, editors. *The Sign of Three: Dupin, Holmes, Peirce* (Bloomington: Indiana University Press, 1983).

Edel, Leon, editor. *The Complete Tales of Henry James*, 12 volumes (London: Rupert Hart-Davis, 1962–4).

Evans, G. Blakemore. 'The "Dering MS" of Shakespeare's "Henry IV" and Sir Edward Dering'. *Journal of English and Germanic Philology* 54 (1955): pp. 498–503.

Evans, G. Blakemore, editor. *Shakespearean Prompt-books of the Seventeenth Century*, 8 volumes (Charlottesville, VA: Bibliographical Society of the University of Virginia, 1960–1996).

Evans, G. Blakemore. 'The Douai Manuscript: Six Shakespearean Transcripts (1694–5)'. *Philological Quarterly* 41 (1962): pp. 158–63.

Evans, G. Blakemore. 'New Evidence on the Provenance of the Padua Prompt-Books of Shakespeare's *Macbeth*, *Measure for Measure* and *Winter's Tale*'. *Studies in Bibliography* 20 (1967): pp. 239–42.

Evans, Patrick. *The Penguin History of New Zealand Literature* (London and Auckland: Penguin Books, 1990).

Evans, Robert C. '"Whome None But Death Could Shake": An Unreported Epitaph on Shakespeare'. *Shakespeare Quarterly* 39 (1988): p. 60.

Ezell, Margaret, editor. *The Poems and Prose of Mary Lady Chudleigh* (New York: Oxford University Press, 1993).

Farrer, Edmund. *The Church Heraldry of Norfolk*, 3 volumes (Norwich: 1893).

F.C.B. 'The Reprint, in 1808, of the First Folio Edition of Shakespeare'. *Notes and Queries* 167 (1853): p. 47.

Fehrenbach, R. J., and E. S. Leedham-Green, editors. *Private Libraries in Renaissance England: A Collection and Catalogue of Tudor and Early Stuart Book-Lists*. Medieval and Renaissance Texts and Studies

(Binghamton, New York: Medieval and Renaissance Texts and Studies; Marlborough: Adam Matthew Publications, 1992).

Ferrell, Lori Anne. 'Extra-illustrating Shakespeare'. *Shakespearean Configurations: Early Modern Literary Studies*, special issue 21 (2013): http://extra.shu.ac.uk/emls/si-21/08-Ferrell_ExtraIllustratingShakespeare.htm (accessed April 2015).

Fitzgerald, Percy. *The Book Fancier or the Romance of Book Collecting* (London, Sampson Lowe, Marston, Searle and Rivington, 1886).

Flatter, Richard. *Shakespeare's Producing Hand: A Study of his Marks of Expression to be Found in the First Folio* (London: W. Heinemann, 1948).

Foakes, R. A., editor. *The Comedy of Errors* (London: Methuen, 1962).

[Folger Shakespeare Library]. *The Folger Library: A Decade of Growth, 1950–1960* (Washington: The Folger Shakespeare Library, 1960).

Fowles, John. *The Collector* (London: Pan Books, 1963).

Freeman, Neil, editor. *The Applause Shakespeare* (New York: Applause Theater and Cinema Books, 1997–2001).

Freeman, Neil, editor. *Measure for Measure* (New York; London: Applause, 1998).

Freud, Sigmund. *Mass Psychology and Other Writings*, translated by J. A. Underwood, introduced by Jacqueline Rose (London: Penguin, 2004).

Freud, Sigmund. *Civilization and its Discontents*, translated by David McLintock (London: Penguin, 2005).

Friedman, William F. and Elizebeth S. Friedman. *The Shakespearean Ciphers Examined: An analysis of Cryptographic Systems Used as Evidence that Some Author other than William Shakespeare wrote the plays commonly attributed to him* (Cambridge: Cambridge University Press, 1957).

Froude, James Anthony. *Oceana, or England and her Colonies* (London: Longmans, Green, 1886).

Furness, H. H. Junior, editor. *The Letters of Horace Howard Furness*, 2 volumes (Boston and New York: Houghton Mifflin, 1922).

Furness, Walter Rogers. *Composite Photography Applied to the Portraits of Shakespeare* (Philadelphia: Robert M. Lindsay, 1885).

Galbraith, Steven K. 'English Literary Folios 1593–1623: Studying Shifts in Format'. In *Tudor Books and Readers: Materiality and the Construction of Meaning*, edited by John N. King (Cambridge: Cambridge University Press, 2010), pp. 46–67.

Galey, Alan. *The Shakespearean Archive: Experiments in New Media from the Renaissance to Postmodernity* (Cambridge: Cambridge University Press, 2014).

Gallup, Elizabeth Wells. *The Bi-Literal Cypher of Sir Francis Bacon Discovered in his works and Deciphered by Mrs Elizabeth Wells Gallup* (Detroit, Michigan: Howard Publishing Co., 1899).

Garber, Marjorie. 'Looking the Part'. In *Shakespeare's Face*, edited by Stephanie Nolen et al. (London: Piatkus, 2003), pp. 156–77.

Garber, Marjorie B. *Academic Instincts* (Princeton, NJ: Princeton University Press, 2001).

Garrick, David. *Florizel and Perdita: A Dramatic Pastoral in Three Acts* (London: J. and R. Tonson, 1758).

[Garrick, David]. *A Catalogue of the Library, Splendid Books of Prints, Political and Historical Tracts of David Garrick Esq.* (London: Saunders, 1823).

Gildon, Charles. *Letters and Essays on Several Subjects* (London, 1697).

Ginzburg, Carlo. 'Clues: Morelli, Freud, and Sherlock Holmes'. In *The Sign of Three: Dupin, Holmes, Peirce*, edited by Umberto Eco and Thomas A. Sebeok (Bloomington: Indiana University Press, 1983), pp. 81–118.

Gollancz, Israel. *A Book of Homage to Shakespeare* (London: Oxford University Press, 1916).

Gollancz, Israel, editor. *In Commemoration of the First Folio Centenary. A Re-setting of the Preliminary Matter of the First Folio, with a Catalogue of Shakespeariana Exhibited in the Hall of The Worshipful Company of Stationers* (London: Oxford University Press for the Shakespeare Association, 1923).

Gollancz, Israel, and M. H. Spielmann, editors. *Studies in the First Folio Written for the Shakespeare Association* (London: Oxford University Press, 1924).

Gosden, Chris and Yvonne Marshall. 'The Cultural Biography of Objects'. *World Archaeology* 31 (1999): pp. 169–78.

Graffius, Jan. 'A Gift from Poetry'. *Times Literary Supplement*, 4 February 2015.

Grafton, Anthony, Deanna Marcum and Jean Strouse, editors. *Collectors, Collections and Scholarly Culture* (America Council of Learned Societies Occasional Paper 48, n.d.).

Grant, Stephen H. *Collecting Shakespeare: The Story of Henry and Emily Folger* (Baltimore: Johns Hopkins University Press, 2014).

[Great Exhibition]. *Exhibition of the Works of Industry of All Nations 1851, Reports by the Juries on the Subjects in the Thirty Classes into which the Exhibition was Divided* (London: 1852).

Greenblatt, Stephen. *Renaissance Self-Fashioning: From More to Shakespeare* (Chicago and London: University of Chicago Press, 1980).

Greg, W. W. *The Shakespeare First Folio: Its Bibliographical and Textual History* (Oxford: Clarendon Press, 1955).

[Grey, George]. Auckland Free Public Library. *Address delivered by Sir George Grey, K.C.B., at the Theatre Royal, Auckland, June 5th 1883. Reprinted from the New Zealand Herald.* (Sir George Grey Collection).

Grigson, Geoffrey. *Collected Poems 1963–1980* (London: Allison and Busby, 1982).

Gringerich, Owen. *The Book Nobody Read: Chasing the Revolutions of Nicolaus Copernicus* (London: William Heinemann, 2004).

Grosart, A. B., editor. *The Poems &c of Richard James* (London, 1880).

Guillimeau, Jacques. *Child-Birth, or the Happy Deliverie of women* (London: 1612).

Gunn, J. A. W., editor. *Benjamin Disraeli Letters*, 10 volumes (Toronto, Ontario; London: University of Toronto Press, 1982–).

Gunn, Simon. *The Public Culture of the Victorian Middle Class: Ritual and Authority in the English Industrial City 1840–1914* (Manchester and New York: Manchester University Press, 2000).

Gurr, Andrew. *Playgoing in Shakespeare's London*, 2nd edn (Cambridge: Cambridge University Press, 1996).

Gurr, Andrew. *The Shakespeare Company, 1594–1642* (Cambridge: Cambridge University Press, 2011).

Gutsche, Thelma. *The Bishop's Lady* (Cape Town: Howard Timmins, 1970).

Habermas, Jürgen. *The Structural Transformation of the Public Sphere: An Enquiry into a Category of Bourgeois Society* (Cambridge: Polity, 1989).

Hackett, Helen. *Shakespeare and Elizabeth: The Meeting of Two Myths* (Princeton and Oxford: Princeton University Press, 2009).

Halasz, Alexandra. *The Marketplace of Print: Pamphlets and the Public Sphere in Early Modern England* (Cambridge: Cambridge University Press, 1997).

Hall, Edith. *Adventures with Iphigenia in Tauris: A Cultural History of Euripides' Black Sea Tragedy* (New York: Oxford University Press, 2012).

Hall, Peter. *Shakespeare's Advice to the Players* (London: Oberon Books, 2003).

Halliwell-Phillips, J. O., editor. *The First Edition of Shakespeare. The Works of William Shakespeare in Reduced Facsimile from the Famous First Folio Edition of 1623 with an Introduction by J. O. Halliwell-Phillips* (London: Chatto and Windus, 1876).

Halliwell-Phillips, J. O. *A Hand-list of the Drawings and Engravings Illustrative of The Life of Shakespeare Preserved at Hollingbury Copse, Near Brighton* (Brighton: private printing, 1884).

Hammerschmidt-Hummel, Hildegard. *The True Face of William Shakespeare: The Poet's Death Mask and Likenesses from Three Periods of His Life* (London: Chaucer, 2006).

Hanmer, Thomas, editor. *The Works of Shakespear: In Six Volumes*, (Oxford: Clarendon Press, 1744).

Hard, Frederick. *Louis B. Wright: A Bibliography and Appreciation* (Charlottesville: University of Virginia Press for the Folger Shakespeare Library, 1968).

Harris, John. *The History of Kent* (London, 1719).

Harrison, Brian, editor. *The History of the University of Oxford*: Volume VIII: *The Twentieth Century* (Oxford: Clarendon Press, 1994).

Hayward, J. C. 'New Directions in the Study of the Falkland Circle'. *Seventeenth Century* 2 (1987): pp. 19–48.

Hazlitt, W. Carew. *Hand-book to the Popular, Poetical and Dramatic Literature of Great Britain: From the Inventing of Printing to the Restoration* (London: J. R. Smith, 1867).

Hazlitt, W. Carew. *The Book-Collector: A General Survey of the Pursuit and of those who have Engaged in it at Home and Abroad from the Earliest Period to the Present Time* (London: G. Redway, 1904).

Hazlitt, William. *The Characters of Shakespear's Plays* (London, 1817).

Heidegger, Martin. *Poetry, Language, Thought*, translated and edited by Albert Hofstader (New York; Evanston; San Francisco; London: Harper and Row Publishers, 1971).

Hemingway, Samuel Burdett. *A New Variorum Edition of Shakespeare: Henry the Fourth Part I* (Philadelphia and London: J. B. Lippincott Company, 1936).

Hewlett, Maurice. *Extemporary Essays* (London and New York: Humphrey Milford, Oxford University Press, 1922).

Highfill, Philip H., Junior, Kalman A Burnim, and Edward A. Langhans. *A Biographical Dictionary of Actors, Actresses, Musicians, Dancers, Managers & Other Stage Personnel in London, 1660–1800*, 16 volumes (Carbondale and Edwardsville: Southern Illinois University Press, 1973–1993).

Hill, George Birkbeck, editor. *Johnsonian Miscellanies*, 2 volumes (Oxford: Clarendon Press, 1897).

Hinman, Charlton. 'Variant Readings in the First Folio of Shakespeare'. *Shakespeare Quarterly* 4 (1953): pp. 279–88.

Hinman, Charlton. 'The Halliwell-Phillips Facsimile of the First Folio of Shakespeare'. *Shakespeare Quarterly* 5 (1954): pp. 395–401.

Hinman, Charlton. 'The Proof-Reading of the First Folio Text of *Romeo and Juliet*'. *Studies in Bibliography* 6 (1954): pp. 61–70.

Hinman, Charlton. *The Printing and Proof-Reading of the First Folio of Shakespeare*, 2 volumes (Oxford: Clarendon Press, 1963).

Hodgdon, Barbara, editor. *The Taming of the Shrew* (London: The Arden Shakespeare, 2010).

Hodges, John C. *The Library of William Congreve* (New York: New York Public Library, 1955).

[Hoe, Robert]. *Catalogue of the Library of Robert Hoe of New York Auction beginning 24 April 1911* (New York: Anderson Auction Company, 1911).

Hoffman, Calvin. *The Man Who Was Shakespeare* (London: Max Parrish, 1955).

Hogan, Charles Beecher. *Shakespeare in the Theatre 1701–1800*, 2 volumes (Oxford: Clarendon Press, 1952–7).

Holgate, C. W. *An Account of the Chief Libraries of New Zealand* (London, 1886).

Holland, Peter. 'Shakespeare Abbreviated'. In *The Cambridge Companion to Shakespeare and Popular Culture*, edited by Robert Shaughnessy (Cambridge: Cambridge University Press, 2007), pp. 26–45.

Honey, Andrew and Arthur Green. 'Met by Chance—a Group of Ten Books Bound for the Bodleian Library in February 1624 by William Wildgoose of Oxford'. Conference paper given at the Men and Books: From Microorganisms to Megaorganisms (Horn II conference), St. Pölten, Austria, 28 April–1 May 2014, forthcoming in the conference proceedings.

Hooper, David, and Ken Whyld, editors. *The Oxford Companion to Chess*, 2nd edn (Oxford: Oxford University Press, 1992).

Howarth, Janet. 'The Edwardian Reform Movement'. In *The History of the University of Oxford*, Volume 7: *Nineteenth Century Oxford Part 2*, edited by M. G. Brock and M. C. Curthoys (Oxford: Oxford University Press, 2000), pp. 822–54.

Hunt, R. W., I. G. Philip and R. J. Roberts, editors. *Studies in the Book Trade In Honour of Graham Pollard* (Oxford: Oxford Bibliographical Society, 1975).

Hunter, G. K. 'The Marking of Sententiae in Elizabethan Printed Plays, Poems and Romances'. *Library* 5th series no. 6 (1951): pp. 171–88.

Hutchinson, Julius, editor. *Memoirs of the Life of Colonel John Hutchinson* (London, 1808).

Hyde, Edward. *The Life of Edward, Earl of Clarendon* (Oxford: Clarendon Press, 1759).

Hyde, Edward. *The History of the Rebellion and Civil Wars in England*, 3 volumes (Oxford: Clarendon Press, 1816).

Ireland, William-Henry. *The Confessions of William-Henry Ireland containing the particulars of his fabrication of the Shakespeare Manuscripts* (London, 1805).

Jackson, H. J. *Marginalia: Readers Writing in Books* (New Haven, Conn.: Yale University Press, 2001).

Jackson, Holbrook. *The Anatomy of Bibliomania* (London: Soncino Press, 1932).

Jaggard, William. *Shakespeare Bibliography: A Dictionary of Every Known Issue of the Writings of our National Poet and of Recorded Opinion Thereon in the English Language* (Stratford-upon-Avon: The Shakespeare Press, 1911).

James, Colonel Sir Henry. *Photo-Zincography* (Southampton: Forbes and Bennett, 1860).

James, Henry. *The Outcry* (London: Methuen, 1911).

James, Henry. 'The Birthplace'. In *The Complete Tales of Henry James*, Volume 11: *1900–1903*, edited by Leon Edel (London: Rupert Hart-Davis, 1964), pp. 403–65.

[Jennens, Charles]. *King Lear. A Tragedy 'Collated with the Old and Modern Editions'* (London: W. and J. Richardson, 1770).

Johnson, David. *Shakespeare and South Africa* (Oxford: Clarendon Press, 1996).

Johnson, Samuel. *Proposals for printing, by subscription, the dramatick works of William Shakespeare* (London, 1756).

Johnson, Samuel, editor. *The Plays of William Shakespeare, in Eight Volumes, with the Corrections and Illustrations of Various Commentators; To which are added Notes by Sam. Johnson*, 8 volumes (London: Jacob Tonson, 1765).

Johnston, Edward D. *The First Folio of Shake-speare* (London: Cecil Palmer, 1932).

Jonson, Ben. *The Cambridge Edition of the Works of Ben Jonson Online* (Cambridge University Press, 2014) http://universitypublishingonline. org/cambridge/benjonson/k/litrecord/litrecord_cary_002/

Jowett, John. '"For Many of Your Companies": Middleton's Early Readers'. In *Thomas Middleton and Early Modern Textual Culture*, edited by Gary Taylor and John Lavagnino (Oxford: Clarendon Press, 2007), pp. 286–330.

Kahrl, George M., and Dorothy Anderson. *The Garrick Collection of Old English Plays* (London: British Library, 1982).

Kerr, Donald Jackson. *Amassing Treasure for All times: Sir George Grey, Colonial Bookman and Collector* (Dunedin, NZ: Oak Knoll Press and Otago University Press, 2006).

Kesson, Andy, and Emma Smith, editors. *The Elizabethan Top Ten: Defining Print Popularity in Early Modern England* (Farnham: Ashgate, 2013).

[Killigrew, Charles]. *Catalogus Librorum in omni fere scientia & facultate prasetantium; ex bibliothecis Caroli Killigrew* (London: Gyles Fletcher, 1725).

King, John N., editor. *Tudor Books and Readers: Materiality and the Construction of Meaning* (Cambridge: Cambridge University Press, 2010).

King, Stanley. *Recollections of the Folger Shakespeare Library* (Ithaca: Cornell University Press for the Trustees of Amherst College, 1950).

Knight, Charles. *Passages of A Working Life During half a Century*, 3 volumes (London: Bradbury and Evans, 1864).

Knight, G. Wilson. *The Wheel of Fire: Interpretations of Shakespearian Tragedy* (London: Methuen, 1949).

Kodama, Mitsuo, editor. *William Shakespeare: The First Folio 1623* (Tokyo: Meisei University Press, 1985).

Kökeritz, Helge, editor. *Mr William Shakespeares Comedies, Histories and Tragedies* (New Haven, Conn.; London: Yale University Press, 1954).

Kraus, H. P. *A Rare Book Saga: The Autobiography of H. P. Kraus* (London: Deutsch, 1979).

Krivatsy, Nati H., and Laetitia Yeandle. 'Sir Edward Dering'. In *Private Libraries in Renaissance England: A Collection and Catalogue of Tudor and Early Stuart Book-Lists*, edited by R. J. Fehrenbach and E. S. Leedham-Green (Binghamton, New York: Medieval and Renaissance Texts and Studies; Marlborough: Adam Matthew Publications, 1992), pp. 137–269.

Lang, Andrew. *The Library* (London: Macmillan, 1881).

Laporte, Charles. 'The Bard, the Bible, and the Victorian Shakespeare Question'. *English Literary History* 74 (2007): pp. 609–28.

Lee, Sidney. 'Letter to the Editor'. *The Times*, 15 March 1901.

Lee, Sidney. *Shakespeares Comedies, Histories, & Tragedies: A Supplement to the Reproduction in Facsimile of the First Folio Edition (1623) from the Chatsworth copy in the possession of the Duke of Devonshire, KG. containing A Census of Extant Copies with some Account of their History and Condition* (Oxford: Clarendon Press, 1902).

Lee, Sidney, editor. *Shakespeares comedies, histories, & tragedies: Being a Reproduction in Facsimile of the First Folio Edition, 1623, from the Chatsworth Copy in the Possession of the Duke of Devonshire, K.G.* (Oxford: Clarendon Press, 1902).

Lee, Sidney. *Notes and Additions to the Census of Copies of the First Folio* (London: Oxford University Press, 1906).

Lee, Sidney. 'A Survey of First Folios'. In *1623–1923: Studies in the First Folio Written for the Shakespeare Association* (London: Oxford University Press, 1924), pp. 78–105.

Lennam, T. N. S. 'Sir Edward Dering's Collection of Playbooks, 1619–1624'. *Shakespeare Quarterly* 16 (1965): pp. 145–53.

Lesser, Zachary and Peter Stallybrass. 'The First Literary *Hamlet* and the Commonplacing of Professional Plays'. *Shakespeare Quarterly* 59 (2008): pp. 371–420.

Lewin, A. M. *Quarterly Bulletin of the South African Library* 5 (1950): pp. 11–16.

Lilly, Joseph. *Catalogue* (London, 1852).

Lilly, Joseph. *Catalogue* (London, 1859).

Lilly, Joseph. *Catalogue* (London, 1860).

Lilly, Joseph. *A Catalogue of a most Interesting and Valuable Assembled of Rare, Curious, and Useful old Books* (London, 1862).

Lilly, Joseph. *Lilly's Catalogue of Rare, Curious, Valuable and Useful books* (London, 1863).

Lilly, Joseph. *Catalogue* (London, 1867).

Lindenbaum, Peter. 'Dispatches from the Archives', *Times Literary Supplement* 2 June 2006.

Loewenstein, Joseph F. 'Authentic Reproductions: The Material Origins of the New Bibliography'. In *Textual Formations and Reformations*, edited by Laurie E. Maguire and Thomas L. Berger (Newark: University of Delaware Press, 1998), pp. 23–44.

London Borough of Southwark. *Shakespeare 1st Folio Tercentenary, 1623–1923: Southwark Commemmoration Exhibition Catalogue* (Southwark, 1923).

The London Shakespeare League. *Tercentenary of the Publication of the First Folio of Shakespeare's Works* (London, 1923).

Loomba, Ania. *Gender, Race, Renaissance Drama* (Manchester: Manchester University Press, 1989).

Loomba, Ania. *Shakespeare, Race, and Colonialism* (Oxford: Oxford University Press, 2002).

Loomba, Ania and Martin Orkin, editors. *Post-Colonial Shakespeares* (London: Routledge, 1998).

Looney, Thomas J. *'Shakespeare' Identified in Edward de Vere, the Seventeenth Earl of Oxford* (London: C. Palmer, 1920).

Lucas, E. V., editor. *Miscellaneous Prose by Charles and Mary Lamb* (London: Methuen and Co. Ltd, 1912).

Lyttelton, George. *The Poetical Works of George Lyttelton* (Edinburgh: 1781).

Madan, Falconer. 'The Duplicity of Duplicates'. *Transactions of the Bibliographical Society* 12 (1914): pp. 15–24.

Madan, Falconer and Gladwyn Turbutt. *The Original Bodleian Copy of the First Folio of Shakespeare (The Turbutt Shakespeare)* (Oxford: Clarendon Press, 1905).

Maguire, Laurie E. 'Composition/decomposition: singular Shakespeare and the death of the author'. In *The Renaissance Text: Theory, Editing, Textuality*, edited by Andrew Murphy (Manchester: Manchester University Press, 2000), pp. 135–53.

Maguire, Laurie E. and Thomas L. Berger, editors. *Textual Formations and Reformations* (Newark: University of Delaware Press, 1998).

Malone, Edmond, editor. *The Plays and Poems of William Shakspeare, in ten volumes; collated verbatim with the most authentick copies*, 10 volumes (London: H. Baldwin for J. Rivington and Sons, 1790).

Martin, Peter. *Edmond Malone: Shakespearean Scholar: A Literary Biography* (Cambridge: Cambridge University Press, 1995).

Massai, Sonia. *Shakespeare and the Rise of the Editor* (Cambridge: Cambridge University Press, 2007).

Masten, Jeffrey. 'Pressing Subjects; Or, The Secret Lives of Shakespeare's Compositors'. In *Language Machines: Technologies of Literary and Cultural Production*, edited by Jeffrey Masten, Peter Stallybrass and Nancy Vickers (London and New York: Routledge, 1997), pp. 75–107.

Masten, Jeffrey, Peter Stallybrass and Nancy Vickers, editors. *Language Machines: Technologies of Literary and Cultural Production* (London and New York: Routledge, 1997).

Mauss, Marcel. *The Gift: The Form and Reason for Exchange in Archaic Societies*, translated by W. D. Halls (London: Routledge, 2002).

McCabe, William H. *An Introduction to the Jesuit Theater: a posthumous work* (St Louis: Institute of Jesuit Sources, 1983).

McKenzie, D. F. *Bibliography and the Sociology of Texts* (Cambridge: Cambridge University Press, 1999).

McKenzie, D. F. 'Typography and Meaning'. In *Making Meaning: 'Printers of the Mind' and Other Essays*, edited by D. F. McKenzie, Peter McDonald and Michael Suarez (Amherst: University of Massachusetts Press, 2002), pp. 199–236.

McKenzie, D. F., Peter McDonald and Michael Suarez. *Making Meaning: 'Printers of the Mind' and Other Essays* (Amherst: University of Massachusetts Press, 2002).

McKitterick, David. ' "Ovid with a Littleton": the cost of English books in the early seventeenth century'. *Transactions of the Cambridge Bibliographical Society* 11 (1997): pp. 184–234.

McKitterick, David. *Print, Manuscript and the Search for Order 1450–1830* (Cambridge: Cambridge University Press, 2003).

Melville, Lewis, editor. *The Life and Letters of William Cobbett in England and America*, 2 volumes (London: John Lane, The Bodley Head, 1913).

Milhous, Judith, and Robert D. Hume. 'Charles Killigrew's Petition about the Master of the Revels' Power as Censor (1715)'. *Theatre Notebook* 41 (1987): pp. 74–9.

Morgan, Paul. 'Frances Wolfreston and "Hor Bouks": A Seventeenth-Century Woman Book-Collector'. *The Library*, 6th series 11 (1989): pp. 179–219.

Morris, Leslie A. *Rosenbach Redux: Further Book Adventures in England and Ireland* (Philadelphia: Rosenbach Museum and Library, 1989).

Morris, Michael. 'Report on the Great Grey Colloquium'. *Quarterly Bulletin of the Library of South Africa* 57 (2003): pp. 50–2.

Moss, Ann. *Printed Common-Place books and the Structuring of Renaissance Thought* (Oxford: Clarendon Press, 1996).

Moston, Doug, editor. *The First Folio of Shakespeare 1623* (New York and London: Applause Books, 1995).

Munby, A. N. L., editor. *Sale Catalogues of Eminent Persons*, 12 volumes (London: Mansell, with Sotheby Parke Bernet Publications, 1971–75).

Murphy, Andrew, editor. *The Renaissance Text: Theory, Editing, Textuality* (Manchester: Manchester University Press, 2000).

Murphy, Andrew. *Shakespeare in Print: A History and Chronology of Shakespeare Publishing* (Cambridge: Cambridge University Press, 2003).

Murphy, Andrew. *Shakespeare for the People: Working-class Readers, 1800–1900* (Cambridge: Cambridge University Press, 2008).

Myers, Fred R., editor. *The Empire of Things: Regimes of Value and Imperial Culture* (Santa Fe: School of American Research Press, 2001).

Neill, Michael. 'Post-Colonial Shakespeare? Writing away from the Centre'. In *Post-Colonial Shakespeares*, edited by Ania Loomba and Martin Orkin (London: Routledge, 1998), pp. 164–85.

Nichols, John, editor. *Literary Anecdotes of the Eighteenth Century*, 9 volumes (London: Nichols, Son and Bentley, 1812–16).

Nolen, Stephanie et al., editors. *Shakespeare's Face* (London: Piatkus, 2003).

Norris, J. Parker. *The Portraits of Shakespeare* (Philadelphia: Robert M. Lindsay, 1885).

O'Neill, SJ, George. *The Clouds Around Shakespeare: A Lecture Delivered before the Royal Dublin Society, February 22 1911* (Dublin: E. Ponsonby Ltd, 1911).

Oldenburg, Scott. *Alien Albion: Literature and Immigration in Early Modern England* (Toronto: University of Toronto Press, 2014).

Osborn, James M. 'Edmond Malone: Scholar-Collector'. *Library* 19 (1964): pp. 11–37.

Paton, Allan Park. *The Tragedy of Macbeth: According to the First Folio* (Edinburgh: Edmonston and Co, 1877).

Paton, Sir Joseph, editor. *The National Shakespeare: A Facsimile of the Text of the First Folio of 1623* (London and Edinburgh: Mackenzie, 1888).

Pearson, David. 'English Book Owners in the Seventeenth Century: A Work in Progress Listing'. http://www.bibsoc.org.uk/content/english-book-owners-seventeenth-century

Perry, William. *A Treatise on the Identity of Herne's Oak, shewing the Maiden Tree to have been the Real One* (London: L. Booth, 1867).

Philip, Ian. *The Bodleian Library in the Seventeenth and Eighteenth Centuries* (Oxford: Clarendon Press, 1983).

Poel, William. 'Shakespeare's "Prompt Copies": A Plea for the Early Texts'. *Times Literary Supplement*, 3 February 1921.

Pollard, A. W. *Shakespeare Folios and Quartos: A Study in the Bibliography of Shakespeare's Plays* (London: Methuen, 1909).

Pollard, A. W. 'The Division of Rare English Books between England and the United States'. *The Library* 20 (1920): pp. 111–19.

Pollard, A. W., et al. '"Facsimile" Reprints of Old Books'. *The Library* 4 (1926): pp. 305–28.

Pope, Alexander, editor. *The Works of Shakespear in Six Volumes* (London: Jacob Tonson, 1725).

Porter, C. and H. A. Clarke, editors. *The First Folio Edition*, 16 volumes (London: Harrup, 1903–8).

Pressly, William L. 'The Ashbourne Portrait of Shakespeare: Through the Looking Glass'. *Shakespeare Quarterly* 44 (1993): pp. 54–72.

Pressman, Jessica. 'The Aesthetics of Bookishness in Twenty-First-Century Literature'. *Michigan Quarterly Review* 48 (2009): pp. 465–82.

Price, Leah. 'Dead Again'. *The New York Times*, 10 August 2012.

Prynne, William. *Histriomastix, The players scourge or actors tragedy... Wherein it is largely evidenced... that popular stage plays... are sinful, heathenish, lewd, ungodly spectacles and most pernicious corruptions* (London, 1632).

Quaritch, Bernard. *Catalogue 81* (London: Bernard Quaritch, 1887).

Quaritch, Bernard. *Catalogue 93* (London: Bernard Quaritch, 1888).

Quaritch, Bernard. *Catalogue* (London: Quaritch, May 1913).

Quaritch, Bernard and William Carew Hazlitt. *Contributions towards a Dictionary of English Book-Collectors*, 14 parts (London: Bernard Quaritch, 1892–1921).

[Quarterly Bulletin of the Library of South Africa]. 'Editorial: The Grey Collection Up for Sale?'. *Quarterly Bulletin of the Library of South Africa* 57 (2003): pp. 51–2.

Rasmussen, Eric. *The Shakespeare Thefts: In Search of the First Folios* (Basingstoke: Palgrave Macmillan, 2011).

Rasmussen, Eric and Anthony James West, editors. *The Shakespeare First Folios: A Descriptive Catalogue* (Basingstoke: Palgrave Macmillan, 2012).

Rhodes, Neil. *Shakespeare and the Origins of English* (Oxford: Oxford University Press, 2004).

Richards, Jennifer and Fred Schurink. 'Introduction: The Textuality and Materiality of Reading in Early Modern England'. *Huntington Library Quarterly* 73 (2010): pp. 345–61.

Roberts, Jeanne Addison. 'Women Edit Shakespeare'. *Shakespeare Survey* 59 (2006): pp. 136–46.

Roberts, Julian. 'The Latin Trade'. In *The History of the Book in Britain*, volume 4: *1557–1695*, edited by John Barnard and D. F. MacKenzie with the assistance of Maureen Bell (Cambridge: Cambridge University Press, 2002), pp. 141–73.

Roberts, Sasha. 'Reading the Shakespeare Text in Early Modern England'. *Critical Survey* 7 (1995): pp. 299–306.

Rogers, Malcolm. 'The Meaning of Van Dyck's Portrait of Sir John Suckling'. *The Burlington Magazine* 120 (1978): pp. 739–45.

Rokison, Abigail. *Shakespearean Verse-Speaking: Text and Theatre Practice* (Cambridge: Cambridge University Press, 2009).

Rosenbach, A. S. W. 'Henry C. Folger as a collector'. In *Henry C. Folger 18 June 1857–11 June 1930*, edited by S. Parkes Cadman (New Haven: privately printed, 1931).

[The Rosenbach Company]. *William Shakespeare: a collection of First and Early Editions of his Works* (Philadelphia: Rosenbach Company, 1951).

Rosenheim, Shawn James. *The Cryptographic Imagination: Secret Writing from Edgar Poe to the Internet* (Baltimore: Johns Hopkins University Press, 1997).

Ross, Robert, editor. *The Collected Works of Oscar Wilde*, 15 volumes (London: Routledge/Thoemmes Press, 1993).

Rowe, Katherine. 'Shakespeare and Media History'. In *The New Cambridge Companion to Shakespeare*, edited by Margreta de Grazia and Stanley Wells (Cambridge: Cambridge University Press, 2010), pp. 303–45.

Rowe, Nicholas, editor. *The Works of Mr William Shakespear; in Six Volumes. Adorn'd with Cuts. Revis'd and Corrected, with an Account of the Life and Writings of the Author* (London: Jacob Tonson, 1709).

Rowe, Nicholas, editor. *The Works of Mr William Shakespear; in eight volumes. Adorn'd with cuts. Revis'd and corrected* (London: Jacob Tonson, 1714).

Ryskamp, Charles. 'Abbie Pope: Portrait of a Bibliophile XXIV'. *The Book Collector* 33 (1984): pp. 39–52.

Sae, Kitamura. 'The role of Women in the Canonization of Shakespeare: From Elizabethan Theatre to the Shakespeare Jubilee'. Unpublished PhD thesis, King's College London, 2013.

Samuels, Ernest. *Bernard Berenson: The Making of a Connoisseur* (Cambridge, Mass.; London: Belknap Press of Harvard University Press, 1979).

Sargent, George H. 'Should Collectors Read Books?' *The Bookman* 49 (1919): pp. 744–9.

Satchell, Thomas. 'The Spelling of the First Folio: A Letter to the Editor'. *Times Literary Supplement*, 3 June 1920.

Savage, Richard, editor. *Shakespearean Extracts from 'Edward Pudsey's booke'* (Stratford-upon-Avon: n.p., 1888).

Schalkwyk, David. *Hamlet's Dreams: The Robben Island Shakespeare* (London: Continuum, 2012).

Schoenbaum, Samuel. *Shakespeare's Lives*, new edition (Oxford: Clarendon Press, 1991).

Schwartz, Lillian. 'The Art Historian's Computer'. *Scientific American*, April 1995, pp. 106–11.

Scott-Warren, Jason. 'Reading Graffiti in the Early Modern Book'. *Huntington Library Quarterly* 73 (2010): pp. 363–81.

Shakespeare, William, *The Norton Facsimile: The First Folio of Shakespeare prepared by Charlton Hinman*, second edition (New York and London: W. W. Norton and Company, 1996).

Shapiro, James. *Contested Will: Who Wrote Shakespeare?* (London: Faber, 2010).

Shaughnessy, Robert, editor. *The Cambridge Companion to Shakespeare and Popular Culture* (Cambridge: Cambridge University Press, 2007).

Shaw, George Bernard. 'Shakespeare: A Standard Text'. *Times Literary Supplement*, 17 March 1921.

Shaw, George Bernard. *The Works of Bernard Shaw*, 30 volumes (London: Constable, 1930–2).

Shell, Alison. *Catholicism, Controversy, and the English Literary Imagination, 1558–1660* (Cambridge: Cambridge University Press, 1999).

Sherman, William H. *Used Books: Marking Readers in Renaissance England* (Philadelphia: University of Pennsylvania Press, 2008).

Sillars, Stuart. *The Illustrated Shakespeare 1709–1875* (Cambridge: Cambridge University Press, 2008).

Smallwood, Robert, editor. *Players of Shakespeare 5* (Cambridge: Cambridge University Press, 2003).

Smith, Helen. '"Rare poemes ask rare friends": Popularity and Collection in Elizabethan England'. In *The Elizabethan Top Ten: Defining Print Popularity in Early Modern England*, edited by Andy Kesson and Emma Smith (Farnham: Ashgate, 2013), pp. 79–100.

Smith, Robert M. *The Shakespeare Folios: The Forgeries of Shakespeare's Handwriting in the Lucy Packer Memorial Library of Lehigh University* (Bethlehem, Pennsylvania: Lehigh University Press, 1927).

Smith, Robert M. 'The Formation of Shakespeare Libraries in America'. *The Shakespeare Association Bulletin* 4 (1929): pp. 65–73.

Smith, Steven Escar. '"Armadillos of Invention": A Census of Mechanical Collators'. *Studies in Bibliography* 55 (2002): pp. 133–70.

Smith, Steven Escar. '"The Eternal Verities Verified": Charlton Hinman and the Roots of Mechanical Collation'. *Studies in Bibliography* 53 (2003): pp. 129–61.

Smyth, Adam. *Autobiography in Early Modern England* (Cambridge: Cambridge University Press, 2010).

Speed Hill, W., editor. *New Ways of Looking at Old Texts: Papers of the Renaissance English Text Society, 1985–1991* (Binghamton: Medieval and Renaissance Texts Society, 1993).

Speilmann, M. H. *The Title-Page of the First Folio of Shakespeare's Plays: A Comparative Study of the Droeshout Portrait and the Stratford Monument* (London: Oxford University Press, 1924).

Spenser, Edmund. *The Faerie Queene*, edited by A. C. Hamilton (New York and London: Longman, 1977).

Spohr, O. H. 'The Grey Collection a Century Ago'. *Quarterly Bulletin of the South African Library* 17 (1962): pp. 5–15.

Staunton, Howard, editor. *Memorials of Shakespeare* (London: Day, 1864).

Steevens, George, and Samuel Johnson, editors. *The Plays of William Shakspere, in Fifteen Volumes* (London, 1793).

Stewart, Susan. *On Longing: Narratives of the Miniature, the Gigantic, the Souvenir, the Collection* (Baltimore, London: Johns Hopkins University Press, 1984).

[Stowe House]. *Catalogue of the Library removed from Stowe House, Buckinghamshire* (S. Leigh Sotheby and Co, 1849).

Strouse, Jean. *Morgan: American Financier* (London: Harvill, 1999).

Strouse, Jean. 'The Collector J. Pierpont Morgan'. In *Collectors, Collections and Scholarly Culture*, edited by Anthony Grafton, Deanna Marcum, and Jean Strouse (America Council of Learned Societies Occasional Paper 48, n.d.).

Tangye, Richard. *Notes of my Fourth Voyage to the Australian Colonies* (Birmingham: White and Pike, 1886).

Taylor, Gary. 'William Shakespeare, Richard James and the House of Cobham'. *Review of English Studies* 38 (1987): pp. 334–54.

Taylor, Gary and John Lavagnino, editors. *Thomas Middleton and Early Modern Textual Culture* (Oxford: Clarendon Press, 2007).

Theobald, Lewis, editor. *The works of Shakespeare: in seven volumes. Collated with the oldest copies, and corrected: with notes, explanatory and critical*, 7 volumes (London, 1733).

Thomas, Julia. *Shakespeare's Shrine: The Bard's Birthplace and the Invention of Stratford-upon-Avon* (Philadelphia: University of Pennsylvania Press, 2012).

Thrumbo, Hurlo. *The Merry-Thought or, the Glass-Window and Bog-House Miscellany* (1731), Augustan Reprint Society 221–2 (Los Angeles: University of California, 1983).

Tillotson, Arthur, editor. *The Correspondence of Thomas Percy and Edmond Malone* (Baton Rouge: Louisiana State University Press, 1908).

Timmins, Samuel. *Books on Shakespeare* (London: Simpkin, Marshall and Co., 1885).

Tooke, John Horne. *Epea pteroenta. Or, the Diversions of Purley*, 2nd edn, 2 volumes (London: printed for the author, 1798–1805).

Trevor-Roper, Hugh. *Catholics, Anglicans and Puritans: Seventeenth Century Essays* (London: Secker and Warburg, 1987).

Trollope, Anthony. *South Africa*, 2 volumes (London: Chapman and Hall, 1878).

Tucker, Patrick. *Secrets of Acting Shakespeare: the Original Approach* (London, New York: Routledge, 2002).

Tucker, Patrick. *First Folio Speeches for Men* (London: Oberon Books, 2004).

Turbutt, Gladwyn. *A History of Ogston* (Higham: The Ogston Estates, 1975).

Twidle, Hedley. 'From *The Origins of Language* to a Language of Origin: A Prologue to the Grey Collection'. In *Print, Text and Book Cultures in South Africa*, edited by Andrew van der Vlies (Johannesburg: Wits University Press, 2012), pp. 252–8.

van der Vlies, Andrew, editor. *Print, Text and Book Cultures in South Africa* (Johannesburg: Wits University Press, 2012).

Vander Meulen, David L., editor. *The Bibliographical Society of the University of Virginia: The First Fifty Years* (Charlottesville: Bibliographical Society of the University of Virginia, 1998).

Vander Meulen, David L. 'A History of the Bibliographical Society of the University of Virginia: The First Fifty Years'. In *The Bibliographical Society of the University of Virginia: The First Fifty Years*, edited by David L. Vander Meulen (Charlottesville: Bibliographical Society of the University of Virginia, 1998), pp. 1–81.

Vaughan, Virginia Mason and Alden T. Vaughan, editors. *Shakespeare in American Life* (Washington DC: Folger Shakespeare Library, 2007).

Veblen, Thorstein. *The Theory of the Leisure Class*, edited by Martha Banta (Oxford: Oxford University Press, 2007).

Voss, Philip. 'Prospero'. In *Players of Shakespeare 5*, edited by Robert Smallwood (Cambridge: Cambridge University Press, 2003), pp. 15–28.

Wadsworth, Frank W. *The Poacher from Stratford: A Partial Account of the Controversy over the Authorship of Shakespeare's Plays* (Berkeley: University of California Press, 1958).

Walker, Charles Clement. *John Heminge and Henry Condell. Friends and Fellow-Actors of Shakespeare and What the World Owes to Them* (London: C. J. Clay and Sons, 1896).

Watson, Nicola J. 'Shakespeare on the Tourist Trail'. In *The Cambridge Companion to Shakespeare and Popular Culture*, edited by Robert Shaughnessy (Cambridge: Cambridge University Press, 2007), pp. 199–226.

[Webster, Paul Francis]. *'Multum in Parvo': The Small Select Library of Paul Francis Webster* (Beverly Hills, California: privately printed, 1972).

Weimerkirsch, Philip J. 'John Harris, Sr., 1767–1832. Memoir by his Son, John Harris, Jr., 1791–1873'. *The Book Collector* 42 (1993): pp. 245–52.

Weiner, Annette. *Inalienable Possessions: The Paradox of Keeping-while-Giving* (Berkeley; Los Angeles; Oxford: University of California Press, 1992).

West, Anthony James. 'How Many First Folios Does the Folger Hold?'.
    Shakespeare Quarterly 47 (1996): pp. 190–4.
West, Anthony James. 'Sales and Prices of Shakespeare First Folios: a
    History, 1623 to the Present'. *Publications of the Bibliographical Society of
    America* 92 (1998): pp. 465–528.
West, Anthony James. 'Constantijn Huygens Owned a Shakespeare First
    Folio'. *Notes and Queries* 55 (2008): pp. 221–2.
West, Anthony James. 'Constantijn Huygens's Shakespeare First Folio:
    the First to go Abroad; now at the Folger'. *Notes and Queries* 60 no. 1
    (2013): p. 49.
West, Anthony James. 'Proving the Identity of the Stolen Durham First
    Folio', *The Library* 14 (2013), pp. 428–40.
West, James Anthony. 'A Model for Describing Shakespeare First Folios,
    With Descriptions of Selected Copies'. *The Library* 21 (1999):
    pp. 1–49.
[Weston House]. *Catalogue of the Sale of the Contents of Weston House*
    (London: Christie's, 1781).
Westwood, Doris. *These Players: A Diary of the 'Old Vic'* (London: Heath
    Cranton Ltd, 1926).
Wheatley, Henry B. *Prices of Books: An Inquiry into the Changes in the Price
    of Books which have Occurred in England at Different Periods* (Detroit:
    Gale Research Co, 1970).
Wheeler, G. A., editor. *Letters of Sir Thomas Bodley to Thomas James*
    (Oxford: Clarendon Press, 1926).
Wiggins, Martin. 'Shakespeare Jesuited: The Plagiarisms of "Pater
    Clarcus". *The Seventeenth Century* 20 (2005): pp. 1–21.
Williams, John Ambrose. *Memoirs of John Philip Kemble, Esq.* (London:
    John Bowley Wood, 1817).
Williams, Samuel D., editor. *Who's Who in Newport* (Newport: Williams
    Press Ltd, 1920).
Williams, William Proctor. 'F1 Coriolanus Fragment Found in 17th
    Century Binding'. *Shakespeare Newsletter* 16 (1966): p. 12.
[Dr Williams's Library]. *A Short Account of the Charity & Library Estab-
    lished under the Will of the Late Rev. Daniel Williams, D.D.* (London,
    1917).
[Dr Williams's Library]. *The Shakespeare First Folio, 1623: The Dr
    Williams's Copy* (London: Sotheby's, 2006).

Willoughby, Edwin Eliott. *The Printing of the First Folio of Shakespeare*, Supplements to the Bibliographical Society's Transactions 8 (Oxford: Oxford University Press for the Bibliographical Society, 1932).

Wilson, John Dover. 'The Task of Heminge and Condell, 1623–1923'. In *Studies in the First Folio Written for the Shakespeare Association*, edited by Israel Gollancz and M. H. Spielmann (London: Oxford University Press, 1924), pp. 53–77.

Wolfe, Jessica. *Humanism and Machinery in Renaissance Literature* (Cambridge: Cambridge University Press, 2004).

Wright, Louis B. *The Folger Library. Two Decades of Growth: An Informal Account* (Charlottesville: University Press of Virginia for the Folger Shakespeare Library, 1968).

Yamada, Akihiro. *The First Folio of Shakespeare: A Transcript of Contemporary Marginalia in a copy in the Kodama Memorial Library of Meisei University* (Tokyo: Yushodo Press, 1988).

Yeandle, Laetitia. 'Sir Edward Dering, 1st Bart., of Surrenden Dering and his "Booke of Expences" 1617–1628'. Published online by Kent Archaelogical Society at http://www.kentarchaeology.ac/authors/020.pdf.

Yeo, Richard. 'An Idol of the Market-place: Baconianism in the Nineteenth Century'. *History of Science* 23.3 (1985): pp. 251–98.

Ziegler, Georgianna. 'Duty and Enjoyment: The Folgers as Shakespeare Collectors in the Gilded Age'. In *Shakespeare in American Life*, edited by Virginia Mason Vaughan and Alden T. Vaughan (Washington DC: Folger Shakespeare Library, 2007), pp. 101–12.

Zucker, Adam. *The Places of Wit in Early Modern English Comedy* (Cambridge: Cambridge University Press, 2011).

Index